True Education

from Birth and for Eternity

A practical guide for following God's beautiful method of education

About the author

Jennifer White, mother of two grown children, embraced God's plan of education when her children were young, and, desiring nothing more than to please the Lord, she devoted all her energies to raising her children for Him. Now that her children are grown, she works with A Thinking Generation as a consultant for young mothers. Drawing from a wealth of experience and study, Jennifer has blessed many parents with practical instruction in God's plan of education. It is her earnest prayer that all who read this book will experience the joy and blessing of following God's ways.

Contents

How to Use this Book

*"Never will education accomplish all that it might and
should accomplish until the importance of the parents'
work is fully recognized, and they receive a training for
its sacred responsibilities." – Education, 276*

If you are picking up this book for the first time, it may be tempting to turn to the section on curriculum, or the one on lesson books, or whatever particular section especially interests you. However, the foundation laid in the early chapters is essential to understanding how to apply the later sections of the book. This book is intended to be read sequentially.

You will find some inevitable redundancy in this book. Unlike traditional education that can be fragmented into different subjects, the many components of God's method of education are like various colors of threads that are woven together into a beautiful tapestry; they are intimately interconnected with all the other components, and it is impossible to separate one thread from another without marring the beautiful whole. Consequently, you will find information about one area of true education explained in one chapter and then expounded upon from a slightly different angle in another chapter. I considered trying to eliminate the redundancy, but after much prayer, I came to understand that the reiteration was valuable. While God's methods of true education are simple – simple enough for all to follow – they are also very different from the ones most of us are accustomed to, and seeing how one component in His plan of education fits into many other areas of His plan can help us to better understand God's very unique method.

Who Should Use This Book

This book was *not* written for the perfect parent.

It's okay if you've made mistakes. It's okay if you don't have it all together. It's okay if you don't have this parenting and educating thing all figured out. You don't have to be a perfect parent to follow God's plan of education. You only have to trust in our perfect God and be willing to follow Him. It is when we recognize our weakness, our mistakes, our deficiencies, and our inadequacies that we become deeply aware of our need for Jesus. We learn that we cannot parent well in our own strength. And we learn that we don't have to. "It is well for us to feel our weakness, for then we shall seek the strength and wisdom that the Father delights to give to His children." [1] It is when we come to Him in humility, recognizing our needs, surrendering our will to His perfect plan, that we are brought into connection with Him and He can reveal His power. Take hold of his perfect power for strength to be obedient, and He will help you. The Savior comes very near to those who consecrate themselves to Him.

It is the privilege and responsibility of every father and mother to educate their children to bring honor to the great Creator and Master of all. God could have chosen another human whom you believe to be more qualified to do this job. He even could have chosen angels to provide the perfect education for your child. But He didn't do that. He chose you.

This book was written for the parent who loves the Lord and wants to follow His ways no matter how different they may be from the ways of the world. "The grace of Jesus Christ will give wisdom to all who follow the Lord's plan of true education." [2]

When To Use This Book

Since true education begins at (or before) birth, ideally, we would learn and understand God's method of education *before* we become parents. Unfortunately, that is not the case for most of us. And God knows this. If, as you read this book, you find aspects of God's method of education that you did not apply at the right time because you didn't know about them, there is no reason to despair. God is great in mercy, and it is not too late. Start implementing God's methods right away, where you are, in the best way you can, adapted as much as possible to the age of your children now, and the Lord will help you.

An important factor in understanding God's method of education is to follow light as it is revealed. God helps us understand today's instruction only as we have obeyed the instruction from yesterday. Therefore, as you read a section in this book and see something that God wants you to implement in your family, do not delay. Do not wait to read the entire book and have all the information. Do not think about all the reasons why obedience will be difficult. Do not think about the obstacles. Do not think about what others will think. Do not hesitate to trust in God. By His grace and with His help, implement His instruction immediately. When you see new light, and you step forward in that light, this step of faith will open up to you an abundance of power and aid in obeying that new direction from God.

How This Book is Organized

This book is divided into sections. Section I covers some of the most vital and foundational elements of God's method of true education. If you don't read any other part of this book, you want to read Section I.

Section II shows how to follow God's schedule for education (what to do when) and exposes some of the common mistakes and myths in traditional education.

In Section III, we look at God's method for building the brain – an important step that is so often neglected in education. When we take care to follow what is laid out in this section, all subsequent learning happens much more effectively and efficiently.

In Section IV, we cover the four lesson books from which God intends a child to learn. Section V looks at the subjects that God wants us to learn. Section VI covers the parents' education.

A parent will find that following the guidelines in Sections IV and V is extremely challenging – if not impossible – without first applying the foundational principles found in the first three sections. But once the foundational steps are in place, using the methods in later chapters becomes natural and joyful.

Other Notes About This Book

For simplicity's sake, I have used the male pronouns (he, him, etc.) when I am referring to children in this book. Just as the word "man" in the Bible often encompasses all of mankind (not only males), my use of the male pronouns encompasses both male and female children. The use of the male pronoun is in no way intended to devalue the female gender in any way. Rather, the reason for this is simplicity in writing and reading. To write he/she, him/her, himself/herself, etc. is tedious and may bog down the reader.

There are many true stories in this book, but I've changed the names in the stories to protect privacy.

Some of the pages in this book may seem to be more geared toward parenting rather than educating children, but God's beautiful method of education means more than inputting information into a child's brain; rather it encompasses the whole child, which includes the development of character and good habits, the nurturing of a relationship with our Savior, and much more.

And finally, any book that touches on the subject of raising and educating children has to walk that painfully fine line between giving useful direction and being discouraging. If the author simply gives you a superficial, cheery pep-talk, then you may walk away happy and encouraged yet without any information that is actually helpful in a practical, day-to-day manner. In contrast, if the book provides solid, fact-based information and instruction, it can sound critical and may discourage the reader. The intention of this book is neither to give you fluff that isn't useful nor information to make you feel guilty or inadequate. God truly cares about how we educate our children, and I share this book in the simple hope that as each of us, day-by-day, learn more of God's will, the light from the beauty of His ways will disperse the fog of doubt and uncertainty, and we will be all drawn closer to our Savior and live lives that fully honor Him.

It was with a tremendous amount of prayer and a solemn realization of the eternal effects of our methods of education that this book was written. I invite you to read the book in the same manner – with much prayer and a deep sense of the eternal consequences of how you choose to educate your child. "Human reasoning alone can never explain the science of education. Spiritual eyesight is required to understand what the true higher education is." [3]

SECTION I
GOD'S BEAUTIFUL METHOD OF EDUCATION

Chapter 1

God's Perfect Method
of Education

"He only who created the mind and ordained its laws can perfectly understand its needs or direct its development." – Education, 276

"ETHAN, have you finished your math assignment?" Mom asked her son.

No answer.

"Ethan, are you done with your math paper?"

"No," groaned Ethan. Mom got up from her desk where she was looking over Meghan's math assignment and walked over to check Ethan's progress.

"Ethan! You've only done two math problems! What have you been doing all this time?"

"It's too haaarrrrd," groaned Ethan again as he slouched sideways in his chair while repeatedly flicking his pencil on his head.

"It's not too hard. Please sit up and do your schoolwork."

"It's so boring. I don't like school. I hate learning!" Ethan protested.

"I hate learning!" Ethan's three-year-old brother echoed from the other room where he was playing. Mom's heart sank. When Meghan, Ethan's older sister, was his age, she loved school. Yes, Meghan had some character issues that Mom was concerned about, and she was beginning to notice Meghan no longer wanted to do things with the family; she only wanted to be with her friends. But at least...

"When can I go outside and play?" Ethan interrupted Mom's thoughts.

Getting Ethan to do his schoolwork was a regular battle for Ethan's mom. He was very distractible and fidgety, and he regularly expressed a strong dislike for anything school-related. The daily struggle was wearing on Mom.

The Dying Love of Learning

The despair felt by Ethan's mom isn't uncommon. Many children struggle to sit still, pay attention, and do their schoolwork. Is this just par for the course? Do some children enjoy learning and others do not? Is there a better way?

Every day, all around the world, millions of toddlers ask what seems like millions of questions.

"Do frogs have fingernails?"

"Are there any ostriches on the moon?"

"Why can't I eat mud?"

"Why are there matches if I'm not allowed to use them?"

"How come I'm not a dog?"

"Why do I have nipples?

"Did you eat trees when you were little?"

"Do fish have eyebrows?" "Why not?"

Some researchers estimate that toddlers ask over 70 questions per day, but at least a few parents would argue that their little one asks that many before breakfast.

Curiosity is something all children are born with. Children don't need to be coerced to learn; they are observant and naturally interested in and curious about life around them. They have active minds and an enthusiastic desire to learn.

But as children get older, this insatiable desire to learn seems to lose some of its urgency. That curiosity seems to fade, the questions grow silent, the desire to learn turns to boredom. Rare is it to find a fourteen-year-old who has an enthusiastic and self-motivated interest in learning. What's even more tragic is that many adults have come to believe that this attitude is normal. "That's the way kids are," they reason.

But this is not how God created children. Something has gone awry. Contrary to what is commonly believed in our modern society, children don't naturally progress from being intensely interested in learning to being apathetic and uninterested. Is it possible that our methods of education are squashing that natural love of learning?

God's Original Design Nearly Lost

From the creation of the world, God gave His people a method of education that retained and nurtured a child's natural love of learning and helped them to develop not only mentally, but also physically and spiritually. His perfect method was designed to produce a people who were "the head, and not the tail,"[1] "a praise and a glory,"[2] and an example to the world of "physical strength and vigor of intellect."[3]

Unfortunately, through the centuries, man's understanding of God's perfect plan of education has become diluted and adulterated, until, sadly, it has been nearly lost.[4] A false system of education has taken its place. This false system of education is the foundation of our modern educational system, and it is also, by far, the predominant and foremost method used in modern-day homeschooling.

The methods of this false system of education subtly suppress a child's love of true learning and his abilities for independent thought. And, of even greater consequence, these educational methods eventually tend to spiritually weaken our children.

Some of these educational methods may seem benign, but this is only because of their subtlety, their prevalence, and our familiarity with them (after all, these methods are those that nearly the entire world currently uses and has been using for thousands of years). But the methodology of this false system is far from innocuous. A child's brain changes physically as a result of how he is educated, and to say that the method used will significantly affect the outcome is a drastic understatement. "Satan has used the most ingenious methods to weave his plans into the systems of education, and thus gain a strong hold on the minds of the children and youth."[5] "By a misconception of the true nature and object of education many have been led into serious and even fatal errors."[6] In fact, "the reason why the youth of the present age are not more religiously inclined is that their education is defective"[7] – we have departed from God's original design.

We are urged, "Now, as never before, we need to understand the true science of education."[8] The Lord has designed His method of education to be used by His people;[9] it is not optional. "We are not at liberty to teach that which shall meet the world's standard or the standard of the church, simply because it is the custom to do so."[10]

More Than We Suppose

God's method of "education means much more than many suppose."[11] God's system of education is more than a mere knowledge of math, history, and science, "more than the pursual of a certain course of study,"[12] more than using a curriculum that is Bible-based or centered on character development, more than simply combining the practical with the academic.

For the education of our children, we find a perfect model in the Word of God. "Lessons of great profit, even in this age of educational progress, may be found in the history of God's ancient people."[13] The God of Heaven was directly involved with the education of the young in ancient Israel,[14] gave specific instructions regarding how it was to be accomplished, and explained the duty of parents to their children. The parents were not to send their little ones away to school to be educated by another; God commanded the parents themselves to teach their children. "In the place of stranger lips the loving hearts of the father and mother were to give instruction to their children."[15] God commanded them to teach their children when they were sitting in their house, when they were walking by the way, when they were lying down, and when they rose up.[16] The parents were to teach their children at all times of the day, through the daily activities of life, through the many object lessons gained in observing nature and in working with their hands in the home and in the field. The child's education was to be such that the practical, the intellectual, and the spiritual would be woven together as a fine fabric, a beautiful tapestry, and everything the child learned was so interwoven into his life that it deeply affected his very being. [17] This real-life, moment-by-moment learning strengthened the intellect and the reasoning skills like no other method can.

Sadly, not all parents in ancient Israel adopted God's beautiful plan of education. [18] Most only partially followed the instructions given by God, [19] "and the sad results are pictured before us in a nation rejected of God." [20]

But there were a few who did value God's very precise ways. There were a few who faithfully considered the sacred responsibility and charge committed to them and carefully followed the directions laid out by the God of Israel in the education of their children. And what were the results of following God's plan of education?

"Wherever in Israel God's plan of education was carried into effect, its results testified of its Author." [21] When families heeded God's instruction, their youth came forth from this education "vigorous in body and in mind, quick to perceive and strong to act, the heart prepared like good ground for the growth of the precious seed." [22] And they remained true to the principles they had learned in early life. [23]

We see an example of this type of education in the life of Daniel. Daniel was only a youth when he was taken away from his parents' home to a heathen land and placed in a corrupt environment that caused many of his peers to quickly fall to temptation. But the education of Daniel had been different from that of most of his peers; his education had been according to God's plan. [24] And at the tender age of fifteen, the age when most youth are yielding to peer pressure, Daniel was unwavering in his commitment to God and firm to resist temptation – even at the risk of his very life.

And though he "had not been educated in the schools of Jerusalem, much less in those of Babylon," [25] he also possessed strength and vigor of intellect, keen comprehension, integrity, "knowledge and skill in all learning and wisdom," [26] and extraordinary reasoning powers. Though he was now living in the educational center of the world surrounded by men of extraordinary knowledge and wisdom,[27]

Daniel stood unrivaled. [28] His abilities exceeded even those of his teachers, and he was extraordinarily qualified to successfully undertake a challenging leadership position in the foreign nation in which he now lived, in "the most magnificent of cities" [29] in "the court of its greatest monarch." [30]

Daniel's parents had followed God's method of education, and Daniel grew to be spiritually, physically, and mentally strong.

The life of Joseph provides another example of the results of God's plan of education. Sold as a slave by his own brothers, a stranger in a heathen land, unjustly accused and cast into prison, Joseph faced "experiences that tested his courage and uprightness to the fullest extent." [31] How was it, at the young age of seventeen, the age when many young people begin to stray from the Lord, that Joseph was able to stay faithful to God? How was he able to rise to such greatness and administer the affairs of the kingdom of Egypt with such wisdom? It was the result of following God's methods of true education. [32]

We see the results of this beautiful plan of education in the lives of the other great men of the Bible, such as Moses, Samuel, and Timothy. [33] And the education of Jesus followed this divine plan. [34]

God's method of education is broad and deep. It is a method of education that is like no other. Conventional methods of education do not need to be modified, improved, or Christianized. We are not to take conventional education and add a spiritual emphasis to it. As God's people, we are to reject the ways of the world and follow God's prescribed methods. "With us, as with Israel of old, success in education depends on fidelity in carrying out the Creator's plan. Adherence to the principles of God's word will bring as great blessings to us as it would have brought to the Hebrew people." [35]

A Better Way

As we learn about God's method of education, because it is so different from what we are accustomed to, we may at first think it is difficult or overwhelming. However, the truth is that God's method, because it works with the natural functioning of a child's brain, is actually easier to use than traditional methods. Not only is it easier, but it takes less time, is more effective, and produces infinitely superior results *if* parents are willing to invest in learning God's ways.

As I was driving down the highway one morning, I noticed some construction happening on the side of the road. Part of the project, apparently, was to move a pile of rocks – a massive pile that was many times the size of a house. A giant excavator was diligently scooping bucketful after bucketful of rock from the pile and loading it into a very large dump truck that, in turn, hauled the rock to its new location.

The pile was so immense, I wondered how many days it would take to move all that rock. I didn't have to wonder for long. When I drove past the construction site later that day, the entire pile was gone. Apparently, the excavator had loaded every last rock into the truck, and the truck had hauled it away. I was impressed with how much work those strong machines could accomplish in a short amount of time.

Now, suppose the manager of that project was new to this type of work. Suppose he wasn't familiar with the necessary steps of obtaining an excavator and a dump truck, and when he looked into the process, he found that it was quite involved. There was so much that was required and so much that he didn't have experience with.

Suppose he decided the whole process was too much trouble and that he didn't want to take the time to learn something new. Suppose he determined that he would get the rock moved in a way that he was familiar with, a way that he had used before. He would move the rock with a wheelbarrow. Imagine how long it would take him to move this rock without the benefit of the strong equipment. It would take months, maybe years. The idea is preposterous. Why should he reject a better, stronger, and more efficient method simply because he wasn't familiar with the method?

Parents often, unintentionally, adopt this same mindset when it comes to educating children. Perhaps because the methods in God's system of education are unfamiliar to them, perhaps because His methods are unlike those that everyone else uses, perhaps because the parents don't have experience with God's educational design, or perhaps because they don't know about His methods at all, many parents, just like the man with the wheelbarrow, decide to follow a method with which they are familiar.

Unfortunately, the negative effects of the familiar methods of education have become so widespread that they are now considered normal. It's normal for a child to have trouble sitting still. It's normal to hear a child say, "I'm bored." It's normal to have to create special, fun, attention-grabbing curricula for children because it's normal for a child to have trouble paying attention. It's normal for a child to forget a large percentage of what he learns in school. It's normal for children to be uninterested in the adult world or in religious things. The effects of deviating from God's perfect plan have become so normal that a child's lack of pleasure in learning doesn't even alarm us. But is this really normal? It's about as normal as spending twelve years pushing wheelbarrows of rock when an excavator can get the job done better and much more efficiently (and with a lot more enjoyment).

There is a better way. Just like that big excavator, God's methods are so much more efficient and effective. Yes, parents will need to make an upfront investment to learn about God's method, and often following His method goes against that with which we are familiar. But God's method of education produces children who love to learn, who are calm and have amazing attention spans, whose eagerness to learn leaves them seldom bored, who don't need to be entertained, and who have a deep interest in the subjects of heaven. Because God's method is in harmony with how a child's brain was designed to function, the child develops a strong, thinking mind. And, just like the strong equipment can get the job done more efficiently, a strong mind will make the process of education happen more efficiently.

God's beautiful system of education is unparalleled; its methodologies are unique; its results are astounding. When used correctly, God's system of education never fails; it will always produce intelligent, capable, resourceful, creative, compassionate, and spiritually-strong young people who possess excellent leadership skills, are self-disciplined, and excel socially – which should not come as a surprise since this method of education has been prescribed by the Creator Himself. This is how children were designed to learn. "He only who created the mind and ordained its laws can perfectly understand its needs or direct its development. The principles of education that He has given are the only safe guide." [36]

Words of Counsel

"The foolishness of God is wiser than men; and the weakness of God is stronger than men." 1 Corinthians 1:25

"Press in the right direction, and make a change, solidly, intelligently. Then circumstances will be your helpers and not your hindrances. Make a beginning. The oak is in the acorn." [37]

Chapter 2

The Whole Child

"And thou shalt love the Lord thy God with all thine heart, and with all thy soul, and with all thy might." – Deuteronomy 6:5

OPENING a book on true education, one might expect to read advice on curriculum and guidelines for what to teach a five-year-old. While this book does provide help in these areas, it doesn't begin there. The reason for this is that true education does not begin with a curriculum, nor does it begin at age five. God's method of education deals with the whole child, begins at birth, and includes a significant amount of preparation before a child is ever introduced to reading or math. These elements are outlined in the next few chapters and cannot be neglected if a parent wants to educate their child according to God's plan.

Conventional systems of education tend to focus on putting information into the mind, and most cultures define education in terms of mental development. But God's plan of education involves the entire being. His method of education involves "the harmonious development of the physical, the mental, and the spiritual powers."[1] Just as a wheel cannot be completely balanced when a spoke is missing from the wheel, nor can a child be balanced when one aspect of his education is missing. "The nature of man is threefold, and the training enjoined by Solomon" – train up a child in the way he should go: and when he is old, he will not depart from it – "comprehends the right development of the physical, intellectual, and moral powers."[2] To properly educate a child, we must educate the whole child – the physical, the intellectual, and the moral.

Advanced Academic Performance

Some may think that focusing on the whole child risks lowering academic standards, but the whole-child approach and high academic performance are not mutually exclusive. In fact, the opposite is true.

The whole-child approach to education engages numerous areas of a child's brain at once, which in turn prompts the development of more connections between brain cells, which strengthens the brain, promotes more effective learning, aids retention and recall, improves competence and proficiency, and facilitates application of what is learned.

Dr. Carla Hannaford, in her book *Smart Moves: Why Learning Is Not All in Your Head,* tells us that true learning is more than intellectual input. "The intricate wiring of the limbic system shows that in order to learn and remember something, there must be sensory input [intellectual], a personal emotional connection [emotional/moral], and movement [physical]."[3]

The Whole Is More Than the Sum of Its Parts

An education that wholly integrates physical, mental, and spiritual development is woefully misunderstood, underused, and undervalued today. The educational practices predominantly used throughout the world – even among most homeschooling families – usually separate the intellectual, physical, and moral education. Spiritual development happens in Bible class or church, physical development in physical education class, and intellectual development in school. Academic studies (such as math, science, history, geography, and social studies) are even further categorized and isolated into separate compartments to be learned at separate times.

God's method of education is naturally integrated and all-encompassing. All academic learning overlaps and overflows into the physical and spiritual areas. The type of physical education that God endorses not only strengthens the body, but also the moral and the mental powers. And spiritual education involves not only character development, but also the expansion and care of the physical and intellectual powers. This is a wonderfully wise design as this approach to education encourages the brain to function as a whole, and a child's learning and thinking abilities are developed to his fullest potential.

The Moral Powers

God has given parents the responsibility to cultivate the moral powers of their children,[4] but what are the moral powers?

Due to the influence of false education, many parents unknowingly confuse the development of the moral powers with the development of the intellectual powers. Consequently, they erroneously believe that they are giving their child a moral education when they read Bible stories to their child or teach their child to memorize Bible verses. While these activities may very well have a valuable impact on the child's moral education, they primarily contribute to the development of the intellectual powers rather than the moral.

The intellectual powers have more to do with the understanding, the logical element of the mind, a knowledge of right and wrong; while the moral powers have their foundation in love and are intimately connected with (if not regulated by) the child's desires, will, and affections.[5] Moral power is strongly interlaced with a deep heart desire for goodness. This heart desire is most effectively developed and nourished through a child's relationship with his parents, which is later transferred to his relationship with his heavenly Father. When parents properly develop the moral powers in their child through their relationship with their child, over time the child's affections are drawn out to God, love is deepened, the heart-desire for right is strengthened, a relationship with his Father in heaven is developed, and faith and trust in Him increases and expands. (I'll discuss how to practically do this in a later chapter.)

It is true that intellectual powers and moral powers walk hand-in-hand, and that the one is affected, nourished, and supported by the other (as well as by the physical development). However, care should be taken to avoid confusing the moral powers with the intellectual powers, otherwise, a parent risks neglecting the cultivation of the moral powers. Without strong affections toward God, all the Biblical knowledge in the world will not make a child morally strong. It is the precious love of Christ that compels us.[6]

The Intellectual Powers

Due to the ubiquitous and all-pervasive influence of false education on modern-day culture, an individual's intelligence is often judged by his degree of academic education or his occupation. Intelligence has come to be synonymous with a scholastic education, so much so that the terms *intelligent* and *schooled* are often used interchangeably. But intelligence and academics are not the same.

Academics are usually limited to areas of study that are typically taught in school, such as the study of languages, science, and mathematics. That which is studied in academics is not always applied in a practical way in everyday life.

Intelligence, on the other hand, while it may include an understanding of academic subjects, is much more comprehensive. Intelligence can be used in a practical manner, and it is not measured by the amount of knowledge one has, but rather by one's ability to acquire, assimilate, and use knowledge. [7] A person can be highly intelligent without formal academic training. In fact, some of the most intelligent people who ever lived (such as Benjamin Franklin, Thomas Edison, and Albert Einstein) either had very little academic training or performed very poorly in school.

"Moral, intellectual, and physical culture should be combined in order to have well-developed, well-balanced men and women." [8] God created humans with incredible intellectual powers, and it is only through His perfect method of education that a child may develop to his fullest potential.

The Physical Powers

The common saying among woodsmen, "If I had four hours to chop down a tree, I'd spend the first two hours sharpening the axe" highlights a valuable lesson. An otherwise difficult job can be made significantly easier if one is willing to invest some upfront effort and time in preparing for the job. One can either spend time and effort sharpening his ax so that the task of cutting down the tree goes smoothly, or one can spend much time and effort trying to cut down a tree with a dull ax.

That same principle holds true for educating a child. A close chemical and biological link exists between a child's daily health habits and the development and functioning of his mental *and* moral powers. When parents first invest time and effort into developing the child's physical constitution (sharpening the ax), the development of his intellectual and moral powers will happen more quickly and more easily.

Focusing on developing the intellect without understanding the impact that the physical habits have on intellectual and emotional development is one of the main reasons for many of the failures of traditional education. "Both mental and spiritual vigor are in great degree *dependent* upon physical strength and activity." [9]

And a lack of understanding of the physical needs of a young child is the cause for many tears, frustration, and learning problems in the school (and homeschool) setting. "In the early education of children, many parents and teachers fail to understand that the *greatest attention* needs to be given to the physical constitution, that a healthy condition of body and brain may be secured." [10] "Right physical habits promote mental superiority." [11]

"There is an intimate relation between the mind and the body, and in order to reach a high standard of moral and intellectual attainment the laws that control our physical being must be heeded." [12] If we want our children to be strong mentally and spiritually, we must prioritize proper physical habits, for "whatever promotes physical health, promotes the development of a strong mind and a well-balanced character." [13]

I'll share some guidelines for proper physical development according to God's plan in the next chapter.

God's Desire

In the beginning, God created man with superior intelligence. "All his faculties were capable of development; their capacity and vigor were continually to increase." [14] Adam's mind was capable of comprehending wondrously complex ideas, [15] and he could probably explain molecular biology, electrochemistry, atomic physics, and kinetic energy with the same ease we can explain how to make a peanut butter sandwich. "Had he remained loyal to God, all this would have been his forever. Throughout eternal ages, he would have continued to gain new treasures of knowledge, to discover fresh springs of happiness, and to obtain clearer and yet clearer conceptions of the wisdom, the power, and the love of God.

"But by disobedience this was forfeited."[16] Because of sin, Adam's moral, physical, and intellectual capacity was greatly lessened.

God desires, through the work of *His* method of education, to restore humans to their original state – not just morally, but also physically and mentally. "To restore in man the image of his Maker, to bring him back to the perfection in which he was created, to promote the development of body, mind, and soul, that the divine purpose in his creation might be realized — this was to be the work of redemption. This is the object of education, the great object of life."[17] "In the highest sense the work of education and the work of redemption are one."[18]

Words of Counsel

"True education is the preparation of the physical, mental, and moral powers for the performance of every duty; it is the training of body, mind, and soul for divine service. This is the education that will endure unto eternal life."[19]

"Education comprises more than a knowledge of books."[20]

"We should not close our eyes to the defects in the present system of education. In the eager effort to secure intellectual culture, physical as well as moral training has been neglected."[21]

"Any effort that exalts intellectual culture above moral training is misdirected."[22]

"Something more is called for than the culture of the intellect. Education is not complete unless the body, the mind, and the heart are equally educated."[23]

"And thou shalt love the Lord thy God with all thy heart, and with all thy soul, and with all thy mind, and with all thy strength: this is the first commandment."[24]

"The physical, mental, and spiritual capabilities should be developed in order to form a properly balanced character."[25]

CHAPTER 3

HEALTHY LEARNING

*"During the first six or seven years of a child's life
special attention should be given to its physical
training, rather than the intellectual." – Review
and Herald, August 1, 1899*

FOUR-YEAR-OLD Daniel was outside constructing roads in the dirt for his little pretend people and animals to travel on when his mother said it was time to go to the kitchen and prepare the midday meal. "Yes, Mother!" he exclaimed enthusiastically as he quickly gathered his stone and stick figures and neatly placed them under a nearby bush so he could find them later.

Daniel's chubby little hands worked carefully as he helped his mother prepare the greens to place in the large cooking pot. When the vegetables were hot and tender, his mother set them on the table along with the warm, cooked lentils and enough bread for everyone. After thanking the God in heaven for His love and provision for them, the family began to eat their simple meal – everyone except for Daniel, who was obviously deep in thought.

After a brief, quiet moment, the little boy asked, "Mother, why can we not have the other food?" Daniel's father knew and understood the thoughts that lie beneath the little boy's simple question. The tables of the nations around them, and even of many of their own people, were often laden with a rich and more flavorful fare than the simple provision daily found on their family's table.

Daniel took a bite of his whole-grain bread as his father gently explained to his little questioner that the God of heaven desired His people to live a life of simplicity, self-denial, and self-control. "It is our duty," Father explained, "to bring our appetite and our habits of life into conformity to natural law." [1] "At our daily meals, Mama and I are educating your tastes and appetite. [2] We are training them to appreciate simplicity. Instruction from the Torah won't make a firm impression upon your heart if it is benumbed by a rich diet." [3]

Seeing that Daniel was satisfied with the explanation, Father asked Daniel a question. "Remember what Mama explained to you this morning just before you began your walk to the water well and you asked for a fig?"

"Yes," recalled the little boy. "She reminded me that it wasn't time to eat. I had already eaten earlier that morning."

"And she told you that your morning meal would give you the energy you needed to be able to wait until the next meal, didn't she?"

Daniel smiled and nodded his head as he took another bite of the soft lentils that tasted quite good to him.

"Were you still hungry when you were finished bringing the water to the house?" asked his father.

Daniel thought for a moment. He couldn't remember being hungry.

Daniel was still trying to remember if he was hungry when his father continued. "We don't choose what to eat and when to eat according to what pleases us; rather, we make those choices for the glory of Jehovah." [4]

"That's called self-control!" Daniel exclaimed as a previous conversation with his mother sprang into his mind.

"That's correct, my son. The desire to advance in the divine life and to perfect holiness in the fear of God are the ruling principles in our life, not appetite." [5]

Father then reminded his little boy of what they had been learning from the Torah about gluttony and of the warnings they had in the history of their people. "It is impossible for any to enjoy the blessing of sanctification while they are gluttonous." [6] "Eating too much of even healthful foods will degrade the higher and nobler faculties that the great God of heaven has given you," Daniel's father explained. This reminded Daniel of thoughts on unselfishness that his mother had shared with him when they were watching the mother bird feed her babies, and so, the conversation wandered off to other topics.

Later that evening during family worship, Father talked about the specific directions that the great God of heaven had given them regarding the offerings they were to bring to Him. No defective or diseased animal should be presented as an offering to a pure and holy God. Only the most perfect animal is to be selected for this purpose. "Our pure and holy God also requires that our habits of eating and drinking be such as to secure the preservation of physical, mental, and moral health, that we may present *ourselves* to the Lord – not an offering corrupted by wrong habits, but – as 'a living sacrifice, holy, acceptable unto God.'" [7]

Daniel had heard his father and mother talk about this topic many times, and his little mind was contemplating those concepts when he heard his father speak again. "We must cultivate habits of self-control and simplicity, that our bodies may be in health, and our minds may be unclouded, so we can preserve the full vigor of every faculty to give to the service of God. We must commit our souls and bodies unto God, to be used for his glory." [8]

While the other parents in their community educated their children in the usual branches of education, thus hoping to ensure success in life, the parents of Daniel were carefully and diligently teaching him of the history of Israel and training him in habits of diligence, integrity, unselfishness, self-control, earnestness of purpose, and steadfastness in adhering to true principles. They taught him of the laws of his own being, of his responsibility as a steward of not only his moral powers, but also his intellectual and physical powers, and of his duty to live uncompromisingly for the honor of the God of heaven. These precious lessons were given to him in both word and example, and Daniel learned them not only in theory, but in reality and in practice.

Daniel thrived amid the loving instruction and example of his parents, and, in turn, he learned to love and obey the God of heaven. But this love and obedience would soon be tested.

Eleven years later and many hundreds of miles away, a foreign king sent his army in the direction of Daniel's home. The army of Babylon intended to invade Daniel's homeland. They succeeded in their purpose and took Daniel and many of his countrymen hostage.

At the tender age of fifteen, [9] Daniel found himself in a strange place, far from his simple home, far from his loving mother and father, far from everything that was familiar to him, far from everything that was dear to him. [10]

Soon after arriving in Babylon, Daniel learned that he and other young captives were selected to be trained to fill important positions in the Babylonian kingdom. To qualify them for the honored position in the king's court, these young men would be subjected to a special, three-year training course that provided extraordinary educational advantages and physical discipline. In order to secure the best physical and mental development that could be obtained, a special diet – the diet that was believed to be the best for physical health and mental vigor – would be provided for them during this training period. The king bestowed a great honor upon them by giving them the royal food to eat, food that was very different from the simple food of Daniel's childhood.

Daniel contemplated these strange new occurrences. Here he was, a worshiper of Jehovah, captive in a strange land whose inhabitants were known for their genius and wealth. Everything had been stripped from him. The boasts of the Babylonians could be heard on every side citing their victory as evidence that their religion, their customs, and their lifestyle were superior to the religion and customs of his people. How could Daniel *not* eat the food provided for him? How could he risk offending the king himself?

Daniel's thoughts transported him back to his childhood. Tears welled up in his eyes as he thought of his loving mother and father who had faithfully taught him of the ways of Jehovah. His parents had demonstrated in their lives what it meant to reverence the laws of God in the heart. He had been taught that his physical, mental, and moral powers all belonged to God. "Daniel's parents had trained him in his childhood to habits of strict temperance. They had taught him that he must conform to nature's laws in all his habits; that his eating and drinking had a direct influence upon his physical, mental, and moral nature, and that he was accountable to God for his capabilities." [11] "Daniel did not long hesitate. He decided to stand firm in his integrity, let the result be what it might." [12] He would honor God even if it offended the king and even if it meant the loss of his life.

Daniel decided that he would talk to the officer in charge of those who would be going through the training. The task in front of Daniel was not an easy one. It took courage and determination. He was not just asking to be excused from the wine and unclean meats; no, he was asking for a completely different diet – the simple diet that, from his childhood, he had learned to be the best for physical, mental, and moral strength. But Daniel "was true, firm, and noble. He sought to live in peace with all, while he was unbending as the lofty cedar wherever principle was involved. In everything that did not come in collision with his allegiance to God, he was respectful and obedient to those who had authority over him; but he had so high a sense of the claims of God that the requirements of earthly rulers were held subordinate. He would not be induced by any selfish consideration to swerve from his duty." [13]

There are some who may think that Daniel was too particular, that he didn't have to be so strict and risk offending the king – and maybe even lose his life. "But those who reason thus will find in the day of Judgment that they turned from God's express requirements, and set up their own opinion as a standard of right and wrong. They will find that what seemed to them unimportant was not so regarded of God." [14] God did not give His requirements to be classified according to perceived importance by human minds. "Those who accept and obey one of his precepts because it is convenient to do so, while they reject another because its observance would require a sacrifice, lower the standard of right, and by their example lead others to lightly regard the holy law of God. 'Thus saith the Lord' is to be our rule in all things." [15]

"The Lord regarded with approval the firmness and self-denial" [16] of Daniel and the handful of other faithful young men, and His blessing attended him. "At the end of the ten days ... not only in personal appearance, but in physical activity and mental vigor, those who had been temperate in their habits exhibited a marked superiority over their companions who had indulged appetite. As a result of this trial, Daniel and his associates were permitted to continue their simple diet during the whole course of their training for the duties of the kingdom." [17]

During the three years of his Babylonian education, Daniel

constantly depended upon the God of heaven for the power to be faithful to the true education he received in childhood. At the end of their three-year training, in their examination with other candidates for the honors of the kingdom, there was found none like Daniel and his companions who remained firm to the principles of God. "At the court of Babylon were gathered representatives from all lands, men of the highest talent, men the most richly endowed with natural gifts, and possessed of the broadest culture that the world could bestow; yet among them all, the Hebrew youth were without a peer. In physical strength and beauty, in mental vigor and literary attainment, they stood unrivaled." [18]

"What if Daniel and his companions had made a compromise with those heathen officers, and had yielded to the pressure of the occasion by eating and drinking as was customary with the Babylonians? That single instance of departure from principle would have weakened their sense of right and their abhorrence of wrong. Indulgence of appetite would have involved the sacrifice of physical vigor, clearness of intellect, and spiritual power. One wrong step would probably have led to others, until, their connection with heaven being severed, they would have been swept away by temptation." [19]

The life of Daniel, who "even in his youth ... was a moral giant in the strength of the Mighty One," [20] presents a lesson for all parents who desire their child's mind to develop to its fullest potential. "A strict compliance with the requirements of God is beneficial to the health of body *and mind*. In order to reach the highest standard of moral and intellectual attainments, it is necessary to seek wisdom and strength from God, and to observe strict temperance in all the habits of life." [21] "The experience of Daniel and his youthful companions illustrates the benefits that may result from an abstemious diet, and shows what God will do for those who will co-operate with Him in the purifying and uplifting of the soul." [22]

"The spirit that possessed Daniel, the youth of today may have; they may draw from the same source of strength, possess the same power of self-control, and reveal the same grace in their lives." [23] "The same mighty truths that were revealed through these men, God desires to reveal through the youth and children today." [24] In this account of the life of Daniel, "we hear the voice of God addressing us individually, bidding us ... place ourselves in right relation to the laws of health." [25]

We, like Daniel's parents, have the wonderful privilege and responsibility of helping our children, through our daily practice, learn to obey God's health laws, thus shaping the habits that are so integral to the development of the intellectual and moral circuitry of their brains. Many don't realize that these laws significantly affect how well a child can learn. They may wonder why so many pages in a book on true education are dedicated to the subject of health. We must remember that children are whole beings. It is impossible to affect one part of their being without affecting another part. Neural function and the healthy development of brain circuits are strongly influenced by a child's health habits. This is why "those who give proper attention to physical development will make greater advancement in literary lines than they would if their entire time were devoted to study." [26]

And, because of the intimate interconnection of the body and the brain, the factors that affect the physical health of a child not only affect his developing intellect and learning abilities, but also his emotional and spiritual health as well. "A close sympathy exists between the physical and the moral nature. The standard of virtue is elevated or degraded by the physical habits." [27] "Whatever affects the body has a corresponding effect on the mind *and* the soul." [28] "Recklessness in physical habits tends to recklessness in morals." [29]

Some are inclined to think of God's requirements as restrictive – as if God's laws will stifle our fun. But God's laws are far from restrictive. His commands "are the dictates of infinite wisdom, goodness, and love." [30] They are protective. "God desires man to be happy, and for this reason he gave him the precepts of his law, that in obeying these he might have joy." [31] If killing and stealing were able to bring us happiness and peace, then God would not have laws against them. The same is true for *all* of God's laws – not only His moral laws, but also health laws. "All the laws of nature – which are the laws of God – are designed for our good. Obedience to them will promote our happiness in this life, and will aid us in a preparation for the life to come." [32] "It was in love that our heavenly Father sent the light of health reform." [33] "God does not require us to give up anything that it is for our best interest to retain." [34] "In all that He does, He has the well-being of His children in view." [35]

"Those who perceive the evidences of God's love, who understand something of the wisdom and beneficence of His laws, and the results of obedience, will come to regard their duties and obligations from an altogether different point of view. Instead of looking upon an observance of the laws of health as a matter of sacrifice or self-denial, they will regard it, as it really is, as an inestimable blessing." [36]

Principles for Healthy Development

There are several factors that contribute to a child's healthy physical development. This section will cover some of the most influential ones.

It is important that parents not only follow God's health principles, but they should also explain the reasons for them to their children. Rather than expecting blind obedience to some arbitrary rules, parents should give their children an intelligent understanding of *why* health laws are to be obeyed so that when the children are not under the guidance of their parents, they can make wise decisions on their own. "God gave to Israel instruction in all the principles essential to physical as well as to moral health, and *it was concerning these principles* no less than concerning those of the moral law that He commanded them: 'These words, which I command thee this day, shall be in thine heart: and thou shalt teach them diligently unto thy children, and shalt talk of them when thou sittest in thine house, and when thou walkest by the way, and when thou liest down, and when thou risest up. And thou shalt bind them for a sign upon thine hand, and they shall be as frontlets between thine eyes. And thou shalt write them upon the posts of thy house, and on thy gates.' Deuteronomy 6:6-9" [37]

Quiet and Simple Life

The first step toward good health for a child is to provide for him a quiet and simple life. "The more quiet and simple the life of the child – the more free from artificial excitement and the more in harmony with nature – the more favorable it is to physical and mental vigor and to spiritual strength."[38] How can we make a child's life quiet and simple?

Parents can cultivate a home environment that is free from clutter, one that minimizes artificial stimuli, such as electronic toys and devices, constant music or other noise, or an abundance of toys and games, and one where learning happens in a natural way instead of through artificial means.

Care should also be taken to avoid overstimulation by engaging in more than one activity at a time, such as giving children a craft to do while they listen to a story (such as is common in children's classes at church). When the young child's brain is given concurrent inputs, it is forced to either block out one of the inputs or switch its attention back and forth between the two – something known as task switching. This type of demand on a child's mind impairs cognitive processes, especially the type of brain processes that involve deep thought and creativity. It can also negatively affect the anterior cingulate cortex, which is an area of the brain that is involved with impulse control, decision making, attention span, and motivation. [39]

In addition to the physical environment, parents can bring a simple and quiet peace to the home through their demeanor. Parents should be quiet and calm. A parent's "gentle, unhurried manner will have a soothing influence that will be of untold benefit to the child."[40]

Quiet and simple also means unrushed. Children need time to ask questions, time to be well-heard, time to process communication, time to think. They need time for relationship and affection. They need calmness and an unhurried atmosphere.

Yet, quiet and simple does not mean inactive. Children were created to be active – very active. An abundance of physical activity, such as running, crawling, jumping, tumbling, and spinning actually enhances brain growth. But this activity can and should be a result of the natural energy of a healthy, strong, and active child whose life includes an abundance of time in nature and healthy work – not a result of pent-up energy that results from too much inactivity, a stimulating diet, or from artificial stimulation (such as media).

Physical Activity

When we want to improve a child's math and reading skills, our first thought may not be to spend less time in the books and more time in physical activity, yet this is exactly what research has found to be beneficial. Even when physical activity replaces a significant portion of academic time, we see improved academic performance. [41]

Research shows that movement improves the functioning of brain cells and protects them from stress and cell death. Physical activity also stimulates the production of new neurons in several areas of the brain involved with learning, problem-solving, planning ahead, the ability to focus, language development, attention span, motivation, emotional processing, and more.

Not only does being physically active assist in the development of various parts of the brain, but it is also a key factor for stimulating the integration of these brain areas so they can work together harmoniously. Any physical activity that involves cross-lateral body movements (movements in which opposite sides of the body work together, such as crawling, hoeing, raking, skipping, and climbing) is especially strengthening to the corpus callosum – a band of nerve fibers that facilitates good communication between the left and right brain hemispheres. This connection between the two brain hemispheres plays an extremely important role in whole-brain thinking; the stronger this connection, the better the two sides of the brain can communicate, and the stronger the thinking abilities.

Physical activity also increases the level of neurotransmitters like dopamine, serotonin, and norepinephrine, all of which boost alertness, augment memory, and improve concentration and ability to focus.

There's yet another reason that movement helps a child learn. Have you ever noticed how children like to spin themselves around and around faster and faster until they are so dizzy that they can barely stand up? Or how they can find endless entertainment doing cartwheels and somersaults and standing on their heads? All of these activities would make an adult feel ill, but God put in children the desire and ability to move like this because these types of movements develop a child's vestibular system and proprioceptive system – two systems in the body that largely impact a child's development.

The vestibular system and the proprioceptive system are systems in the body that are closely involved with learning. Among their many functions, these systems are involved with vision and eye function, holding a pencil properly, fine motor control, coordination, hand-writing, reading, the ability to focus and pay attention, sensory processing, integration of auditory and visual senses, spatial orientation, the ability to sit still, and much more. Well-developed proprioceptive and vestibular systems also enhance the development and integration of all other senses and may even help prevent learning disabilities. Asking a child to do academic work before his proprioceptive or vestibular systems are sufficiently developed has been compared to attempting to put one's shoes on before their socks. The brain and body are not ready, and the learning will suffer.

How do we incorporate more physical activity into a child's day? Parents don't need to include a physical education class in their child's daily schedule. There is no need for a daily regimen of toe touches, push-ups, running around the house, or jumping jacks. The type of physical activity that God's method of education enjoins is not an hour of calisthenics or aerobics, but rather practical, useful work and time outside in nature. [42] (More on this in later chapters.)

Does this mean that a child should be allowed to run wild like a little tornado and never be required to sit still? Not at all. An abundance of movement should be incorporated into a child's day, but most of this movement should be purposeful movement, not wild, uncontrolled movement. There are times, such as in church, at mealtime, or when visiting in someone's home, that a child needs to be able to sit still. Strenuous activity of the large muscles of the body promotes small muscle development, which in turn contributes to a child's ability to sit still. This means that the more physical activity a child engages in, the easier it will be for that child to sit still. If a child engages in several hours of outdoor activity every day, helps with the daily work of the household, gets sufficient sleep, eats a healthy diet, lives a healthy lifestyle, and is emotionally secure, he will be active, but his activity can be controlled and calm. And, when necessary, he will be able to sit quietly for long periods of time.

That said, parents should remember that, in general, our un-healthy, inactive, academically-oriented society expects children to be more sedentary than God created them to be. While inactivity and passivity may be attractive to adults, these inactive periods do very little for a child's brain development, and parents should minimize them as much as possible.

"Physical culture is an essential part of all right methods of education. The young need to be taught how to develop their physical powers, how to preserve these powers in the best condition, and how to make them useful in the practical duties of life. Many think that these things are no part of school work; but this is a mistake. The lessons necessary to fit one for practical usefulness should be taught to every child in the home and to every student in the schools." [43]

Sunshine

Being physically active provides a number of benefits, and when the activity is performed outdoors, the benefits are multiplied. [44]

Exposure to sunlight stimulates capillary growth and frontal-lobe function, as well as the production of serotonin and dopamine – two neurotransmitters that increase a child's ability to be calm and to focus. And research suggests that exposing the skin and eyes to sun-light may stimulate brain cell growth and overall brain development, and may enhance motor learning and memory. [45]

To receive sufficient exposure to the sun, children should spend several hours a day outdoors. "Outdoor exercise is best." [46]

Fresh Air

"In order for children and youth to have health, cheerfulness, vivacity, and well-developed muscles and brains, they should be much in the open air." [47] "The health cannot be preserved unless some portion of each day is given to muscular exertion in the open air." [48]

Fresh, outside air has a vitalizing effect on the entire body, [49] and especially the brain. [50] The electrically charged ions that are found in fresh outdoor air – especially in the air around moving water, plants, and trees – stimulate the growth of brain cells. They also produce biochemical reactions that increase levels of serotonin in the brain. Serotonin facilitates better brain function and contributes significantly to the regulation of mood and cognition. [51] The results include a sense of serenity or calmness, better brain growth, improved concentration, better memory, and improved learning. [52] Indoor air is deficient in these brain-boosting ions, and it usually has a suboptimal balance of oxygen, carbon dioxide, and nitrogen.

Children should spend several hours a day outdoors, and there is no need to limit access to fresh air in the winter months. "If children are well clothed, it will benefit them to exercise freely in the open air, summer or winter." [53]

"Fresh air is the free blessing of Heaven, calculated to electrify the whole system." [54]

Nature

Nature is more of an actual need for children than many realize. Our Creator chose for the first humans "the surroundings best adapted for their health and happiness. He did not place them in a palace or surround them with the artificial adornments and luxuries that so many today are struggling to obtain. He placed them in close touch with nature." [55] "The pure air, the glad sunshine, the flowers and trees, the orchards and vineyards, and outdoor exercise amid these surroundings, are health-giving, life-giving." [56] The mental, the moral, and the physical – the whole child – thrive in the beautiful atmosphere of God's creation.

"For the first eight or ten years of a child's life the field or garden is the best schoolroom, the mother the best teacher, nature the best lesson book." [57] (We'll look at this topic more in depth later in this book.)

Cheerfulness and Its Companions

Proverbs 17:22 tells us, "A merry heart doeth good like a medicine: but a broken spirit drieth the bones." This counsel isn't an old wives' tale. Feelings of love and cheerfulness increase endorphin levels in the body, boost the immune system, reduce the risk of contracting viruses and infections, decrease the stress response, and promote better sleep at night. [58]

"Courage, hope, faith, sympathy, love, promote health and prolong life. A contented mind, a cheerful spirit, is health to the body and strength to the soul." [59] "Parents, let the sunshine of love, cheerfulness, and happy contentment enter your own hearts, and let its sweet, cheering influence pervade your home. Manifest a kindly, forbearing spirit; and encourage the same in your children, cultivating all the graces that will brighten the home life." [60] "Gratitude, rejoicing, benevolence, trust in God's love and care – these are health's greatest safeguard." [61]

Schedule

"To everything there is a season, and a time to every purpose under the heaven" (Ecclesiastes 3:1).

The circadian rhythm (the body's natural internal clock that regulates the daily cycle of many biological processes) was given to us by God as a support for health and happiness. "In every family there should be order, and regular habits. There should be a fixed time to rise in the morning, a time for breakfast, and a time for prayer," [62] "a fixed time for morning and evening worship," [63] specific times for work, for outdoor activities, for bath time, bedtime, and the other activities that are done on a daily basis. This course of action cooperates with the functioning of circadian rhythm and leads to improved physical health (including good digestion, proper cleansing of the blood, and even superior muscle strength) and better brain function (including better mood, better integration of the different areas of the brain, and better learning). [64]

Two areas of regularity that most significantly affect a child's brain development and behavior are eating times and sleeping times. "Irregular hours for eating and sleeping sap the brain forces." [65] "Regularity should be the rule in all the habits of children." [66]

Children thrive with predictability in their lives. Predictability reduces stress in the brain and helps it recover from stressors, which in turn helps children with behavior regulation. Knowing what comes next in their day and what time to expect certain activities gives children a sense of security and assists with the regulation of cortisol production (which affects the developing brain). Children whose daily activities follow a regular schedule tend to be more patient, calm, and attentive, and better behaved overall.

As parents strive to help their family live life on a regular schedule, they should be careful not to impose an unrealistic schedule on their child. Children usually need more time for everyday activities than do adults. Tight schedules discourage exploration, experimentation, and learning, and don't allow enough time for a child to think and contemplate. For example, bedtime can certainly be at a set time every evening, but there should be sufficient time allotted in the schedule so that a four-year-old has enough time to ask his twenty-six questions at family worship, sing a good-night song to all the birds at the birdfeeder, test out his walking abilities with both of his legs in one pajama leg, go to the bathroom eight times, snuggle with his parents, and all the other things a little four-year-old mind needs to have time to do for good brain development. The daily schedule should have plenty of padding, and it should also be somewhat flexible so that important opportunities, such as character-building moments, don't have to be neglected in order to stay on schedule. A good schedule is not a rigid slave master that allows no time for valuable detours from the normal course, but rather the scaffolding that supports and contributes to the organization of a well-functioning family.

Another area in which parents may mistakenly inflict inappropriate schedule demands is in the area of breastfeeding times. Babies can and should be fed on a regular schedule, but that schedule should be in harmony with a baby's biological needs, which may vary slightly from day to day and significantly from month to month, and often vary from the parents' desires and needs. Breastmilk digests quickly, and much damage can be done by allowing a baby to cry from hunger because there are yet twenty minutes until the scheduled feeding time.

Sometimes parents also have unrealistic expectations when it comes to a baby's sleep. Babies are not physiologically equipped to sleep through the night, and frequent night wakings are not only biologically normal but also healthy for a baby. [67] The need for nourishment, comfort, and reassurance in the night is not a selfish demand but an actual need. (More on this topic later.)

Physical Touch and Proximity

Research provides clear evidence that an abundance of loving, physical touch is a true biological need and is critical to proper physical, mental, emotional, and moral (spiritual) development. [68]

During the early months and years of life, numerous physiological systems are being developed – including the stress response system, the endocrine systems, the oxytocin system, the vagus nerve, and the immune system. Affectionate touch and maternal closeness are crucial for the proper development of each of these systems. [69] Children who receive an abundance of affectionate touch demonstrate superior neurological development and functioning, better behavior, better emotional regulation, better attentional processing, and better memory than children who do not receive this physical nurturing.

The absence of this physical connection can be confusing and detrimental for babies because they are not equipped to manage such a scenario.

Because physical touch plays an important role in early brain development, [70] babies and children who do not receive sufficient physical touch tend to have higher levels of the stress hormone cortisol (which reduces immune function and hampers learning), lower levels of oxytocin and vasopressin (important hormones that are linked to emotion and social bonding [71]), and underdevelopment of the prefrontal cortex, serotonin receptors, the self-regulatory system. [72] Underdevelopment of these systems translates to more difficulties with self-control, motivational regulation, empathy, reasoning, planning, problem solving, organizing, focus, and emotional regulation.

God designed infants to be physically connected with their mothers. This is one reason that babies are born helpless, unable to do anything for themselves. Human infants are completely dependent on someone else to feed them, keep them warm, protect them from danger, comfort them, and even transport them from place to place. This is God's original, simple, and practical design, and this design is no accident since, in the absence of modern-day, artificial aids (such as strollers, baby carriers, bottles, etc.), this developmentally-early birth necessitates that a mother have physical contact with her baby often, if not nearly continually. Human babies were not created and are not biologically equipped to be without continual, loving, maternal contact, and they don't develop as well without it. Research shows that even *short-term* separation from mom dysregulates multiple biological systems, leads to elevated levels of stress hormones in the baby, and has been associated with "many behavioral, immunological, and physiological consequences." [73] These negative effects are intensified in boys. [74]

An abundance of tender, physical touch is important for optimal physical, mental, and emotional development in children.

Proper Clothing

"In order to have good health, we must have good blood; for the blood is the current of life. It repairs waste and nourishes the body. ... The more perfect the circulation, the better will this work be accomplished." [75] Properly clothing the body assists good blood circulation. "At every pulsation of the heart the blood should make its way quickly and easily to all parts of the body. Its circulation should not be hindered by tight clothing or bands, or by insufficient clothing of the extremities." [76]

"The feet and limbs, being remote from the vital organs, should be especially guarded from cold by abundant clothing," [77] such as warm socks to keep the feet warm. "The limbs ... demand greater protection than the other parts of the body. ... [W]hen the limbs are left unprotected or are insufficiently clad, the arteries and veins become contracted, the sensitive portions of the body are chilled, and the circulation of the blood hindered." [78]

And, of course, "it is important also that the clothing be kept clean. The garments worn absorb the waste matter that passes off through the pores; if they are not frequently changed and washed, the impurities will be reabsorbed." [79]

Water

Water is specifically needed for cerebral circulation and for cushioning and lubrication of the brain tissue. [80] Sufficient water intake promotes better memory and attention, better mood, improved concentration, better emotional self-regulation, and superior performance on tasks that involve psychomotor skills. [81]

The body needs pure water. Juice and other fluids do not supply the body's needs as does water. "In health and in sickness, pure water is one of Heaven's choicest blessings." [82]

To keep the brain adequately hydrated, avoid drinking water (or other fluids) with meals; water should be taken in between meals when the body can most efficiently use it and when it will not impair digestion by diluting the digestive fluids.

Water intake upon arising in the morning is especially beneficial as the body is most dehydrated at this time. In addition, water is needed at least 30 minutes before breakfast to prepare digestive fluids that the stomach will need to digest breakfast.

Water is beneficial for the outside of the body as well. Bathing improves circulation, helps the skin dispose of toxins, and more. "Frequent bathing is very beneficial, especially at night, just before retiring, or upon rising in the morning. It will take but a few moments to give the children a bath and to rub them until their bodies are in a glow. This brings the blood to the surface, relieving the brain; and there will be less inclination to indulge in impure practices." [83] "Most persons would receive benefit from a cool or tepid bath every day, morning or evening. ...The mind and the body are alike invigorated. The muscles become more flexible, the intellect is made brighter." [84]

Feeding the Brain

Many parents underestimate the tremendous effect a child's diet has on his learning and his behavior.

"The relation of diet to intellectual development should be given far more attention than it has received." [85] The enteric nervous system (located in the digestive system) has moment-by-moment, direct communication with the brain, which means that "whatever is taken into the stomach affects not only the body, but ultimately the mind as well." [86] "The brain and nerves are in sympathy with the stomach. Erroneous eating and drinking result in erroneous thinking and acting." [87]

Diet also has a molding and transforming effect on "moral health." [88] "You cannot arouse the moral sensibilities of your children while you are not careful in the selection of their food." [89] "The spiritual as well as the mental and physical powers suffer under the influence of unhealthful food. The conscience becomes stupefied, and the susceptibility to good impressions is impaired." [90]

"Indulged appetite is the greatest hindrance to mental improvement and soul sanctification." [91] This is the very reason that the enemy of our souls is constantly attempting to entice and confuse in the area of diet.

The only way to ensure good health is to eat the *simple* diet that our Creator designed us to eat. "Grains, fruits, nuts, and vegetables constitute the diet chosen for us by our Creator. These foods, prepared in as *simple* and natural a manner as possible, are the most healthful and nourishing." [92] Humans cannot improve on God's perfect plan, and efforts to do so often lead to errors and – sooner or later – negative consequences.

What Should a Baby Eat?

Starting in infancy, one of the most significant ways to promote not only physical health, but also good development of the intellectual and moral circuitry of a child's brain is through breastfeeding. In addition to providing important nutrients, enzymes, hormones, and antibodies, breastfeeding also colonizes the baby's gut with beneficial gut bacteria that promote long-term health *and* have a positive influence on temperament, behavior, and cognitive functioning. [93]

(*Please understand that this information is not intended to dishearten mothers who did not breastfeed their baby – a child can still develop well even if he is not breastfed. This information is provided to inform mothers who are expecting or currently breastfeeding of the many advantages breastfeeding provides for a child.*)

Human breastmilk contains nerve growth stimulators that facilitate the development of the central nervous system. Breastmilk also contains stem cells, which pass through the gastrointestinal tract into the blood of the baby and travel to various organs, including the brain, where they become functioning brain cells.[94] Research shows that these and other characteristics exclusive to breastfeeding work together in a harmonious manner to promote development in areas of the brain associated with language, cognition, and emotional function.[95] The resulting structural differences in the brains of breastfed babies (compared to children who were formula-fed or received a combination of formula and breastmilk) contribute to superior emotional and mental intelligence throughout life.[96]

Research also shows that *extending* the period of time in which a child is breastfed is directly associated with increases in both verbal IQ and performance.[97]

One of the most astoundingly brilliant design characteristics of human breastmilk is that it is a complex, living fluid, and its composition is constantly changing over the course of years, months, weeks, days, hours, and even minutes (!) in order to precisely provide for the varied needs of a developing baby.[98] Our amazing Designer has created mother's milk to perfectly match the exact needs of the developing child down to the very minute that those needs arise! For example, in the daylight hours, breastmilk contains higher levels of energy- and activity-promoting hormones and neuroactive amino acids;[99] while nighttime milk is rich in the sleep-inducing hormones[100] – which explains why breastfeeding a baby at night can help a baby fall back asleep. Nighttime milk also contains an extra dose of tryptophan, a brain-development hormone,[101] since it is during the night hours that most of the brain growth that facilitates learning occurs.[102] "In early life, tryptophan ingestion leads to more serotonin receptor development,"[103] which translates to better learning throughout a child's life. Our great Designer placed these hormones in mother's milk and the receptors for these hormones in the baby's body because He knew exactly what a baby needed.

Breastfeeding is unparalleled in providing optimal nutritional, immunological, *and* emotional nurturing for a baby. "Human milk is not simply a food but rather a complex, human infant support system."[104]

"The best food for the infant is the food that nature provides."[105]

As the Child Grows

In the first few months, a baby's digestive system is not yet equipped with the digestive enzymes needed to digest any food other than breastmilk. Accordingly, breastmilk should be the only food for infants for *at least* the first six months of life, and many experts "recommend that two *more* months of breast milk *alone* be encouraged."[106]

If at all possible, breastfeeding should be continued for two years or longer,[107] even after complementary foods (solids) are introduced, as breastfeeding is a valuable source of bioactive compounds that provide nutrition, disease protection, and more for a child for as long as breastfeeding continues.[108]

Breastmilk is constantly synchronizing with a child's changing needs as he grows. For example, the breastmilk of a mother of a toddler contains significantly higher concentrations of total protein and healthy fats than does breastmilk made for a younger baby.[109] It is also significantly higher in lactoferrin,[110] immunoglobulin A, and other immune-boosting factors[111] that combat bacterial, viral, fungal, and parasitic infections – which may come in handy when the toddler starts taste-testing all the shoes in the house. And when a breastfeeding toddler gets sick, the number of white blood cells in the mother's milk spikes, which will help that child get well quickly.[112]

In addition, extensive research shows a positive correlation between cognitive achievement and the number of months and years breastfeeding continues.[113] The research also shows that breastfeeding duration has a positive influence on the social-emotional development of a child.[114]

Parents should wait to introduce complementary foods until their baby shows definite signs of readiness, such as the emergence of teeth, good hand-to-mouth coordination, loss of the tongue thrust reflex, the ability to chew, etc. When the child *is* old enough to eat complementary foods and begins to show an interest, very small amounts of soft fruits, such as bananas or soft pears, can be given to the child at family mealtime.

If parents wait until a baby is physiologically mature enough to eat complementary foods, there is no need to puree food or to purchase premade baby food; babies have been thriving without homemade and commercially-prepared baby food for thousands of years before blenders and baby food companies came on the scene. Studies show that pureed food is less nourishing to a baby's gut microbiota and is more likely to produce a picky eater. [115]

These soft foods should be introduced slowly. By doing so, it will be several months before baby is actually relying on solid food for nutrition, and parents should remember that if the child is still being breastfed, he is receiving more than sufficient nutrients (as well as helpful antibodies and other disease-prevention components [116]) from the breastmilk.

Whenever possible, it is best to allow a baby to feed himself. It may seem like baby is just making a mess, but there is a significant amount of hand-eye coordination and brain development that occurs when a baby feeds himself. This hands-on activity also allows him to experiment and develop good cause-to-effect reasoning and motor skills. [117] And children who are allowed to feed themselves tend to be less picky about their food. [118] Perhaps most importantly, allowing a baby to feed himself permits him to pace his eating. Adults tend to rush the eating process, thus discouraging sufficient mastication and pause between bites. They also tend to overfeed a baby. Allowing a baby to feed himself provides him with the important opportunity to learn how to regulate his appetite and to stop eating when he has had enough. Coaxing a child to eat more than he wants is not only unnecessary but is also bad for his health, as it can upset the development of proper appetite regulation.

When a baby has been eating soft fruits for a while without any problems, soft, starchy vegetables, such as cooked potatoes, squash, or sweet potatoes, may be added to the child's diet. Later, whole grains that have been well-cooked (cooked for several hours [119]) and other vegetables may be added. "These foods, prepared in as simple and natural a manner as possible, are the most healthful and nourishing." [120]

The child's diet should be kept plain, using only one or, at the most, two kinds of foods at a meal. A simple diet that limits the variety of foods at one meal has been shown to enhance the absorption of various nutrients that assist with brain functioning. [121]

There is no need to add butter (or butter substitutes), oil, sweeteners (even so-called healthy sweeteners), condiments, seasonings, or other taste-enhancers to a young child's food. Children should be given "only plain food, of that quality that would preserve to them the best condition of health." [122] This simple food will train a child's palate to relish the flavors of the healthful, nourishing foods provided for us by our Creator.

Foods to be Avoided

There are a few foods that should be avoided due to their detrimental effects on the physical and moral development of a child and their tendency to hamper brain functioning. [123]

Caffeine and Related Chemicals

Caffeine and its related chemicals [124] that are found in chocolate and other cocoa products, some tea, mate, some energy food and beverages, coffee (both caffeinated and decaffeinated), and colas should have no place in a child's diet. These are all psychoactive compounds that alter the biochemistry of the forebrain and can affect learning and memory. [125]

Refined and Concentrated Sweeteners

Sugar and other refined or concentrated sweeteners (such as agave, brown rice syrup, molasses, stevia, coconut sugar, etc.) hinder the functioning of the body systems, including the brain. They also inhibit the functioning of the hippocampus, a part of the brain that plays a vital role in learning. [126] In addition, sweeteners create an imbalance in the gut microbiota, which has a strong influence on brain development, mood, behavior, and health. [127]

"It is better to let sweet things alone. Let alone those sweet dessert dishes that are placed on the table. [We] do not need them. [We] want a clear mind to think after God's order." [128]

Other Refined Foods

A refined food is a food from which fiber and other nutrients have been removed. For example, wheat and wheat flour are whole foods, but removing fiber and other nutrients results in a refined food – white flour. Sugar cane is a whole food, but removing fiber and other nutrients results in a refined product – sugar. Oranges and other fruits are whole foods, but removing the fiber and other nutrients from these fruits results in refined products – orange juice and other fruit juices. Olives are a whole food, but removing fiber and other nutrients results in a refined food – olive oil. These are just a few examples of refined foods; a high percentage of the food occupying our modern-day grocery store shelves are refined products.

The consumption of refined foods impairs hippocampus and endothelial function, hinders the blood's ability to absorb and deliver oxygen to the brain cells, and negatively affects brain development, thinking skills, and attention span. [129] God designed food to be consumed in its unrefined, unprocessed form and "prepared in as simple and natural a manner as possible." [130]

Animal products

"In choosing man's food in Eden, the Lord showed what was the best diet." [131] "Grains, with fruits, nuts, and vegetables, contain all the nutritive properties necessary to make good blood," [132] and "in order to have good health, we must have good blood; for the blood is the current of life." [133]

Research shows that the intake of animal products causes a negative shift in the gut microbiota ecology. This impairs health, affects thinking, and promotes changes in the brain that can disturb mood and negatively affect learning. [134] Animal products also tend to weaken the higher-thinking skills of the brain and strengthen the lower propensities, impulses, and passions. [135]

Cheese, which contains amines and fatty acids that cause irritation to the nerves and the gastrointestinal tract, is especially harmful and "should never be introduced into the stomach." [136]

Spices

While herbs are generally healing in nature and offer many benefits to health, spices are irritating to the entire body system, [137] are linked to a number of diseases, [138] and have an especially deleterious effect on the central nervous system. [139] Many spices also have the potential to negatively affect the gut microbiome, and a healthy gut microbiome plays an essential role in good brain function. [140]

As a general rule, spices are usually derived from the bark, buds, roots, or aromatic seeds of plants. On the other hand, herbs are usually derived from the leafy parts of herbaceous plants. Herbs include basil, bay leaf, chives, cilantro, dill weed, marjoram, mint, parsley, rosemary, sage, savory, tarragon, and thyme. Spices include allspice, anise, cassia, cardamon, cayenne pepper, chili powder, cinnamon, cloves, cumin, horseradish, mace, mustard, nutmeg, pepper (black and white), poppy seeds, and turmeric. [141] Any peppers that contain capsaicinoids (the most common of which is capsaicin, an irritant alkaloid that gives peppers their pungent flavor) are also included in the category of spices. This includes peppers such as banana peppers, pepperoncini, Anaheim, poblano, cayenne, and others. Sweet bell peppers contain little to no capsaicin and are not considered a spice.

Alcohol, Vinegar, and Other Fermented Foods

The fermentation process produces waste products that are toxic to the body. These waste products cause irritation to the digestive system and the nervous system, make the blood impure, and increase the risk of disease. [142] They also have a dulling effect on the brain cells, cause poor memory, and promote cravings. [143] In addition, the liver and kidneys suffer as the body attempts to rid itself of the waste products.

Vinegar is one example of a product that results from food fermentation. The basic component of vinegar is diluted acetic acid, which is a waste product in the human body. This acid causes damage to the gastric mucosal barrier, negatively affects digestive health, can damage blood capillaries and increase capillary permeability, setting the stage for ulcers, gastritis, vitamin deficiencies (especially vitamin B12), infection with Helicobacter pylori, and other health problems. [144]

The foods that are highest in nutrition are those that are eaten in their fresh, natural, and unprocessed state. [145]

Baking Soda and Baking Powder

Baking soda and baking powder (which is a mixture of baking soda and an acid-reacting material) alter the pH of the blood, have an irritating effect on the organ systems, promote inflammation, and cause an imbalance in physiology. [146]

To cooperate with God in your child's physical, mental, and spiritual development, these foods should be avoided and replaced with the simple diet our Creator has given.

When to Eat

Just as important as what a child eats is *when* he eats. "Regularity in eating is of vital importance. There should be a specified time for each meal." [147] The digestive processes and the digestive organs both influence and are strongly influenced by the body's circadian rhythms. [148] Eating at regular times assists the body in the synthesis of several important hormones, optimizes certain metabolic functions, and helps the body most efficiently use nutrients from food. [149]

"Eat for strength, in due season" (Ecclesiastes 10:17).

In Between Meals

One of the surest ways to help a child enjoy healthful food is to eat on a regular schedule and avoid all in-between-meal snacks. "Irregularities in eating destroy the healthful tone of the digestive organs, to the detriment of health and cheerfulness. And when the children come to the table, they do not relish wholesome food; their appetites crave that which is hurtful for them." [150]

The process of digestion is designed to function in a very precise, organized, and step-by-step manner. The entire process takes several hours to fully complete and includes the very important regeneration and recuperation phase. "Any defect in one phase of digestion hampers another." [151] Even a small bite of food taken in between meals interferes with this orderly process, weakens the system, and hinders proper digestion and assimilation.

The disruption of the digestion process also causes fermentation of the contents of the digestive system, and toxic chemicals (such as aldehydes, alcohols, amines, and esters) are produced. These chemicals have a negative effect on the liver, kidneys, [152] and the brain and other nervous tissue, which results in a dulling effect on the brain cells. Consequently, thinking processes, learning, and memory consolidation are inhibited. [153]

"Regularity in eating is very important for health of body and serenity of mind. Your children should be allowed to eat only at regular meal time." [154] "Never should a morsel of food pass the lips between meals." [155] "They should not be allowed to digress from this established rule." [156]

Breakfast

"Make your breakfast correspond more nearly to the heartiest meal of the day." [157] A healthy breakfast improves the ability to concentrate, strengthens mental performance, [158] and reduces the risk of disease.

Evening Meal

"When we lie down to rest, the stomach should have its work all done, that it, as well as the other organs of the body, may enjoy rest." [159] Allowing the digestive system a period of rest in the evening and through the night increases natural growth factors in the brain (which generates the growth of new neurons), [160] improves neuroplasticity (the ability of neural networks in the brain to grow and reorganize), [161] improves memory, and improves brain structure and function overall. [162]

If a large meal is eaten in the evening, "intestinal fermentation is much more likely to occur during the slower digestion of the evening, especially during sleep." [163] This not only leads to compromised digestion and hindered waste removal from cells, but it also causes an irritation of the nerves in the digestive system, which negatively affects brain functioning.

For optimal health and cognitive functioning, supper should "be very light, and of food most easily digested." [164] Fresh fruits, with the addition of a small portion of properly-cooked grains if needed, are the foods best suited for supper. [165] Avoid vegetables or other foods that take longer to digest. [166] This approach will ensure a sweet sleep and the best brain function.

Quantity

While it is, of course, important that children are provided with as much food as they need, "parents often make a mistake by giving their children too much food." [167] Encouraging your child to eat more than he needs or desires – even of the healthiest foods – is a tax on the body and hinders the functioning of many of the body organs, including the brain, which in turn can interfere with learning and behavior. [168]

At times, it may seem like your little one couldn't possibly be eating enough to sustain life. However, children often don't need as much as their parents think they do, and it is very common for children to go through phases when their body simply doesn't need as much food.

Trying to coerce the child to finish his meal not only makes meal-time a stressful time for the child (and parent), but it also conditions a child to override his natural, built-in mechanism for knowing when he has had enough food, which can contribute to eating disorders or problems with overeating in later years. If a child says that he is full and does not want to finish his meal, a parent should respect this. There is nothing disobedient or rebellious about not finishing one's food. Parents should recognize that an individual (including a child) is able to have a better sense of the fullness of his own stomach than can someone else (including parents). If a child does not eat in between meals and is not permitted to eat junk food, he will eat as much as he needs – without a parent's pleading, cajoling, coaxing, or bribing.

The Simple Diet that Our Creator Has Given Us

Parents may wonder why a child can't sit still during church, why he fights with his siblings, or why he throws temper tantrums.

Science has discovered an irrefutable link between a child's diet and his behavior. While diet usually isn't the only cause of misbehavior, it plays a more significant role than many parents realize. "Parents wonder that children are so much more difficult to control than they used to be, when in most cases their own ... management has made them so. The quality of food they bring upon their tables, and encourage their children to eat, is ... weakening the moral and intellectual faculties." [169]

"The diet affects both physical and moral health. How carefully, then, should mothers study to supply the table with most *simple*, healthful food, in order that the digestive organs may not be weakened, the nerves unbalanced, or the instruction which they give their children counteracted." [170] "It is best, both for our physical health and for our spiritual advancement, to observe simplicity in diet." [171]

"Daniel's clearness of mind and firmness of purpose, his strength of intellect in acquiring knowledge, were due in a great degree to the *plainness* of his diet in connection with his life of prayer." [172] We are living in an age of moral degeneracy. "If ever there was a time when the diet should be of the most *simple* kind, it is now." [173] And yet there was never a time when rich food and drink have been so readily accessible. "Satan is no novice in the business of destroying souls. He well knows that if he can lead men and women into wrong habits of eating and drinking, he has gained, in a great degree, the control of their minds." [174]

There is no shortage of health trends offering wonderfully-sounding promises of health, but most of these are not in agreement with the simple diet that God has given humans. [175] There is no diet or supplement that can benefit the physical, mental, and moral health as can a *simple*, plant-based diet. [176] "The Lord intends to bring his people back to live upon simple fruits, vegetables, and grains." [177] A diet that consists of "plain food, prepared in the simplest manner" [178] will not only provide good health and facilitate good brain development, but, because of its effect on the mind and morals, will also aid in the formation of characters fit for heaven.

Sleep

Sufficient and proper sleep is an important ingredient in good brain development. During sleep, primarily in the hours before midnight, a child's brain balances brain chemicals, restores correct harmony between the nervous system and the other body systems, and transfers information from temporary memory storage to long-term memory storage. Without proper sleep in the *early* hours of the night, a child won't be able to learn at his true potential. [179]

How To Help a Baby Get Proper Sleep

Infants are born without fully set circadian rhythms, [180] but breastfeeding is designed to help remedy that. [181] Because of its remarkable ability to program infant circadian rhythms, breastfeeding – especially nursing a child to sleep – is the best method for helping an infant learn to sleep well and at the right time. [182] The increase of sleep-promoting hormones in breastmilk at night (described in the previous section, "Feeding the Brain") not only helps a baby to obtain brain-building sleep, but it also helps develop a baby's circadian rhythm and programs his body and brain to sleep at the right times and for the right length of time. Falling asleep at the breast also provides closeness and comfort for a baby that is conducive to the development of emotional security, which is associated with optimal brain growth.

Another help for getting a baby to sleep well at night is to ensure he gets plenty of outside time every day. Studies show that infants who are exposed to an abundance of sunlight develop stronger circadian rhythms and tend to sleep longer at night. [183] In addition, mom should include her infant in her regular daily activities, as infants who are active at the same time of day as their mothers quickly develop healthy circadian rhythms. [184]

A baby should not be given food other than breastmilk in the evening to help him sleep better at night. Unlike breastmilk, which digests well whether a baby is upright or lying down, solids don't digest properly when a baby is in a horizontal position and consequently can damage the digestive system.

To help encourage the regular production of melatonin (a hormone that helps with sleep), babies should sleep in a dark room during the nighttime hours without nightlights or other light sources. However, for daytime naps, babies should sleep in a well-lit room to help them have better-regulated circadian rhythms. There is no need to have a special, quiet place for baby to take naps. From birth, babies are able to nap in bright light and surrounded by noise and movement. And if mom carries her baby in a baby wrap and takes her baby with her wherever she goes, the baby continues to be able to nap-on-the-go and sleep anywhere and in any environment.

How Much Sleep Does a Baby Need?

Total sleep requirements vary greatly from baby to baby and child to child, and due to cultural influences, many parents have a misconception about how much sleep little ones actually need. While some parents make the mistake of not ensuring that their child obtains sufficient sleep, many parents try very hard to get their babies on a strict sleep schedule and put a lot of effort into getting their child to sleep more than he actually needs.

Understandably, getting their baby to sleep through the night is usually one of the top priorities for parents of infants; however, parents should be aware that "sleeping through the night is not biologically normal" [185] for a baby, nor is it necessarily healthy. [186] In fact, waking frequently through the night provides many benefits for a baby. Night wakings may actually protect the infant from SIDS (sudden infant death syndrome – also called cot death). [187] Long, deep sleep, though relieving to tired parents, is potentially dangerous for a baby since babies don't as readily awaken from a deep sleep if they aren't getting enough oxygen.

Night wakings also provide the opportunity for the child to breastfeed. An infant's stomach is extremely small compared to the amount of nutrition he needs at this stage of rapid growth. Human breastmilk, which God perfectly designed for the growing infant's undeveloped digestive system, digests quickly and is low in calories, and night feedings are necessary to provide for the growing infant's physical needs. They also safeguard a mother's milk supply, since night feedings prompt the mother's body to produce more milk. In addition, nighttime breastmilk contains valuable components that supply important nutrients for brain and psychomotor development. It also contains hormones that help establish healthy circadian rhythms.

Feeding a baby in the night can be tiring for mom; however, it can be made less tiring if the baby sleeps in a co-sleeper bassinet [188] adjacent to the parent's bed or in the same bed as the parents (provided the bed is made safe for the baby), and mom can nurse the baby while lying down in bed. Keeping the baby close at night has been shown to have a positive impact on the quality of sleep for the baby [189] and provides other benefits as well. A baby's brain and nervous system are wired to respond positively to maternal smells, as well as the sound of her breathing. [190] When a baby is in such close proximity to his mother that he can smell her, hear her breathing, and feel her movement, he experiences improved cardiorespiratory stability, better thermoregulation, better nutritional absorption, less stress, and optimal balance of hormone levels. [191] Epidemiological studies have shown that co-sleeping drastically reduces an infant's chances of dying from SIDS. In fact, rates of SIDS are the lowest in cultures with the highest rates of bed-sharing. [192] Next to his mother's body is the healthiest environment for an infant.

Sleep for Children

For children, there are a few other factors that can help them go to sleep quickly and sleep well. These include an abundance of time outside; [193] emotional security; plenty of sunshine (especially morning sun); [194] living life on a regular schedule; and a healthy, whole-food, plant-based diet, free from stimulating foods that increase the production of adrenaline and cortisol and work contrary to melatonin (such as spices, caffeine, refined foods, vinegar).

It is also important to avoid the use of screen-based devices completely, as these devices disrupt circadian rhythms, raise cortisol levels, and suppress the production of melatonin. [195] They reduce the quality of sleep, decreasing the amount of time spent in slow-wave sleep and rapid-eye movement (REM) sleep – two stages of the sleep cycle that are essential for good cognitive functioning. Children seem to be especially sensitive to the negative effects of screen-based devices on sleep quantity and quality. [196]

Avoid sound machines, sleep machines, white noise, and other artificial sleep helps as there are some potential long-term consequences to their use. The continuous artificial noise from sleep machines can negatively alter a child's natural auditory processing and provoke a stress response in the brain that causes an increase in cortisol levels (a stress hormone) and a decrease in dopamine levels. Low dopamine levels and high levels of cortisol can contribute to behavioral issues and inhibit learning. In addition, relying on these artificial sounds to fall asleep and stay asleep creates a sleep association in the young, malleable, and developing mind of a child. Because his brain learns to associate the process of going to sleep with the noise of the sleep machine, the natural development of the ability to fall asleep or go back to sleep if he wakes up in the night is hindered. And, with the use of these aids, children don't learn to sleep through regular, common noises of life.

An early bedtime is beneficial for children (and parents). [197] Going to bed early increases the brain's production of melatonin, cooperates with the body's natural circadian rhythm, helps children learn better, and tends to increase feelings of happiness, cheerfulness, and alertness. [198]

How can you know if your child is getting enough sleep? Some children need more sleep than others, and individual needs for sleep change slightly day to day, week to week, and year to year. There is no magic number of sleep hours that can be set for a child. If you are using the tips mentioned above and your child is not overstimulated by media, environment, and/or unhealthful food, then he will generally go to sleep within a few minutes of going to bed (especially if he has the comfort and security of a parent's presence as he goes to sleep). If twenty minutes pass and the child is still not asleep, parents should reconsider the amount of sleep they believe their child needs (or whether any lifestyle factors are causing overstimulation). If a child is truly sleep deprived, there will be noticeable signs. Rubbing his eyes in the evening, having a hard time waking up in the morning, or falling asleep during family worship or other times in the day when the child should normally be awake are good indicators. Being grouchy can be a sign of insufficient sleep, but it isn't necessarily a dependable gauge since there can be many other contributing factors.

Health Habits and Intellectual and Moral Development

Due to the strong influence of the body upon the development of the brain and morals, the subject of health cannot be separated from the subject of education. "The body is the only medium through which the mind and the soul are developed for the upbuilding of character. Hence it is that the adversary of souls directs his temptations to the enfeebling and degrading of the physical powers." [199]

"It is not mimic battles in which we are engaged. We are waging a warfare upon which hang eternal results. We have unseen enemies to meet. Evil angels are striving for the dominion of every human being. Whatever injures the health not only lessens physical vigor but tends to weaken the mental and moral powers. Indulgence in any unhealthful practice makes it more difficult for one to discriminate between right and wrong, and hence more difficult to resist evil." [200]

"Let mothers place themselves without delay in right relations to their Creator, that they may by his assisting grace build around their children a bulwark against dissipation and intemperance. If mothers would but follow such a course, they might see their children, like the youthful Daniel, reach a high standard in moral and intellectual attainments, becoming a blessing to society and an honor to their Creator." [201]

Words of Counsel

"The laws which God has established for the well-being of the physical structure are to be treated as divine. To every action done in violation of these laws a penalty is affixed. The transgressor is recorded as having broken the commandments of God." [202]

"Transgression of physical law is transgression of the moral law; for God is as truly the author of physical laws as He is the author of the moral law. His law is written with His own finger upon every nerve, every muscle, every faculty, which has been entrusted to man. And every misuse of any part of our organism is a violation of that law." [203]

"The right balance of the mental and moral powers depends

in a great degree on the right condition of the physical system." [204]

"Our bodies are Christ's purchased possession, and we are not at liberty to do with them as we please. All who understand the laws of health should realize their obligation to obey these laws which God has established in their being. Obedience to the laws of health is to be made a matter of personal duty. We ourselves must suffer the results of violated law. We must individually answer to God for our habits and practices. Therefore the question with us is not, "What is the world's practice?" but, "How shall I as an individual treat the habitation that God has given me?" [205]

CHAPTER 4

A SECURE FOUNDATION

"Love is the best teacher." – Fundamentals of
Christian Education, 58

WHEN it comes to learning, with our society's focus on educational methods, curriculum quality, and aptitude of teachers, we tend to overlook one absolutely vital factor that critically influences – perhaps more than any other factor – a child's ability to learn.

Scientific research is abundantly clear that emotional security is an important factor for optimal brain development and a child's ability to learn well. [1]

The Brain's Priority List

The young brain views emotional security as a fundamental need of survival – not just healthy functioning, but *survival*. The developing brain places emotional needs on the same level of importance as it does food, air, and other physical needs. This means that the development of emotional security is top priority for a child's brain; and, if necessary, the brain will seek to establish this security to the neglect of other important functions, including cognition. When a child's emotional security is threatened, learning will suffer while the brain attempts to adapt to its situation.

Emotional Security Promotes Brain Development

The emotional center of a baby's and a young child's brain has a profusion of neural fibers that connect and communicate with many other areas of the brain, including those involved with learning. A secure emotional relationship with a loving mother (or permanent mother figure) who is consistently available stimulates optimal development of these neural connections.

Note: While the father plays a crucial role in a child's healthy development, research indicates that a deep emotional bond between a mother and her baby is the most central ingredient to emotional security, emotional health, long-term mental health, and future success for a child. [2] *"The tenderest earthly tie is that between the mother and her child. The child is more readily impressed by the life and example of the mother than by that of the father; for a stronger and more tender bond of union unites them. Mothers have a heavy responsibility."* [3] *They can do a beautiful work "in molding the minds of their children."* [4] *This does not negate the responsibility of the father and the essential contribution he makes in nurturing his child, but it does help us to see how crucial is the mother's role.*

Studies show that children with a secure emotional attachment to their mothers have larger and better-developed hippocampi (a brain structure responsible for learning, memory, attention regulation, and more) than children who do not have this secure emotional attachment. [5] They also tend to have larger grey matter volume in the temporoparietal junction (a brain area involved with information processing, self-control, empathy, and selflessness). [6] And they exhibit more advanced development of the prefrontal cortex (responsible for higher-level cognitive processes, such as decision making, problem solving, planning, organizing, prioritizing, ability to focus, behavior regulation, emotional regulation, impulse control, and more). [7]

A *lack* of consistent, warm, and intimate nurturing negatively affects many areas of the brain, and is associated with a decrease in brain volume, alterations in brain organization of chemical receptors, and even brain cell deaths. [8]

How to Create Emotional Security

How can parents provide emotional security for their children? It may seem obvious to a parent that their baby is safe, valued, and loved, but parents must learn to provide security for their baby in ways that translate to security in the baby's mind.

Babies are born physically, emotionally, socially, and spiritually vulnerable. This was no mistake on the part of our Creator. This period of time in which infants are so vulnerable gives parents the opportunity and privilege of lovingly and compassionately caring for these helpless little ones in a way that provides for their every need – not just their physical needs, but also for their emotional, social, and spiritual needs – in order to bind their little one's hearts to theirs and, in turn, to God's.

Here are some of the primary ways that parents can cultivate emotional security in their child.

1. Mothers, breastfeed your baby.

Breastfeeding provides much more than nutrients for a baby. The skin-to-skin contact, the hormone release, and other factors that naturally happen when a baby is held in his mother's arms as he nurses from her breast have a calming effect on baby, bring about strong feelings of love and security for a baby, and encourage a strong emotional bond between mother and child. Children who experience this bonding in babyhood tend to be more emotionally secure, have better emotional regulation and better behavior, have better mental health, and exhibit superior conflict resolution abilities than those who do not. [9]

2. Keep your baby with you.

Before the age of about 8 months, babies do not have an understanding of an important concept that adults take for granted. That concept is called object permanence, which is the awareness that people (and other things in life) still exist even when they are out of sight. This means that before this age, when Mom walks out of the room, a baby may think that he has forever lost the most important person in his life. Obviously, this can cause a tremendous amount of stress and anxiety for baby. Research shows that even short-term separation from mother can lead to elevated levels of stress hormones in babies, which negatively impact the production and survival of new brain cells, alter the organization of neurotransmitter receptors, and increase oxidative stress in the brain (which can damage brain cells). [10] Frequent and/or prolonged exposure to elevated stress hormones can hamper the functioning of areas of the brain involved with behavior regulation, decision making, emotion processing, empathy, impulse control, resistance to temptation, problem solving, and learning. [11]

Babies *can* be trained to adapt to the absence of their mother. They adapt to such a situation by detaching emotionally and thus weakening the maternal bond. But since this infant-mother bond is a key factor and crucial ingredient in a baby's emotional, intellectual, and spiritual development, parents should avoid pushing a baby's brain to adapt in this direction.

Babies are born with a strong instinct to seek closeness and connection and have a physical, emotional, mental, social, and spiritual need to be with their mothers.

3. Respond to your baby's communication.

From birth, babies are primed and ready for social input and are continually trying to communicate their feelings and emotional needs to their parents, moment by moment. [12] No, they don't communicate in a manner that adults are accustomed to communicating, but they do communicate via facial expressions, eye contact/avoidance, noises, body language, and cries (especially if the aforementioned attempts at communicating are unsuccessful in evoking a response). [13]

Consistent, prompt, loving, and compassionate parental responsiveness to a baby's desire for communication boosts the development of brain areas involved with emotional security and promotes a stronger bond between child and parents. [14] If crying and other forms of communication are not met with an attentive and caring response, blood flow in the baby's brain shifts away from higher-order brain development toward survival mechanisms, which undermines his brain's capacity to develop in the areas that are designed to develop at that time. [15]

When a baby cries, he is not misbehaving (even if that crying is in the middle of the night when his parents want to sleep); he is communicating just as God designed him to communicate and attempting to ensure his emotional well-being by asking for connection with, and comfort from, his parents. Since a baby cannot talk, and a baby's other forms of communication can be difficult to understand, how else can a baby communicate with his parents?

A child's drive to communicate can be stifled through behavioral conditioning, but he will suffer emotionally, intellectually, socially, physically, and spiritually if he can't dependably connect and communicate feelings and thoughts with an individual who he knows loves and cares for him.

Parents can help their baby feel secure by taking the time and making the effort to learn to understand their baby's communication and to promptly respond to him in gentle, calming, reassuring ways. Sometimes it can be difficult to correctly understand a baby's cues, but when parents – especially mothers – spend an abundance of time with their infant, consistently interacting with him, they can grow in their understanding of their baby's communication. [16] It is helpful to note that the great majority of a baby's communication is expressed through body movement, which can be best discerned by the mother if she is holding her baby. In addition, research shows that the more a mother responds positively to a baby's babbling, the better a baby learns to communicate in ways that the parents can understand. [17] Without this deep level of understanding of their baby's communication, parents may think that a baby is crying to be annoying or demanding or manipulative. But as parents grow to understand what a baby is trying to communicate, they may learn that a cry, rather than an effort to manipulate, is really a plea for connection, understanding, comfort, love, affection, reassurance, security, or relief from discomfort.

Can we teach a baby to self-soothe? The ability to think analytically, rationally assess a situation, and mediate a response is not yet developed in babies. So, when a baby feels discomfort – whether it's hunger, sadness, loneliness, or fear – he does not have the physiological capabilities to rationally deal with that feeling. In other words, self-soothing is a physical impossibility for an infant. This is why God created babies to cry when they feel a need. God intended for babies to rely on their parents for comfort.

There may be times when, no matter how hard they try, parents are unable to understand why their baby is crying, and regardless of how much comfort a parent gives the baby, he still cries. When this is the case, parents can be reassured that gentle attempts at soothing the baby (such as *quietly* holding the baby) are still comforting to him, even if he does continue to whimper. Research shows that babies who cry alone experience significant surges in stress hormones that can impair proper brain development, hamper learning, and inhibit the development of self-regulation; however, babies who are held in their mother's arms while they are crying do not experience the same increase in stress hormone levels.

Parents can shape the heart and brain of their baby by how they communicate with him. When parents (especially the mother) are consistently present and responsive, the brain's systems develop as they were intended to develop, and the child can grow in emotional security and emotional maturity.

4. Be generous with physical connection.

As mentioned in Chapter 3, babies have an intrinsic biological need for nearly constant physical connection and abundant affectionate touch. [18] God designed babies to be held, carried, and cuddled by loving human arms, not supported and transported in plastic containers otherwise known as baby carriers, strollers, bouncy seats, activity chairs, swings, and baby walkers. Research shows a strong correlation between nurturing physical touch and emotional maturity, healthy physiological development, higher moral capacities, better behavioral regulation, and positive social behavior. [19]

5. Be a friend to your child.

As your little one grows, be a friend to him. Laugh at what he finds funny, be amazed at what amazes him, and be interested in what he is interested in.

When your toddler is telling you – for the seventeenth time – the hour-long story about the frog that jumped *reeeeaaaalllly* high, and you have plenty of other seemingly more important things to do, stop what you're doing, look him in the eyes, and listen to him. Though this story may not be important to you, it is very important to your child, and it is even more important to him that you listen to him. In his little stories and scores of questions, your child is really asking, "Is what I have to say important? Are you interested in what interests me? Do I matter to you?"

Treasure each and every moment with your little one. Use every interaction as an opportunity to connect. These interactions promote emotional security in the heart of a child because they send the message that you are interested in him, and there is no other person who he more wants to be interested in him than you.

6. Work together.

For all ages, time together can create a strong bond. Parents can include a toddler (and even a baby) in their daily activities, such as washing dishes, preparing meals, cleaning the car, working in the garden, cleaning the house, doing laundry, maintaining the vehicle, and more. Even if the child cannot help much, just the fact that he is with you and feels as if he is a valuable part of the work is beneficial to him emotionally and intellectually – emotionally because of the bond that is formed, and intellectually because he is learning much about life by observing you and imitating you.

Abandon the results-oriented mindset and embrace the value of relationship. You may think that your baby is too young to help you fold clothes, but include him anyway. Give him some clothes to fold. It doesn't matter if he doesn't fold them correctly or if he can fold them at all; just the fact that he is *holding* some clothes while you are holding (and folding) clothes, creates a connection between you and your baby and builds the foundation for you to teach him to cooperate and work with you. When working in the garden, give your little one a safe tool to dig the dirt with. For a baby, this can be a spoon; or, for the toddler, a spade can be a fun tool. At every meal prep time, give your little one a job he can do. Even two-year-olds can wash potatoes, break the lettuce into the bowl, or add water to the beans. Yes, he will probably make a mess, but as you help *him* clean up the mess, he is learning valuable lessons of responsibility, cause-to-effect reasoning, and cooperation. And you are building the bond that develops emotional security.

For the older child, rather than sending him to clean his room, go *with* him and work *together*. You can help him clean his room, and then he can help you clean your room. Talk with him while you work. Express an interest in his interests. Ask his opinion about something. Share with him your thoughts. Tell him what you read that morning in your devotional time with God. All the activities of daily life can be bonding experiences if done together.

7. Play together.

God admonishes parents to learn selflessness, retain their own youthful feelings, and play with their children. [20] This does not mean taking a child to the playground and watching him play; this means actually playing *with* your child.

Run through the yard with him. Play in the mud with him. (Go ahead and get dirty; it won't hurt you.) Laugh with him at the funny bug crawling on the tree limb. Climb trees with him. Play hide-and-seek with him. It doesn't matter that he hides behind the same tree every time and is still stunned at your ability to find him; playing together with your child creates a bond and a connection between you and your child, strengthens your relationship, helps your child feel understood, and shows him that you love him and are interested in his happiness.

8. Avoid negative socialization.

Children need proper socialization, but parents often mistake socialization for something that must happen between peers. Peer socialization usually does damage to a child's emotional security. The single most beneficial type of socialization a child can get is socialization within his own family. "He who made us ordained that we should be associated in families, and the child nature will develop best in the loving atmosphere of a Christian home." [21] The relationship a child develops with his parents is *the most* important relationship from an emotional development standpoint.

We'll look at this topic more in-depth later in this book.

9. Avoid praising your child too much.

"Children need appreciation, sympathy, and encouragement, but care should be taken not to foster in them a love of praise." [22] "Praise, flattery, and indulgence have done more toward leading precious souls into false paths than any other art that Satan has devised." [23]

Praise can actually undermine a child's sense of emotional security as it sends a message to the child that he must appear a certain way, act a certain way, or accomplish something to be valued. Some parents try to work around this negative effect by praising a child for his efforts (instead of the results of his efforts), but this approach still hinges a child's value on something he does.

Praise turns the child's attention towards himself. In contrast, parental responsiveness and loving companionship, combined with genuine appreciation, sympathy when needed, and encouragement in difficulty, show a child that he is valuable, build emotional security, and draw his heart toward his parents (and, in turn, toward God).

10. Be mentally and emotionally present.

Children are quick to discern whether you are fully engaged or only half-there. They may not verbally protest your lack of attentiveness, but their sense of emotional security suffers a weighty blow. Rather than seeing the daily tasks, activities, and interactions with your child as mundane responsibilities that just need to be accomplished, take hold of these precious moments to interact and be completely present with your child. Put away the phone and other distractions. You have relatively few hours with your child before he doesn't need you so much anymore. Don't waste these precious moments being only half present.

These various factors for developing emotional security are essential elements of true education (and are steps that can be taken immediately, wherever you are in your child's development). With the constant companionship of the ones that he loves and knows love him, a child can feel safe, secure, and protected – which means he can focus on all the other fascinating aspects of life, like learning.

An Investment

Creating emotional security in children takes time, effort, and a degree of self-sacrifice on the part of the parents – especially the mother. But, in the words of Pam Leo, author of the book *Connection Parenting*, we either "spend time meeting children's emotional needs … or we spend time dealing with behaviors caused from their unmet needs. Either way, we spend the time."[24] It seems more prudent to act on the plan of prevention.

This investment not only benefits children, but it also benefits parents. Parenting shapes the character of the parents just as much as it does the character of a child. As parents study the character of our heavenly Father and learn "to represent God's disposition"[25] (one of justice, tender compassion, and constant care for His children) to their children and learn to show them "Christlike tenderness, and unselfish love,"[26] they "find their own hearts subdued and melted."[27] By beholding Christ, selflessness and love begin to develop and grow in their own heart. Parents learn to "have a spirit and character akin to His,"[28] and the beautiful results will be manifested not only in the home, but also in the church and in society.[29]

The time and effort spent nurturing a child is the most profitable investment you can ever make. It is an investment that yields beautiful and peaceful results. You will never regret it.

Spoiled?

Providing emotional security in babyhood is often confused with the act of spoiling a baby, but the two are very different. Providing for a baby's emotional needs does not spoil a baby any more than providing for his physical needs does. No rational person would ever suggest that a parent should withhold from a baby what is necessary for his physical health. Without sufficient healthy food, clean water, protective shelter, etc., a baby may survive, but he will not thrive. Likewise, parents should not withhold from a baby that which he needs for emotional security; if they do, the baby may survive, but he will not thrive.

Research has shown that a baby's emotional needs *are* actual physical needs. Without consistent physical contact and maternal responsiveness, a baby experiences elevated stress hormones, reduced oxytocin release, reduced sensitivity to neurotransmitters (including serotonin), and other biochemical effects that can impact his physical health and invite disease later in life.[30] These physiological responses also affect the neurodevelopment of a child, which can then negatively affect his emotional, behavioral, social, and cognitive development.[31] There is no such thing as giving a baby too much connection and affection; the more a baby gets, the healthier he will be.[32]

Providing for a child's emotional needs doesn't mean that

parents are permissive and allow behavior that is out of harmony with God's principles. Parents can be generous with physical affection, be consistently present, respond to their child's communication, and otherwise provide for his emotional needs without indulging, spoiling, or neglecting to discipline their child.

Children should not be permitted to have their own way when that way is out of harmony with God's will, but tenderly holding a baby when he wants to be held is perfectly in harmony with God's will and His character. God never requires parents to withhold love, affection, care, attentiveness, and tenderness from a child. Not allowing a child's will to control the parents does not mean withholding that which is good from the child.

In order for parents to understand the difference between providing for a child's emotional needs and spoiling the child, they first must understand the difference between needs and non-needs. Affection, physical touch, warmth, shelter, interaction, comfort, and proper nourishment (including, for a baby, in the middle of the night) are actual, God-given needs and are good for – even essential for – healthy physical, emotional, and spiritual growth. Providing for these needs does not spoil a child. On the other hand, permitting a child to do something or have something that is *not* good for him is spoiling him. For example, allowing a child to have the blue blanket because he doesn't like the green one, buying him the expensive shirt because he doesn't like the one you were going to buy him, allowing him to choose the biggest apple or the most comfortable seat, or permitting him to be inconsiderate of others is spoiling him. Not teaching him to cheerfully help with the daily duties is spoiling him.[33] Admiring him for his cuteness, permitting him to argue, whine, or complain, allowing him to be selfish, or permitting him to be disrespectful is spoiling him. Giving him ice cream (or other unhealthful food), allowing the well-meaning grandma to shower him with toys, giving him rewards for work that he hasn't done (otherwise known as an allowance) are all forms of indulgence. When parents "indulge them [their children] in what they know is *not for their good*, the children soon lose all respect for their parents, all regard for the authority of God or man."[34] There are many other forms of spoiling a child, but providing for a child's emotional needs is *not* one of them.

Parents must also recognize that it is often easier to give a child something he *doesn't* need than it is to give him something he *does* need. For example, breastfeeding and/or comforting a little one in the middle of the night is not easy, but this is something babies and children actually need. To give a child what he desires in this situation is not spoiling him. On the other hand, allowing a three-year-old to play when he should be helping with the chores is easier than patiently and consistently teaching him to help. But playing when he should be helping is *not* something a child needs. To give a child what he desires in this situation *is* spoiling him.

It often takes far more effort to raise a child in a non-indulgent manner than it takes to spoil him. But it is the parents' duty to train their "children so as to make their [the children's] ways pleasing to God,"[35] not to train them to make their ways pleasing to the parents.

A child feels secure when he sees that his parents will take care of his every need. This includes not only his need for tenderness, comfort, and attentiveness, but also his need for consistency and firm decisiveness based on solid principles. Children who see that their parents guide them from a place of authority under the guidance of the God of heaven and consistently choose what is best for them (even if it means denying him the dessert that everyone else at the church social is eating) tend to be happier and more emotionally secure. [36]

Children need to have clear boundaries, they need to know what is expected of them, and they need to see that their parents love them enough to confidently and firmly enforce those boundaries. It is common for a child to test boundaries, but when his boundary testing causes those boundaries to collapse, he does not feel secure. The same is true if his boundary testing causes impatience, frustration, or anger in his parents. A child needs to know that his parents are in control – both of *his* well-being *and* of their own behavior. Your child may not act like he is happy when you kindly, firmly, definitively, consistently, and matter-of-factly tell him you won't buy that toy for him, but when a child is emotionally secure, restrictions are actually comforting for him. Deep down, he feels assured and comforted when he finds confident leadership in you.

"There are two ways to deal with children, – ways that differ widely in principle and in results. Faithfulness and love, united with wisdom and firmness, in accordance with the teachings of God's word, will bring happiness in this life and in the next. Neglect of duty, injudicious indulgence, failure to restrain or correct the follies of youth, will result in unhappiness and final ruin to the children, and disappointment and anguish to the parents."[37] Parents can "be firm, but kind."[38] They can "win the affections of their children by their sympathy and tender care, ... yet be firm and decided in their government."[39] "Let the home government be just and tender, full of love and compassion, yet firm and true. Do not permit one disrespectful word or disobedient act."[40] Not even one.

Clingy?

Won't a baby who is held often and is with his mother continually grow up to be overly dependent on his mother? Overly needy? Shy? Clingy?

An immense amount of research clearly shows that "meeting a child's dependency needs is the key to helping that child achieve independence."[41] "Responsive and contingent parenting produces securely attached children who show more curiosity, self-reliance, and independence."[42] Babies "who develop secure attachments to their mothers in the first year of life are more competent as toddlers in peer interaction, exploration, and play behavior, and are more enthusiastic and persistent in approaching problem-solving tasks."[43] They tend to be more resilient and socially competent. Even for the child whose personality is naturally shy or timid, the emotional security he gains from being with his mother provides him with what he needs to have the confidence to learn to be independent.

When the child does *not* have the security of developing that stable bond with his mother, the instability created in his mind causes his survival instincts to kick in, and his brain attempts to adapt emotionally. He learns that he must take care of himself, protect himself, and provide for his own emotional needs since, from his immature perspective, others do not. The results manifest themselves in several ways. The child may become self-sufficient and preoccupied with himself (which leads to selfishness, disobedience, lack of conside- ration for others, etc.) and exhibit a lack of desire to cooperate. Or he may become worrisome, fearful, and easily overwhelmed. Or he may be controlling. [44] Or, even worse, he may exhibit a combination of these traits.

An even more difficult situation is when a mother provides security for her child most, but not all of the time. Separation anxiety is often worse for a child who experiences inconsistencies in a parent's attentiveness and availability. This child is usually overly emotional, easily overwhelmed, whiny, and clingy. He may cry easily and be difficult to comfort. To remedy clinginess, parents should be intentional to provide *extra* and more consistent emotional security. For example, the mom should be continually with her child and initiate picking him up and holding him long before he asks to be held. She should hold the child so much that he develops a sense of security and eventually gets tired of being held and seeks independence. In other words, the best way to cure clinginess is to give a child even *more* security than he is actually looking for.

The research is clear. Children who are provided with a secure connection with their parents and allowed to achieve independence at their own pace are more secure in that independence than are children who are pushed into independence.

God's Representatives

Children desperately need to feel secure. There will be (and *should* be) difficulties and disappointments in a child's life, and an eight- or nine-year-old child will be better prepared to bravely face and manage those daily challenges if he has been given a solid base of emotional security in the early years of life.

And no matter the age, in every difficulty, a child should always know that his parents are his safe and loving place. He should know that they are there for him – not to solve his problems or to remove the difficulties, but to be a comfort and protection for him. This will teach him to find his comfort and protection in God when he is older.

It is a basic fact of brain development that young children need to experience something to be able to understand it. And as God wants every one of us to understand what it is to have a relationship with Him, He has not overlooked the children. In His great wisdom, He has designed a way by which a child can understand relationship – by experiencing it with their parents. Relationship is not taught in a class. It is experienced. God gave parents to children to help them experience who God is and what God is like. God gave parents to children to help them *experience* how to have a relationship with Him. As a parent, you have the beautiful privilege of standing in the place of God to your child. As you are consistently available to your little one, you are teaching him of the companionship of Christ, of the One who has said, "I will never leave you or forsake you." You are teaching him that God is always there for His children. You are teaching him to turn to his Savior for love and security, to depend on Him for all his needs, to turn to Him with all his cares. You are educating your child in the most valuable way.

Words of Counsel

"By the cords of unselfish love bind them to you and to Christ."[45]

"Home influence should be soothing, elevating, and refining. Oh, how many children have parents, yet are in complete orphanage as far as right training is concerned!"[46]

"There has been altogether too little attention paid to our children and youth, and they have failed to develop as they should in the Christian life."[47]

"Fathers and mothers, in the home you are to represent God's disposition. You are to require obedience, not with a storm of words, but in a kind, loving manner. You are to be so full of compassion that your children will be drawn to you. Keep them away from the society of those children who are disobedient and unruly, and then God can impress their minds. As the right work is done in the home, parents will find their own hearts subdued and melted."[48]

SECTION II
GOD'S EDUCATIONAL
SCHEDULE FOR YOUR CHILD

CHAPTER 5

GOD'S PERFECT SCHEDULE

"The more slowly trees grow at first, the
sounder they are at the core, and I think the same is
true of human beings." – Henry David Thoreau

SEVEN-YEAR-OLD Henry is supposed to be practicing writing, but it's difficult to tell whether he's making much progress or not. With one knee on his chair, the other one nearly reaching the floor, his torso curved to one side, and his left arm reaching around to the back of his seat, it's unlikely his penmanship is very good anyway.

Henry is a bundle of energy, continually wiggling, spinning, hopping, and jumping. Henry's parents feel worn out by his constant activity, and getting him to sit still to do his school work is draining every last bit of energy they have left. In reality, Henry's parents may be fighting a losing battle. Unfortunately, the more they try to coerce, persuade, or force Henry to sit still and focus, the more difficulties Henry is going to have with learning (and the more difficulties his parents are going to have teaching him). Henry's brain and body are simply not ready to sit still and do schoolwork.

In traditional education, the proverbial cart is years ahead of the horse when we expect a young child to do academic study before his brain and body are sufficiently equipped to do this type of work. Consequently, instead of being easily pulled by the horse, the cart must be pushed along with much effort, frustration, and inefficiency.

Earlier Isn't Better

In the United States, most children begin school around four to five years of age; in some countries, the school entrance age is as young as three, while others as late as seven years. Is there a best age to begin academic learning? Are there benefits to beginning school at an early age? Does a child do better in school if he gets a head start on reading, writing, and arithmetic? Are there any negative effects of early academic learning?

When researchers look at the relationship between the age of starting school and academic performance in later years, they consistently find that children who begin academics at a later age attain *higher* achievement scores than those who start early. For example, studies performed by the International Association for the Evaluation of Educational Achievement which examined the relationship between the school starting age and reading performance of children from thirty-two different countries found that, when assessed at the age of fourteen, children who started school at a later age had better reading skills than those who began school at an early age. [1]

We see more evidence of the advantages of beginning academics at a later age in the educational history of Finland. In the past, most children in Finland began school at a much later age than other schools around the world. They also had shorter school hours and had significantly more recess time (typically outdoors, regardless of the weather). Yet at fifteen years of age, Finnish children consistently scored among the top nations of the world on the Programme for International Student Assessment (PISA).

Many studies conducted across the world demonstrate the same results: Children who begin academics around four or five years of age often show initial academic advantages over those who begin at a later age, but by around age ten to twelve, these initial advantages are reversed. The children who begin academics later perform better scholastically and achieve significantly higher school grades than those who began academics at the usual age.

Research shows that even the most carefully planned early education programs eventually (usually by age eleven) result in lower academic performance, a sharp increase in learning disorders, and more behavioral issues than programs in which academics begin at a later age. [2]

Developmental neuroscience explains why this is so.

Some Assembly Required

At birth, the baby's brain has the basic architecture, but much growing and changing still occurs in the brain from babyhood well into adulthood. These changes, which are essential to the optimal functioning of the brain, happen in a very precise and scheduled manner and in an exact sequence prescribed by our Creator.

While certain areas of the brain are quite mature and ready for use at a very early age (such as those involved in relationship learning and character development), the brain areas that facilitate academic learning don't even *begin* to be ready for dependable use until around age eight in girls and age ten in boys. And the brain areas involved with deductive thinking and abstract understanding (which are necessary for many areas of academic learning) do not begin to develop until around age eleven to twelve. Furthermore, integration of the various areas of the brain (so they can work together in a coherent, organized, and efficient manner) doesn't begin until around age twelve. [3]

God designed for parents to give full attention to building emotional security, strengthening the emotional bond between parents and child, creating solid health habits, and developing good character in the early years. He did not design these years to be used for academic learning.

What happens in the brain when we ask a young child to engage in academic-type thinking?

When Kaylee was four years old, her parents could easily see that she was a very bright little girl. She could already recite the alphabet and count to twenty. Eager to learn, creative, and curious, she was constantly asking questions and loved to have her parents read to her. Kaylee's parents noticed her thirst for learning, and when she turned five, they purchased a good, Christian curriculum and started homeschooling her. Kaylee enjoyed her school time, and, from all outward appearances, everything was going well. But something interesting was happening in Kaylee's brain.

Because Kaylee was only five years old, the areas of her brain designed to be used for formal academic learning had not yet matured, and so the brain had to adapt and use other areas of the brain that *were* more developed but weren't designed for academic learning. Kaylee did well in her schoolwork, but the neural pathways were being formed in incorrect areas – areas that were not well-suited for the type of learning that was being asked of her. Consequently, her academic learning never became as proficient as it could have been had her parents waited until her brain was ready for formal academics. And other areas of learning suffered as well.

But My Child Loves School!

Kaylee seemed to really enjoy school, hence her mom and dad had no reservations about moving forward in her schooling, but parents should remember that a child's *desire* for academic learning is not necessarily connected to a child's *readiness* for academic learning. Our modern culture that revolves around indoor, book- and screen-based activities and requires very little physical exertion in the outdoors promotes a premature interest in reading and other academic subjects. This interest, however, is not an indication that the brain is ready for this type of learning. Readiness happens on a divinely designed schedule.

Most cultures have arbitrary ages at which children are expected to learn to count, or to read, or to be able to do multiplication. But who decided on these ages? It wasn't God. We are told that "the only schoolroom for children until eight or ten years of age should be in the open air, amid the opening flowers and nature's beautiful scenery, and their most familiar textbook the treasures of nature." [4] Engaging in academic tasks before this age goes against natural mental and physiological development. Following God's schedule of brain development and waiting until the areas of the brain important for academic learning are mature before trying to teach academics means that a child can develop in the beautiful symmetry that God intended for him.

Other Concerns

In addition to its effects on brain development, veering from God's schedule brings other negative consequences.

General Physical Development

Henry isn't the only child who has trouble sitting still. This urge to move is a natural predisposition of every young child. God placed in children a desire to move since physical activity promotes the development of the brain (and various systems of the body).

As we saw in chapter 3, a strong and healthy physical constitution lays the foundation for proper and full development of the mind. Many of the regions of the brain that are responsible for movement are also involved with higher-level thinking. The better these brain regions are developed through healthful physical activity in the early years, the stronger will be a child's thinking abilities in the later years. This is why "during the first six or seven years of a child's life special attention should be given to its physical training, rather than the intellectual."⁵

Our present-day, sedentary, indoor-focused culture is so inured to screen and book-based learning that parents must be intentional about providing sufficient outdoor, physical activity for their young child. Desk- and book-style learning should not be allowed to steal time that should be devoted to building the large muscles and developing a strong physical constitution. The process of developing a healthy foundation requires that a child spend several hours a day over the course of several years engaged in physical activity, but the investment is not in vain since once a strong physical constitution is in place, academic learning can move forward with true mastery and at an unparalleled pace.

Fine Motor Development

The fine motor skills of the small muscles and nerves in the hand and fingers are not developed enough for academic work until about nine to ten years of age, and even then, their development is dependent on preliminary development of the larger muscles, such as those of the trunk, legs, and arms. An abundance of physical activity (i.e., *not* sitting at a school desk) during the first eight to ten years of childhood promotes good development of not only the larger muscles, but also the smaller muscles, bones, and nerves. Not allowing sufficient time for the full development of these small muscles, bones, and nerves before requiring academic activities causes unhealthy stress and strain on the child and on the fine motor system.

Eye Health

Reading, writing, and other types of close-up work before around age of eight to nine places demands on the visual faculties that can cause eye inflammation and elongation, which can lead to myopia (near-sightedness) and permanent damage to the eyes. [6] Waiting until the eyes have developed before teaching reading or writing significantly reduces the risk of developing myopia.

Auditory System Development

A child's auditory system is still developing well into adolescence, and until this development reaches a certain point of maturity, a child may struggle to distinguish certain sounds from others. A lack of this ability can frustrate a child's attempts at learning phonics and reading.

In addition, unlike an adult's auditory system, which has the ability to be selective in the way it processes sound, a child's imma- ture auditory system is designed to process *all* input. This can make tuning out distracting background noise and focusing on the task at hand particularly challenging for a young child. However, this keen alertness is not a design flaw that needs to be trained out of the child; God designed a young child's senses to be alert and actively interested in all that is around him to help him learn. As the child gets older, the auditory system gradually becomes more selective, and the child develops the ability to focus.

Ability to Internalize Concepts

As three-year-old Caroline was helping set the table for lunch, I could hear a sweet, little voice: "I get the pwate aaaand ... I ... and I put it on the table aaaand ... now I need a fork aaaannnnndddd ... then ... umm ... a spoon and then [looking around] ... now I need ... I need anover pwate."

Adults can process thoughts – even deep, complex thoughts – all in the mind; no words need to be spoken. However, children do not have this ability; many of the thought processes that a child expe- riences are not fully experienced unless he can verbalize them. This means that children have an actual need to talk their way through many thinking processes. A little one doesn't jabber his way through his day just to annoy his parents; rather, speaking his thoughts is an essential part of cognitive development and creates physical connections in the brain that help with later academic learning. Requiring pencil-and-paper learning before the child has developed the ability to internalize concepts not only makes learning difficult for the child, but it also inhibits the full and proper development of internalizing thoughts.

Intersensory Perception

Intersensory perception is the ability to take information from one of the senses, such as the visual sense, and integrate and coordinate it with information from another of the senses, such as the tactile sense, to form a unified perceptual understanding. Adults use intersensory perception nearly every moment without thinking about it; this is how we experience life. A very basic example is when we are having a conversation with someone. If we are looking at the person, we can both hear him speaking and see his mouth moving in the shape of the sounds of his speech. Our visual and auditory senses integrate and coordinate the information taken in. If we were to see the person's mouth move in a way that didn't match the sounds that we heard, our intersensory perception would alert us that something is awry.

A child is born with a degree of intersensory perception, but this perception must be developed through an abundance of real-life, physical, hands-on, multi-sensory experiences with the world around him. When we confine a child to a desk and schoolwork, we limit these practical experiences and thus inhibit the full and proper development of his intersensory perception.

Proprioceptive System

Research shows that "in order for a child to be able to sit still, pay attention, and visually remember the shapes of letters and numbers, the child first needs to have developed his or her proprioceptive system."[7] This system takes time to mature and is not fully developed until about age eight in girls and age ten in boys, and even then, it won't develop well without an abundance of physical activity. (See Chapter 3 for more information.) Writing letters and numbers and sitting still at a desk can be particularly challenging and frustrating for a child before this system is fully developed.

Emotional Confidence, Stability, Security, and Maturity

In their report "Reading in Kindergarten: Little to Gain and Much to Lose," education professor Nancy Carlsson-Paige and her colleagues warn that "when children have educational experiences that are not geared to their developmental level ... it can cause them great harm, including feelings of inadequacy, anxiety and confusion." [8] Unfortunately, children tend to blame themselves (usually subconsciously) for the difficulty and confusion they experience, which, in turn, can lessen their desire to learn.

Because both sufficient time and the correct environment are needed for the proper development of all these systems, "for the first eight or ten years of a child's life the field or garden is the best schoolroom, the mother the best teacher, nature the best lesson book." [9]

Boys

I recently had a discussion with a child psychologist who told me that her days are filled with parents who are desperately trying to fix their unhappy, unruly children. Four-year-olds who are fearful and anxious. Six-year-olds who are fidgety and unable to focus. Eleven-year-olds who are angry. Fourteen-year-olds who are withdrawn and rebellious or depressed. While she sees plenty of girls in her practice, the number of boys outweighs the number of girls by more than two to one. Are boys just more prone to misbehavior, or is there something in our child-raising and educational methods that is contributing to this epidemic of troubled boys?

God designed the boy brain to develop differently than the girl brain. [10] The stress-regulating circuitries of the brain mature more slowly in boys than in girls. [11] The structures and functions necessary for traditional academic learning also mature later in boys than in girls. And boys require much more physical activity for proper brain development than do girls. These, and the many other dissimilarities between boys and girls, mean that boys are even *more* susceptible to the negative effects of early academic learning than are girls.

Why this difference in brain development between boys and girls? Did God make a mistake? Not at all. This difference in developmental schedule between boys and girls is a beautiful part of God's perfect design. God designed men to be the spiritual leaders of our homes and our churches. [12] This is a high and noble responsibility and one that a boy doesn't just wake up to one day and find himself equipped to handle. Because God designated the first few years of a child's life for relationship development, character building, and spiritual growth, and because He designed boys to grow to become spiritual leaders, God in His wisdom gave boys the extra years to develop the strong foundation they would later need to fill the role God designed them to fill. Placing boys in school at an early age interrupts and hinders the natural, God-designed progression of brain development.

Left Behind?

Many parents worry that delaying their child's academic instruction will mean that their child will fall behind in his education. The reality is that the exact opposite is true.

Waiting to begin academic study until the corresponding areas of the brain are mature and ready to tackle academic subjects means that a child will learn in a fraction of the time that it takes a child to learn using the traditional educational timeframe. And he will "quickly pass early entrants in learning, behavior and sociability." [13] "When children are given time to develop ... their minds will more readily grasp difficult concepts in school, and less time will be spent learning a subject that might have taken them much longer to learn at an earlier age." [14]

Let's look at a couple of real-life examples.

Thomas started school at age four. He learned to multiply single-digit numbers at age eight and three-digit numbers at age ten (with the help of his mom, some workbooks, and much practice).

Ten-year-old Carter has never seen a multiplication table, opened a workbook, or done a math problem on paper. Yet, when his mom asked him how many apples they needed to pick from their apple trees so they could share twenty with each of the thirteen families in their church, he quickly replied, "About 260." When his dad asked him how many potatoes the family should plant if their family ate about 100 pounds of potatoes a year, and the variety they planted produced about four pounds per plant, he answered, "We need to plant twenty-five. But if we planted three extra plants, then we would have twelve pounds to share with Mrs. Webster!"

Around the time that Carter turned twelve, his mom showed him how to multiply and divide three-, four-, and five-digit numbers on paper. After a total of eleven minutes of instruction, Carter had mastered the skill with stunning accuracy and proficiency, and he quickly and easily moved on to more advanced mathematics.

How can this even be possible? It's not only possible, but it is very common and to be expected when a child is raised using the methods of true education and we give the areas of the brain that are responsible for academic learning the time and environment they need for proper development and maturation before beginning academic instruction.

Dr. Raymond Moore asserts that much of what "children now learn early can be more quickly and efficiently learned at a later age – with less repetition, apathy, and frustration." [15] Research shows that "children who embark later on literacy and numeracy programmes quickly catch up," [16] and "because the children's minds are ready to learn, they actually end up ahead of the game when started later." [17] In addition, waiting until a child's brain is ready means he will approach academic learning with confidence and proficiency as he is enabled to grasp concepts quickly and efficiently.

When our late-starter Carter was seven years old and didn't know how to sit down with a workbook and add numbers on paper like all the other seven-year-olds around him could, it may have seemed that Carter's academic education was deficient. But appearances can be misleading. Carter's parents were following God's method of education – a method that strengthens the mind, body, and moral powers while cooperating with the natural schedule of development of the child's mind. His education was far from deficient. In his early years, Carter's parents were helping him develop a solid foundation and sturdy framework for better brain functioning and robust thinking abilities. They were helping him develop depth of thought and moral strength. These factors made all future educational endeavors more efficient and more successful. Children who are educated using this method become avid learners with exceptional capacity to understand and apply what they learn.

And what about Thomas and other children who begin school at age four or five? As they progress in their education, most can do the math on paper and produce the correct answers because they were taught to do so. But many of them do it without a full understanding of how the skill can be applied in a variety of situations. Even after completing countless workbook pages on the subject of mathematics, when confronted with similar problems in a practical, real-life context, most struggle to take what they were taught and apply it.

Rather than spending three, four, or five years teaching a child basic academic skills, we could and should wait until the child's brain structures that are involved with academic learning have matured, and then we can teach those skills in a fraction of the time.

The child's brain is not a big box that needs to be filled, and the sooner you get started filling it, the sooner it will be full. True education, true learning, is not about filling a child's mind with information; rather, it is about helping a child's brain develop as it was designed to develop so he can think and think well.

But, some parents reason, what will others think when my six-year-old cannot read or do math like the other children? If parents would understand the solemn responsibility which rests upon them in raising their children according to the Lord's standards, "their anxiety would not be to know how they can educate their children so that they will be praised and honored of the world, but how they can educate them to form beautiful characters that God can approve." [18]

It's time to pause, take a step back, and ask ourselves the question, "What exactly are we trying to achieve?" If parents desire to raise their little one to be spiritually strong in his later years, they will use the early years for what they were intended to be used for. Delaying *academic* instruction does not mean delaying a child's education. The Lord has given parents plenty to teach a child before age eight to ten – so much that there really isn't time left for that math workbook! For the young child under age ten, parents should concentrate on building the emotional bond, developing a strong physical constitution, building character, answering the child's many questions, [19] and nurturing the child's relationship with God. When we cooperate with the God-created, natural development schedule of children's brains, we are not delaying a child's education. Everything is right on time!

Words of Counsel

"True education is not the forcing of instruction on an unready and unreceptive mind." [20]

"In the earliest years of the child's life the soil of the heart is to be carefully prepared for the showers of God's grace." [21]

CHAPTER 6

THE EDUCATION OF THE CHARACTER

"The greatest and most essential education is that which results in the formation of a true character." – The Signs of the Times, March 23, 1891

JOHN and Lisa were doing some improvements on their house, and being the skilled handyman that he was, John was doing most of the work himself. One of the projects involved building a small deck outside the back door and pouring a concrete sidewalk that would connect the deck to the driveway. Over the course of several evenings, John laid out where the sidewalk would go, removed the sod and soil, added gravel to prepare the bed for the sidewalk, and built a strong, wood framework to hold the concrete while it set. When he was finished with his preparatory work, he called the local concrete company and scheduled them to bring the concrete truck the next Monday.

Early Monday morning, John went outside to look things over and make sure everything was ready for concrete. Seeing that all was in place, he decided to work on the deck while he was waiting for the truck. At precisely 9:00, he heard the rumble of the truck turning into the driveway. Less than an hour later, the truck had emptied its load into the sturdy forms that John had built. So far, so good.

The deck project was looking really good too, and John really wanted to screw the last few boards in place before he moved on to the concrete. The concrete was still quite wet, so he decided that he had time. Just a couple more boards on the deck ... and a couple more ... he was making great progress! Now, if he could just saw off the ends of the boards so they were all even, then it would look amazing. He picked up his saw and made straight and tidy cuts. The deck was looking great. He stood back to admire his work when he suddenly remembered the sidewalk. He grabbed his concrete tools from the garage, hustled over to the sidewalk, and thrust his rake into the concrete to start the leveling process, but was met with firm resistance. With all the time that had passed, the concrete was no longer wet and easily moved. It had begun to set.

Anyone who has any experience with concrete (and even those without) will recognize that John was focused on the wrong job at the wrong time. Though he was anxious to get the deck built, in reality, that project could have been worked on at any time. There aren't many time-sensitive factors involved in deck building. The concrete, on the other hand, was a job that needed to be done at a certain time. Waiting too long could mean trouble.

The job of character building is like the job of pouring concrete. "Children can be molded when they are young,"[1] but molding and shaping become more and more difficult as the months and years pass by. On the other hand, there is no timeframe in which academics must be learned. Math and other academic subjects can be learned at age thirteen just as easily (and often more easily) as they can be learned at a younger age.

There are stages or periods in brain development during which brain cell connections are more receptive to a particular type of learning than at any other time of life. After a particular period, re-wiring those connections is very difficult. The critical period for the development of character, conscience, morals, and self-regulation is from birth through about age seven.[2] Character development *does* continue throughout life, but deep-rooted development in these areas is most efficient and effective in the early years and comparatively challenging in the later years. In other words, once this critical period has passed, conscience and character can be adjusted and refined, but much more effort is required than would have been necessary if those adjustments were made in the early years.[3] This is perhaps the most important reason why the early years should revolve around that which pertains to character building, not academics.

Not a Second to Lose

Can't parents mold their child's character and teach him academics at the same time?

I know a man who grows tomatoes for a living. He grows and sells thousands of tomatoes every year. Let's suppose that early one spring, the owner of a local restaurant asked my tomato-growing friend if he would grow 8,000 pounds of specialty tomatoes for the restaurant, and the restaurant would pay him ten times as much for the specialty tomatoes as he could normally earn. How do you think the tomato grower would respond? Even though it would mean long hours and a lot of work for him to grow that many tomatoes, he would be happy to do so because he would earn quite a bit of extra income with this opportunity. Now, if his goal is to produce 8,000 pounds of specialty tomatoes, do you think he's going to spend his spring days painting the barn? No, of course not. This is a unique opportunity for him and growing that many tomatoes is a big job for just one man. Logically, his focus is going to be to get the tomatoes plants growing so the tomatoes are ready at the time the restaurant owner needs them. And he would restructure his priorities in order to do so.

Similarly, growing beautiful characters in our children is a big job. And we have a short and limited season in which that can be done. "Childhood is the season in which the most abiding impressions may be made. What the child sees and hears is drawing deep lines upon the tender mind, which no after circumstances in life can entirely efface." [4] "During the first years of their lives is the time to work and watch and pray and encourage every good inclination. This work must go on *without interruption*." [5]

Without interruption.

Character development is a full-time job and cannot be interrupted by the intrusion of formal academic learning without negative consequences. "The labour due to your child during the first years of his life will admit of no neglect." [6]

Considering the amount of time and effort it takes to solidly develop good character traits in a child and the fact that the "cement begins to harden" around age seven, it is dangerous to misappropriate these precious early years that God has designated specifically for the purpose of moral character development and use them for subjects that can be easily learned, and even better learned, at a later age.

"The future happiness of your families and the welfare of society depend largely upon the *physical* and *moral* education which your children receive *in the first years of their life.*" [7]

The Highest Education

Your child may excel in school, go to the best college or university, and get a well-paying job, but no matter how successful your child is in this world, he can take none of that worldly success to heaven. "A character formed according to the divine likeness is the only treasure that we can take from this world to the next. ... How important, then, is the development of character in this life." [8] The education of the character is an essential aspect of true education and the most important work of parents. If we want to cooperate with God in the work of true education, then much of our focus will be on good character development.

What is Good Character?

"There are many who have not a correct knowledge of what constitutes a Christian character." [9] Character is not the equivalent of courtesy, politeness, and kindness (though a good character does include these traits). Character cannot necessarily be detected through outward appearances or even actions as it does not consist only of external behavior. While outward behavior is often an indication of what's in the heart, children can quickly learn what is expected of them and behave accordingly without a true heart change. Some children exhibit good behavior so they can get approval from Mom or Dad, or so they can avoid punishment. While this outward behavior can be pleasing to parents, wise parents will be more concerned about a child's motives and values than his outward actions.

Character goes much, *much* deeper than how a child acts. Character begins with the thoughts and the feelings. "If the thoughts are wrong, the feelings will be wrong. And the thoughts and feelings combined make up the moral character." [10] Since the combination of thoughts and feelings make up the character, then to correctly shape the character of a child, the parents' focus should be on the thoughts and feelings.

We often approach character formation backwards. "The great danger is in neglecting a heartwork." [11] We encourage good behavior and correct bad behavior, and we think we are shaping the character. While this approach certainly can have a positive influence on character, a "from-the-inside-out" approach is much more effective. "True character is not shaped from without, and put on; it radiates from within." [12]

The nurturing of the thoughts and feelings can be a challenging, full-time job, and that's why God has directed parents to take up this work in the early years and allow nothing to distract them from this sacred work. "Heart education is of far more importance than mere book learning." [13] In these precious first few years of life, "the mind is most susceptible; and so the very first lessons are of great importance. These lessons have a powerful influence on the formation of character. If they are of the right stamp, and if, as the child advances in years, they are followed up with patient perseverance, the earthly and eternal destinies will be shaped for good. This is the word of the Lord, 'Train up a child in the way he should go; and when he is old, he will not depart from it.' Proverbs 22:6." [14]

Nurturing Character on the Prevention Plan

All through the Scriptures, we can see clearly that God is a God of prevention. He prefers to prevent evil rather than correct it. For example, in Psalm 119, He instructs us how to prevent sin – by hiding His word in our heart. [15] In Ephesians 6, He tells us what we should do ahead of time so that we may be "able to stand against the wiles of the devil." [16] In Exodus 15:26, God explains how we can prevent disease. In Proverbs 27:12, we are told that the prudent person sees danger and hides himself, but the simple go on and suffer for it. The book of Revelation tells us of the things that must soon take place so we can prepare for them. [17] In contrast, the false system of education is constantly dealing with correction instead of prevention. We see evidence of this in the oceans of how-to-discipline-your-child books that offer a panoply of creative (and not-so-creative) ways to correct bad behavior.

God loves the good; hence, preventing the bad is important to Him. As representatives of God, parents should also work on the prevention plan. In character development, parents should focus on preventing bad behavior to minimize the times in when they must correct it.

There are many ways we can work on this peaceful plan of prevention. I'll briefly touch on a few here.

1. Nurture emotional security.

Children who experience a strong mother-child bond and loving parental responsiveness tend to have better development of the higher-order brain systems, which enables them to have better emotional regulation. They also tend to have a more tender, sensitive conscience, [18] which in turn can give them a strong desire to do what is right. In addition, emotional security triggers the release of a natural chemical called oxytocin in the young child, which increases feelings of trust and connectedness in the child toward his parents, which, in turn, translates to a higher degree of cooperation and obedience. (See Chapter 4 for more information on emotional security.)

2. Build relationship.

Research demonstrates that the parent-child bond is one of the most significant predictors of how willing a child is to embrace parental instruction and values. [19] "Children with a close emotional bond with parents have greater respect for their parents and respond more favorably to their directions and discipline." [20]

When a child's little heart is bound to the heart of his loving parent, he will be more deeply receptive to his parent's guidance. As Pam Leo states, "The level of cooperation parents get from their children is usually equal to the level of connection children feel with their parents."

3. Spend time in nature.

"It is a law of the mind that it gradually adapts itself to the subjects upon which it is trained to dwell." Therefore, if we help our little ones to dwell upon Jesus, their minds will gradually adapt themselves to His beautiful character. This is the key to becoming like sweet Jesus. How can we help a little child's mind dwell on Jesus? "God has revealed Himself to us in ... the works of creation." [21] "The impress of Deity ... is seen upon the lofty mountains, the fruitful valleys, the broad, deep ocean." [22] Spend time with your child in nature (outside, not in a book). In "the birds caroling in the leafy branches, the flowers of the valley, the lofty trees, the fruitful lands, the springing grain, the barren soil, the setting sun gilding the heavens with its golden beams," [23] a little child cannot but see the beautiful character of God.

4. Give special attention to physical habits.

"The relation that exists between the mind and the body is very intimate. When one is affected, the other sympathizes." [24] "Both mental and spiritual vigor are in great degree dependent upon physical strength and activity; whatever promotes physical health, promotes the development of a strong mind and a well-balanced character." [25] "The physical, mental, and spiritual capabilities should be developed in order to form a properly balanced character." [26]

Because physical habits, such as diet, sleep, and regularity, affect the upbuilding of character, "the adversary of souls directs his temptations to the enfeebling and degrading of the physical powers." [27] When we don't prioritize proper health habits, we hinder the character-building process.

5. Be attentive.

"Don't get your church pants dirty!" I heard the mother call toward her six-year-old boy, Austin, as he ran through the church yard with the other children. Mom and Dad, knowing that the other children were well-behaved children with good morals, were not concerned about keeping their children by their side nor monitoring their interactions with the other children and could finally enjoy some relaxing time chatting with friends after a church dinner. When I noticed one of the little girls trip and fall, I walked across the yard to comfort her. It was then that I overheard an eight-year-old girl dare Austin to see how close he could get to the road without his parents noticing. Austin stopped running to process this thought. He seemed slightly perplexed for a moment, as if he was wondering why he would want to try to do something without his parents' knowledge. Austin's parents had invested much in their children's upbringing.

They were careful in their example to their son, they faithfully taught him of the love of God and His perfect ways, they were careful in his education, his health, and the many other factors that would influence his character. And, as a result, Austin had developed into a sweet little boy with a good character and pure thoughts and motives. But at six years of age, it was difficult for him (as it would be for any child) to clearly discern Satan's influence and resist negative suggestions without his parents' help.

Sadly, Austin's parents were unaware that Satan was placing suggestions into their little boy's mind – thoughts of disobedience that he had never had before now, thoughts that he could have resisted at a later age, but that were confusing to him at the tender age of six. Dirt on the child's pants is but little consequence compared to the soiling of his character.

One of the biggest mistakes parents make is not being sufficiently attentive to their children. Parents are admonished to "carefully and prayerfully study the characters of their children," [28] but how can they do this if they are not with them in their work, in their play, in their everyday activities? Character building "must be a daily, hourly work." [29] Parents would reap great rewards (and save much heartache) if they would be careful to be with their children and be attentive to what they are hearing, seeing, saying, and doing. "Parents should not be so much engaged in other things that they cannot give time to patiently discipline the developing minds of their charges." [30] They "should allow nothing to come between them and the obligation they owe to their children." [31]

Mothers especially should not allow themselves to become absorbed in other responsibilities and activities as to neglect being with their children. [32] "The children need the watchful eye of the mother." [33] "It should be her delight to keep her children in her presence as much as possible." [34] The mother must shape her children's character moment by moment. "She must allow nothing to divert her mind." [35] "The mother should be with her children as much as possible, and should sow precious seed in their hearts." [36] Without the mother's presence to guide them *at the right time*, the seeds of bad character habits can be sown in the hearts of her children without her knowledge, and she is often ignorant that these seeds are growing in the heart of her child until many years later when she begins to see the harvest.

All children – from the best behaved to the worst behaved – need the constant, loving watch care of their parents.

6. Prioritize correctly.

Give character development the attention it deserves. Parents, what are your priorities in life? Do you have time to raise your child for God's kingdom, or is a career more important to you? Do you prefer spending time on social media instead of socializing with your little one? Are you working for your child's salvation, or are you busy working on other projects?

"Earthly treasures must pass away; but nobility of character, moral worth, will endure forever. If the work of parents be well done, it will through eternity testify of their wisdom and faithfulness." [37] "It will pay in the end for mothers to make the formation of the characters of their children their first and highest consideration, that the thorns may not take root and yield an abundant harvest. God calls upon mothers to become co-workers with him in the formation of the character of their children." [38]

"Mothers, you are developing character. Your compassionate Redeemer is watching you in love and sympathy, ready to hear your prayers, and render you the assistance which you need in your life-work." [39]

Too Late?

While the early years are the time when character formation is the most easily accomplished, if you have an older child and you've missed this important opportunity for character development, do not despair. The Lord is compassionate. "The precious Saviour, who understands our heart-struggles and the weakness of our natures, pities, and forgives us our errors, and bestows upon us the graces which we earnestly desire." [40] Use the steps outlined in this chapter, adapting them to an older child. Ask the Lord for wisdom, do all in your power to redeem the time, and God will help you.

The True Object of Education

We read in the book *Education*, "In the highest sense the work of education and the work of redemption are one." [41] What a contrast from our traditional views of education!

"The true object of education is to restore the image of God in the soul." [42] "To bring man back into harmony with God, so to elevate and ennoble his moral nature that he may again reflect the image of the Creator, is the great purpose of all the education and discipline of life." [43]

It is a privilege to cooperate with God in this work.

Words of Counsel

"No higher work was ever committed to mortals than the shaping of character." [44]

"The lessons learned, the habits formed, during the years of infancy and childhood have more to do with the formation of the character and the direction of the life than have all the instruction and training of after years." [45]

"There is no chance work in this life; the harvest will determine the character of the seed that has been sown. Mothers may neglect present opportunities, and let their duties and burdens fall upon others, but their responsibility remains the same, and they will reap in bitterness what they have sown in carelessness and neglect." [46]

"The work of wise parents will never be appreciated by the world, but when the Judgment shall sit, and the books shall be opened, their work will appear as God views it, and will be rewarded before men and angels. It will be seen that one child who has been brought up in a faithful way, has been a light in the world. It cost tears and anxiety and sleepless nights to oversee the character-building of this child, but the work was done wisely, and the parents hear the 'Well done' of the Master." [47]

"The dangers of the young are greatly increased as they are thrown into the society of a large number of their own age." [48]

"What work is more essential than that of a mother in educating her children for practical life and in molding their character for the future, immortal life?" [49]

SECTION III
GOD'S METHOD FOR BUILDING THE BRAIN

CHAPTER 7

A Thinking Mind

"Education is not the learning of facts, but rather the training of the mind to think." – Albert Einstein

I got them all right!" Julia danced around the dining room tabl waving her vocabulary quiz in the air.

"Good for you!" her mom replied with a smile. Julia was a good student and usually received perfect scores on her school assignments. It was clear to friends and family that Julia was doing very well in her schooling. But was Julia really learning? Was she learning how to think? Was she strengthening her mind according to God's plan?

Later that day, Julia and her family were reading a passage from the Bible for worship when they came across the word *forbearance.* Dad asked Julia if she knew the meaning of the word. When Julia responded that she did not, and her dad asked her to figure out the meaning based on the context, she became frustrated and impatient. Julia excelled at vocabulary quizzes, memorizing the multiplication tables, and test-taking, but if asked to figure something out, think deeply, or reason through something, she would quickly give up or get frustrated.

Thinking Deficit Disorder

Conventional educational methods condition children to become dependent upon direct instruction for learning – whether from a teacher, through textbooks, via videos, or other man-made educational materials. With this type of education, a child learns to be a passive learner, to think superficially, and to echo what others have said or written.

This type of learning – dependent learning – may help a child acquire specific knowledge quickly, but a child educated in this environment has little need to discover knowledge on his own or in a practical way. He has no need to extract the meaning of or application for this knowledge. He does not have to be an independent thinker; he only needs to repeat what someone has taught him. He does not have to understand what he is doing and why he is doing it; he only needs to give the right answers and complete the assignment. The child quickly learns that his responsibility is not to observe, think, and reason, but rather to follow a predetermined learning sequence in order to achieve purported success. This type of learning is not designed to create strong thinkers but merely reflectors of others' thoughts. Children in this environment often do well in the school setting, but they tend to lose the ability to engage in the process of independent thought and meaningful learning on his own.

Dependent learning is attractive – to both children and adults – because it's easy for the brain. It requires little effort and no real thinking. We teach and/or learn what someone tells us to teach and/or learn, and when we are done with that, we are done teaching and/or learning. It is the easy way of teaching and learning. But it is not God's method of true education.

More important than being able to produce the right answer on a test is a child's ability to think, to understand, to reason, be able to apply what he learns in any number of situations, and to be able to figure out how to do something without being taught.

Fruit of the Tree of Rote Knowledge

The consequences of false educational methods extend far beyond how well a child does academically. A child who doesn't learn to think and reason for himself is at risk for becoming weak not only in mental power, but also in moral power. [1] His mind "becomes incapable of vigorous, self-reliant effort, and is content to depend on the judgment and perception of others." [2] And, unfortunately, "the mind that depends upon the judgment of others is certain, sooner or later, to be misled." [3]

God's plan of education uses methods and practices that, though vastly different from traditional methods, strengthen the child's mind so that he not only learns more efficiently, but he also learns to reason independently and intelligently. Children with these skills are not easily led astray by negative influences, such as peer pressure. They have stability of character. Their minds are strong and well developed. [4] They are capable "of thinking, acting, or deciding for themselves" [5] and know how to put forth "independent action from firm principle." [6] They "possess breadth of mind, clearness of thought, and the courage of their convictions." [7] They grow up to be "strong to think and to act." [8] They are those who "are masters and not slaves of circumstances," [9] and they grow to be those "who bear responsibilities, who are leaders in enterprise, and who influence character." [10]

Strong to Think

"Where did you learn to do that?"

Ben, a skilled software developer who had recently started his own software company, was in the middle of rebuilding the engine of his truck when his friend, Luke, stopped by. Over the years, Luke had enjoyed Ben's talent as an accomplished musician, but he didn't know that he also had skills as a diesel mechanic. A few months later, when Ben and Luke were planning a mission trip together, Luke also learned that Ben could speak three languages fluently. A year later, when Ben became engaged to be married and built his own home, Luke also discovered Ben had several additional practical skills, including being a very talented custom cabinet maker.

"Where did you learn to do that?" inquired Luke. "Did you take classes somewhere?"

"No."

"Then, how do you know what you're doing?"

"I just figured it out," Ben replied.

When Barbara Rogoff, Distinguished Professor of Psychology at the University of California, Santa Cruz, was doing research in a Mayan community where she worked for over forty years, she noticed that not only were the very young girls (as young as age four) able to weave, but they were remarkably skilled and able to accomplish extremely complex and intricate weaving patterns. Barbara remarks, "When I asked mothers 'How do you teach your daughters to weave?' they replied, 'I don't teach them to weave, they just learn.'" [11]

Perhaps you have heard someone say, "I can't. I don't know how." "I never learned to do that." "That's not my talent." "No one taught me how to do that." "I didn't learn that in school." "I've never taken classes on that." "I'd like to know how to do that, but I don't have anyone to teach me." This is the mentality cultivated by false education. But for a child who has strongly developed his thinking skills through the methods and environment of true education, not being taught how to do something becomes an irrelevant factor.

True education – true learning – involves higher-order cognitive skills, such as the ability to figure out how to do something without being taught, solve tough problems that don't have one right answer, and make complex connections between new information and previously learned concepts and combine the various factors into a coherent whole so that what is learned can be used and applied in new, unfamiliar contexts.

This may sound like a type of learning that would be covered in a college class, but when a child is raised using the methods of true education, his mind becomes so active and strong that, instead of being dependent upon others to teach him, he becomes capable of learning in any situation. He gains an abundance of useful knowledge and skills quickly without being taught. He develops such robust thinking abilities and extensive reasoning powers that all learning becomes extraordinarily and exceptionally efficient and accelerated, and he grows to become a competent, active agent of his own intellectual development.

The Work of True Education

"It is the work of true education to ... train the youth to be thinkers, and not mere reflectors of other men's thought." [12] There are several elements of true education that strengthen the brain and help a child to be a thinker. We'll look at five of them below and a couple more in the following two chapters.

1. Use God's timing and methods.

The habit of deep thinking is most easily and effectively established at a young age. If parents want their child to be able to think well, they will avoid using sit-down academic work (which fosters linear thinking) for their child before the age of eight to ten and instead cooperate with God's method of education by focusing on emotional security, relationship, character development, and health habits in the early years. (See Chapters 2 through 6.)

True education is like a beautiful tapestry – the many threads of which are intricately woven together to make a perfect whole. There is an intimate interconnection between a child's ability to think well and his physical habits, his emotional health, and his character development. We cannot pull out a thread without spoiling the beautiful pattern. We cannot neglect *any* of the elements of God's method of education without spoiling the beautiful whole.

2. Use real life more than textbooks.

Children learn far better from real and practical experiences of life than they do from textbooks. One simple example of the difference between learning from real experiences and learning from a textbook can be seen in how a child can learn to cook.

When Jenna was a young child, her mother decided she should learn to cook. To accomplish this, suppose that Jenna's mom signed her up for a cooking course that required her to read and study five recipes a week and then take a test on what she learned. In the first week, she would study several main dish recipes, such as rice and beans, pasta with sauce, and stir-fry. Then, at the end of the week, she would take a test that asked questions such as, "What are three ingredients commonly used in stir-fry?" And "How long should you cook beans so that they are tender?"

This knowledge may have been useful, but this knowledge alone wouldn't make her a good cook. In addition, the approach would have been terribly boring, and she could have learned this very same information in a much more practical way.

Suppose instead of enrolling Jenna in a cooking course, her mom simply allowed her to experiment in the kitchen. Every day, she would actually cook foods like rice and beans, pasta with sauce, and stir-fry. Through these real-life experiences, she would obtain a practical knowledge of how long beans need to cook to be tender. She would get hands-on experience with what seasonings make stir-fry taste amazing and which ones make it taste like pumpkin-pie-flavored broccoli. And, if she needed help, had questions, or wanted to learn additional information, she could use a recipe book or a how-to-cook book for reference.

Through her daily experiences, through her mistakes and successes, through her experimentation with a variety of cooking challenges, she would learn about how different ingredients function in different dishes. She would come to understand how those ingredients work with each other. She would learn how to combine ingredients in a particular way to bring out completely new flavors. She would gain a knowledge of cooking tools and how they work. And, as she put that new knowledge into practice, that experience would enable her to learn even more. With this practical experience, the skill of cooking would become instinctive and intuitive, and she would not only be equipped to whip up delicious meals with ease (and without the aid of the step-by-step guidelines of a recipe), but she might also create her own well-designed recipes and maybe even eventually write a cookbook.

And, more importantly, through this practical experience, she would improve her abilities to observe, analyze, reason, evaluate, and think through every decision she made in the kitchen to ensure that the food came out right, thus strengthening her mind.

Taking a rote cooking course as described in the first example is very similar to the approach that false education uses when trying to teach a child academic subjects. We give a child the information that someone has determined that he needs to know, tell him to read and study it, then test him on his memory of it. Unfortunately, this method stifles the need for fully developing deep thinking skills and is an effective way to cultivate superficial learning.

Unlike two-dimensional, pencil-and-paper learning, real-life learning is broad, multi-dimensional, and engaging. It creates a more extensive network of connections in the brain and facilitates better anchoring of information in the neural networks. According to John Taylor Gatto, former New York State Teacher of the Year, "When children are given whole lives instead of age-graded ones in cellblocks, they learn to read, write, and do arithmetic with ease, if those things make sense in the kind of life that unfolds around them."

3. Focus on knowledge that can be used.

Nearly every student who has ever sat through a class on trigonometry has asked the seemingly ubiquitous, schooldays question: "When will I ever use this?" The question is valid. Much of what is taught in a typical educational setting will be forgotten in just a few months, and of the very little that is remembered, even less is actually used.

The reality is that most children aren't convinced that they will ever need to know how many feet above the earth they will be twelve seconds after they jump out of a plane at 10,000 feet. For many students, the most he will use any of the out-of-context information that is dished out to him on a daily basis is on the test next week. And because the information is currently irrelevant to the child, it gets filed superficially in the brain, thus conditioning a child for superficial learning.

True education focuses on knowledge that can actually be used.

4. Practice thinking.

Just as practicing the piano can help one strengthen one's piano-playing abilities, so practicing thinking can help one strengthen one's thinking abilities. With this in mind, children should be allowed to think and act for themselves as much as is possible and appropriate. Parents should "properly [direct] them to think and act for themselves as their own capacity and turn of mind will allow, that by this means they may have growth of thought, feelings of self-respect, and confidence in their own ability to perform." [13]

This does not mean that parents should leave their children free to do whatever they want to do, free to make all their own choices and decisions unguided by the wisdom of an adult. It simply means that parents should seek appropriate opportunities to allow their child to learn to think through practical experiences.

One of the best ways to do this is through practical work. "Practical work encourages close observation and independent thought." [14] The acquisition of solid reasoning skills, problem-solving skills, and observational skills is the direct result of a child's trial-and-error engagement with the practical things in life. Attempting to pick up something that is too heavy for him, combining various ingredients into a mixing bowl, hammering a nail, attempting to repair a broken tool or appliance, and similar activities provides him with authentic feedback and real-life consequences.

Practical work engages and develops the brain like no textbook, workbook, or curriculum can.

In addition, in their daily conversations with their young child, parents can ask him "think questions." At first, use very easy, logic questions such as, "If we can't see Grandma's house right now, does that mean that it isn't there?" "If *this* book is blue, does that mean *all* books are blue?" (You can even have him go find another book to prove his answer.) Beginning with easy questions that have obvious answers makes the conversations fun, which means that your child will be more likely to want to have more "think conversations," and you can gradually move on to progressively more challenging questions.

5. Minimize reliance on memorization.

In our modern system of education, a student who is adept at memorizing and reiterating facts is considered a good student because this skill enables him to produce correct answers on tests. However, while it is valuable to store useful information in our memory, rote memorization is a linear process that uses only a small section of the brain at one time and does little in the way of connecting the various structures of the brain. It often fails to provide a student with a comprehensive understanding of information, how various aspects of the information relate to one another, or how to apply the knowledge in different contexts. "In short, rote memory does not require thinking." [15] The negative effects are seen not only in a child's intellectual development, but in a child's moral development as well. "The education that consists in the training of the memory, tending to discourage independent thought, has a moral bearing which is too little appreciated. As the student sacrifices the power to reason and judge for himself, he becomes incapable of discriminating between truth and error, and falls an easy prey to deception. He is easily led to follow tradition and custom." [16]

To help a child be a thinker and not a reflector, avoid methods of learning that depend heavily on memorizing; instead, focus on connected understanding and practical application. Encourage your child to explore, experiment, think, evaluate, reason, innovate, and problem solve. When we encourage a child to truly learn instead of just filling his brain with information, more connections are made in the brain, and thinking skills are strengthened.

True Learning

With superficial learning, knowledge is received; with true learning, knowledge is discovered. With superficial learning, the learner is given facts; with true learning, the learner searches for meaning. Superficial learning is limited because it reflects the knowledge and skills of the teacher; true learning is limitless. Superficial learning tends to depend upon external motivation; true learning cultivates and nurtures intrinsic motivation. With superficial learning, the child may do well on textbook problems that have a similar theme, but if he is asked to apply what he has learned in a whole new setting or situation, he may struggle to do so. With true learning, a child is enabled to discern how new information has application in other contexts. With superficial learning, the child memorizes the dots; with true learning, he connects the dots.

We owe it to our children to not shackle their thinking powers with the restrictive and hindering methods of false education. We must enable our children to think.

Words of Counsel

"The many branches which students are induced to take up in their studies, holding them from the work for years, are not in the order of God." [17]

"Every student needs to understand the relation between plain living and high thinking." [18]

"Close reasoners and logical thinkers are few, for the reason that false influences have checked the development of the intellect. The supposition of parents and teachers that continued study would strengthen the intellect has proved erroneous; for in many cases it has had the opposite effect." [19]

CHAPTER 8

CREATING A BRAIN-BUILDING ENVIRONMENT

"I never teach my pupils. I only attempt to provide the conditions in which they can learn." – Albert Einstein

COLORFUL pictures and eye-catching charts were strategically hung on the wall of the cute homeschool room. A large world globe and entertaining geography games were invitingly displayed on the side table. Two tall bookshelves filled with interesting books were on the other side of the room. Educational games were neatly stacked in one cabinet, and another cabinet was dedicated to a rainbow of art supplies and crafts. Brightly-colored Bible lessons, nature books, and coloring pages were perched on the center table, and along a wall was a construction system equipped with blocks, tools, and fasteners, as well as a play kitchen with pots, pans, measuring cups, pretend food, and all sorts of fun things for creative experiences. Madelyn and Alexander were homeschooled, and, in their parents' effort to make sure their children received a superior education, they were careful to create a rich learning environment for their children. In addition to supplying Madelyn and Alexander with a wide variety of educational material in their home, Mom and Dad also provided once-a-week music lessons for their children. Many would say that these children were privileged to have such a wonderful learning environment.

The problem is that Madelyn and Alexander were bored. And any serious learning was uninteresting to them.

Their well-meaning parents had tried to provide them with an environment that would enhance their children's education, but what is typically defined as a "learning rich" environment doesn't necessarily translate into better learning outcomes. Children who are furnished with an abundance of learning aids don't have to tap into their own creativity or invent their own mental imagery, and consequently, they generally don't learn how to learn without external stimulus or prompting.

The consequences? The young brain, though at first intrigued by all the interesting material, gradually becomes passive and lazy, and its natural, inborn tendency to seek out its own learning opportunities is stifled. Creativity is extinguished. Attention span is diminished. Independent thinking is hindered. And the love of learning for the sake of learning begins to melt away. Children in this type of environment gradually lose the enthusiastic, observant, self-initiated learning that was so prominent in early toddlerhood. A quiet walk in the woods, an unillustrated book, an unexciting conversation, a simple lesson is boring to them. Contrary to what parents are led to believe through the numerous influences surrounding us in our modern culture, this artificially-enriched environment tends to suppress individual genius.

Building the Brain

How well a child learns is significantly affected by his environment. The child's environment molds the development of his brain. Thankfully, parents can create for their child an environment – a physical, emotional, and intellectual climate – that capitalizes on and nurtures the child's natural, inborn love of learning. How can they do this? This chapter covers several of the various components that contribute to a healthy learning environment for a child.

1. Live a quiet and simple life.

In the book *Education*, we read, "The more quiet and simple the life of the child – the more free from artificial excitement and the more in harmony with nature – the more favorable it is to physical and mental vigor and to spiritual strength." [1]

Research shows that the constant activity and continual sensory input of our modern life vie for a child's attention and hinder the development of deep thinking, but a quiet and simple environment enhances his learning, improves his attention span, and strengthens his observational skills. [2] The peace, restfulness, calmness, and tranquility of a quiet and simple life provide the child's mind with what it needs to process and reflect and to grow and develop. "Plain living is indispensable to high thinking." [3] "If Christian parents lived in obedience to the requirements of the divine Teacher, they would preserve simplicity in eating and in dressing, and would live more in accordance with natural law." [4] "They would not then devote so much time to artificial life." [5]

2. Maintain neatness and order.

Another important component that contributes to a healthy learning environment is neatness and order. The young brain is sensitive to visual distractions such as clutter. Clutter decreases a child's attention span and retention and hinders the depth to which a child can process intellectually and emotionally. This clutter can be physical clutter or mental clutter, or both. A lack of organization and/or an abundance of things (even good things) add to physical clutter. Screen-based devices, a lack of schedule, and an abundance of activities can contribute to mental clutter.

3. Provide an environment that allows a child to communicate.

As mentioned in Chapter 5, young children do not have a well-developed ability to internalize thoughts, and so they often verbally express what's going on in their minds. As children mature, they develop the skill of inner speech; but in the early years, they need an environment that allows for this verbal chatter, as it is important for brain development.

In addition, for children young *and* old, much brain development can happen in a home in which good communication is practiced between children and parents. An abundance of free and mutual interaction with a responsive parent helps develop brain areas involved with perception, social skills, empathy, visual imagery, music skills, non-verbal thinking, and spirituality. [6]

4. Get rid of the desk and the schoolroom.

Neat rows of desks that seat neat rows of children who are all looking at the same page in the same book may seem like the perfect educational climate, but this type of environment is not compatible with how a child's brain functions or with how God designed a child to learn. Movement is a precursor to all learning. Moving not only helps the child's brain to develop properly, but it also puts the brain in learning mode. Sit a child at a desk and his brain development and learning potential plummet rapidly.

5. Minimize the entertainment factor.

One hundred and fifty years ago, very few children had toys – at least not what we would typically consider to be toys. Instead, children created their own forms of amusement. They spent their time exploring the woods, observing the adults in their lives (a significant form of entertainment for children in the past), working with their parents, making dolls from scrap cloths, floating leaf boats down the stream, and inventing an endless array of fun out of natural materials like sticks, mud, and stones. With their active imaginations, a large, empty box became a house or a store. Three chairs lined up became a train. Kitchen pots and utensils became musical instruments. In many cultures around the world, children still maintain this type of play and creativity. All without the direction or help of adults. Or Legos.

Perhaps there is nothing wrong with toys, games, and other forms of artificial entertainment, but just as cake and ice cream will lessen a child's appetite for carrots and kale, so will entertainment lessen a child's appetite for discovering, experimenting, and learning. In fact, one of the greatest inhibitors to motivation and the development of thoughtful creativity in a child – and perhaps the development of the mind in general – are toys. Research shows "the fewer toys a child has, the better he is able to focus, the more creativity he develops, and the longer he plays before becoming bored." [7]

"Read the history of Abraham, Jacob, and Joseph, of Moses, David, and Elisha. Study the lives of men of later times who have most worthily filled positions of trust and responsibility, the men whose influence has been most effective for the world's uplifting. ... How many of these were reared in country homes. They knew little of luxury. They did not spend their youth in amusement." [8]

6. Provide an age-integrated environment.

The learning environment in God's method of education centers in the family (immediate family and, ideally but not necessarily, extended family) where life is lived with people of various ages with varying levels of knowledge, assorted skills, differing talents, and diverse personalities.

This mixed-age environment, which follows the Biblical example for educating our children, [9] nurtures a spirit of cooperation, promotes a sense of responsibility, encourages maturity, cultivates the development of empathy, and more. While providing emotional and social benefits, multigenerational relationships also provide intellectual benefits. Research shows that children who learn in mixed-age environments experience deeper learning, develop better language and communication skills, and academically outperform those grouped by age. [10]

In the real world, humans regularly interact with other humans of different ages. The school years are the only time of life when humans are segregated by age. Since, to be successful in life, we must daily interact with people both older and younger than we are, it only makes sense that, to prepare our children for success, we raise them in an age-integrated environment.

7. Include reference material.

Children are naturally curious, and simple, basic reference material can give you a resource to help answer the many questions your child may have that cannot be answered through hands-on experience.

Have on hand at least one large, good-quality dictionary (a book, not an electronic device) and one set of encyclopedias or other reference books on useful topics (again, print books) so you and your child can look up answers to his questions such as, "What's the difference between an ocean and a sea?" or "How far away is the sun?" A world atlas, a world globe, and other maps are also very helpful. At breakfast, when your child notices that the sticker on his kiwi says, "Product of New Zealand," you can get out a map and discover where this country is. A handbook on the English language (or the language you speak) is also an important component of a good learning environment. In addition, be sure to have a Bible concordance and all of the Spirit of Prophecy books, as well as an index to these writings.

Also helpful, but not necessary, are a map of the night sky, a few basic science textbooks (such as biology, anatomy, and physics), and a gardening book or two. When your child stubs his toe on a rock, you can turn to the anatomy book to find out which blood vessels, nerves, or bones may have been injured. If he is curious about why his ball falls to the floor faster than a piece of paper, you can read about the effect of air resistance in your physics book. If he wants to know where the fish go in the winter, you can read about animal habitats in your biology book.

Whether your child is three years old or fifteen years old, much can be learned through the avenue of curiosity. And by searching for the answers to these questions together, you are modeling not only how to learn, but also an eagerness to learn.

Though reference material is valuable and can be helpful in learning, parents should keep this counsel in mind: "The multiplication of books, even books that in themselves are not harmful, may be a positive evil. With the immense tide of printed matter constantly pouring from the press, old and young form the habit of reading hastily and superficially, and the mind loses its power of connected and vigorous thought."[11] "One of the chief causes of mental inefficiency and moral weakness is the lack of concentration for worthy ends."[12] Reference books can be helpful for answering curiosity questions, but don't let them crowd out real-life experiences that strengthen the mind.

8. Avoid digital devices.

Studies using fMRI neuroimaging reveal that the use of paper and print material instead of digital devices results in more robust brain activation in multiple brain areas, better memory recall, stronger conceptual understanding, and better application and integration of knowledge gained.[13]

Exposing the developing brain to digital devices inhibits optimal integration of the different areas of the brain and negatively affects higher-order cognitive functioning. We tend to see more attention deficit disorders, increased impulsivity, and decreased ability to self-regulate in those who spend more time on screen-based devices. A child's use of these devices can impair learning and lead to lower scores on language and thinking tests. Research has also shown an association between the use of digital devices and premature thinning of the brain's cortex, the area of the brain related to critical thinking and reasoning.[14]

Children have lived for thousands of years without these devices, and they do just fine without them.

9. Make the home a place where angels love to dwell.

"Above all things else, let parents surround their children with an atmosphere of cheerfulness, courtesy, and love. A home where love dwells, and where it is expressed in looks, in words, and in acts, is a place where angels delight to manifest their presence." [15] "The home should be to the children the most attractive place in the world, and the mother's presence should be its greatest attraction." [16] An environment such as this provides peace and security for a child, which allows his brain to focus on learning.

I'm Bored

It was a beautiful day outside, but Madelyn and Alexander were sitting in the living room feeling quite bored.

"Why don't you and Madelyn go outside to play?" Mom suggested.

"There's nothing to do outside," mumbled Alexander.

"It's boring outside," echoed Madelyn.

Despite the abundance of time, attention, and affection this dedicated and loving mom gave to her children, and the host of games, toys, books, and other forms of entertainment they had available to them, boredom was a common complaint from both Madelyn and Alexander.

At another home a few miles away from that of Madelyn and Alexander, there is a very different scenario. We knock on the front door of this home, but there is no answer. We hear something, so we knock again, only to realize that the noise is coming from the backyard. Walking around the house, we see Evelyn and Benjamin playing in their backyard. If their wet clothes and massive pile of collected sticks, dried leaves, green leaves, grass, and thin vines are any indication, it looks like they've been there for quite a while. The noise we heard was sweet, innocent, belly-shaking laughter coming from the children. Evelyn and Benjamin are designing and building pretend boats from their stock of raw material and then testing their designs in the turbulent waters of the seaway ... er, puddle. Every design is well-thought-through, improving on the previous design, and masterfully constructed. But, given the giggles and squeals we hear, it is apparent that the testing process is also providing the highest form of entertainment as each ship is christened in the waters of the deep.

Inside the home of Evelyn and Benjamin, you won't find a toy room; in fact, you would have to look hard to even find any toys. And yet, these two little ones never complain of boredom. One day you may find them climbing trees, another day they are building forts with sticks, and another day they and their mom may be gone for several hours as they explore the treasures in the woods and the field near their house. No entertainment from store-bought toys can compare with the imaginative and creative fun that Evelyn and Benjamin daily concoct in their simple and natural environment.

But play doesn't absorb all of their day. Both Evelyn and Benjamin are actively involved in the responsibilities of cooking, laundry, cleaning, gardening, and more. They both engage in their responsibilities cheerfully because each of these duties is a fun part of their day. One of eight-year-old Evelyn's favorite activities is inventing recipes in the kitchen and testing them on her family. Four-year-old Benjamin loves anything that involves working in the garden and has done extensive research (for a four-year-old) on the best conditions for growing his favorite variety of potatoes. The previous summer, they helped their dad rebuild an old lawnmower, and this year Benjamin is learning to change the oil in the car. These children believe that working can be fun, exciting, challenging, and fulfilling all at once. The parents of these two little ones have never heard the boredom cry from their children, and these children love to learn.

Children thrive on a quiet and simple lifestyle. We don't need to ignite a child's love of learning; we just need to provide the right environment to keep it burning.

Words of Counsel

"The more simple the order of a well-regulated household, the happier will that home be." [17]

"Our artificial habits deprive us of many blessings and much enjoyment, and unfit us for living the most useful lives." [18]

CHAPTER 9

THE MOST IMPORTANT ELEMENT

"I was inspired by an amazing workbook in elementary school that changed my life." – No Child Ever

THERE is one more very important element for building your child's brain, so important that I've devoted a separate chapter to focus on this component alone. It's an element that contributes more to the healthy development of your child's mind than any other factor, an element that most ensures success in learning, an element that is absolutely essential for optimal cognitive development – and yet, it is an element that is most often overlooked.

A child's brain is most primed for learning when in the context of relationship. And the most important relationship for a child is the relationship with his parents.

This absolutely crucial element in your child's education is YOU.

God Designed Learning to Happen in Relationship

Research shows that children who learn in a cooperative, supportive, and loving family environment with an abundance of free and mutual interactions with their parents learn more quickly, achieve higher cognition, experience better memory retention, and have superior attention regulation than children who do not have an intimate and interactive relationship with their parents. [1] In the book *Education* we read: "In all true teaching the personal element is essential." [2]

Children were created with the need for connection and relationship and with a "desire for sympathy and companionship." [3] This is why God placed children in families. "He who made us ordained that we should be associated in families, and the child nature will develop best in the loving atmosphere of a Christian home." [4] God designed children to learn in the context of the family relationship – not a relationship with a textbook, an educational video, or a curriculum, but a relationship with their parents.

The Learning Environment of the Greatest Educator

In the original plan in the Garden of Eden, we see that God Himself came to commune – to communicate on an intimate level – with Adam and Eve. This was how they were to learn of God. This was how their characters were to be developed. This was how they were to gain knowledge and learn of the world around them. "Adam and Eve received knowledge through direct communion with God."[5] God didn't sit them in a classroom and give them a lecture about His knowledge, His wisdom, and His character, filling their mind with information. He didn't hand them a curriculum or a workbook or an instructional video and then go about His other important duties. No. He came personally to be with them. He walked and talked with them. It was through *communion* with Him that they were to learn.[6]

When the children of Israel were on their journey from Egypt to the Promised Land, and God wanted to teach them His ways, how did He do so? "'Let them make Me a sanctuary,' He said; 'that I may dwell among them.'"[7] God knew that the best way to teach them was to be *with* them.

And when Jesus – the greatest Teacher this world has ever known – was on this earth, how did He teach? Jesus used true education – relationship-based education – in the teaching of His disciples. When Andrew and John wanted to learn of Jesus, He invited them to come and dwell with Him, and they *abode* with Him. The small group of men known as his disciples became the "family of Jesus,"[8] and He lived with them, ate with them, walked with them, and worked with them. "They were with Him in the house, at the table, in the closet, in the field. They accompanied Him on His journeys, shared His trials and hardships, and, as much as in them was, entered into His work."[9] Through this daily communion with them, in the context of this relationship with Him, they observed Him and learned from Him. Jesus came to know them personally, and they came to know Him. As He developed a relationship with them, their hearts became tuned to His, and this is how He could teach them.

Jesus used this same method when He wanted to teach the little children. "Christ ... took little children in his arms, and descended to the level of the young. His large heart of love could comprehend their trials and necessities, and he enjoyed their happiness." [10] It was because of this connection with Jesus that the children readily responded to Him and learned from Him. Through the perfect example of Jesus, we can see that the most effective way to teach children is through a warm connection with them.

Outsourcing

We live in an age where outsourcing is a regular part of life. We pay someone else to change the oil in our car, someone else to mow our lawn, someone else to fix our appliances, someone else to handle our finances, someone else to grow our food, and sometimes we even pay someone else to prepare our food. There may be advantages to outsourcing the common tasks of life, like fixing the washing machine, but there are serious negative effects that come when we outsource our children's education. Even the best Christian schoolteacher – let alone an educational video or an inanimate curriculum – is unable to connect with the heart of a child in the way that God designed his parents to. Children need positive, consistent, and deep emotional involvement and connection with the ones who know them better than anyone else. This connection nurtures brain growth and catalyzes healthy development and learning.

Substitutes for Parents

An even worse situation than outsourcing is that of substitutes for parents. Every child, from the very shy child to the most gregarious and outgoing, has a strong, deep-seated desire to belong. Children have a natural propensity to look for this belonging, this relationship, with their parents; but if they don't find a sufficiently fulfilling relationship with their parents, they will look for it in others. [11]

Sadly, modern parents think it is normal for young people to be peer-oriented and uninterested in their parents. But this was not God's original design. For thousands of years, parents and children shared lives, shared experiences, and shared hearts. There was mutual consideration of both the older members of the family and the younger. Family values were passed down from generation to generation within the context of close family relationships. In religious instruction and socializing, age groups were not segregated as they are in today's modern society; children and parents engaged in these activities together. All of life was lived as a family unit.

But, in the modern structure of many cultures, children are deprived of the identity that comes from inter-generational socializing and everyday living. And because a sense of belonging is a deep-seated need for them, children and youth instinctively generate their own culture and belonging among their peers.

This is all part of the enemy's plan. He knows that our children will suffer many negative effects by substituting the trusting and harmonious parent-child connection with peer-to-peer relationships. And he knows he doesn't need to physically separate parents and children; he only needs to emotionally separate them. When this happens, instead of turning to their wise and experienced parents for instruction, guidance, and example, children turn to their own peers – individuals whom God never intended to be placed in the parenting role. [12]

One of Satan's greatest lies is that the rebellious teen years are an inevitable part of growing up. God's design is not for the parent-child relationship to grow more distant as the child grows older, but rather that it thrive and grow even closer and more enjoyable in the teen years and beyond. True education provides for solid, warm, and continuous parent-child connection that nurtures both relationship and learning and leads to healthy psychological and social development.

Parents, if you want your children to learn to think, be secure and confident, to develop good character, to have a close relationship with God, "watch and pray, and make your children your companions." [13]

A Higher Education

Parents must remember that "it is not the highest work of education to communicate knowledge merely, but to impart that vitalizing energy which is received through the contact of mind with mind, and soul with soul." [14] In God's method of education, parents build a deep relationship with their child, daily bringing the mind of the child into communion with the mind of the parent, thus preparing the child for the higher education where "the mind of man is brought into communion with the mind of God, the finite with the Infinite. The effect of such communion on body and mind and soul is beyond estimate. In this communion is found the highest education. It is God's own method of development." [15]

Parent, you are the most valuable factor in your child's education because it is you who stands in the place of God to your child. [16] Don't outsource this privilege to someone or something else.

A Child's Heart

My friend and I were taking a walk in the woods when suddenly her son, Anthony, enthusiastically sprinted toward the very muddy, very large puddle and jumped into the middle of it. Squealing with delight, he wiped the mud off his cheek (he really just smeared it, but it was a good try), and went back for seconds. I waited to hear what his mom's reaction would be. Would she tell him to stop? Would she scold him for getting his clothes muddy when he didn't have any clothes to change into?

She gave none of these responses. Rather, she joined him.

Within seconds, she was also quite muddy (although Anthony was definitely more talented in this activity). Anthony's mom had a deep connection with her child. And it showed – not just in her willingness to jump in mud puddles, but also in *his* willingness to do what she wanted him to do. When Anthony's mom later asked him to go wash his shoes off in the hose, he quickly and willingly complied. When she asked him to wait patiently while we finished our conversation, he did so with a cheerful and polite attitude. When she told him that he couldn't play with the dog because he needed to help put things into the car and prepare to go home, there was no whining and no arguing.

It *is* possible to be your child's parent and also his friend at the same time, and there has never been a generation when children so desperately needed their parents' time, love, and friendship.

Besides the many advantages for brain development, spending time with your child helps build spiritual strength. To teach a child truth, his heart must be open to receive it. How do we open the heart of the child? Through relationship. The child's heart is open to those with whom he is friends. If he is friends with his peers, his heart will be open to receive what his peers tell him. But if he is friends with his parents, his heart will be open to receive what his parents tell him. Every parent should strive to be "very best friends" [17] with their child.

Your child does not need to know how to do polynomial division to develop and grow into a secure and successful adult, but he does need *you*. He needs you to help him learn who he is, who God is, how much he is loved, and what is his purpose here on this earth. He needs you because when you spend time with him and delight in his companionship, he learns that he is valuable and loved – by you and by God. He needs you because *you* – not a math book, not a history lesson, not a curriculum, not even a Bible story – are the one who can lead him to Christ. And, ironically, when parents make relationship a priority, not only do children learn the most valuable and eternal lessons, but, because of the positive effect that relationship has on their brains, they also learn polynomial division better.

The book *Education* tells us that it is only by "the communion of mind with mind and heart with heart" [18] that the work of true education can be accomplished. True education is not something you do *to* your child; rather, it is something you do *with* your child. The time a parent spends with their child *is* education!

Art Linkletter is reported to have said, "I once asked a five-year-old what he would take with him to heaven, and he replied, 'I would take my parents because I think that up there they would have more time to spend with me.'" Parents, please don't let these few precious moments you have with your child slip by without investing your time and energy in creating a solid relationship with him.

Words of Counsel

"The heart of the child is tender and easily impressed; and when we who are older become 'as little children,' when we learn the simplicity and gentleness and tender love of the Saviour, we shall not find it difficult to touch the hearts of the little ones and teach them love's ministry of healing."[19]

"The mother's time belongs in a special manner to her children. They have a right to her time as no others can have."[20]

"Some parents do not understand their children and are not really acquainted with them. There is often a great distance between parents and children. If the parents would enter more fully into the feelings of their children and draw out what is in their hearts, it would have a beneficial influence upon them."[21]

"Parents should encourage their children to confide in them, to be open and frank, to come to them with their difficulties, their little daily annoyances, and when they are perplexed as to what course is right, to lay the matter before their parents, and ask their advice. Who are so well calculated to see and point out their dangers as godly parents? Who can understand the peculiar temperaments of their children as well as they? The mother who has watched every turn of mind from infancy, and is acquainted with the natural disposition, is best prepared to counsel her children."[22]

"Parents, give your time to your children."[23]

SECTION IV
GOD'S LESSON BOOKS

CHAPTER 10

HEAVEN-APPOINTED LESSON BOOKS

"Real success in education depends upon the fidelity with which men carry out the Creator's plan." –
Patriarchs and Prophets, 595

EDUCATING children is an important responsibility. "No work ever undertaken by man requires greater care and skill than the proper training and education of youth and children." [1] Do you feel inadequate for this responsibility? Does it seem overwhelming? Do you wish that God would give you a set of lesson books to help you? Thankfully, He has done just that.

In the book *Education*, we are told, "Jesus followed the divine plan of education." [2] And then we are told what lesson books were used in His education. His education provides a pattern for us to follow. What could be more perfect for our children than lesson books straight from heaven? What could grow the brain more? What could educate a child better? What better lesson books than those chosen by God Himself?

The results of being educated with these lesson books are shown in the life of Jesus. "The child [Jesus] grew, and waxed strong in spirit, filled with wisdom: and the grace of God was upon him." [3] When Jesus grew to adulthood, the people "were astonished at His teaching." [4] "Never before spoke one who had such power to awaken thought, to kindle aspiration, to arouse every capability of body, mind, and soul." [5] And these same educational lesson books will produce superior results for your child. We are promised, "every child may gain knowledge as Jesus did." [6]

God's lesson books are "full of instruction." [7] Infinitely superior to traditional lesson books, they provide an unsurpassed framework for learning. They also provide much of the reason, motivation, and content for learning.

What are these lesson books? Where can we get these lesson books?

Continuing in the same paragraph in the book *Education*, we discover what they are: useful work, the study of the Scriptures and of nature, and the experiences of life. [8] These four Heaven-appointed sources of instruction are "God's lesson books, full of instruction to all who bring to them the willing hand, the seeing eye, and the understanding heart."[9]

Crossing the Stream to Fetch Water

There is a story of an old village in Europe that was located beside a large, ever-flowing, spring-fed stream. This stream flowed with an abundance of clean, clear water all year round and supplied the little village with all the water they could want.

About a mile or two beyond the flowing stream was a larger, neighboring village that, being not so privileged as to be situated close to this large stream, had a well that supplied the needs of the people in the village. The water from the well was not as good as the water from the flowing stream, and because there was only one well, the villagers often had to wait in line before they could draw water, but the well sufficed to provide for the needs of that larger village.

Due to intermarriages between the two villages, there were many women native to the well-bearing village who now lived in the stream-supplied village. Every day, these women would arm themselves with a couple of sturdy buckets and an old cotton towel and head toward the stream. But when they arrived at the stream, instead of drawing from the clear, clean water, they sat down to remove their shoes and stockings. Carrying buckets in one hand and shoes and stockings in the other, they carefully navigated their way over the rocky stream. When they reached the other side, they again sat down, dried their legs and feet with their cotton towel, donned stockings and shoes, and continued on toward the other village to collect water from the well.

When asked why they didn't simply get water from the flowing stream that was not only closer to their new home village but also provided better water, they replied, "This is the way I've always fetched water, and this is the way most people get water, so I believe it's a good way."

When we are accustomed to one method, we sometimes have difficulty comprehending that another method can be not only better but also easier. Likewise, when we've been educated in false educational methods, we may have difficulty comprehending that God's lesson books provide better learning than does traditional education. However, if parents seek to learn, understand, and apply God's beautiful methods of education and trust in the One who has provided the abundantly flowing stream of wisdom and knowledge, they will soon find that His ways indeed are not only better but also easier.

Nothing Missing

Ever since Lucifer rejected God's authority and convinced Adam and Eve to do the same, humankind has been attempting to exalt their own ideas as better than God's simple methods.

In this modern world where certain educational goals are stressed to the point of unthinking obsession, much more important aspects of education are strangely and sadly neglected. And because of this strong and deep-rooted societal influence on our ideas of education, we often fail to understand how comprehensive and efficacious God's methods really are. This may explain why, after learning of the complex beauties of God's system of education and how His ways will strengthen the mental capacities of a child and will grant that child unlimited capacity to learn, a parent will often with a puzzled expression ask, "But how will my child learn _____?"

Parent, you can let go of your fears that God's method is in some way inferior. A child will not end up "uneducated" by following the methods of the greatest Educator. There are no holes; nothing is missing in His system. The One who is the source of all wisdom did not recommend a method of education or a set of lesson books that were lacking. God's divine plan of education is perfectly suited for the optimal development of the human mind. "He only who created the mind and ordained its laws can perfectly understand its needs or direct its development. The principles of education that He has given are the only safe guide." [10] The mind of a child who is educated using this method will grow and expand far beyond what any other method could even dream of. Why would we ever want to replace God's perfect lesson books with lesson books made by man?

In the next few chapters, we will take a closer look at each of these perfect lesson books and how to use them.

CHAPTER 11

GOD'S LESSON BOOK OF
EXPERIENCES OF LIFE

"Learning is experience. Everything else is just information." – Albert Einstein

MOM had fed baby Olivia, finished her own breakfast, and cleaned up the dishes, and now it was time for school. The subject for the day? Talking.

Mom sat six-month-old Olivia in her baby seat and pulled out her flashcards, video lessons, and workbook from her "Learning to Talk" curriculum and proceeded with Lesson 1 on learning how to talk. They faithfully continued this daily "school time" until, at about eleven months old, baby Olivia started forming her first words. Olivia was learning how to talk! Mom told all her friends and relatives and everyone in her homeschool chat group about how impressed she was with the "Learning to Talk" curriculum, and soon many others were using this method with their babies as well.

Sound silly? Do babies need flashcards, workbooks, and video lessons to learn how to talk? Of course not. Babies who live in an environment in which talking is a daily activity of life will naturally learn this skill, without any special curriculum. Not only will they learn to talk, but in the right environment, within a few short years, they will even learn correct pronunciation, proper sentence structure, and correct grammar if that is what they have been exposed to. [1] What's more, children who live in a bilingual or multilingual environment often learn to speak *more* than one language. And all this happens without a single class on talking.

If we stop to think about the complexity of the task of acquiring a vocabulary of thousands of words and using them correctly so that they comply with hundreds of cultural norms and grammatical rules, the thought may be overwhelming. That's a lot to learn without a single flashcard! Yet a child takes on this challenge without hesitation, and acquires all of this learning as a result of simple experimentation in and through everyday life.

Real-Life Learning

Because of the influence of traditional educational methods, most people hold the view that children learn when they are seated at a desk and taught by a teacher. But this "I-teach, you-learn" approach does not correspond with how a child is designed to learn. In fact, this method hinders learning. For a child to truly learn – to build sturdy brain architecture, make solid brain connections, and apply what has been stored in the brain – he needs practical experiences in which he interacts with the real world.

We see an example of experiential learning in how children learn to talk. Experiential learning allows children to learn in the way that is most natural to the functioning of a child's brain – by connecting concepts with real-life experiences.

Experiential learning is brain-building. It is a whole-brain activity. It engages all of the senses and many areas of the brain at once. It enhances the development of the prefrontal cortex, thus strengthening cognitive processes such as memory, planning, focus and attention, decision-making, problem-solving, and self-control. And it facilitates superior organization of connections between neurons, providing for a broader, more meaningful, and more authentic understanding than can be accomplished with pencil and paper.

Starving the Brain

Passive or two-dimensional learning in which a child learns through written instruction is usually quite attractive to adults – the child is sitting at a desk, the workbook or the textbook is doing the work of instructing, and the progress is quantifiable or easily measured and tracked. But learning at a desk with books, paper, and pencil starves a child of the real-life, sensory experiences that his brain is nourished by; and this method of education does not promote nearly as much brain development in a young child as does experiential learning.

Consider these two examples of how a child can learn fractions.

Ellie is homeschooled, and her parents use a typical homeschool curriculum. With this curriculum, Ellie is introduced to fractions at age seven, and she daily practices what she's learned in a workbook. Using this method, it takes Ellie several years to fully understand the concept and be able to solve math problems that involve fractions.

Four-year-old Savannah is learning fractions in a very different way – she's gaining the concept of fractions through incidental con- versation and everyday activities (the lesson book of experiences of life). Before her dad leaves for work in the morning, Savannah and her family enjoy breakfast together. Sometimes she and her dad share a banana – Dad gets half and Savannah gets half. If Savannah's sister wants some, Dad tells Savannah to divide the banana into thirds. Later, Savannah and her mom and sister spend time working in the garden, talking about the beautiful birds that God has made as well as the trees, flowers, and all the wonderful plants in their garden. This morning, they have some marigolds to plant, and Savannah asks if they could plant some of them beside her special tomato plant. Mom suggests they plant two-thirds of the flowers with the tomato plant and one-third of them in the flower bed. After their work is finished, they play in the water from the hose for a while. The flowers on the other side of the house need to be watered, so Mom asks Savannah to fill her bucket halfway with water and take it to the flowers before they go into the house to prepare lunch.

Savannah and Mom prepare some vegetables and sandwiches for lunch and talk about how the vegetables are good for their bodies and how well the lettuce grew in their garden this year. Mom cuts her sandwich in half and then carefully hands the knife to Savannah and instructs her to cut her sandwich in half also to make it easier to eat. Then, since she was enjoying this hands-on fun, Savannah cuts each sandwich half in half again. Mom tells her that her sandwich is now cut into quarters and teaches her how to add fractions by asking her what would happen if she took three quarters of her sandwich and added one quarter of the sandwich.

Through these and other simple, everyday conversations and activ- ities, the concept of fractions becomes solidly embedded in Savannah's brain without any formal instruction or even an awareness that learning was occurring – and long before fractions are generally taught in school.

But Savannah is learning far more than fractions through these everyday experiences. She's also learning communication skills as she converses with her parents. She's learning to share as she and her family share bananas at breakfast. She's learning observation skills as she watches how her parents do things. She's learning knife skills as she practices cutting her sandwich. She's also learning responsibility, diligence, unselfish service, and cooperation. Numerous brain connections are being created, and her prefrontal cortex is being strengthened, which means that all future learning will happen more easily and more efficiently for Savannah.

Conversely, learning fractions in the way they are typically taught – two-dimensionally – teaches only one thing: fractions. And it doesn't even do that very well, as most children don't know how to apply the knowledge in practical life. This two-dimensional work is not in accordance with the way a child is designed to learn, and the brain struggles to fully process the information.

The Long and Short of Memory

There is yet another problem with two-dimensional learning. In traditional education, there is much concern among educators about learning loss – the tendency for children to forget what they have been taught if they aren't continually practicing and reviewing it. The concern is valid. Most research shows that over summer vacation, students lose (on average) between 25 to 30 percent of what they learned in the school year.

Why do children so quickly forget what was taught to them? Two-dimensional learning goes against a child's natural brain function. When the information a child is given is not connected to something he is experiencing in real life, his brain has difficulty storing the new information in a way that it can be easily retrieved, because the new information has nothing to connect with –nothing to which it can attach. This is why in traditional education new information must be reviewed and practiced over and over and over in order for the child to remember it. Review in textbooks. Practice on worksheet after worksheet. Review at the end of a chapter. Review before a test. Review after summer break. There is so much repetition, practice, and review that a student using false methods of education requires twelve or more years to learn what a child who follows God's method can often learn in just a few years. Without meaningful context, a child may remember information long enough to get the answers correct on a test, but he will not retain what he learns very well or for very long, and he will struggle to know how to apply what he has learned in different contexts.

Some would argue that at least a portion of the information will be remembered. But if you had a bucket that consistently lost about 30 percent of the water that you put in it, would you not look for another method to transport the water? There are better ways to teach a child.

Peter Gray, PhD, research professor at Boston College, states, "Very little is learned in a few months of school that is remembered over time. There is even evidence that the skills schools are most concerned about – literacy and numeracy skills – are actually more deeply learned in out-of-school activities than in school." [2] For a child to learn something well enough that he can remember it and apply it in any given situation, he must experience it.

Dependent Learning

False educational methods not only require constant repetition and review, but they also are inextricably dependent upon the teacher (or the parents). If the teacher doesn't teach, the child doesn't learn. This means that in a homeschooling setting, the mother must work two full-time jobs – homeschooling and mothering. More often than not, this approach leads to an exhausted mama and homeschool burnout.

When a child's education follows God's methods (which includes the environment and principles covered in Chapters 2 through 9), and the child learns through God's lesson book of the experiences of life, a child will do an amazing amount of learning on his own (thus removing a huge burden from the mother). In addition, because experiential learning strengthens the brain, a child learns faster, and he better remembers what he has learned.

Creativity vs. Right-Answeritis

Real-life learning also greatly enhances creativity, which is helpful for academic success. We tend to think of artists and musicians as the creative people, but the usefulness of creativity goes far beyond the fields of art and music. Successful engineers, architects, writers, physicians, and research scientists generally score high on creativity tests as well because these careers require the ability to generate original ideas and to analyze and evaluate those ideas as to whether they are of value to the particular application.

Textbooks, worksheets, and curricula put learning in a box – or on a piece of paper – flattening the imagination and creativity of the child. They inevitably send the message that textbooks, worksheets, and curricula are all there is to learning. Fill out this worksheet, and the job is done. Finish the textbook, and that subject is completed for the year. Complete the curriculum, and school has been accomplished. Over time, the once inquisitive mind of a child adapts to this two-dimensional type of education. When this happens, a child usually stops exploring, observing, and creating and settles into the job of accomplishing what is required. He develops the mental condition I call "right-answeritis," and settles into knowing the right answer instead of growing the higher mental processes of problem solving, reasoning, analyzing, interpreting, and understanding.

God's method of education is not two-dimensional. It is multi-dimensional. It is broad, deep, creative, and well-rounded. And a multi-dimensional, broad, deep, creative, and well-rounded education produces multi-dimensional, broad, deep, creative, and well-rounded thinkers.

Books vs Real-Life

Historically, the Chillihuani children in the Peruvian Andes have provided an example of the benefits of experiential learning. Until recent years, these children grew up extensively and intrinsically involved in the experiences of daily life alongside their parents, and though they received very little formal schooling, they showed extraordinary intelligence, talent, skills, and academic achievement, and they consistently surpassed their schooled agemates in academic abilities. [3]

We see another example in Brazil where researchers noted that carpenters who received practical experiences yet little schooling had a better understanding of mathematical concepts and were amazingly skilled at solving problems relevant to their work than were carpenter apprentices who took classes specifically designed to teach those concepts. [4]

In a school experiment in the U.S., when children were instructed to learn the different parts of a plant, those who had *experience* with gardening remembered the lessons much better than those who had never gardened. In reading class, poor readers who had also had experience with bird watching scored higher on a reading comprehension test about bird habitats than strong readers who had not taken the class.

Psychologists who observed workers at a packing plant noted that workers who had received comparatively little formal schooling were able to rapidly execute complex mental mathematical calculations (with virtually no errors) in their work with ease and to a degree that the more highly-schooled workers couldn't even begin to match. [5]

No Books?

None of the above is to say that books are not useful. Books are a valuable learning tool, and much learning can be gained from books, especially once a child has reached twelve to fourteen years of age and has a solid foundation in practical, experiential learning. But books are an inadequate substitute for God's lesson book of the experiences of life. When the act of learning is confined to books, learning becomes a spectator sport. A child *views* what is learned instead of *experiencing* it. The consequences? The child's brain disengages, and thinking deeply becomes difficult.

We are warned that "the study of books will be of little benefit, unless the ideas gained can be carried out in practical life." [6] "Even an acquaintance with facts and theories important in themselves is of little value unless put to a practical use." [7] "If you gain ever so much knowledge, and yet fail to put that knowledge to a practical use, you fail of your object." [8]

Instead of reading books, a child should be encouraged to do, to experience, to experiment, to problem-solve, to reflect, to think. The child who engages in real-life activities with his parents, such as cooking, gardening, budgeting, planning, as well as going to the grocery store, the bank, the hardware store, has the potential to learn and understand math, science, and many other academic subjects much better than could ever be hoped for in the typical educational environment that centers on workbooks and other two-dimensional material.

If you want to grow your child's brain, include him in the daily activities of life. It may look like your little one is simply doing a load of laundry, but the reality is, if you use God's method of education, your child is actually embarking on a research program in which he is observing and collecting data, producing hypotheses, conducting field experiments using control groups, examining how the manipulation of one independent variable leads to a change in a dependent variable, analyzing data, extricating patterns, constructing theories, and making countless synaptic connections in his amazing, growing brain.

Experiential Learning and Spiritual Growth

"He wasn't raised this way." The parents of a seventeen-year-old were sitting beside me, feeling distraught and frustrated. They had raised their son in a Christian home. They had taught him the difference between right and wrong. But from the description they gave, the actions of this young man would leave one to believe otherwise. "This is not how we raised him," his mother expressed in tears. My heart ached for these parents. They had really tried to raise their child to be a Christian.

How many times have you heard someone say, "I know I should exercise more, but ..." or "I know I should be more patient, but ..." or "I know I should eat healthier, but ..." or "I know I should be more organized, but ...."? The disconnect between *knowing* and *doing* is a serious epidemic in our modern society, and unfortunately, this disconnect even affects Christians in their Christian walk. There is a disconnect between *knowing* what's right and *doing* what's right.

God tells us that when we are hearers of the Word and not doers, we deceive ourselves. [9] What's even more disturbing is that, even though this attitude is considered by God to be sinful, [10] there is very little concern for this ever-widening gap between knowing and doing (at least not until we face serious consequences). The disconnect between knowing what to do and actually implementing that knowledge has become so common, so normal, so expected, that not only is no one alarmed at the breach between the two, but we are often surprised when someone actually goes against cultural expectations and applies what he knows to be right.

But what causes this disconnect?

In false education, learning is detached from practical life. Reading is taught during reading class, science during science class, and math during math class. What is learned is removed out of the context of ordinary, practical, day-to-day activities and placed in its own compartment. There is little, if any, connection between what is learned and its application in everyday life.

Because the methods of false education create a disconnect in the mind of a child between what he is taught and what he does, even if a child seems to be learning well in church, Bible class, and family worship time, when his mind is not accustomed to *applying* knowledge in real-life situations, what he learns becomes a mere sterile abstraction – not something that would necessarily apply to his life. False educational methods have conditioned him to disconnect knowledge from practice. As the child grows, the gap between knowing the teachings of the Bible and allowing its teachings to change the everyday thoughts, decisions, and actions becomes wider and wider until, eventually, Biblical knowledge is divorced from the transformation that Christ desires to make in the heart through communion with Him.

When a child is four years old and excited about learning, parents are often eager to get him started in some sort of book learning. But they should remember that there are long-term ramifications of allowing book learning to intrude upon the time that God designed for practical learning. We may not see the results for several years, but when they do appear, reversing the negative effects can be difficult.

The need for practical application is absolutely essential for children. If we want God's truth to sink deeply into the hearts of our children, we would do well to make all learning real, practical, and blended with their daily experience.

How to Make Learning Practical

While most people are still waiting for the day that they will use $(x^2+8x+1)(9x^2-10x+15)$ in real life, many academic skills *are* useful in everyday life. So, how do parents make academic skills practical for a child?

1. Include your child in everyday activities.

Everyday environments and activities are the ideal classroom and instructors for a young child. Home is equipped with a number of laboratories, such as the kitchen, the garden, and the garage; and children can find real-life resources in their parents, grandparents, aunts, uncles, neighbors, and friends. One does not need to manufacture artificial settings in order for a child to learn. Real-life learning is the same method a child uses to learn many skills in life, including how to walk, how to put on his socks, how to tie his shoes, and how to brush his teeth. When a parent demonstrates the skill and incorporates it into the everyday life of the child, he will learn it.

A simple example is the above story of how Savannah learned the meaning of the term *half.* When her mom told her that she was going to cut her sandwich in half, her active brain registered that word and connected it with her mom's actions. Through this small life experience and others, a child may quickly comprehend the meaning of the word without any formal teaching taking place. If the concept of *half* can be learned in everyday life, then so can the concept of one-third, one-sixth, one-eighth, and thirteen-sixteenths. And without a single textbook, a child can learn fractions and learn them at a deeper level than he ever could have were he confined to a desk and told to learn it from a book.

Numbers can be learned in the kitchen, in a building project, and in everyday work. Children can learn to read through the incidental encounters with project instructions, words on maps, recipes, product packages, etc. They can learn science in the great outdoors, through gardening, and through cooking. On a simple shopping trip, a child can learn mathematics (calculating the price per quantity of something), social studies (interacting with people and discussing things you see), health (determining the healthiest foods to buy), and science (why are some vegetables wilting and others fresh?). As children work with parents in the garden, they learn science (as they learn about plants, insects, and soil health), mathematics (as they count seeds, calculate how many seeds to plant in an area, and calculate area and square footage), and communication skills all rolled into one activity. Real-life situations not only promote better learning by engaging multiple senses simultaneously, but they also help with character building as real-life activities provide many opportunities for the child to learn to be attentive, diligent, industrious, helpful, careful, patient, and more.

Using real objects, interacting with people, and exploring in nature gives the brain the ability to gain knowledge about how things in the world work. These types of experiences form prolific beneficial brain connections and help a child learn how to think, solve problems, and generate new thoughts and ideas.

2. Exhibit an enthusiasm for learning.

It is a law of the mind that one will learn something more quickly and more thoroughly when one is happy and eager to learn it. [11] Cooperating with this law will help children learn much more in just a fraction of the time.

For a very young child, life is fascinating. (Just watch a two-year-old as he stands mesmerized by the spin cycle on the washing machine.) "From the earliest moments of their life the children are learners." [12] They are also imitators. By our actions and attitude, we can inadvertently put a damper on a child's intrigue. (For example, I recently observed an adult mindlessly smash a spider that a little child was enjoying watching.) Parents can nurture a child's love of learning by demonstrating a desire to learn themselves.

Avoid the false education mindset in which the focus is on the right answer instead of on the joy that can be experienced in the learning process. For example, if you want your child to learn music, rather than signing your child up for piano lessons, one of the first steps you should take is to show an interest in music yourself – even if you can't play a musical instrument. The goal is not to impress your child with your amazing musical abilities; the goal is to show your child enthusiasm for learning. Sit at the piano or another instrument and have fun trying to pick out a tune. Laugh at your mistakes and get excited at any inkling of a recognizable tune. By your example, your child will learn that music – and learning – is enjoyable.

With the blessing of a positive environment surrounded by a family who is interested and interesting, a child will learn eagerly and often surprise parents with what they know.

3. Communicate with your child.

Savannah's learning of fractions was facilitated not only by her real-life experiences but also by her parent's communication with her. Talk with your child. Include him in plans for the day, for the next day, and for the week. Involve him in solving problems. Talk to him about what Dad is doing at work, about why you made the decision to move to the home you currently live in, about the food you're going to buy for a needy neighbor. As you prepare lunch together, talk about how the food was grown and, if you didn't grow it yourself, how it made its way to you. In everyday, casual conversation, talk about how to be honest and trustworthy, how to be content, how to be compassionate. Ask for his opinion about things. Ask him questions that don't have a yes or no answer. Ask questions about things that neither you nor your child knows about, then brainstorm to think of ways you can learn the answer together. (Encourage options such as experimenting, researching in books, or asking someone. Avoid using the internet to find answers as this method requires very few brain resources.) All these activities will engage his brain and get it in "think" mode.

Be careful to not shut down communication by expressing impatience if your child doesn't have much to say or doesn't give the response you want. And avoid telling him what he should say or think. Also, take care to not burden or weary the child by overdoing it. Take cues from the child as to whether he is interested and engaged in the

conversation; if he's not, don't force it. There is a big difference between asking a question or mentioning something interesting versus
drowning your child with a flood of questions, pouncing on every
potential object lesson, and giving exhaustive dissertations on every
topic that comes up. When raised with methods of true education,
a child's active mind is always learning; there is no need to force a
learning lesson into every activity of the day.

4. Encourage observation.

An observant mind is always learning. The skill of observation
helps a child develop strong cause-to-effect reasoning. It assists in
the development of a child's ability to extricate patterns, compare
these patterns with others that have been observed, and classify objects – skills that are beneficial in the study of mathematics, reading,
language, music, and many other subjects. Observation also tends to
enrich a child's vocabulary since an observant child notices the words
he hears and how those words are used, and, due to the enhanced
memory that is developed through observational skills, he remembers
those words and is able to use them intelligently.

Following all the principles of God's method of education will
help develop the skill of observation in a child. In addition, parents
should also encourage this skill in their child and take care to arrange
the day to allow sufficient time for opportunities for observation.
The learning opportunities found in careful observation cannot be
scheduled. (I talk more about cultivating the skill of observation
later in the book.)

5. Answer your child's questions.

Children are full of questions, and these questions are part of
the way that God designed children to learn. Welcoming questions
supports and encourages curiosity that leads to an abundance of
learning.

When your child asks a question, don't be concerned if you don't
know the answer. Finding the answer and learning together can
be a fun experience and teaches your child methods of discovering
answers to questions.

Even if you *do* know the answer, occasionally you may want to use the question as a conversation starter, an opportunity to experiment, or a reason to pull out some reference books. Not only does this provide you with more information about the subject than perhaps you could have given, but it also models to your child the love of learning. Just be sure to avoid making every single question an intense learning opportunity, or your child may begin to think twice before asking you another question.

6. Provide a need-to-know.

Eight-year-old Lillian had no interest in learning the metric system, and neither did her parents have an interest in teaching her about this system of measuring, as they lived in the United States where nearly all measurements are given in Imperial units. At a church dinner one week, someone served a vegetable casserole that Lillian liked very much, and so she politely asked the creator of the casserole if she could have the recipe. The next day, while attempting to make the casserole herself, she discovered that all the measurements were given in milliliters and grams – units of measurement that she had never used before.

Lillian suddenly had an interest in learning the metric system.

Lillian and her mom retrieved a reference book from the bookshelf and found an explanation on the metric system as used in cooking. By the time she was finished with the recipe, she understood the metric system of measuring (at least how it pertained to cooking) quite well, and every spare moment she had for the next week, her mom found her studying and experimenting with other metric measurement units.

A couple of weeks later, her older brother asked Dad how long the garden beds were as he was making plans for the next gardening season. When Dad said he wasn't sure, Lillian responded, "Ten meters."

"Ten meters? How do you know that?" her brother asked.

"I measured them last week," she responded.

"Well, I was kind of hoping for a measurement in feet."

"Oh. I think that would be just over 30 feet," Lillian replied.

Because she had a need for the knowledge – a purpose for learning – Lillian learned this system of measuring well and became quite proficient at it. While the isolated and seemingly irrelevant material in a child's school textbook usually presents no reason for learning, real life presents innumerable need-to-know situations. Parents can also *create* need-to-know situations to help a child learn something. When a need for knowledge exists before the knowledge is presented, children learn very quickly.

7. Look for learning opportunities.

While parents should resist trying to make every moment an intense learning opportunity ("Mom, can I just turn the light on one time without you saying that Jesus is the light of the world?"), they certainly should look for opportunities from which they can teach a child something valuable. Short learning moments, rather than long lessons, are best for keeping the child's interest.

Many parents feel that they are not creative enough to come up with ideas on their own, but if they will only, through prayer and time in God's Word, put themselves in a place where God can communicate with them, He will give them wisdom and ideas that are perfectly fitted to their child's needs.

8. Always apply what you learn.

"Your education should continue during your lifetime; every day you should be learning and putting to practical use the knowledge gained." [13]

The Results of Real-Life Learning

True education does not compartmentalize learning. Rather than teaching math during math class, reading in reading class, health principles in health class, Bible during Bible class, and moral lessons in family worship time, true education recognizes that every waking hour can be a learning time.

The results?

A child learns that there is no limit to learning. He learns that learning is a fascinating part of life and that learning happens continually throughout the day, every day, year-round, and throughout life.

Instead of seeing math as a collection of dry, lifeless, and uninteresting data, formulas, and imaginary and irrelevant problems on paper that have no relationship to his life ("When am I ever going to use this?"), a child comes to view math as a very practical tool that he can use to overcome obstacles, to discover intelligent and efficient methods for doing things, to keep an accurate account of his own resources, [14] and even learn what it means to be a steward for God.

Instead of science being an exercise in the memorization of technical terms and uninteresting facts that don't seem to have any relevance to anything, the study of science provides intensely interesting insight into the world around him and the body he lives in. A child discovers fascinating answers to questions his active brain has been pondering, and his heart fills with gratitude as he comes to understand more clearly the rich meaning and purpose of life, in addition to the greatness of the God he loves.

Instead of the study of history being a boring repetition of facts and data about people he doesn't know and events that he doesn't care about, learning about history provides him with an understanding of where he came from and why he is here, gives him a deep insight into the great controversy between Christ and Satan, helps him to see all things from the perspective of eternity, gives him a fascinating look at how God has had His hand in all the events of history, aids him in understanding "how wonderfully we are bound together in the great brotherhood of society and nations," [15] and helps him to see "how great an extent the oppression or degradation of one member means loss to all." [16]

Instead of geography being a list of places where he's never been and cares nothing about, a child gains a meaningful understanding of the different cultures, environments, and landscapes around the world. He learns to respect those who live differently than he does, which significantly contributes to the character traits of humility, empathy, and kindness. And he becomes interested in how the work of God is moving forward in other areas of the world.

Instead of the study of language being a plethora of confusing rules to memorize and boring essays to write, language becomes an exciting, beautiful, and engaging tool for clearly and easily communicating his thoughts and ideas to those around him, as well as a means for spreading the beautiful gospel of Christ to the world.

And when parents use God's lesson books to educate their child, the effects will also be revealed in the child's spiritual growth. Charles Spurgeon, one of England's most notable ministers of the nineteenth century, said, "The religion of mere brain and jaw does not amount to much. We want the religion of hands and feet." [17]

Real-Life Learning

When a baby learns to talk, he does not learn this new skill because a parent sits him down and teaches him to talk. Nor does he learn to talk so he can get good grades or get a college scholarship. He does not learn to talk because he may use this skill sometime later in his career. And he does not learn to talk so he can develop self-discipline. Rather, he learns to talk because his experience of living with his family causes his brain to realize that the skill of talking is *relevant* to his life. It is a useful tool. The ability to talk has *practical* relevance in his life.

We can fill a child's mind with an abundance of knowledge, but unless the information is relevant to his life, most of this knowledge goes in one ear and out the other, floating around in the brain just long enough to help him pass a test. Instead of educating our children with useful knowledge, we educate them to forget.

Real-life experiences generate greater brain cell activity, engage multiple neural networks simultaneously, build connections between many areas of the brain at once, and develop the higher mental processes (reasoning, thinking, problem solving, analyzing, etc.), all of which result in better brain function and greater learning capacity.

When we use God's lesson books, we cooperate with how God designed a child's brain to learn, and we see learning rise to a whole new level.

Words of Counsel

"The study of books only cannot give students the discipline they need. A broader foundation must be laid." [18]

"A return to simpler methods will be appreciated by the children and youth. Work in the garden and field will be an agreeable change from the wearisome routine of abstract lessons, to which their young minds should never be confined." [19]

"The time, means, and study that so many expend for a comparatively useless education should be devoted to gaining an education that would make them practical men and women, fitted to bear life's responsibilities. Such an education would be of the highest value." [20]

CHAPTER 12

GOD'S LESSON BOOK OF NATURE

*"I love to think of nature as an unlimited broad-
casting station, through which God speaks to us
every hour, if we will only tune in." – George
Washington Carver*

GOD'S lesson books – useful work, the study of the Scriptures and of nature, and the experiences of life – are the perfect educational books for your child. In this chapter, we're taking a look at the wonderful lesson book of nature and how to use this lesson book for the development of your child's brain.

The Education of a Great Man

He was a skilled musician who performed before royalty. He was a great composer who wrote songs and poems that are still loved and sung 3,000 years after his death. But his talents were not confined to the arts. He was highly intelligent, he was a brilliant planner, and he was a competent organizer and leader. He was also a talented architect and designed a massive and beautiful edifice that was famous throughout the nations of the world. Full of wisdom and understanding, he was selected to be a ruler of a great nation when he was only thirty years old, and he became one of the greatest kings in all history. He was a fearless warrior with exceptional military skill, winning numerous battles, thus expanding Israel's territory and making it a great nation. But perhaps his greatest accomplishment was when God said of him, "I have found David the son of Jesse, a man after mine own heart." [1]

David was clearly a successful, highly educated man. Where did he receive his education? How did David become qualified to be such a successful man and great king? Did he receive his education at one of the elite schools? Was he prepared for his great accomplishments and intense responsibilities through training in the best educational centers of his day?

David's education came from God's lesson books, including the one called nature. As the young boy kept watch over his father's flocks, "before him spread a landscape of rich and varied beauty. The vines, with their clustering fruit, brightened in the sunshine. The forest trees, with their green foliage, swayed in the breeze. He beheld the sun flooding the heavens with light, coming forth as a bridegroom out of his chamber and rejoicing as a strong man to run a race. There were the bold summits of the hills reaching toward the sky; in the faraway distance rose the barren cliffs of the mountain wall of Moab; above all spread the tender blue of the overarching heavens. And beyond was God. He could not see Him, but His works were full of His praise. The light of day, gilding forest and mountain, meadow and stream, carried the mind up to behold the Father of lights, the Author of every good and perfect gift." [2]

Through his immersion in nature, David perceived "daily revelations of the character and majesty of his Creator [that] filled the young poet's heart with adoration and rejoicing. In contemplation of God and His works the faculties of David's mind and heart were developing and strengthening for the work of his afterlife." [3] On the grassy slope beside the sheep, by the pools of clear water, amid the forest trees, God gave David a thorough education, strengthened his heart and mind, enriched him with wisdom and talents beyond his years, and prepared him "to take a high position with the noblest of the earth." [4] Through communion with nature and with God, David "proceeded from strength to strength, from knowledge to knowledge." [5]

Nature is a potent and effective lesson book that has the power to shape and strengthen the mind and prepare your child for that which God is calling him.

Nature – God's Wonderful Educator

Neuroscientists have discovered that when children observe and explore in the context of nature, learning capacities increase rapidly. In fact, time in nature actually changes the physical structure and the functional organization of the brain.

By bringing our children in contact with nature, their minds come in contact with the mind of the Infinite. God, the Creator of nature, is the "source of all knowledge," [6] and the more closely we connect a child with this Source of all knowledge, "the more he can be advantaged *intellectually* as well as spiritually." [7] "Through His creation we become acquainted with the Creator. And so the book of nature becomes a great lesson-book." [8]

Time in nature has been a part of God's method of education from the beginning. Moses, Samuel, Joseph, Daniel, and many others all learned amidst God's created works. "In early ages, with the people who were under God's direction, life was simple. They lived close to the heart of nature. Their children shared in the labor of the parents and studied the beauties and mysteries of nature's treasure house. And in the quiet of field and wood they pondered those mighty truths handed down as a sacred trust from generation to generation. Such training produced strong men." [9]

Nature was also a significant part of the education that Jesus received. "He found recreation amidst the scenes of nature, gathering knowledge as He sought to understand nature's mysteries." [10] "Day by day he gained knowledge from the great library of animate and inanimate nature. He who had created all things, was now a child of humanity, and he studied the lessons which his own hand had written in earth and sea and sky. The parables by which, during his ministry, he loved to teach his lessons of truth, show how open his spirit was to the influences of nature, and how, in his youth, he had delighted to gather the spiritual teaching from the surroundings of his daily life." [11] An education through the lesson book of nature had a powerful effect on the mind of the child Jesus. The results? "Never before spoke one who had such power to awaken thought, to kindle aspiration, to arouse every capability of body, mind, and soul." [12]

In the educational methods of the greatest Educator the world has ever known, we have a perfect example of how to teach. "During His ministry Jesus lived to a great degree an outdoor life," [13] and immersed in the natural outdoors, Jesus was able to turn the thoughts of his students "from the artificial to the natural." [14] He "bound up His precious lessons with the things of nature. The trees, the birds, the flowers of the valleys, the hills, the lakes, and the beautiful heavens ... were all linked with the words of truth." [15] "The Great

Teacher brought His hearers in contact with nature, that they might listen to the voice which speaks in all created things. ... The birds of the air, the lilies of the field, the sower and the seed, the shepherd and the sheep – with these Christ illustrated immortal truth." [16]

"So we should teach." [17]

It is the Creator's design that "the fields and hills – nature's audience chamber – should be the schoolroom for little children. Her treasures should be their textbook." [18] "Mothers, let the little ones play in the open air; let them listen to the songs of the birds, and learn the love of God as expressed in his beautiful works." [19] "Let the children learn to see in nature an expression of the love and the wisdom of God; let the thought of Him be linked with bird and flower and tree." [20]

Spending time in nature is not an optional part of true education, not a side help, not an enrichment activity. It is one of God's four lesson books designed for the education of our children and is *essential* for proper brain development and true learning.

At What Age Should Learning from Nature Begin?

Abundant time in nature should be a regular part of a child's day from babyhood. "So far as possible, let the child from his earliest years be placed where this wonderful lesson book shall be open before him. Let him behold the glorious scenes painted by the great Master Artist upon the shifting canvas of the heavens, let him become acquainted with the wonders of earth and sea, let him watch the unfolding mysteries of the changing seasons, and, in all His works, learn of the Creator." [21]

"The little children should come especially close to nature." [22] "In no other way can the foundation of a true education be so firmly and surely laid." [23]

Is There a Curriculum *for* That?

Unless a child has been indoors for most of his little life or has been accustomed to being artificially entertained, learning from nature is something that will come quite naturally to him – no curriculum needed. Give a child free rein in the great outdoors among the dirt, trees, puddles, creeks, wild flowers, and rocks, and it won't be long before you find him digging, climbing, splashing, exploring, creating, or simply observing and otherwise growing his developing mind. He will thrive in nature and will learn from this lesson book quite naturally.

But what if your child isn't an outdoor magnet? What if you've never really spent time in nature yourself? How can you teach your child from nature if you don't know anything about nature? Does this all seem overwhelming? Do you sometimes wish that someone could help you teach your child? Or maybe even do some of the teaching for you? God is willing to do just that. Through the medium of nature, God wants to send a personal tutor to your child to help him learn. Nature itself is an amazing teacher – far greater than most realize. We are told that nature "is a living teacher, instructing constantly," [24] and can teach you and your child far more than the best human teacher, book, or curriculum this world has to offer.

"The mountains, the rivers, the stones, are full of truth. They are our teachers. The instant the Lord bids nature speak, she utters her voice in lessons of heavenly wisdom and eternal truth." [25] The Scriptures bid us to, "Speak to the earth, and it shall teach thee," [26] "ask now the beasts, and they shall teach thee; and the fowls of the air, and they shall tell thee," [27] "and the fishes of the sea shall declare unto thee." [28] "We are not merely to tell the child about these creatures of God. The animals themselves are to be his teachers." [29] You don't need to know anything about nature in order for your child to learn through nature. Nature itself will teach your child!

And as if that were not enough, our heavenly Father has given us yet another teacher. We have the promise that through nature, "Christ himself will be your teacher." [30] The Creator Himself will teach you and your child.

You may be tempted to search for a resource to guide you, to help you learn from nature. But this may only prove to be a handicap. Even "men of the greatest intellect cannot understand the mysteries of Jehovah as revealed in nature." [31] How could a man-made resource with its inherent limitations be better than being instructed by the Creator Himself? Why settle for a nature curriculum, for man-made instruction, when you have Christ Himself to instruct you?! What better teacher could we ask for? In fact, because of the countless – literally countless – learning opportunities in nature, there really is no curriculum, no course, no guide that could provide you with even a fraction of the learning you can gain directly from the infinite wisdom of our great Creator.

In addition, there are many components of nature that cannot be planned nor can they be experienced through a book, a video, or other forms of media. The invigorating aroma of the pine needles, the gentle breeze caressing your cheek, the delight as a dragonfly alights on your arm and looks up at you through his goggle-like eyes, the drum of a grouse that makes you feel like you're hearing your own heartbeat somewhere out in the woods, the occasional tiny raindrop moistening the back of your hand, the ever so subtle and gradual changes in the color of the tree bark through the seasons, the giant shadows of the tiny lady bug as he takes an evening stroll across the meadow path, the noticeable cooling of the air as you walk down a hill, and the very brief moment of silence as the entire woodland community pause to listen – these and more are all experiences that can be had only when one actually steps outside into the classroom of nature with the expectancy and anticipation of being charmed by the Creator of nature Himself.

Parents must recognize that books and other man-made resources are inferior and inadequate substitutes for God's true lesson book – the one He designed for parents to use to instruct their children. Nothing can compare with being *in* nature live and real-time. Nature has an influence that is powerful, yet impossible to fully understand or explain. "The heavens declare the glory of God. The stars speak of him. The sun, the ruler of the day, and the moon, with its softer light, declare His glory." [32] When we spend time in God's creation, "every nerve and sense will respond to the expressions of God's love in His marvellous works." [33]

Where to start? Just go outside with your child, take a leisurely walk, and look around. The first few times may seem boring, but as you continue to spend time in nature, observing, and trying to learn from nature, "the light of heaven will quicken the mind." [34] Ask the Lord to open your eyes and the eyes of your child to His lesson book of nature. You can learn straight from the Source just as David did. God "is speaking to your senses and impressing your soul through His created works. Let your heart receive these impressions, and nature will be to you an open book, and will teach you divine truth through familiar things." [35] "As the dwellers in Eden learned from nature's pages, as Moses discerned God's handwriting on the Arabian plains and mountains, and the child Jesus on the hillsides of Nazareth, so the children of today may learn of Him." [36]

Benefits of Spending Time in Nature

Time in nature is not merely for the purpose of getting exercise outdoors or burning up some of that childhood energy (although that can certainly happen). And, while one can learn some valuable facts about nature during outdoor time, even this is not the purpose of spending time outdoors. Time in nature provides dynamic learning components that cannot be duplicated in an indoor environment and imparts immeasurable intellectual, physical, social, spiritual, and emotional benefits. The value of time in nature extends into all facets of childhood development and beyond.

1. Nature stimulates brain development.

Due in part to the positive effects that the different components of nature (such as phytoncides, microbes, the air's negatively-charged ions, and other as yet unknown factors) have on the health of the brain, children who spend much of their childhood in nature develop stronger thinking skills, which translate to higher short-term and long-term academic achievement. [37] Both correlational and experimental research have demonstrated nature's positive effects on cognitive performance. [38]

"We should contemplate God in nature – study His character in the work of His hands. The mind is strengthened by becoming acquainted with God, by reading His attributes in the things which He has made." [39]

2. Time in nature reduces behavioral problems.

Studies have shown that exposure to nature can improve impulse control and self-discipline, [40] can reduce anger outbursts and aggression, [41] and is associated with increases in happiness, positive social interactions, a sense of meaning and purpose in life, and a decrease in mental distress. [42]

3. Experience in nature helps develop endurance and perseverance.

Very few things in nature are push-button-instantaneous. Indoor life, with its "a + b = c" problems and linear solutions, doesn't offer the type of challenges that require the thinking, endurance, and perseverance that outdoor life does. Activities in nature evoke effort from both brain and muscle and provide a number of challenges without scripted solutions. Consequently, children who spend an abundance of time outdoors tend to be more persevering and more resilient.

"Nature's voice is the voice of Jesus Christ teaching us innumerable lessons of perseverance." [43]

4. Nature can teach lessons of responsibility, compassion, and stewardship.

In your outdoor explorations in nature, you are sure to come across insects, butterflies, spiders, and other living creatures. Observing these creatures with your child gives you the opportunity to teach your child about his responsibility to treat those lesser than he with respect, compassion, and consideration. If your child wants to pick up these creatures or take them home with him, talk to him about how that might feel to the creature and how he might feel if someone did that to him. Teach him how to observe God's creation from the angle of compassion, stewardship, and responsibility. Instilling in your child a sense of responsibility for God's creatures will also engender in him a sense of his responsibility toward God.

5. Time in nature can enhance listening skills.

"The beauties of nature have a tongue that speaks to our senses without ceasing," [44] and the thousands of voices in creation have something to say to your child. From the most obvious like the melodious songs of the birds, the shrill peeps of the tree frogs, the buzzing ring of the cicadas, the cheerful chirps of the crickets, the gurgling water in a stream, the stiff snorting of a deer, the chatter of a squirrel, the echoing call of an owl, the staccato drumming of a woodpecker, and the solemn roll of the deep-toned thunder ... to the sounds that only the more discerning can hear, like the soft crumpling of leaves as a wild creature cautiously walks through the woods, the whisper of the wind as it moves the tree branches, the singing of the sand in the sand dunes, a squishy salamander making its way through the vegetation, and the extremely rare sound of silence, "nature's ten thousand voices speak his praise." [45]

6. Nature cultivates curiosity.

Curiosity opens the mind to learning and is connected with improved observational skills. The skill of observation has been shown to improve thinking and learning skills.

Transplanting a child from the restrictive and limited environment of the indoors to the freeing and limitless expanses of the great outdoors brings an abundance of opportunities for cultivating curiosity, wonderment, and a love of learning.

If your child has not had much exposure to the artificial world of toys and screen-based devices, much learning through curiosity will come naturally, but you can also encourage this process. Go outside and find a quiet place to watch and listen. Watch a spider build a web. Look at the patterns on the leaves of the trees. Observe the insects going about their work on the ground beside you. Listen to the birds. Which bird is singing which song? Why is that bird throwing wood chips out of that dead tree? When do birds sing most? Do some birds sing at different times than other birds?

7. Time outside helps develop the vestibular and proprioceptive systems.

Movement is essential for the proper development of the vestibular and proprioceptive systems (see Chapter 3), and when that movement happens on the varied terrain of the great outdoors, development is enhanced. The many objects in nature that a child can push, lift, dig, roll, drag, climb on, swing on, clamber over, line up, take apart, or otherwise use as curiosity leads him offer innumerable opportunities for superior development of these systems. Too much time indoors on flat, predictable surfaces does not provide a child with the stimulation needed for good development.

8. Outdoor time leads to better eye health.

Rates of myopia in children have been increasing steadily over the past several years, and this may be attributed in part to the number of hours children spend indoors. During childhood, the eyes are still developing, and two important factors in helping the eyes to develop properly are exposure to full-spectrum sunlight and long-distance viewing. Research shows that an abundance of outdoor time in which a child can view objects that are at a distance (such as treetops, clouds, and hills on the horizon) in the natural light significantly decreases the risk of developing myopia.

Time in nature also helps the eye muscles to develop properly as the varying scenes of nature – from the far away white clouds to the red bug crawling up his arm – provides the child with opportunities to view objects in a wide range of colors and at varying distances.

9. An abundance of outdoor time promotes better sleep.

Studies show that exposure to phytoncides (a natural substance given off by plants) and sunlight enhances the quality and duration of sleep, helps regulate the circadian rhythm, and improves sleep patterns. [46]

10. Time outside promotes better health overall.

Our bodies were not designed to spend hours and hours indoors. Sunshine, fresh air, phytoncides, the various bacteria and microorganisms in dirt, and many other components of nature play a crucial role in many body processes, including strengthening the immune system, building strong bones, regulating circadian rhythms, balancing hormones, developing a healthy gut microbiome, preventing and treating depression, maintaining healthy blood sugar levels, and promoting proper brain functioning. "In order for children and youth to have health, cheerfulness, vivacity, and well-developed muscles and brains, they should be much in the open air." [47]

11. Nature teaches a child to trust and obey his Heavenly Father who loves him.

"Christ pointed His disciples to the lilies of the field and the birds of the air, showing how God cares for them, and presented this as an evidence that He will care for man." [48] "If we will but listen, God's created works will teach us precious lessons of obedience and trust. From the stars that in their trackless courses through space follow from age to age their appointed path, down to the minutest atom, the things of nature obey the Creator's will. And God cares for everything and sustains everything that He has created. He who upholds the unnumbered worlds throughout immensity, at the same time cares for the wants of the little brown sparrow that sings its humble song without fear." [49] Help your child "to notice the evidences everywhere manifest in nature of God's thought for us, the wonderful adaptation of all things to our need and happiness." [50] Teach him that "every green leaf, with its delicate veins, every opening bud and blooming flower, every lofty tree stretching upward to heaven, the earth clothed with its carpet of living green, is an expression of the love of God" [51] for him.

12. Nature nurtures a one-on-one, personal relationship with God.

It's one thing to learn about God, and quite another to *know* Him personally. As parents, we desire for our children more than just a knowledge of who God is; we want our children to truly know God as a personal friend. We can give this gift to our children through nature. In nature, God reveals Himself to a child in a unique and extraordinary manner. Time in nature allows a child to "become acquainted with the Creator" [52] in a way that no other experience will equal. [53]

It is in nature that "we hear the voice of God." [54] "In the song of the bird, the sighing of the trees, and the music of the sea, we may hear His voice who talked with Adam in Eden in the cool of the day. And as we behold His power in nature we find comfort, for the word that created all things is that which speaks life to the soul." [55] "The green fields, the lofty trees, the buds and flowers, the passing cloud, the falling rain, the babbling brook, the glories of the heavens, speak to our hearts, and invite us to become acquainted with Him who made them all." [56] "As we come close to the heart of nature, Christ makes His presence real to us, and speaks to our hearts of His peace and love." [57]

Surround your child with the wonderful works of God, and his mind will be lifted from the things that are seen to the things that are unseen. Nature is a supreme source of divine revelation. "In this study the mind expands, is elevated and uplifted, and becomes hungry to know more of God and His majesty." [58] What parent doesn't want this for their child?

How Much Time?

How much time should children spend outdoors in nature? Many experts believe that children need a bare minimum of an hour a day, but preferably three or four hours or more, for proper brain development, reduced risk of myopia, and good physical and mental health. [59]

Sometimes parents become concerned that the amount of time spent outdoors is taking away from time that their child should be doing schoolwork, and to compensate for this fear, they try to make every moment a learning opportunity. But, while parents should indeed watch for valuable teaching opportunities, they should keep in mind that instead of being spoon-fed object lessons, children need time to playfully experiment, quietly observe, and deeply contemplate when in nature. Discussion is good, and children can learn much through a parent's guidance, but even in quiet hours in nature, the child is being educated. His observational skills are being trained, he's developing superior thinking skills, he's learning patience, self-control, respect, and other valuable character qualities, he's developing an understanding of who he is and who his Creator is, and so much more.

Don't rush your child. Allowing him the time he needs to play and explore in nature is growing his brain and body. If you find yourself bored after spending two hours throwing stones in a creek, remind yourself that your child's brain is not bored. On the contrary, this is one of the most beneficial activities you can provide for your child in terms of brain development.

Together Time

It may be tempting to send your child outside to play, but in doing so, you miss precious opportunities. Instead, the majority of your child's outdoor time should be spent with you, his parent.

"Mothers cannot employ their time better than in occasionally roaming over hill and dale with their children, to view the natural opening buds and blooming flowers, the lofty trees, and the variety of rich and beautiful productions of nature. This will give mother and children opportunities for exercise, and to become acquainted with God as seen in nature. God demands of parents that they do the important work he has intrusted to them in the education and formation of the characters of their dear children." [60]

What to Do

We live such an indoor life these days that some children find it difficult to know what to do outdoors; however, a generation or two ago, no one had to tell a child what to do outside. The grass and trees, the water and the mud, the sticks and the rocks begged children to come and play with them, and children eagerly accepted the invitation.

How can we restore a child's receptivity to the inviting voice of nature?

One of the first steps is to simplify life. Make the indoors less attractive and less demanding. Expel from your life the competing clamor of media, an abundance of toys, and other forms of artificial entertainment.

Remember that your child will likely take cues about how he should feel about nature from you. Your attitude toward the great outdoors sets the tone for his attitude. When your child spots a vernal pool in the woods, resist the nagging thoughts of muddy shoes and dirty laundry. Rather, embrace the fun and learning that a simple water hole can bring. Splash in the water and watch your children look at you with a whole new level of admiration. Or stoop down and explore the wonderful and abundant world living in its murky depths. Notice how the frogs jump suddenly out of nowhere, protecting themselves from you before you even knew they were there. Contemplate how the tiny, legless blob of squirmy tadpole will one day become the clever and prudent frog with legs that jet him forty times his body length in the blink of an eye. Be awed by the amazing combination of biology and physics in the creation of the water strider. Watch a worm steadily, patiently, and humbly continuing its duties seemingly unaffected by your interest in it.

Take a walk and observe the leaves blowing in the breeze, and ask your child if he notices the different shapes and textures of the different kinds of leaves. Place a leaf boat in a stream and watch it float away. Pick a particular tree and observe it closely and in detail through the various seasons. See if you can spot a bird hiding in the trees and follow its journey through the air. Listen to the birds and try to mimic their sounds. Sing your own songs of praise to your Creator. Gently feel the petals of the little wild flowers in the grass and talk about how they feel. Talk about their colors. Lie down in the grass and look at the clouds and appreciate their beauty. Talk about what the clouds are made of. Talk about how the grass feels. Discover what's crawling between the blades of grass. Discover what's living under the big rocks and the little ones. Watch a turtle or a lizard warm itself in the sun. Listen to a tree creak and moan in the winter. Watch a thunderstorm rolling in.

Jump from rock to rock to cross a stream. Balance on fallen logs in the woods. Or find trees to climb, rivers to wade through, and grape vines to swing on. Crawl under the low branches of the evergreen trees to see what it's like under there. Climb onto tree stumps and jump off. Take a child-led hike. Find a river to walk in. Smell the dandelions and squish mud between your toes. Listen for the rattling call of a kingfisher and watch him as he scans the water with his binocular vision and swiftly makes a dive to catch a fish. Watch a sandpiper as it nods and teeters its way along the shore of a lake. Listen to a pair of mourning doves sing a duet. Be in awe of the maneuverability of the falcon or hawk as it soars through the air and then suddenly goes into an aerial dive at incredible speed.

The Educating of a King

"The study of textbooks alone cannot afford students the discipline they need, nor can it impart true wisdom." [61] Children need the education that can be had only through experience in nature, in the open air, surrounded by the works of God. "An education amid such surroundings is in accordance with the directions which God has given for the instruction of youth." [62]

What a privilege we have to educate our children in the same schoolroom that was used to educate the great King David. What a privilege to use the same textbook that was used to educate David for his noble position as the king of Israel. What a privilege to have the same teacher as did David.

"God speaks to you through His created works. Will you listen to His voice? Will you become acquainted with God in nature?" [63]

Words of Counsel

"The only school-room for children from eight to ten years of age should be in the open air, amid the opening flowers and nature's beautiful scenery. And their only text book should be the treasures of nature. These lessons, imprinted upon the minds of young children amid the pleasant, attractive scenes of nature, will not be soon forgotten." [64]

"In the growth and development of nature, learn the principles of Christ's kingdom. Thus the light of heaven will quicken the mind. Christ himself will be your teacher." [65]

"In the loveliness of the things of nature you may learn more of the wisdom of God than the schoolmen know." [66]

"Take time to go with the children into the fields, and learn of God through the beauty of His works." [67]

"Take them out in the morning, and let them hear the birds carolling forth their songs of praise. Teach them that we too should return thanks to the bountiful Giver of all for the blessings we daily receive." [68]

"Teach them the ministry of the flowers. Show them that if Jesus had not come to earth and died, we should have had none of the beautiful things which we now enjoy. Call their attention to the fact that the color and even the arrangement of every delicate bud and flower is an expression of the love of God to man, and that affection and gratitude to their heavenly Father should be awakened in their hearts for all these gifts." [69]

"The things of nature are the Lord's silent ministers, given to us to teach us spiritual truths." [70]

"Next to the Bible, nature is to be our great lessonbook." [71]

CHAPTER 13

GOD'S LESSON BOOK OF
USEFUL WORK

"We should work because it is the Lord's will concerning us" [Ephesians 4:28]. – George Müller

IN this chapter, we will look at another of the Heaven-appointed sources of instruction – the lesson book of useful work – and how to use this lesson book to educate a child.

Little five-year-old Mariana carefully placed several pieces of squash in the oven while her mom washed the knife and cutting board. Mariana took a minute to look around the kitchen, apparently checking to see if there was anything left for her to do, before she headed out to the porch to sweep up the sawdust where her older brothers, Samuel and Isaac, were engaged in a building project. A few minutes later, Samuel noticed that Isaac was almost out of nails and ran off to the garage to get some. Mariana quickly leaned the broom against the house, picked up Samuel's sandpaper, and continued the work of smoothing the wood while her brother went to get the nails. After the wood project was finished, Mariana, Samuel, and Isaac went into the house to wash their hands. Mariana noticed Mom was folding laundry and sat down beside her to help. Samuel smelled a delicious aroma coming from the kitchen and went to see what was for lunch when he noticed that the squash in the oven was done, so he pulled a serving plate off the shelf to place the squash on while Isaac set the table. While Mom and Mariana were finishing folding the laundry, the boys gathered the last few items for lunch, and then the family sat down to eat together.

Whether they knew it or not, Mariana, Samuel, and Isaac were getting a good education in God's lesson book of useful work.

The Connection Between Work and Academic Success

Because they want their child to do well in school and to be successful in life, parents often fill their child's time with academic work, music lessons, homeschool co-ops, academic summer programs, science camps, leadership classes, college prep programs, and pre-college classes. But, in their effort to give their child the advantages they think he needs to be successful, they crowd out one important factor that has been shown to be an excellent precursor to success in life – practical work.

Teaching children how to work from an early age and daily involving them in the household responsibilities provides more benefits than just a smooth-running household. Work has a positive influence on a child's brain development, academic success, and success in adulthood.

Benefits of Useful Work

1. Useful work promotes brain development

Research has discovered a strong connection between physical activity and superior brain development and function.[1] Physical activity is critical to the development of the cerebellum, the hippocampus, the corpus callosum, and many other areas of the brain that are essential for learning. Physical activity has also been found to significantly improve executive function in children.[2] (Executive functions are the higher-level cognitive processes that include decision making, problem solving, planning, organizing, prioritizing, cognitive flexibility, behavior regulation, emotional regulation, impulse control, and focus and attention.) This means that children who spend several hours a day engaged in physical activity will learn better and more quickly in one hour of study than those who study for several hours but aren't regularly involved in physical activity.

But not all types of physical activity benefit the brain equally. The most favorable brain development occurs when physical activity is in the form of useful work.[3] "The exercise that develops mind *and* character, that teaches the hands to be *useful*, and trains the young to bear their share of life's burdens, is that which gives physical strength, *and* quickens every faculty." [4] "The mind educated to enjoy useful labor becomes enlarged." [5] Useful work not only engages the physical powers, but it also engages the mental powers (and often even the moral powers) and strengthens many areas of the brain that are specifically used for learning – especially those that are used for reading, writing, mathematics, creative thinking, and language abilities.

This is one of the main reasons why Abraham, Jacob, Joseph, Moses, David, Elisha, and many others "who have most worthily filled positions of trust and responsibility" [6] were able to be so successful in life. "They early learned to work, and their active life in the open air gave vigor and elasticity to all their faculties." [7]

"Daily, systematic labor should constitute a part of the education of youth. ... Much can now be gained in this way. In following this plan the students will realize elasticity of spirit and vigor of thought, and in a given time can accomplish *more* mental labor than they could by study alone." [8]

2. Practical work is a key ingredient to long-term mental health.

An abundance of research shows that regular practical work in the lives of children makes them happier and is a strong predictor of good mental health and higher life satisfaction in later years. [9]

When parents expect their child to help with the daily duties of running a household, when the child sees that the home functions more smoothly with his help, he learns to feel that he is a needed and valued part of his family, and he develops a sense of belonging that is crucial to his emotional well-being. [10]

Research shows that children who regularly help with family chores develop greater confidence in their ability to learn, greater capacity to cope with failure, and more confidence in their abilities to overcome difficulties (including academic challenges) than those who don't help with family work. [11] Many experts believe that these qualities are a greater indicator of educational success than other educational advantages, such as intelligence. [12]

"God ordained that the beings he created should work. Upon this their happiness depends."[13]

3. Practical work prepares a child for success in life.

Success in life requires skills beyond the ability to study for a test and get good grades. If a person cannot budget his time, be self-motivated, be organized, take care of his things (such as a car or household appliances), work in cooperation with others, and be responsible, life will be difficult for him. Daily involvement in useful work helps develop these valuable life skills in a child and prepares him at a young age for success in real life. In fact, one study "determined that the best predictor of young adults' success in their mid-20s was that they participated in household tasks when they were three or four."[14]

4. Practical work teaches self-discipline.

Practical work provides many opportunities for a child to practice self-discipline as he often must delay gratification, plan ahead, practice time management, and persevere in order to complete a task in time.

5. Practical work improves a child's ability to pay attention and focus.

Often, when a child struggles to focus and pay attention in school, parents may reprimand, remove privileges, create pay-attention practice drills, or even seek out medical treatments. But these approaches only address the symptoms. They do not treat the cause of the problem.

Children need to engage in an abundance of practical, physical work in order to develop attention span and the ability to focus. And they need several years of this type of work before they will have the focused attention needed for sit-down academic work. Children who daily engage in useful physical work develop exceptional attention spans (often better than most adults in our modern society). On the other hand, sedentary work (such as schoolwork) does nothing to help with the development of focused attention. And screen-based devices hinder this development even more.[15]

6. Physical work is healthful for the body.

God created us to be physically active and useful. We cannot have good health unless we use our being in the way that it was created to be used, and "nothing can increase the strength of the young like proper exercise of all the muscles in useful labor." [16] Young children absolutely need large motor activities like digging in the garden, hauling firewood, carrying a laundry basket full of clothes, hanging laundry on the clothesline, carrying a full watering can, bringing in groceries, and scrubbing the floor for proper development of both the body and the brain.

7. Work teaches appreciation and respect.

Parents don't set out to raise children to have ungrateful attitudes, but many of our parenting practices unintentionally encourage a sense of entitlement in our children that is inevitably connected with a lack of gratitude. When a three-year-old's laundry somehow just gets washed and placed in his closet, when a four-year-old's dishes from lunch somehow get clean without his help, when a five-year-old's meals just show up on the table at meal time, a child can quickly develop a sense of entitlement.

Not requiring a child to help with work that he is capable of doing sends the wrong message as to what is the parent's role in the parent-child relationship. Rather than being the one who is there to guide and teach him, a parent becomes the one who is to be his servant and cater to his needs.

Children who are not required to help with the daily responsibilities of the home tend to be more selfish, self-centered, and disrespectful than those who are. Instead of developing a sense of responsibility, obligation, and gratitude toward their parents, these children come to expect things to be done for them. In fact, "it is often the case that the more their parents do for them the more ungrateful they are, and the less they respect them." [17] And "those children for whom parents do the most, frequently feel under the least obligation toward them." [18]

Being a daily part of all of the family's chores is a great antidote to the attitude of entitlement. When a child learns that he is a needed part of a properly functioning household and that things aren't somehow accomplished without any effort on his part, he gains respect and appreciation for the work that goes into the smooth functioning of the household.

8. Practical work helps teach teamwork.

Being able to work in cooperation with others as a productive member of a team is an important life skill, and this skill can be effectively developed as a child learns to work in cooperation with other family members. While it is good for each member of the family to have his own individual chores, too many fixed jobs that are solely the responsibility of an individual (instead of the family's responsibility) can cultivate too much of an independent, self-centered, selfish spirit. "Why do I have to do that? That's Tommy's job!" Or, "I already did my chores. Why can't *you* put away the dishes?"

Doing chores *together* can do much to promote the skill and attitude of teamwork and teach children how to work cohesively and cooperatively. For example, if everyone is working, side by side, preparing a meal together and then, after the meal, cleaning up together, a team spirit inevitably develops since no one eats until the meal is ready and no one leaves the kitchen until it is fully clean. This type of scenario means that members of the family team are naturally accountable to each other, and there are consequences when one member of the team doesn't fulfill his responsibilities. Learning these lessons at home where character flaws can be corrected will prevent many difficulties later when a child is grown and others do not have the same patience and care for him.

9. Working together as a family bonds a family emotionally.

I recently heard a mom lament that she didn't have much time to spend with her four children because she was too busy with laundry, cleaning, and cooking. But these household tasks don't need to take away time from our children; rather, they can facilitate *more* time together as a family. Doing all the activities of life together helps put parents and children on the same page, promotes a sense of mutuality, and has the potential to create many special moments and develop strong bonds.

10. Useful work can develop the trait of unselfishness.

In addition to taking care of responsibilities around the home, the family can spend time helping a neighbor and others who are in need. Helping others can cultivate unselfishness and teach gratitude, as well as teach social skills and enhance a child's world perspective – especially if the work is done in a different community or culture and among people of different races and backgrounds than his own.

Helping others prepares the heart and character for heaven and for the society of angels who are always working unselfishly to bless and help us. "The satisfaction children will have in being useful, of denying themselves to help others, will be the most healthful pleasure they ever enjoyed." [19] "No recreation helpful only to themselves will prove so great a blessing to the children and youth as that which makes them helpful to others." [20]

11. Useful work is a safeguard against temptation.

"Parents should remember that occupation is essential for children. If their hands are kept active in useful employment, a door will be closed against the temptations of Satan." [21] "Idleness is a curse." [22] In fact, "inaction is the *greatest* curse that ever came upon youth." [23] "Much sin results from idleness. Active hands and minds do not find time to heed every temptation the enemy suggests; but idle hands and brains are all ready for Satan to control, and parents should teach their children that idleness is sin." [24] "If parents neglect to turn their children's energies into useful channels, they do them great injury, for Satan is ready to find them something to do." [25] "Therefore train your children to useful work." [26]

12. Practical work gives a child purpose in life.

The realization that God has a high calling on his life does not come suddenly when a young person reaches young adulthood; the concept that he has a purpose in life must shape his thinking from a young age. A life of play and indulgence does nothing for instilling this message in a child, nor does most academic study. But useful work, like helping maintain a smooth-functioning household, repairing an elderly neighbor's porch, fixing an automobile, or making a meal for a sick friend, gives a child the intrinsic satisfaction of doing something that has meaning and worth. These activities elevate his thinking and build a lasting sense of purpose in his heart. If taught correctly and from a young age, a child will see work not as drudgery but as a challenge worth engaging in.

13. The proper balance of mental and physical work helps children understand the Bible properly.

We generally don't connect useful work with the ability to comprehend God's Word correctly (and also better remember what is learned), but useful work does have this effect. When the brains and muscles are exercised proportionately, "the youth can then bring to the study of the word of God healthy perception and well-balanced nerves. They will have wholesome thoughts and can retain the precious things that are brought from the word. They will digest its truths and as a result will have brain power to discern what is truth."[27]

14. A life filled with practical work engenders a spiritually mature young person.

There is a strong connection between practical work and spiritual maturity. "Children, for their own ... moral good, should be taught to work."[28] Children who are trained to be capable and useful develop "characters of industry, frugality, and moral worth, which lie at the foundation of success in the Christian life."[29]

Indolence will "grieve the Spirit of God and destroy true godliness. A stagnant pool becomes offensive; but a pure, flowing brook spreads health and gladness over the land."[30]

An Indispensable Part of God's Method of Education

The lesson book of useful work plays a fundamental and indispensable role in God's perfect method of education. "Many think that these things are no part of school work; but this is a mistake. The lessons necessary to fit one for practical usefulness should be taught to every child."[31] "An education derived chiefly from books leads to superficial thinking. Practical work encourages close observation and independent thought. ... It develops ability to plan and execute, strengthens courage and perseverance, and calls for the exercise of tact and skill." [32]

Even when God created Adam and Eve and placed them in Paradise, He gave them work to do because He knew that a "life of useful labor is indispensable to the physical, mental, and moral well-being of man." [33] After sin entered the world, useful labor was still a crucial part of a healthy and happy life. Those who followed God's instruction "still pursued the plan of life that He had appointed in the beginning. Those who departed from God built for themselves cities. ... But the men who held fast God's principles of life dwelt among the fields and hills. They were tillers of the soil and keepers of flocks and herds, and in this free, independent life, with its opportunities for labor and study and meditation, they learned of God and taught their children of His works and ways." [34] For God's chosen people, "this was the method of education that God desired to establish." [35] "It was required that every youth should learn how to work." [36] He desired for them to "possess a knowledge of practical life, and be not only self-sustaining, but useful. This was the instruction which God gave to his people." [37]

This daily, practical work was also an integral part of the education of Jesus. "In childhood his hands were engaged in useful acts." [38] "He was obedient and helpful in the home." [39] "As soon as He was old enough to handle tools, He shared the burden of caring for the family," [40] and "He learned the carpenter's trade, and worked with His own hands in the little shop at Nazareth." [41] "Christ was in his child life and youthful life an example to all children and youth." [42]

"So with the great majority of the best and noblest men of all ages. Read the history of Abraham, Jacob, and Joseph, of Moses, David, and Elisha. Study the lives of men of later times who have most worthily filled positions of trust and responsibility, the men whose influence has been most effective for the world's uplifting.

"How many of these were reared in country homes. They knew little of luxury. They did not spend their youth in amusement. ... They early learned to work, and their active life in the open air gave vigor and elasticity to all their faculties." [43]

What was the result of this type of education? Did the time spent in useful labor detract from their intellectual education? Did it cause these men to be uneducated and unprepared for success in life? On the contrary. "When called to their lifework, they brought to it physical *and mental* power, buoyancy of spirit, ability to plan and execute, and steadfastness in resisting evil, that made them a positive power for good in the world." [44] What good parent wouldn't want this for their child?

How to Teach Children to Enjoy Work

Some feel that expecting children to do chores at an early age is robbing them of their childhood and adding unnecessary responsibility to a time in their life when they should be carefree. But to a young child who is trained in the methods of true education, work is a joy, a privilege, and even fun – especially when that work is done with the sweet companionship of his parents. "Even when quite young, [children] may begin learning to work, and they will be happy in the thought that they are making themselves useful." [45]

How can parents ensure that their child enjoys work?

1. Start early.

"As early in life as possible children should be trained to share the burdens of home." [46] "The mother should be the teacher, and home the school where every child receives his first lessons; and these lessons should include habits of industry. Mothers, let the little ones play in the open air; let them listen to the songs of the birds, and learn the love of God as expressed in his beautiful works. ... But let them also learn, even in their earliest years, to be useful. Train them to think that, as members of the household, they are to act an interested, helpful part in sharing the domestic burdens, and to seek healthful exercise in the performance of necessary home duties." [47]

Research consistently shows that the earlier parents begin involving a child in the practical functioning of the household, the more natural it will be for a child to take initiative to work, and the more the child will enjoy work. [48] If a baby or toddler doesn't have too many toys and other distractions, he usually *wants* to be involved in any activity that the parent is doing – whether it be sweeping the floor or working in the garden or cooking a meal. When parents cheerfully encourage this help (even if his efforts are more messy than helpful), the child learns that working with his mom and dad is a happy and very normal part of everyday life. Yes, it's faster to set the table yourself than to watch your two-year-old carry every single spoon from the kitchen drawer over to the table. One. By. One. Yes, it's easier to prepare a meal yourself than to clean almond butter out of your toddler's eyelashes. Yes, your child may slow down your progress, but that progress is not as important as your child's well-being. And if you don't include your child in the chores when he is young, he is much less likely to want to be included in the chores later.

As early as a few months old, a baby can help with work around the house. When you're doing laundry, give your little one clothes to put in the washing machine too. When sweeping the floor, give him a small broom. Toddlers can wash the carrots, tear lettuce leaves, or put the potatoes into the saucepan (before it is placed on the stove). When you are washing dishes, let your toddler rinse them. (It's okay if he gets some water on the floor. He can also learn to clean up his messes.) With a parent's help, a small child can learn to plant and care for a garden, harvest the food, check the air in an automobile tire, change a tire, change the oil in a car, wash a car, install shelving, make basic plumbing repairs, build something with wood, and participate in other useful manual skills. If you are doing a job that you don't think he can help with, ask the Lord to help you think of ways your child can contribute.

Instead of trying to get the chores done during naptime, save work for when your little one can help, recognizing that encouraging his help at an early age means he will feel that he is a needed part of the family and will more willingly help when he is older. When children understand that they are genuine contributors to a well-functioning home and family, helping is only natural. At a young and impressionable age, if parents present work as a privilege, as an honor, children will learn to enjoy work.

2. Do everything together.

"Young children love companionship and can seldom enjoy

themselves alone."[49] Play together, go outside together, run errands together, talk together, sing together, laugh together ... and work together.

In cultures where the children work alongside the adults, willingness and initiative to help are more prevalent than in cultures where children are motivated to help by the use of rewards, "mock excitement, praise, and other motivators."[50] For example, researchers have observed that in the Mayan culture where children contribute extensively to the family work, harmonious collaboration between all members of the family is prioritized, and the children seldom, if ever, work alone.[51] Instead, work is a family activity that involves children of all ages (even those who can barely walk). As one researcher expressed, "Children's sense of belonging and responsibility to the family seemed to be the driving forces in their contributions, as they pay attention to the needs of the family and take the initiative to learn and help."[52]

I have noticed the same in my personal observations of children around the world. Children who grow up with a sense that they are a needed part of the family more naturally and willingly help than those who are rewarded or praised for their help. In this collaborative environment, children express that they enjoy helping with the family work, and they help without being asked to do so. No bribing. No coaxing. No allowance. No chore charts. No threats. No consequences. Just willing cooperation.

Working together can also facilitate proper instruction in good work habits since the parent is present to gently guide the child and correct his negligence or mistakes. "Solomon did not say, '*Tell* a child the way he should go, and when he is old, he will not depart from it.' But rather, 'Train up a child in the way he should go, and when he is old, he will not depart from it.'"[53] This training involves shoulder-to-shoulder life with our children, gently guiding, directing, and discipling by example.

We can give to our children few gifts as valuable as our companionship. "Mothers should seek to make themselves companionable to their children, and be able to keep their little ones interested, by providing suitable employment for their minds and hands."[54] "Let the mother teach her children to be her willing helpers gladly assisting her to bear life's burdens."[55] "If the children share the labor with their mother, they will learn to regard useful employment as essential to happiness."[56]

3. Minimize the distractions.

For a small child, a broom is a toy. A dust cloth is a toy. And washing dishes can be loads of fun. Work and play are often synonymous. But when children are surrounded with other forms of entertainment, they gradually become accustomed to being entertained and no longer find joy and fun in work. The more artificial entertainment a child has, the more easily he will become bored with work.

"Children and youth who are allowed to devote much of their time to amusement and pleasure-seeking are never really happy,"[57] but children who have fewer artificial sources of amusement tend to find more pleasure in life. In addition, they tend to have longer attention spans, be less selfish, and develop more perseverance – which helps them better enjoy chores. If you want your children to enjoy doing chores, minimize the toys and maximize the happy time doing things together.

4. Allow the child to try.

Little ones often like to try to put on their own shoes, dress themselves, and carry things. Avoid hovering over your child and doing things for him before he asks for help. Even if your very young child wants to do something that you know to be too difficult for him – such as dishing out his own food or carrying a heavy item – as much as possible, allow your child to try, even if things get a little messy. Do not tell him it's too heavy for him or too hard for him. The process of trying nurtures in a child a desire to persevere and work.

5. Be sure your child makes genuine contributions.

Allow your child to make genuine contributions to the work at hand. When it's time to prepare dinner, don't give your child a play bowl and spoon or other cooking toys. Give him some real work to do. Let him help make dinner. When it's time to clean up from the meal, don't wash the table first and then hand your child a cloth so he can "help" wash the table after you've already cleaned it. Wash the table together. When it's time to work in the garden, don't give your child a toy rake; give him a real one. Children who understand that they can provide valuable contributions to the family just like everyone else tend to be more willing to help.

6. Create an age-integrated, Christ-centered environment.

In our current culture, it is common – even expected – for children to have their own special activities, their own special books, their own special dinner menu, their own special breakfast cereal, their own special classes, their own special entertainment, their own special music, their own special apps, their own special lives. Researchers observe that "where children are segregated from mature family responsibilities, they contribute minimally, they seldom take initiative in family work, and their mothers assign them their 'own' chores to do and rarely expect children's help without adult management."[58] This approach to child-raising has produced self-centered children who have a strong sense of entitlement and little understanding of what it means to live a useful life in which they work with and serve others.

While this age-segregated-child-indulgent mindset may seem normal to us, it is not how God created children to live. Throughout history, children grew up living life alongside adults. In many cultures around the world, this is still the case. Children are not entertained and segregated into their own special anything. Rather, they grow up as an integral part of and a collaborative contributor to the family (and often the community). The lives of children are woven into the everyday lives of their parents and other adults around them. Through the observation of and friendship with the adults in their lives, children's lives are enriched, and they gradually develop a number of important skills. They learn how to cooperate and work with others, how to communicate with people of varying ages, and how to behave appropriately. And they regularly take initiative to work and be helpful.

Avoiding the child-centric environment does not mean that parents revert to adult-centered parenting in which parents adopt the mentality that life is strict, disciplinary, and fun-free. Far from it. When parents replace the child-centric mindset with a "Christ-centered" one in which imitating Christ in His service for others becomes their focus, they recognize that children are individuals to be unselfishly loved, nurtured, listened to, and respected. With this approach, children learn that they are valued members of the household. Parents who adopt this age-integrated, Christ-centered approach to child-raising find that children are less selfish and more cooperative and eager to work.

7. Maintain order and organization.

Research shows that children who live in a disorganized and unscheduled family and home environment have more difficulty learning, ordering their thoughts, regulating their emotions, and staying focused than those who live in orderly homes. They also score higher on measures of problem behaviors and learned helplessness. [59] All these factors make it difficult for a child to feel motivated about work. While a home should never be so regimented and inflexible that individual feelings and needs cannot be considered and the social joys of the home are set aside, all family members should cooperate in maintaining a well-ordered home.

8. Encourage thinking and observation.

Unfortunately, it's easy to make the mistake of using a false-education mindset when trying to teach our children to do useful work. "Lizzy, you wash dishes. John, you sweep the floor. Andrea, you put the food away." When children become accustomed to someone telling them what to do, they do not need to observe, reason, or think for themselves. This may be a great way for the parents to get things done, but it is a terrible way to develop the ability to think or to enjoy work.

"The education of children should not be like the training of dumb animals; for children have an intelligent will, which should be directed to control all their powers." [60] We may tell a child to sweep the floor, and if he promptly sweeps the floor, he may "appear to be well trained," [61] and we consider him a good, obedient child. But if we, by always telling a child what needs to be done, neglect to train the thinking powers, his "mind [is] not called out, that it might expand

and strengthen by exercise." [62] He does not learn to be observant and recognize needs on his own, nor does he learn to help on his own initiative. Training children "without properly directing them to think and act for themselves" [63] will cause them to be "deficient in moral energy and individual responsibility." [64] Far better would it be to instead engage a child's reason and intellect by patiently and consistently teaching him, from a young age, to be observant of the needs of others and to find joy in acting on those observations.

The cultivation of the skills of thinking and observation should happen, not just at the time when parents want their child to work, but all throughout a child's day and in different activities of life. Helping a child learn to be observant and to understand what he is doing and why he is doing it is far more valuable than getting a child to simply complete a task.

9. Enjoy work.

Approached correctly, children really can find deep satisfaction in work. But if parents think of work as drudgery, the children will also. Cultivate a positive attitude toward work. Never use work as a punishment. Make daily work a regular and enjoyable part of life together, and work will have a happy tone. And children will "find their greatest pleasure in helping father and mother." [65]

10. Elevate work.

"If children were taught to regard the humble round of every-day duties as the course marked out for them by the Lord, as a school in which they were to be trained to render faithful and efficient service, how much more pleasant and honorable would their work appear. To perform every duty as unto the Lord, throws a charm around the humblest employment." [66]

Too Late?

If you have an older child and did not teach him to work when he was young, the love for work can still be developed to some degree when he is older. Begin with tasks that personally affect your child, such as cleaning his room, preparing lunch, or doing his laundry. *Do these jobs with him* and try to make the work and the time together enjoyable. Gradually add more work into his day, still doing everything together. Minimize the distractions, such as media and games, and never use work as a punishment. And, of course, talk with your child about the benefits and blessings of useful work.

Allowance?

Allowances, as an unconditional sum of money regularly doled out, can negate many of the positive effects of including work in a child's life. Unconditionally providing your child with an allowance fosters in him a sense of entitlement and hinders learning about the relationship between time, effort, and money. But what about an allowance that is given in exchange for a child doing chores?

One of the goals of parenting is to help a child to view the maintenance of "a well-ordered, well-disciplined family"[67] as a *family* responsibility – one that he and his siblings participate in just as much as the parents do, one that he and his siblings have as great a stake in as his parents do. In other words, we want our children to play a responsible role in maintaining a well-ordered home.

"The family firm is a sacred, social society, in which *each* member is to act a part, each helping the other. The work of the household is to move smoothly, like the different parts of well-regulated machinery."[68]

With this mindset, it is not the parents' job to maintain order and the child's job to create disorder; rather, it is the responsibility, privilege, and desire of *all* members of the family to maintain an orderly home. When a child views the functioning of the home from this angle, the job of raising children is no longer a constant battle between the parents (team bigs) and the children (team littles). Rather, it becomes a beautiful, harmonious, cooperative pursuit in which parents and children are on the same team, aiming for the same goal. All the family members work together for the good of the family.

With this attitude and understanding, just as Mom doesn't get paid to do the laundry, and Dad does not get paid to mow the lawn, the children don't get paid to help with home responsibilities either.

These chores are part of their contributions to the family unit – to the functioning of a well-ordered home. The children are important components of the family, and they view helping with the responsibilities of the home as a privilege of every member of the family. It's just what the members of a well-ordered family do for each other. When everyone contributes, the household runs smoothly, and all gain a sense of being a contributing part of the family unit.

Giving a child an allowance hinders the development of this mutually cooperative attitude and sends the message that keeping the home running smoothly is the parent's responsibility; therefore, if anyone else contributes to this, he should be paid for it. It can also send the message that keeping the home running smoothly is such an undesirable task that he must be paid to do it. Research shows that any extrinsic reward (such as allowances) undermines the cultivation of a child's motivation to help. [69] Research also shows that children who are rewarded for doing chores tend to be less altruistic. [70]

A child should be taught from an early age that helping around the home is a wonderful privilege that he shares as a member of a loving family.

Earning Money

In order to teach a child valuable lessons in life, such as budgeting, unselfish giving, debt avoidance, and financial responsibility, he will need some spending money. If we don't give a child an allowance, how will he learn the skills involved with money management?

Gabe's mom was a little embarrassed when her seven-year-old son, armed with his newly-purchased screwdriver flopping around in one of the pockets of his father's too-big tool belt that was dragging from his hips, headed out the back door and crossed the field to go see their neighbor. Gabe had a business plan, and today was the day he determined to embark on his plan. He was going to offer his carpentry services to his neighbors, Mr. and Mrs. Williams. Mom quickly gave Mrs. Williams a ring and told her that Gabe was coming for a visit, and assured her that she should not feel bad about sending Gabe home. About thirty minutes later, Gabe did come home. He had no extra cash in his pockets, but he was not discouraged. Rather, he put the screwdriver and tool belt away and came to sit by his mom, who was nursing his baby brother. "Maybe I need more tools before I can earn money as a carpenter," he suggested to his mom. "How much do nails cost? And a hammer?" Before Mom could answer, Gabe jumped up from the sofa and said, "I know! I'll sell some of the onions from my garden to earn money for a hammer!" And off he went to pull the onions that he planted a few months previous.

Gabe didn't earn a fortune that day or that week or that year. But he did learn some valuable lessons about business, planning ahead, money management, the benefits of determination, and more. Gabe started several business ventures during his growing-up years, and eventually started and operated a very successful accounting firm. Gabe was not born with an entrepreneurial spirit; his parents began teaching him about the concept of financial independence from a very young age when they encouraged him to purchase everyday items he needed with his own money and also suggested ways that he could earn money, such as starting his own garden plot and selling his produce. And Gabe greatly benefited from those early lessons.

How to Help a Child Earn His Own Money

"There are many ways in which children can earn money them-selves,"[71] and parents should teach their children how to do just that.

One of the healthiest ventures for the child is to sell garden produce that he has grown. He could also start plants and sell the plants themselves. He could offer snow removal to the neighbors, or rake leaves, or pull weeds for them. Or he could bake healthful bread and sell it. Parents tend to underestimate what their young child is capable of learning how to do. In my research for this book, I met more than one child who began repairing lawn mowers on their own before age nine. Several others had their own businesses building and selling bird feeders. One young person made and sold organic garden compost. I heard of a young boy who loved music, and even before he could play the piano, he learned how to tune pianos. By the time he was eleven years old, he had a thriving piano-tuning business. If your child has an interest in starting a business that neither he nor you knows anything about, take a trip to the library, check out some books on the topic, and begin learning together. Once your child has some basic knowledge, find someone who can help him learn more as an apprentice or give him opportunities to learn via trial, error, and practice.

Be sure that, as you are coaching your child in his money-earning endeavors, you don't mar the lessons on financial responsibility that will come up several times in the process of learning to earn his own money. He should purchase all of his own materials with his own money, and he should pay those who help him (including his parents) a fair wage. If you succumb to the temptation to give free financial or physical help to your child in his business venture, you will steal from him the opportunities to truly learn the many valuable lessons that running his own business can teach him. In addition, work for pay should be done for those outside the family (such as neighbors and friends). Selling his wares to family members usually does not do much for teaching a child to run his own business. Also, family responsibilities should not be allowed to be neglected in order to provide the child with enough time to earn his own money.

Benefits of Learning Financial Responsibility

Working to earn money teaches a child many valuable lessons and skills. Below are just a few.

1. Working for pay helps teach money management.

One of the worst things a parent can do for their child is become a human ATM, handing out money whenever their child wants or needs something. Few experiences can teach a child about responsible money management more than requiring that he use his own funds to buy items he needs or wants. When a child must work for what he wants or needs, he quickly learns, in a very concrete way, the relationship between money, time, and things. He gains an appreciation for the work that is required to purchase the things he has in his home, he develops a sense of financial responsibility, and he learns long-term planning.

2. Working for pay can help a child appreciate delayed gratification.

Studies have shown that the ability to delay gratification translates to higher rates of success in life, in academics, and in relationships, and is associated with a more solid sense of self-worth, fewer addictive tendencies, and more adaptive coping skills. [72] Earning money to buy what he needs gives a child the opportunity to practice denying himself immediate pleasures to achieve a more valuable reward in the future. The weeks or months of saving, the patience required, the sacrifice of other purchases along the way, all are important lessons that prepare a child for his future as a responsible adult who can function wisely in an adult world.

3. Earning money can improve social skills.

Often, earning his own money necessitates that a child learn to deal with various situations and people diverse in age and background. Being able to interact with people of all ages and from all walks of life is a valuable skill that will prove a blessing in his adult life.

4. Working for pay can encourage unselfishness.

Sometimes parents give their child money to put in the offering plate at church, thinking they are teaching their child to give, but this doesn't really teach a child unselfish giving. The child is simply giving away the parent's money – no self-sacrifice required.

If a child has his own money to manage, he can be early taught to regularly support missionaries, buy gifts for others, and give to those who are needy without depending on his parents' resources. Parents must take care to nurture this attitude of unselfish giving since, without this guidance, the money he earns has the potential to actually encourage selfishness and worldly ambition. But when parents from the very beginning instill in a child the understanding that he is a steward of his talents (which include money, time, strength, and ability), then earning money can be an activity and lesson in unselfish giving.

Learning to Live for Christ

"God has placed us here not to live for our own amusement, but to do good, to bless humanity, to prepare for heaven." [73] "In all the teachings of Christ, he sought to impress upon the minds of his hearers that their happiness did not consist in self-gratification and amusements, but in the cultivation and exercise of *useful* lives in self-denying benevolence, as he was giving them an example in his own life." [74]

"Every student should devote a portion of each day to active labor. Thus habits of industry will be formed and a spirit of self-reliance encouraged, while the youth will be shielded from many evil and degrading practices that are so often the result of idleness. And this is all in keeping with the primary object of education; for in encouraging activity, diligence, and purity, we are coming into harmony with the Creator." [75]

Scheduling Useful Work into Your Child's Day

There was a lot of activity going on in Angela's home, but she was oblivious to it all as she was in bed with a sore throat and a fever. That evening, her husband came home from work to find a perfectly clean house, all the laundry clean and folded, and a meal waiting for him on the table. He had barely taken off his coat when his three children ran to him, eager for hugs and to tell him about their day. "Mom is not feeling well," eleven-year-old Michael related in a serious tone.

"I know," replied Dad. "When I called her, she said that the three of you were taking very good care of her."

"We took her water to drink and put a cloth on her head," seven-year-old Naomi said. "And we cleaned the house."

"And we made you dinner," chimed in three-year-old Josiah.

Does this seem like a dream? It's a true story.

At first, it may seem difficult to fit teaching your child to work into your already busy day, but removing other activities from the schedule to have time to focus on discipling your children comes with an abundance of rewards that will repay your efforts a thousand times over. And those rewards don't have to take years before they start coming in. Even little three-year-old Josiah took a responsible and useful role in cleaning the house, doing the laundry, and preparing the meal.

Teaching a child to work and daily engaging in useful work is an essential part of true education. "Children should be taught to have a part in domestic duties. They should be instructed how to help father and mother in the little things that they can do. Their minds should be trained to think, their memories taxed to remember their appointed work; and in the training to habits of usefulness in the home, they are being educated in doing practical duties appropriate to their age. ... Parents who love their children in a sensible way will not permit them to grow up with lazy habits, and ignorant of how to do home duties." [76]

"If you want your children to bless you, teach them to be useful and self-denying." [77] Limit entertainment, and instead, teach them to find joy and amusement in useful, practical work. "The education essential for the performance of life's practical duties is the noblest education your children could have." [78] If you want your children to be well-educated, to be happy, to honor God, to bless you, and to be a blessing to humanity, teach them to work.

Words of Counsel

"The most essential education for youth is a knowledge of the branches of labor important for practical life." [79]

"Education does not consist in using the brain alone. Physical employment is a part of the training essential for every youth. An important phase of education is lacking if the student is not taught how to engage in useful labor." [80]

"The greatest benefit is not gained from exercise that is taken as play or exercise merely. There is some benefit derived from being in the fresh air, and also from the exercise of the muscles; but let the same amount of energy be given to the performance of helpful duties, and the benefit will be greater, and a feeling of satisfaction will be realized; for such exercise carries with it the sense of helpfulness and the approval of conscience for duty well done." [81]

"Every man, woman, and child should be educated to practical, useful work." [82]

"All should find something to do that will be beneficial to themselves and helpful to others. God appointed work as a blessing, and only the diligent worker finds the true glory and joy of life." [83]

CHAPTER 14

GOD'S LESSON BOOK OF THE SCRIPTURES

"A thorough knowledge of the Bible is worth more than a college education." – Theodore Roosevelt

THE education of our children may be gained directly from the Heaven-appointed sources – from useful work, from the study of the Scriptures and of nature, and from the experiences of life. These are God's lesson books. In this chapter, we will look at the lesson book of the study of the Scriptures.

There is much to learn from the Scriptures – much more than many realize. "In its pages are found history the most ancient; biography the truest to life; principles of government for the control of the state, for the regulation of the household – principles that human wisdom has never equaled. It contains philosophy the most profound, poetry the sweetest and the most sublime." [1]

"The Bible is God's great lesson book, his great educator." [2]

The Message We Send

In a survey of 10,000 middle and high school students, when asked about what was more important to them – (1) achieving at a high level, (2) their own happiness, or (3) caring for others – almost 80 percent of the students reported that achievement and happiness were more important than caring for others. [3]

Nearly every parent would argue that these are not the values they are teaching to their children. So, where did students get such self-centered views?

Although most parents intend to raise their children to be thoughtful and caring, the message parents *intend* to send is often drowned out by the message they *actually* send. A typical student in the United States spends well over 10,000 hours in the classroom in his nine years in primary and lower secondary education. [4] (This figure varies by country, but in most countries, children spend a lot of time in school.) When so much time is invested in a child's academic education, the child logically learns that academic success must be the priority – a higher priority than a good character.

Christian parents may try to remedy this misalignment of priorities by adding spiritual instruction to their child's life. They go to church, they have family worship, they read the Bible with their child, and they send their child to a Christian school or choose a Bible-based homeschool curriculum. But even with all this added spiritual input, children still spend well over twice as many hours in academic instruction as they do in spiritual instruction.

In our efforts to prepare our children for success in this life, are we neglecting to prepare them for something of greater consequence? Where will this child spend most of his existence? In college? In the workforce? Or as a citizen of heaven? College, career, and success in this life are temporary. One day, everything on this earth will pass away, and our children will stand before God. How much time are we spending preparing our children for citizenship in heaven?

In the time of Christ, the gospel that Jesus presented was a stumbling block to the Jews because they wanted the Messiah to establish His kingdom here on this earth. They wanted success here in this world. They had lost sight of the better world that they should have been preparing for and, instead, were investing in what was visible and tangible. We scoff at the ignorance of the Jews, yet perhaps we are making the same mistake. We want our children to be successful here on this earth, and so we invest much in making that happen. In a sense, we attempt to establish heaven on earth for our children, all the while losing sight of the fact that there is a better world that we should be preparing them for.

When academic achievement is so highly valued by parents and so much energy is funneled toward that goal, whether parents intend to send this message or not, a child learns that worldly success is more important than preparing for heaven.

To make matters worse, all this time studying academic material shapes the child's mind in a way that parents never intended it to. "It is a law of the mind that it gradually adapts itself to the subjects upon which it is trained to dwell."[5] After spending ten to twelve years with his mind thinking about algebra, diagramming sentences, long division, parts of speech, political history, social science, and other academic subjects, a young person becomes conditioned to think on temporal matters, and he struggles to comprehend the relevance of God and eternal matters to his life. And eternal matters become uninteresting to him.

If parents want their children to have a realistic perspective of life, eternity, and their destiny, they must, by their words, actions, attitude, and priorities, impress upon their children the transient nature of this world. The ultimate goal of this life here on earth is to prepare ourselves and others for eternal realities. This goal doesn't render obsolete the needs of everyday life here. We still need to work, eat, sleep, interact, and we should still teach our children the skills they need for living in this world. But when we keep our priorities where God desires them to be, when we seek first the kingdom of God, then the ultimate goal – preparing for eternity – orients and aligns all of our other activities in life. It keeps them in their proper place and gives them a purpose.

The world is in chaos. Tomorrow is uncertain. "All time devoted to that which does not cause the soul to become more conformed to the likeness of Christ, is so much time lost for eternity, and this we cannot afford; for every moment is freighted with eternal interests."[6] Are we preparing our children for earthly success or heavenly success?

God's Priorities

"To many, education means a knowledge of books; but 'the fear of the Lord is the beginning of wisdom.'"[7] In God's method of education, eternal interests are the highest goal, the highest aspiration.

At every age and every stage of a child's life, the Bible should hold the uppermost place in his education, and it should occupy the greatest amount of study time in comparison to any other academic subjects. "Whatever else is taught in the home or at school, the Bible, as the great educator, should stand first. If it is given this place, God is honored, and He will work for you in the conversion of your children." [8]

Benefits, Advantages, and Success

If a child spends more time learning from the Bible than he does learning any other subject, will he fall behind in his academic education? Actually, quite the opposite is true.

"As a means of intellectual training, the Bible is more effective than any other book, or all other books combined." [9] "If the Bible were studied as it should be, men would become strong in intellect." [10] The Bible so strengthens the mind that, when it plays its rightful leading role in true education, it enables your child to learn all other subjects more easily and more quickly. The study of the Bible develops "breadth of mind, a nobility of character, and a stability of purpose that is rarely seen in these times." [11] "As a book to discipline and strengthen the intellect, to ennoble, purify, and refine the character, it is without a rival." [12] In fact, the Bible "is the only sure means of intellectual culture." [13]

"No scientific works are so well adapted to develop the mind as a contemplation of the great and vital truths and practical lessons of the Bible. No other book has ever been printed which is so well calculated to give mental power." [14] "From it strength may be received for the intellect." [15]

"There is nothing so ennobling and invigorating as a study of the great themes which concern our eternal life. Let the youth seek to grasp these God-given truths, and their minds will expand and grow strong in the effort. It will bring every student who is a doer of the word into a broader field of thought, and secure for him a wealth of knowledge that is imperishable." [16] "Studied and obeyed, the word of God would give to the world men of stronger and more active intellect than will the closest application to all the subjects that human philosophy embraces." [17]

How to Use the Lesson Book of the Scriptures

We see in the childhood of Jesus a beautiful pattern of how a little child should learn the Bible. He did not have a curriculum or Bible lessons. He did not have illustrated Bible story books or Bible crafts. Rather, He learned the Scriptures from the lips of His mother and through the lesson book of nature. [18] And this method was so beautifully effective, so touched the heart of the boy Jesus, that it developed in Him a love and desire to learn from the Scriptures on His own. "In His youth the early morning and the evening twilight often found Him alone on the mountainside or among the trees of the forest, spending a quiet hour in prayer and the study of God's word." [19]

How did the mother of Jesus so compellingly teach the Scriptures to her child? She followed the method given in Deuteronomy. We can do the same.

1. Prepare your heart.

The sixth chapter of the book of Deuteronomy instructs that there is some preparatory work to be done in the parents' hearts in order for the parent to teach their children well. "As a preparation for teaching His precepts, God commands that they [His words] be hidden in the hearts of the parents. ... Our instruction to them [the children] will have only the weight of influence given it by our own example and spirit." [20]

Notice in the quote above that our influence takes two forms: our example and our spirit.

A child will be influenced by the example of the parents because when God's Word is in the heart in a way that the parent is transformed by it and it controls every decision, every thought, and every action, a child sees how applicable the Scriptures are to the daily, everyday life. The Bible becomes very real to him, and his heart will be open to its instruction.

A child will be influenced by the spirit of the parent because "when the grace of God reigns within, the soul will be surrounded with an atmosphere of faith and courage and Christlike love, an atmosphere invigorating to the spiritual life of all who inhale it." [21] This atmosphere cannot be manufactured on our own; it is the grace of God reigning within that produces it. When a parent is surrounded by this atmosphere, it has a powerful influence on the child.

2. Prepare the child's heart.

How can parents plant in the heart of the child a love for God and a desire to follow Him? How can we help a child to fall in love with God's beautiful Word and be able to say with the psalmist, "Oh, how I love Thy law; it is my meditation all the day"? [22]

Before the seed of truth is planted in the heart, the soil of the heart must be prepared to receive it. It must be made receptive.

How do we make the heart receptive?

The heart is made receptive through relationship. [23]

The first two to three years of a child's life (and especially the first few months) are a crucial period for this heart preparation. It is during these years that the areas of the brain that are involved with spirituality, emotion, and relationship grow rapidly (more than at any other time of life) and have the greatest potential to prepare a child's heart to receive and appreciate the love of Christ in his later years. An intimate mother-child bond that includes secure connection, affection, and tender closeness creates billions of neural connections in the brain of a child that increase psychological readiness for a close connection with a Being who loves him. The deeper, more consistent, more intimate, and more tender a child's relationship is with his mother, the greater his capacity for a deep, consistent, intimate, and tender relationship with his Savior.

Note: Parents of children who have passed these early years may be comforted knowing that, while the first few years are the most effectual period for this heart preparation, it is never too late to invest in relationship. More time, self-sacrifice, determination, commitment, and dedication are required at a later age; but at any age, connection and relationship are powerful tools to open the heart to the truth. (See Chapter 4 for more on this topic.)

These neural connections are not developed by reading the Bible or the children's Bible lesson to a child (although parents certainly should do that). Spiritual instruction without the emotional and relational aspects tends to develop the intellectual powers without the development of the spiritual powers. The results? Children "have an intellectual knowledge of the truth, but their hearts are untouched with the genuine fervor of the love of Christ," [24] and when they are older, they are more likely to reject what they were taught when they were young. Due to the influence that false education has had on our thinking and on our child-rearing practices, this problem is very common.

False education teaches via the input of information. The idea is that if we expose a child to sufficient information, he will learn. If we get through all the chapters in that lesson book, if we cover the material, then we have accomplished our goal. There is a tendency to adopt the same approach when teaching the Scriptures to our children. We think that if we give a child a good Bible curriculum, if we take him to church, if he can say all his memory verses, if he knows all the Bible stories, then we have accomplished our goal. With the information-based mindset of false education, we focus on the information *about* God instead of a connection *with* God. While there is an inherent power in God's Word that may affect a child through exposure, approaching the Bible with a false-education mentality will not help a child develop a true and lasting relationship with his heavenly Father. It neglects the heart. We must remember that "the gospel does not address the understanding alone. If it did, we might approach it as we approach the study of a book dealing with mathematical formulas, which relate to the intellect alone. ... Its aim is the heart." [25] "The perception and appreciation of truth ... depends less upon the mind than upon the heart." [26] "A mere intellectual assent to the truth is worthless." [27]

Worthless.

The deepest truths are felt by the heart, not the intellect. The writers of the Bible knew this. When David said that God put gladness in his heart, when Solomon said to let thine heart keep the commandments, when Jesus said that evil thoughts come out of the heart and blessed are the pure in heart, they were not just using figures of speech. It is not the bare letter of the Word that a child needs; it is the Word opened and applied to the *heart*.

How do we ensure that the Scriptures reach a child's heart?

A well-known and respected religious leader "was once asked how old a child must be before there was reasonable hope of his being a Christian. 'Age has nothing to do with it,' was the answer. 'Love to Jesus, trust, repose, confidence, are all qualities that agree with the child's nature. As soon as a child can love and trust his mother, then can he love and trust Jesus as the Friend of his mother. Jesus will be his Friend, loved and honored.'" [28]

As the child grows, this connection, this bond, can be nourished and strengthened through time spent together (working together, playing together, etc.), communication, and affection. Research shows that the quality of the relationship that parents have with their children is one of the most significant indicators of the impact that their instruction (Biblical and otherwise) will have on their children. [29] The closer the bond between parent and child, the more open the child will be to moral instruction from the parent. This means that if you want your children to be eager for spiritual instruction, focus less on the actual instruction and more on your relationship with them. Bind their heart to yours. [30] "By the cords of unselfish love bind them to you and to Christ." [31]

Children are not buckets to be filled or products to be measured; they are souls to be nourished. We do not want little robots who can say their memory verses on autopilot with little understanding or concern for what those words of Scripture mean to them personally, having the form of godliness but without the power. [32] We want the power that comes from God's Word to reach a receptive and willing heart – one that hungers and thirsts after righteousness, loves God fully, and desires to serve Him. "An intellectual knowledge of the truth is not enough; we must know its power upon our own hearts and lives." [33]

When a child's heart belongs to Christ, the sanctifying power of the Word is seen in the life of the child, and the truth is "carried into every phase of practical life." [34] The child will love the Bible and the

Author of the Bible, and he will love authentically and enthusiastically. He will not be bored and uninterested in the Bible or subjects of a spiritual nature. Rather, the words of Scripture will inspire and animate him. "The heart that is surrendered to God, loves the truth of God's word. ... The carnal mind finds no pleasure in contemplating the word of God, but he who is renewed in the spirit of his mind, sees new charms in the living oracles; for divine beauty and celestial light seem to shine in every passage." [35]

"Our religion must be something more than a head religion. It must affect the heart, and then it will have a correcting influence upon the life." [36]

3. Make the majority of Biblical instruction oral in nature.

Due to the influence of false education, we have become a visual- and text-dominated culture, and we equate teaching and learning with books. But, in ancient Israel, "in both the school and the home much of the teaching was oral" [37] – not because the people could not read (most could read very well), but because oral instruction nurtures the element of relationship so important to God, and it more fully integrates His Word into the practical life.

This activity – talking about the Scriptures with their children – is one of the duties that God directly and specifically gave to parents. As we have seen, the sixth chapter of Deuteronomy tells parents to put God's Word into their *own* hearts and then *talk* (not read) about God's beautiful Word with their children. When parents, in their relationship with their children, practically talk about God's Word with them, they are making God real and personal to their children.

This is not to say that books should not be used at all, but there is no man-made resource that possesses the indescribable strength and power to provide for the spiritual needs of a child as does the means that God has ordained. When we use a lesson or a program or other materials to do the job that God gave to parents, we are not fulfilling our God-given, parental duty of being a conduit of God's love, wisdom, guidance, and instruction to our children.

In addition to its ability to nurture relationship and be better integrated into practical life, oral learning cooperates with how a young child learns and is more conducive to the strengthening of the brain than is written instruction. Children don't need books with an abundance of pictures to keep their attention. God has given children amazing imaginations and a remarkable ability to create their own pictures in their minds as they listen to His word. The type of listening in which the child supplies his own visuals strengthens his thinking abilities and grows the attention span.

When parents follow God's instruction in Deuteronomy and hide His Word in their hearts, God's Word becomes a part of who they are. Every thought and action are governed by the Bible, and its truths naturally permeate into the incidental conversation of everyday life. [38]

When your two-year-old is sitting on your lap snuggling with you, tell him of when the mothers brought their children to Jesus so he could bless them. Tell him of how Jesus "gathered them in his loving arms,"[39] and how the children loved to climb up onto His lap. As you prepare a meal with your three-year-old, tell him of when Jesus fed the five thousand. As you work in the garden with your four-year-old, tell him how God planted a garden for Adam and Eve. You may not think you can develop these ideas on your own, but when *your* heart is prepared through submission to Christ and study of His word, God will give you thoughts to impart to your child. "The lessons that we ourselves learn from Christ we should give to our children, as the young minds can receive them, little by little opening to them the beauty of the principles of heaven. Thus the Christian home becomes a school, where the parents serve as underteachers, while Christ Himself is the chief instructor." [40] Conversations like these don't need to be forced, planned, or structured; when Jesus has our heart, our thoughts are of Him, and these conversations can be quite natural and normal. [41]

4. Don't waste the early years.

"There are no influences so potent as those which surround us in our early years." [42] Because of this, not one moment of the precious early years should be wasted on storybooks, ABC books, and similar books designed for children. Instead, tell your children the story of Jesus and His love. "Let all your efforts be for their salvation. Act as though they were placed in your care to be fitted as precious jewels to shine in the kingdom of God." [43]

5. Use the stories in the Bible

"In all that men have written, where can be found anything that has such a hold upon the heart, anything so well adapted to *awaken the interest of the little ones*, as the stories of the Bible?" [44] Parents can verbally tell these stories to their children over and over. They can also read the stories to their children from the Bible and from *Christ's Object Lessons* [45] and the books in the *Conflict of the Ages Series*. [46] In this way, the child hears the same stories repeatedly yet in different words, thus deeply impressing them upon his mind and heart. As you tell and read the stories, talk about them with your child. Help him see the relevance of them to him, using examples from your family's everyday life.

6. Make it practical and applicable.

God gave us the command to diligently teach our children when we're sitting in our house, when we walk by the way, when we lie down, and when we rise up, [47] not only because we should teach our children all the time, but also because children were designed to learn everything – whether academic or spiritual – through practical, everyday life.

The teaching of God's Word should not be an event (such as family worship, Bible class, or church) but rather a lifestyle.

If we want our children to be Christians, "our religion should be made practical." [48] "The lessons of the Bible have a moral and religious influence on the character, *as they are brought into the practical life*." [49] "Its principles are to be interwoven with all their experience." [50]

"It is not enough merely to speak to your children of spiritual things. They must see you exemplify the principles of Christianity in your home." [51] "The power of divine grace should control all the regulations of the household. Let it be seen in your simplicity in dress and in the preparation of your food. All these things, as well as the society you choose, the amusements in which you indulge, and the whole round of duties of daily life, will have an abiding influence upon the characters of your children." [52] "The religion of the Bible must be brought into the large and the little affairs of life." [53] All decisions, choices, and actions must be guided by God's Word, not by our own reasoning, our own logic, or our own desires. "Religion must be woven into every part of the home life if we would see the results that God has designed as the fruit of following His way." [54]

Practical application is absolutely essential for children. It is the practical, daily experiences that shape a child's thoughts and feelings, which in turn mold his character and make him who he is. [55] Children need the practical lessons of the Bible "brought into the daily experience in practical life," [56] or the lessons in God's word will mean very little to them. The two-dimensional instruction from a Bible-instruction curriculum will not have anywhere near the impact on a child as will real-life experiences in which a child sees the truth lived before his very eyes.

True education doesn't merely teach a child the truth; it also enables the child to *experience* the truth personally. It is only when our spiritual life is one with our practical everyday life that our children will be truly educated in God's way.

"If you do not make the sacred teachings of God's word the rule and guide of your life, the truth will be nothing to you. Truth is efficient only as it is carried out in practical life." [57]

"Parents, bring practical godliness into the home." [58]

7. Make it a priority.

Life is busy, and it's easy to allow matters of lesser importance to take center stage. But if we want our children to make God a priority in their lives, we must model this attitude in our own lives. Jesus told us in the sixth chapter of Matthew to seek *first* the kingdom of God. "The teaching of the Bible should have our freshest thought, our best methods, and our most earnest effort." [59] If God's messages are a priority to us, we will not begin our day without hearing from Him, we will not end our day without hearing from Him, and we will seek to hear what He has to say to us many times throughout the day.

If you feel that it is challenging to fit an abundance of God's

Word into your life, ask God for wisdom to know which areas of your life need to be trimmed to make time for that which is truly important. We owe everything to our precious Savior, and there is not a moment in our day that our heavenly Father is not thinking about us and caring for us. We are a priority to Him; it is our privilege to make Him our priority.

8. Don't forget the purpose.

There is a vast difference between knowing *about* someone and *knowing* someone. A child may know all about God. He may know His commandments. He may recite entire chapters of the Bible. He may understand God's principles extremely well. But knowing about God and knowing Him are two different things.

Our children need more than to know the Scriptures; they need to know the One who gave the Scriptures. It is by teaching the Scriptures through the avenues of relationship and practical life that we can best help our children truly *know* God. And the more we know God, the more we love Him. [60]

"In His prayer to the Father, Christ gave to the world a lesson which should be graven on mind and soul. 'This is life eternal,' He said, 'that they might know Thee the only true God, and Jesus Christ, whom Thou hast sent.' John 17:3. This is true education." [61]

What About Bible Memorization?

While we should help our children memorize Scripture, a word of caution is in order when it comes to methods of memorization.

Memorizing and reciting Bible verses does not necessarily mean that true, meaningful learning has occurred. When done incorrectly, memorization tends to bypass the reasoning and thinking processes of the brain. When this happens, the information that is memorized gets stored as insignificant knowledge. This type of memorization trains the brain to prefer surface and superficial knowledge rather than rich, meaningful, in-depth, true understanding.

True learning requires reasoning, thinking, understanding, and application. True Bible learning happens only when a child thinks about, understands, and applies the principles of Scripture in the practical aspects of his daily life.

So, should we encourage children to memorize Scripture? Yes! But long before we do so, we should first, through concrete application in daily life, help them to develop a deep, meaningful, and *practical* understanding of the particular passage in the Bible that we want them to memorize. When the concept in a Bible verse has practical application in the life, the child's brain will have a scaffolding to which the words of the Bible verse can attach during the process of memorization, thus making memorization easier and avoiding rote and superficial learning.

Bible Games, Bible Bowls, Bible Contests

Learning from the Bible should always be a joy and a pleasure and have rich meaning in a child's life. When a child loves God's Word, there is no need to use games and other forms of entertainment to motivate a child to study the Scriptures. Bible games and contests, more often than not, stimulate a love for the game, for the competition, and for the rewards of winning, instead of inspiring a love for the Bible. We are warned that "the offering of rewards will create rivalry, envy, and jealousy; and some who are the most diligent and worthy, will receive little credit. Pupils should not try to see how many verses they can learn to repeat; for this brings too great a strain upon the ambitious child, while the rest become discouraged." [62]

We do not want to simply fill our children with knowledge; we want them to be filled with love for Christ. We want our children to study the Bible because they love it, not because they've been extrinsically motivated by worldly methods. And we certainly don't want to replace the sacredness of Scriptures with a spirit of competition. Let's inspire our children with a desire and passion for God so they *desire* to spend time in His Word.

Family Worship Time

While learning from the Bible should primarily be of a practical nature, and Biblical instruction should be given all throughout the day, there is also much that can be gained through family worship time. "In arousing and strengthening a love for Bible study, much depends on the use of the hour of worship." [63]

This time should be enjoyable and interesting. "The hours of morning and evening worship should be the sweetest and most helpful of the day. Let it be understood that into these hours no troubled, unkind thoughts are to intrude; that parents and children assemble to meet with Jesus, and to invite into the home the presence of holy angels."[64] However, the morning and evening worship times should not take on an entertaining nature. They "should be treated with the greatest solemnity and reverence, yet all the pleasantness possible should be brought into them."[65]

As parents follow the instruction in Deuteronomy chapter six, children receive an abundance of Biblical instruction all throughout the day; hence, there is no need to make worship time long. "Let the seasons of family worship be short and spirited. ... When a long chapter is read and explained and a long prayer offered, this precious service becomes wearisome, and it is a relief when it is over."[66] Rather, "let the services be brief and full of life, adapted to the occasion, and varied from time to time."[67] Adapt the content of family worship to the spiritual needs of the family at that particular time. "Let all join in the Bible reading and learn and often repeat God's law. It will add to the interest of the children if they are sometimes permitted to select the reading. Question them upon it, and let them ask questions. Mention anything that will serve to illustrate its meaning. When the service is not thus made too lengthy, let the little ones take part in prayer, and let them join in song, if it be but a single verse."[68]

In family worship time, "Christ should be set forth as 'the chiefest among ten thousand,' the One 'altogether lovely.' Song of Solomon 5:10, 16. He should be presented as the Source of all true pleasure and satisfaction, the Giver of every good and perfect gift, the Author of every blessing, the One in whom all our hopes of eternal life are centered. In every religious exercise let the love of God and the joy of the Christian experience appear in their true beauty."[69]

The Duty of Parents

Our children must "be rooted and grounded in divine truth. Their attention should be called, not to the assertions of men, but to the word of God. Above all other books, the word of God must be our study, the great textbook, the basis of all education; and our children are to be educated in the truths found therein, irrespective of previous habits and customs. In doing this, teachers and students will find the hidden treasure, the higher education." [70]

The Word of God "gives such instruction that parents need not err in regard to the education of their children; but it admits of no indifference or negligence. The law of God is to be kept before the minds of the children as the great moral standard. When they rise up, and when they sit down, when they go out, and when they come in, this law is to be taught them as the great rule of life, and its principles are to be interwoven with all their experience. They are to be taught to be honest, truthful, temperate, economical, and industrious, and to love God with the whole heart. This is bringing them up in the nurture and admonition of the Lord. This is setting their feet in the path of duty and safety." [71]

"Make the word of the living God your lessonbook." [72]

Words of Counsel

"Heart education is of more importance than the education gained from books." [73]

"By a misconception of the true nature and object of education many have been led into serious and even fatal errors. Such a mistake is made when the regulation of the heart or the establishment of right principles is neglected in an effort to secure intellectual culture, or when eternal interests are overlooked in the eager desire for temporal advantage." [74]

"Many think that they must consult commentaries on the Scriptures in order to understand the meaning of the word of God, and we would not take the position that commentaries should not be studied; but it will take much discernment to discover the truth of God under the mass of the words of men." [75]

"Study not the philosophy of man's conjectures, but study the philosophy of Him who is truth. No other literature can compare with this in value." [76]

"The truth as it is in Jesus can be experienced, but never explained." [77]

SECTION V
GOD'S SYLLABUS

CHAPTER 15

CHOOSING GOD'S SYLLABUS

*"The foolishness of God is wiser than men; and the
weakness of God is stronger than men." –*
1 Corinthians 1:25

IN Section I of this book, we looked at some of the most essential
elements of God's method of true education. These elements lay a
solid foundation for proper development and true learning. Section II
covered God's schedule for education – what to do when. In Section
III, we looked at the practical and spiritual importance of teaching
your child to think, as well as God's method for building the brain
so that all learning happens effectively and efficiently. In Section
IV, we covered the four lesson books from which God intended a
child to learn.

The principles outlined in these four sections are absolutely vital
components in God's method of education and cannot be neglected
if a parent wants to educate their child according to God's plan.

This section (Section V) will consider several valuable subjects
that God wants a child to learn and how they can be learned in the
context of God's four lesson books. Parents should keep in mind
that these subjects are only a very small part of the whole – they
are not the sum and substance of true education. You will find that
information in Sections I through IV.

God's Standards vs the World's Standards

Well-meaning parents often ask questions that basically go like
this: "What does my child need to learn in grade two?" "What does
my child need to know to graduate from high school?" The questions usually stem from the parents' concern that their child gains
the required knowledge at the time when it is required of him. But
perhaps the questions we should be asking are *who* is requiring this
information, and *why* is it being required?

There are standardized benchmarks in the false educational system. But who has prescribed these criteria? Are the subjects typically taught in school even what a child needs to learn? Or are they part of an arbitrary conventionality that has been ordained by those who do not know God or His purpose for His children?

Much of what is considered expected and normal in our modern educational system is a fabricated protocol that is based on very little science or intelligent educational philosophy. Yet, we sometimes – consciously or subconsciously – feel bound by these worldly conventions and standards. God instructs us that "we are not at liberty to teach that which shall meet the world's standard or the standard of the church, simply because it is the custom to do so. The lessons which Christ taught are to be the standard."[1] Instead of asking the questions, "What does my child need to know to pass fifth grade?" or "How can I be sure my child knows everything he needs to know to get into a good college?" or "How do I prepare my child to compete in the modern world?" every Christian parent should ask, "How does God want me to educate this child that He has lent to me?" Rather than asking, "What does the world want my child to learn?" we should ask, "What does God want my child to learn?"

Following "common, worldly lines"[2] of education will "prevent us from grasping true educational principles."[3] "The divine principles and modes of working are widely different from those of the world."[4] In educating our children, we must not "reason after the manner of the world and copy its plans and imitate its customs. ... In thus doing, [we] will not meet the mind of the Spirit of God."[5]

"By conforming entirely to the will of God, we shall be placed upon vantage ground, and shall see the necessity of decided separation from the customs and practices of the world. We are not to elevate our standard just a little above the world's standard; but we are to *make the line of demarcation decidedly apparent.*"[6]

"Christ taught in a way altogether different from ordinary methods, and we are to be laborers together with Him."[7]

The Object of Education

We were created in the image of God. [8] The object of education is "to restore in man the image of his Maker, to bring him back to the perfection in which he was created, to promote the development of body, mind, and soul, that the divine purpose in his creation might be realized." [9] This objective must be kept constantly in view through all areas of a child's education.

"Much time and money are spent by students in acquiring a knowledge that is as chaff to them." [10] "Many spend years of their life in the study of books, obtaining an education that will die with them. Upon such an education God places no value." [11] All that a child learns should contribute to his eternal welfare. Our goal and focus of a child's education should be to prepare him to be a citizen of heaven – "for entrance into the higher school." [12] We should not waste time teaching our children "that which God does not require them to know" [13] through methods that God has not ordained.

The next several chapters outline the subjects of study that are included in God's method of education. As you read, keep in mind that these subjects are to be learned through God's four lesson books – useful work, the study of the Scriptures and of nature, and the experiences of life. [14]

Words of Counsel

"There is an education which is essentially worldly. Its aim is success in the world, the gratification of selfish ambition. To secure this education many students spend time and money in crowding their minds with unnecessary knowledge. ... Much of the education at the present time is of this character. The world may regard it as highly desirable; but it increases the peril of the student." [15]

"All unnecessary matters should be weeded from the courses of study, and only such studies placed before the student as will be of real value to him." [16]

CHAPTER 16

AGRICULTURE

"Our model citizen is a sophisticate who, before puberty, understands how to produce a baby, but who at the age of thirty will not know how to produce a potato." – Wendell Berry

GOD'S plan of education was set forth from the beginning, when man was first created, and in His plan, "the garden of Eden was not only Adam's dwelling, but his school-room."[1] God's plan is still the same. The garden and the orchard are to be a child's "schoolroom."[2] "Study in agricultural lines should be the A, B, and C of the education given in our schools. This is the very first work that should be entered upon."[3] Agriculture is not an "extra" in true education; rather, it is an essential. It is foundational.

Agriculture and Education

There are countless reasons why agriculture is an essential component of true education. The next few pages will cover only a fraction of them.

1. Agriculture improves thinking skills.

"No one can succeed in agriculture or gardening without attention to the laws involved. The special needs of every variety of plant must be studied. Different varieties require different soil and cultivation, and compliance with the laws governing each is the condition of success."[4]

For example, kale loves the cold and can be harvested even in very cold, snowy weather, but basil turns brown as soon as the weather even hints at chilliness. Sugar-snap peas require an abundance of water; black-eyed peas will die if you give them too much water. Melons need full sun; parsley grows well with a little shade. Okra needs heat to mature; too much heat will make rapini bolt. A gardener must learn these rules and, at the same time, remember that there are no hard-and-fast rules. The degree to which a plant will perform as expected depends upon a multitude of factors, such as the composition of the soil, nighttime temperatures, whether the plant is mulched or not, the various microclimates in a garden, the health of the individual plant, and more. And to add even more complexity to the already complex (yet-to-be-written) garden rulebook, with every season comes a new set of considerations – frost dates, rainfall, temperature swings, and pest pressure all vary greatly from one year to another.

Agriculture is never, ever a rote activity; there is always some new variable, some surprise element. And this is why agriculture improves thinking skills. One cannot unthinkingly follow a prescribed set of prefabricated rules and expect everything to grow well. To be successful at agriculture, one must *think*. Agriculture strengthens the thinking powers in a way that no book or class or curriculum is capable of.

2. Agriculture cultivates the love to learn.

In our modern culture, fear of failure (which can stifle the love of learning and hinder deep thinking) has become common among children. Yet, this fear is uncommon – or at least less common – among those who grew up gardening. Perhaps this is because trial and error, failures and successes, and various elements beyond our control are normal and expected components of agriculture. Sometimes plants don't perform as anticipated, weather can foil even the best-laid plans, and pests can cause entire crop failures. Mistakes will be made, disappointments will come. Yet children who grow up involved in agriculture learn that much enjoyment can be found in gardening when one accepts the mistakes, failures, and imperfections and embraces the experiences that agriculture provides. And these experiences can help children learn that there are hidden gifts – or lessons – to be gained from both the successes and the failures.

Research shows that children who are actively engaged in garden projects show improved attitudes towards learning and education. [5] Agriculture can help a child learn to love learning for the sake of learning and to see failure not as a definer of who he is but as a tool to improve his abilities. And children who embrace failure and love to learn grow to become highly self-motivated and intelligent adults.

3. Agriculture improves cause-to-effect reasoning.

God has instructed parents to teach their children cause-to-effect reasoning. [6] Agriculture is a simple, yet remarkably effective, way to develop proficient cause-to-effect reasoning skills. If you want to eat carrots, you have to plant carrot seeds. If you want those seeds to grow well, you must take care of them. Even a toddler can grasp this concept when he sees it before his very eyes.

Likewise, in the process of planting and harvesting, children quickly learn that food doesn't magically appear on the grocery shelves or the table. Someone had to grow that food. Someone had to plant it, water it, nourish it, weed it, care for it, and harvest it. Cause-to-effect reasoning gets a major workout in the garden and orchard.

4. Agriculture improves attention spans.

Unlike most other components of our modern life, growing a garden or an orchard is not a quick process. We cannot push a button to produce a cantaloupe, and producing a pecan requires several years. This is one reason why children who regularly engage in agriculture tend to have longer attention spans.

5. Agriculture strengthens academic skills.

Agriculture gives a child hands-on experience in biology, chemistry, ecology, physics, climate science, math, logic, planning, and, of course, horticulture. Studies show that children who regularly engage in agriculture develop better problem-solving skills, perform better on academic tests, have improved science understanding, and are overall better learners compared with children who do not regularly engage in agriculture. Agriculture also allows children to exercise their curiosity, and curiosity is the fuel that drives the love of learning.

6. Agriculture teaches planning.

Children can be impulsive and impetuous, but these traits don't fare well in a garden and orchard. Because blueberries don't grow in a day, one must learn to be thoughtful and plan ahead if one wants to eat blueberries on his cereal.

7. Agriculture teaches responsibility.

Agriculture teaches a child responsibility better than any puppy can. Children naturally learn through the dynamic, yet persistent, nature of a garden that there is no such thing as an excuse for avoiding duties. Weeds don't stop growing just because you don't feel like pulling them. Tomatoes will rot on the vine if you don't pick them on time. Sweet potatoes will taste terrible if you don't harvest them before cold weather comes. There are no excuses in agriculture – a job is a job, and that job must be done regardless of whether one feels like doing that job or not.

8. Agriculture teaches industry and diligence.

No farmer ever plowed a field by turning it over in his mind. The experience of eating fresh, flavorful, and tender garden potatoes for lunch that you have personally planted, cared for, and harvested with your own hands provides a tremendous sense of satisfaction that is highly motivating toward the development of industry and diligence.

9. Agriculture teaches obedience.

As a child learns that obedience to God's natural laws causes the earth to produce its treasures, so will he also learn that obedience to His moral law produces a beautiful character. [7] A child must obey the rules of the Creator if he desires to see good results from his labors. No matter how much he wants a cucumber seed to yield a watermelon, it will not happen. No matter how much he dislikes picking strawberries, he can't eat them for breakfast if he doesn't pick them first.

Engaging in agriculture cultivates this habit of obedience in a child. [8]

10. Agriculture strengthens the body.

Research shows that children need contact with the soil for optimal health. Getting their hands in the garden soil exposes children to numerous beneficial bacteria and other microorganisms that help develop a healthy immune system, contribute to a more diverse gut microbiome, and more.

And, of course, agriculture provides the family with the wonderful rewards of healthy, fresh produce that benefits the body in more ways than we know.

11. Agriculture strengthens the character.

Work in the garden and orchard develops a good character far better than any book or curriculum can. "The constant contact with the mystery of life and the loveliness of nature, as well as the tenderness called forth in ministering to these beautiful objects of God's creation, tends to quicken the mind and refine and elevate the character." [9]

12. Agriculture helps a child know God and promotes spiritual growth.

Teaching a young child spiritual concepts can be challenging, but agriculture can open up a child's understanding of these subjects in a very concrete way. "The same principles run through the spiritual and the natural world." [10] "The operations of agriculture illustrate the Bible lessons." [11] "The unseen is illustrated by the seen." [12]

As you work in the garden with your child, you can compare cultivating the soil of the garden with cultivating the soil of our heart in order to make a welcoming place for the seed of truth. [13] When you and your child plant seeds and tiny sprouts appear, you can explain to him that the seed dies in order to give life to a new plant. [14] As you watch your plants grow, you can talk to your child about how they are growing by a power that is not our own and how "it is the Lord that gives the virtue and the power to the soil and to the seed." [15] "As we cultivate the soil day by day, we may learn precious spiritual lessons" [16] and watch our children's understanding of God and who He is grow in awe and wonder.

The garden and the orchard and "the produce gathered through the blessing of God" [17] are to a child "a living parable" [18] "from which spiritual lessons can be made plain and applied to the necessities of the soul." [19]

"The cultivation of the soil is good work for children and youth. It brings them into direct contact with nature and nature's God."[20] Every child should learn how to cultivate various crops and how to plant and care for fruit trees. "The care of the trees, the planting and the sowing, and the gathering of the harvest are to be wonderful lessons for [them]."[21] "The same God who guides the planets works in the fruit orchard and in the vegetable garden,"[22] and "when the students employ their time and strength in agricultural work, in heaven it is said of them, Ye 'are laborers together with God.' 1 Corinthians 3:9."[23] What a beautiful way to help our children to know their Creator!

I Don't Know How!

How can parents involve their child in agriculture if they don't know anything about agriculture themselves?

A book on agriculture can be helpful, but there is no need for extensive instruction in agriculture before you begin. The false education mindset tells us that we need a class on agriculture to learn agriculture. But the true education mindset tells us that learning can happen in a number of ways, and one of the best ways (especially for children) is through practical experience. (See Chapter 11.) Find a little piece of earth. Dig it up. Plant some seeds. Experiment. And learn from your experiences. Learning agriculture through practical experience teaches not only agriculture, but it also develops the abilities to observe, reason, and think.

"Wisdom will be learned by failures, and the energy that will make a beginning gives hope of success in the end."[24]

In addition, we have the promise that the great God of heaven will bend down to teach us as we work in agriculture. "Of him who cultivates the soil the Bible declares, 'His God doth instruct him to discretion, and doth teach him.' Isaiah 28:26"[25] "He who taught Adam and Eve in Eden how to tend the garden, desires to instruct men today."[26]

If we seek the Lord for wisdom, are careful to reason from cause to effect, and are diligent to learn from experience and failures (three important factors in true education), our knowledge will grow from barely knowing how to place a seed in the soil to understanding how to care for the plants, when to plant for the best results, how to prevent plant diseases, how to harvest, the best ways to properly preserve the harvest, and more.

Learning Together

Work *together* with your child. It's alright if he drops fifteen beet seeds into one tiny hole, pulls the lettuce instead of the weeds, and harvests tomatoes while they are still green; kindly and patiently teach him. Allow your child to use real garden tools – not the little plastic toy ones. Talk to him about "what the Bible says about agriculture: that it was God's plan for man to till the earth; that the first man, the ruler of the whole world, was given a garden to cultivate; and that many of the world's greatest men, its real nobility, have been tillers of the soil. Show the opportunities in such a life." [27] No worries if you feel like you do not know much; talk to your child about what you do know, and the Lord will reveal more to you as you continue to use His ways.

Enjoying Agriculture

Agriculture should be made enjoyable. In fact, we are told that gardening can provide amusement for our children. [28] "We should so train the youth that they will love to engage in the cultivation of the soil." [29] "We should so train the youth that they will love to work upon the land, and delight in improving it." [30] How can we do this?

One important key is to include your child in *all* aspects of agricultural projects. Involve him in *every* small detail of your agriculture adventure – planning the garden layout, learning about the characteristics of each variety of plant, choosing the varieties to grow, deciding how much to grow, cultivating the soil, watering, pulling weeds, harvesting, and eating the produce. When a child is involved with all the varied aspects, he will be much more enthused about the project than if his only job is to weed three days a week.

Another factor is to begin young. When children grow up working in the garden or the orchard every day, they learn that these activities are a normal part of everyday life and seldom question this fact. Even a crawling baby can be involved in the garden activities. Allow him to sift through the dirt with his hands, to feel the texture of the plant leaves, to smell the ripening tomato, or pull the potatoes out of the ground that you uncover with your spade.

And another key to making agriculture enjoyable is to grow food that you and your child like to eat. If your child dislikes broccoli but loves strawberries, he will be more motivated to put his energies into growing strawberries than broccoli.

And finally, have a cheerful attitude about it yourself. "We should work the soil cheerfully, hopefully, gratefully, believing that the earth holds in her bosom rich stores for the faithful worker to garner, richer than gold or silver." [31] Get excited about it. Celebrate with every single carrot you pull. Thank God for every harvest of kale. Cheer for every potato you find hidden in the earth.

There are rich life lessons and deep insights to be gained through cooperating with God in agriculture. These lessons and insights cannot be explained with mere words. They must be experienced to be had. The garden and the orchard provide lessons that "will impart knowledge in the culture of the soul," [32] and will prepare a child "for a place on the Lord's farm in the earth made new." [33]

Words of Counsel

"There is wisdom for him who holds the plow, and plants and sows the seed." [34]

"The hoe and the shovel, the rake and the harrow, are all implements of honorable and profitable industry." [35]

"Both teachers and students would have much more healthful experience in spiritual things, and much stronger minds and purer hearts to interpret eternal mysteries, than they can have while studying books so constantly, and working the brain without taxing the muscles." [36]

"No line of manual training is of more value than agriculture." [37]

"In the study of agriculture, let pupils be given not only theory, but practice." [38]

CHAPTER 17

ANATOMY AND PHYSIOLOGY

"Men go abroad to wonder at the height of moun-
tains, at the huge waves of the sea, at the long
courses of the rivers, at the vast compass of the
oceans, at the circular motion of the stars, and pass
by themselves without wondering." –
St. Augustine

HEALTH, anatomy, and physiology are very practical subjects for a child. Even a toddler can readily learn about his ears, skin, stomach, heart, eyes, bones, muscles, and so forth. These are things that he has daily, practical, and tangible experience with. He can feel his heart beating. He can hear his stomach "grumbling." He can see horripilation on his skin when his arms are cold. He can feel and see the functioning of his elbow joint. He daily uses his eyes and ears in a very practical way. He can watch a scratch on his knee heal, and he can learn about how he can cooperate with God in helping it to heal.

In daily life, through the very practical and concrete means of engaging in health-promoting habits, a child can learn how to keep his body in a healthy condition. "From the first dawn of reason the human mind should become intelligent in regard to the physical structure." [1] When he is eating brown rice, teach him that whole grains provide his body with nutrients he needs to grow strong. When he is eating fresh berries or papaya, teach him that fresh fruits keep his immune system strong. When he is playing outside with you, teach him that fresh air helps digestion and cleans his lungs and that sunshine strengthens his bones. When he wakes up in the morning and thanks God for a good sleep, teach him that sleep re-energizes his brain. When he drinks water, teach him that water helps his blood flow better. When he is waiting until mealtime to eat, teach him that avoiding food in between meals keeps his stomach and brain healthy. When you help him live life on a schedule, teach him that doing his daily activities on a schedule helps his body organs to properly prepare for each of their functions.

Is It Really That Important?

In the education of our children, how essential are the subjects of anatomy, physiology, and health? "A knowledge of physiology and hygiene should be the basis of all educational effort." [2] "What study can be more important for the young than that which treats of this wonderful organism that God has committed to us, and of the laws by which it may be preserved in health?" [3] It is "of the highest importance that among the studies selected for children, physiology occupy an important place. All children should study it. And then parents should see to it that practical hygiene [the science concerned with the prevention of illness and maintenance of health] is added." [4] And "the relation of the physical organism to the spiritual life is one of the most important branches of education. It should receive careful attention in the home and in the school." [5]

How to Teach

Just as with every other subject that God wants children to learn, anatomy and physiology can be learned quite well through God's lesson books.

Rather than teaching rote memorization of the components and functions of the various systems of the body, the study of anatomy and physiology should focus on how to live in obedience to God's health laws. Children should be taught "that the laws that govern our physical organism, God has written upon every nerve, muscle, and fiber of the body. Every careless or willful violation of these laws is a sin against our Creator." [6] This understanding is "of far greater value to the student than are many of the technicalities commonly taught." [7]

Parents should take the time to explain to their children the *reason* for obeying God's health laws. We don't want our children to simply comply because obedience has been drilled into them or "because we said so." We want our children to do what is right because they love and trust God's beautiful ways. Helping children see the wisdom in God's teachings requires an investment of time and effort. We must help them to see that "in all that [God] does, He has the well-being of His children in view." [8]

Children who live healthfully because they desire to honor their Creator have learned infinitely more about anatomy and physiology than those who "can tell just how many bones there are in the human frame, and correctly describe every organ of the body, and yet ... are as ignorant of the laws of health, and the cure of disease." [9]

"Explain the structure, nature, and function of each organ, and the relation it bears to life; the right manner of use ... and show them how to live so that they may make the body a fitting 'temple of the living God!'" [10] If you don't know the functions of the various parts of the body, an anatomy and physiology book can be helpful. However, care should be taken to keep the learning practical.

Parents should remember that true learning always includes application. A child must be able to connect new knowledge with authentic and practical experiences of life. (See Chapter 11.) This means that when the parent teaches the child that outdoor exercise is beneficial, they should regularly engage in it. When the parent teaches the child that "sugar is not good for the stomach," [11] their actions must be consistent with their words. Children are quick to detect inconsistencies. There must not be a disconnect between what is learned and what is practiced in life.

When a child reaches about eight to ten years of age (depending on the child), if he has a good foundation in the practical lessons of anatomy and physiology and is practicing God's health principles in his life, instruction from books can also be included. Read the book *The Ministry of Healing* together as a family. The chapter in the book *Education* entitled "Study of Physiology" and the periodical *The Health Reformer* also provides a wealth of information. [12] "Form a home reading circle, in which every member of the family shall lay aside the busy cares of the day and unite in study." [13]

What to Teach

Here are some of the basic lessons a child should learn. For additional guidance, refer to Chapter 3 in this book, as well as the books mentioned in the previous paragraph.

Healthful Living

A child should be taught the importance of health principles (such as those outlined in Chapter 3) and how to apply them. These valuable lessons are learned in everyday life through what is practiced in the home. Parents should also take the time to discuss with their children the reasons for these health practices.

Structure and Function of Parts of the Body

"To become acquainted with the wonderful human organism, the bones, muscles, stomach, liver, bowels, heart, and pores of the skin, and to understand the dependence of one organ upon another for the healthful action of all" [14] as well as the practical application of this knowledge in keeping the body healthy are important parts of true education.

Natural Remedies

Every child "should understand what to do in case of sickness." [15] And just as God's method of education is different from the world's method, so is God's method of treating illness different from that of the world. "Pure air, sunlight, abstemiousness, rest, exercise, proper diet, the use of water, trust in divine power – these are the *true* remedies." [16] "The beneficial effects of the proper use of water" [17] and its use "to relieve pain and check disease" [18] should be thoroughly taught. In addition, "the Lord has given some simple herbs of the field that at times are beneficial; and if every family were educated in how to use these herbs in case of sickness, much suffering might be prevented, and no doctor need be called." [19] And "one of the most beneficial remedies is pulverized charcoal." [20]

"Every person should have a knowledge of nature's remedial agencies and how to apply them. It is essential both to understand the principles involved in the treatment of the sick and to have a *practical* training that will enable one rightly to use this knowledge," [21] all the while keeping in mind that "it is far better to *prevent* disease than to know how to treat it when contracted." [22] Children "should understand the importance of guarding against disease by preserving the vigor of every organ and should also be taught how to deal with common diseases and accidents." [23] Children should also be taught to avoid counterfeit natural remedies.

Separating Truth from Error

There is no shortage of information about health in our world today. For every one of God's amazing and beautiful truths, the enemy has a counterfeit, and most of his counterfeit methods *appear* to be just as amazing and beautiful. Because Satan's health teachings are so similar to God's and bring so many good results, it can be difficult to distinguish between Satan's methods and God's.

"God calls upon fathers and mothers to become intelligent in regard to the laws which govern physical life, that they may know what are and what are not correct physical habits." [24] How can parents do so when we are constantly bombarded with so much confusing misinformation about health? God has promised to give wisdom to those who obey Him; [25] hence, the first step in discerning truth from error is to follow the light we have. There is a wealth of valuable, error-detecting information in the periodical *The Health Reformer*, the book *The Ministry of Healing*, and the chapter in the book *Education* entitled "Study of Physiology." Read and study them with your children. When we obey that which God has revealed and determine to not swerve to the left or right from His commands, He will guide us concerning that which is not clearly revealed.

Practical Physiologists

"Mothers should be practical physiologists, that they may teach their children to know themselves, and to possess moral courage to carry out correct principles in defiance of the health-and-life-destroying fashions." [26] "Teach your children the principles of true health reform." [27]

The laws of health were given to us by the Creator Himself, and they are His laws. "Nothing that concerns the health of the human agent is to be regarded with indifference." [28] "Since the laws of nature are the laws of God, it is plainly our duty to give these laws careful study. We should study their requirements in regard to our own bodies and conform to them. Ignorance in these things is sin." [29]

Words of Counsel

"Students devote years to different educational lines; they become engrossed in the study of the sciences and of things in the natural world; they are intelligent on most subjects, but they do not become acquainted with themselves. They look upon the delicate human organism as something that will take care of itself; and that which is in the highest degree essential, – a knowledge of their own bodies – is neglected." [30]

"Children are to be trained to understand that every organ of the body and every faculty of the mind is the gift of a good and wise God, and that each is to be used to His glory. Right habits in eating and drinking and dressing must be insisted upon." [31]

"A judicious mother will act in training her children, not merely in regard to her own present comfort, but for their future good. And to this end she will teach her children the important lesson of controlling the appetite, and of self-denial, that they should eat, drink, and dress in reference to health." [32]

"It is woman's right to be qualified to direct the expanding minds of her children. It is her right to have an understanding of her own and her children's organisms, that she may know how to treat her children, and save them from the poisons of doctors' drugs. She may adore her gracious Creator as she contemplates how beautifully and simply nature carries on her work when she is not interfered with. She may be an intelligent nurse and physician of her own dear children, instead of leaving their precious lives in the hands of stranger physicians." [33]

"Teach your children the principles of true health reform. Teach them what things to avoid in order to preserve health." [34] "All should have an intelligent knowledge of the human frame." [35]

"Every youth should learn how to regulate his dietetic habits, – what to eat, when to eat, and how to eat." [36]

"It is important for them to understand the relation that their eating and drinking, and general habits, have to health and life." [37]

CHAPTER 18

HEALTHFUL COOKING

"It is highly essential that the art of cookery be considered one of the most important branches of education." – Counsels on Health, 145

THE skill of cooking is a science and an art, and God regards the preparation of healthful food as "a science above all other sciences"[1] and "one of the most essential arts."[2] "It is a branch of education which has a most direct influence upon health and happiness,"[3] and learning to cook healthfully is an essential component of true education. "This talent should be regarded as equal in value to ten talents; for its right use has much to do with keeping the human organism in health."[4]

Laying the Foundation

"Do not neglect to teach your children how to cook. In so doing, you impart to them principles which they must have in their religious education. In giving your children lessons in physiology, and teaching them how to cook with simplicity and yet with skill, you are laying the foundation for the most useful branches of education."[5] "There is religion in good cooking."[6] "Our bodies are constructed from what we eat; and in order to make tissues of good quality, we must have the right kind of food, and it must be prepared with such skill as will best adapt it to the wants of the system."[7]

When Should This Education Begin?

Cooking is one of the first skills that a child should learn, and lessons in cooking should take precedence over academic instruction or music lessons. "Mothers, instead of seeking to give your daughters a musical education, instruct them in these useful branches which have the closest connection with life and health. Teach them all the mysteries of cooking. Show them that this is a part of their education, and essential for them in order to become Christians."[8] "Before children take lessons on the organ or the piano they should be given lessons in cooking."[9]

What Should a Child Learn to Cook?

What should a child learn to cook? Children do not need to know, nor should they be taught, how to make cookies, cakes, pies, puddings, and other rich or fancy food; rather they should be taught to prepare *simple*, healthful food. They should know how to take produce from the garden or orchard and prepare it in a simple, wholesome, and appetizing manner. "To make food appetizing and at the same time simple and nourishing, requires skill," [10] and every child should be taught that skill.

The Benefits

The skill of cooking is foundational to further education. Cooking together can help a child learn math concepts, build language skills, increase attention span and ability to focus, improve creativity, develop patience, learn science and economics, develop cause-to-effect reasoning, improve fine motor skills and coordination, and develop decision-making skills and the ability to plan. As a child grows older, time in the kitchen will also help him to learn to read (as he reads recipes) and write (as he creates grocery lists, meal plans, or even his own recipes).

Children who regularly participate in the preparation of meals are more able to appreciate the effort that goes into their daily meals. They also tend to cultivate a more adventurous palate. And, perhaps most importantly, working together in the kitchen can build a closer bond and develop a collaborative spirit between parent and child.

How To

Once again, God's lesson books (especially the experiences of life and useful work) are perfect lesson books for teaching a child how to cook. Take your child into the kitchen with you when you are preparing meals. You will, of course, need to allow more time for meal preparation as little hands that are learning may not work as efficiently as yours, but that time will be abundantly rewarded.

Be sure to set your kitchen up for safety. For very young children, ensure that sharp knives and cleaning supplies are out of reach. Be sure to have handles of pots and pans turned toward the back of the stove to avoid accidentally bumping or tipping the pot or pan over. Avoid carrying anything hot with a toddler underfoot. And, of course, you should be in the kitchen with your young child at all times, supervising and ensuring his safety. With common-sense precautions, working together in the kitchen can be safe, fun, rewarding, and educational.

Age Two

A child as young as two years old can learn, through your example and instruction, many valuable cooking skills. A little one can stand on a chair or safety stool and wash produce, snap green beans or asparagus, tear lettuce for a salad, spread nut butter on toast, pull leaves off of strawberries or tomatoes, stir food, put water into a measuring cup, open containers, peel garlic, mash food with a fork or potato masher, add ingredients to a mixing bowl or a saucepan, scoop avocado flesh out of the half-shell, and more.

This is a good age to teach a child the importance of not tasting food or licking his fingers while cooking. Even a two-year-old can comply with this rule. Not only is this a basic sanitary rule, but it will also help a child develop self-control (an essential character trait for a Christian), as well as temperance, good reasoning, unselfishness, and patience. Instructing your child as to the reason for not eating in between meals also gives the opportunity to teach him physiology.

Age Three

A three-year-old can be taught how to bake foods such as potatoes, squash, and sweet potatoes, how to steam vegetables such as broccoli or kale, how to cook legumes, how to make bread, [11] and how to properly cook grains. [12] He can also begin to learn how to weigh and measure food. For example, if a recipe calls for three cups of oats, he can learn how to choose the correct measuring utensil, how to properly scoop the oats from their container using the measuring cup, how to level the oats to the top of the measuring cup, and how to count so as to add the correct number of cups of oats.

Parents should give opportunities for the child to develop motor skills by allowing him to transfer food from one container to another.

Expect spills; these minor mistakes will help a child develop cause-to-effect reasoning, especially if the child is expected to help clean up the spills.

Another essential skill that can be taught at this age is how to avoid wasting food. "There should be careful study that the fragments of food left over from the table be not wasted."[13] Since a child should never be coaxed to eat more than he wants (see Chapter 3), he can be taught creative ways to use the leftovers. "Study how, that in some way these fragments of food shall not be lost. This skill, economy, and tact is a fortune."[14]

Age Four

Most four-year-old children can be taught to use a safety knife to cut soft foods like bananas, cucumbers, strawberries, and cooked potatoes. (A food holder that holds the food while a child cuts can be helpful for safely keeping little fingers out of the way.) Use this opportunity to teach your child proper knife use and safety skills. For example, he should be taught to hold the knife carefully and correctly and to keep the point of the knife facing away from him. He should be taught where to put his free hand if not using a food holder. (The fingers of the hand that is holding the food should be curled under in the shape of a claw to keep fingertips out of danger.) He should also be taught when to press down to cut, when to use a sawing motion to cut, and how to use the tip-fulcrum method of cutting. If a child learns to handle a safety knife properly, then the transition to a regular knife will go more smoothly and naturally.

A four-year-old can also learn how to use a vegetable peeler to peel produce and how to use a whisk and other kitchen tools.

A child of this age should be directly involved with healthy meal planning, which would include deciding on a menu for the week and making a grocery list. Through these planning sessions, a child can be instructed on what constitutes a healthy meal, what constitutes a healthy diet, and how to make good dietary decisions.

Age Five

While caution, careful instruction, and constant supervision are in order when teaching a child to use a sharp knife, most five-year-olds are very capable of learning to safely handle a kitchen knife to slice, dice, or chop most foods. If you don't think your child is quite ready for learning to use a knife, there are several safety tools available, such as a food holder that holds the food while a child slices it, thus keeping little fingers out of the way while the child cuts food. Crinkle cutters can also be used instead of a knife, as they are easier for a child to grip.

Age Six

By age six, a child is capable of learning just about any kitchen skill with adult assistance and can be a great help in the kitchen (especially if he's had the foundational learning mentioned above in ages two through five).

Age Seven

If you have involved your child in the kitchen from his toddler years, he should now be ready to learn to plan a variety of healthful meals and prepare them with minimal help from his parents.

Tips for Happy Cooking Lessons

Every child is different, and there can be a wide range of skills within each age group, so use good judgment to adjust and customize your kitchen tasks to suit each child's maturity level.

Don't worry about messes and mistakes. Trial and error are part of the fun and contribute to learning. Have cleaning cloths nearby for your child to use if he spills something, and be flexible and patient if he measures or cuts incorrectly. As far as possible, try to refrain from criticizing your child's efforts too much or redoing his work. If he drops his rubber ball into the pot of soup, by all means, fish it out; but if the lettuce pieces are not perfectly bite-size, or the tomatoes turn to mush as he cuts them, don't stress. No one will suffer terribly if the salad isn't just right.

Keep in mind that you will have more success with involving your child in cooking responsibilities if he engages in cooking the meals on a *daily* basis rather than designating a special day on which it is his responsibility to help with the cooking.

What If I Don't Know How to Cook?

What if you don't know how to cook? A parent's lack of cooking skills gives even more reason for a child to learn how to cook! Many parents who teach their child this skill at a young age find that the child enjoys cooking so much that, within a few short years, he takes responsibility for this job, and the parents now do very little of the cooking.

But how can you teach your child to cook if *you* don't know how to cook?

Give your child a start by teaching him what you do know. Get a healthful recipe book and make a few of the recipes together. (Begin with the easier recipes. Don't try "14-Step Eggplant Involtini with Basil Pesto and Vegan Almond Ricotta" as your first dish.) Once your child has gained some basic skills and practice in the kitchen, give him some guidelines and allow him to experiment. He may have a few "fails", but children raised using the methods of true education have strong cause-to-effect reasoning and quickly learn from their mistakes. They tend to be good thinkers and very resourceful. And they are often able to figure out how to do quite a bit on their own without being taught. (See chapter 7.)

With some experience and encouragement, he will soon become an accomplished cook!

Words of Counsel

"The science of cooking is an essential science in practical life."[15]

"Mothers should teach their children how to cook. What branch of the education of a young lady can be so important as this? The eating has to do with the life."[16]

"When your daughters have families of their own, an understanding of music and fancy work will not provide for the table a well-cooked dinner."[17]

CHAPTER 19

LANGUAGE

*"O Lord, open thou my lips; and my mouth shall
shew forth thy praise." – Psalm 51:15*

ONE of the fundamental branches of learning is language study."
[1] "Unless we can clothe our ideas in appropriate language, of
what avail is our education? Knowledge will be of little value to us
unless we cultivate the talent of speech; but it is a wonderful power
when combined with the ability to speak wise, helpful words, and to
speak them in a way that will command attention." [2] "He who knows
how to use the English language [or whatever is his native language]
fluently and correctly can exert a far greater influence than one who
is unable to express his thought readily and clearly." [3]

In addition to these infinitely important reasons for good language development, research shows that having good language skills
in the toddler years leads to good reading, mathematics, and writing
ability in the later years. [4]

There are several components to language study. These include
grammar, vocabulary, communication skills, voice culture, and reading
skills. All of these are learned very well using God's lesson books.

Laying the Foundation

Before beginning any language study, parents should first be
sure to lay a good foundation. Parents can do that by consistently,
promptly, intelligently, and lovingly communicating with their baby
and toddler. Though the little interactions between parent and child
may not seem significant to the parent, they have a remarkable impact
on the areas of the brain that are directly involved in the development
of language, communication skills, academic learning, and social skills
later in the child's life. (See Chapter 4.)

In addition, an abundance of physical activity in the early years
also helps lay a solid foundation for language learning. A well-developed connection between the left and right sides of the brain is

critical for the development of good language skills, and this connection is strengthened by daily engaging in whole-body activities,
especially that which involves cross-lateral body movements (movements in which opposite sides of the body to work together, such
as crawling, climbing, hoeing, raking, skipping). (See Chapter 3.)

Learning Correct Grammar

Grammar is the code that makes language work, and correct
grammar is foundational for clear communication. Children should
be taught to use language "correctly in speaking, reading, and writing.
Too much cannot be said in regard to the importance of thoroughness
in these lines." [5] "Before attempting to study the higher branches of
literary knowledge, be sure that you thoroughly understand the simple
rules of English grammar [or the grammar of your native language]
and have learned to read and write and spell correctly. Climb the
lower rounds of the ladder before reaching for the higher rounds." [6]

How can you teach your child correct grammar?

A young child does not need language books or a curriculum
to learn proper grammar. Because God created in children a keen
ability to observe and to imitate, they learn good grammar best by
listening to their parents and those around them use good grammar
in everyday conversation.

What if the parents don't have good grammar? Since the parents'
communication with their child in the first four to six years of the
child's life will determine whether or not proper grammar comes
easily to the child in later years, the parents should get a grammar
book for *themselves* so they can brush up on proper grammar and
speak correctly with their child. If parents have good grammar, then
a child who engages in daily conversation with his parents will grow
up with good grammar, and he will not need to relearn grammar
later in life.

With this solid foundation, when a child reaches twelve or thirteen years of age, he should go through an advanced grammar book
to confirm and solidify what he has learned in everyday life, as well
as to discover any finer details of grammar learning that he didn't

learn about. This book learning should not begin before the age of ten to twelve years, and it cannot replace what the everyday use of correct grammar teaches. With a good practical foundation, that which can be learned from a book will not need to take many years.

Learning Vocabulary

When little four-year-old Madison and her family were watching her uncle repair the roof of his house, she expressed that the ladder looked to be "precariously perched" on the side of the house. Her aunt looked at the little girl with a surprised look. "How do you know such a big word?" her aunt asked.

"What word?" replied a puzzled Madison.

Madison didn't know *precarious* was a big word that only adults used; she only knew that it was a normal word in the everyday language in her family. Madison's father used the words *precarious* and *precariously* often in his everyday communication. "That block is balanced precariously on top of your block tower, Madison!" "That trail slopes at a precarious angle. I don't think we should ride our bikes down there."

Children have a greater capacity for building an extensive vocabulary bank than most parents realize; their active little minds are quick to decipher the meaning of accurately descriptive words when used in context. Since children learn what they live better than what they are taught, they best develop a rich vocabulary through immersion in intelligent and meaningful conversation, not through direct instruction or a weekly vocabulary test. "Talk to your children as if you had confidence in their intelligence." [7] A child can learn the word *train* just as well as he can learn the word *choo-choo*. If your child is old enough to notice that it's raining outside, then he is old enough to learn the word *precipitation*.

In addition to speaking to your child in an intelligent manner, set aside a few minutes every day to read to your young child from the King James Version (or similar translations) of the Bible and from the Spirit of Prophecy books. No other books can develop the mind as well as these writings can.

A rich vocabulary is a solid bedrock upon which to build overall language proficiency. Children with a broad vocabulary tend to be more proficient in all areas of academics and are better enabled to understand advanced reading material. And, because the skills of listening, speaking, reading, and writing are easier to perform with a well-developed vocabulary, a child who possesses a broad vocabulary is able to communicate better.

Keep in mind that a rich vocabulary does not mean superfluous words, fancy expressions, or jargon that unnecessarily complicates and bogs down communication. In addition, while we don't want to oversimplify our communication with our children, we should always make sure that our children understand what we are saying to them. When Jesus taught his hearers, He never introduced complex and bewildering postulations or high-sounding words to dazzle his hearers; rather, He used language that was precise, descriptive, and illustrative, yet so simple, practical, and unencumbered with unnecessary complexities that even the children could understand. A rich vocabulary, rather than complicating communication, should add clarity and detail to the communicated message so it can be comprehended with accuracy. It should enable one to "use words which express their thoughts clearly and forcibly." [8]

When we give a child the gift of a rich vocabulary, we enable him to clothe his thoughts with language that is precise, descriptive, and illustrative, to replace "common, cheap expressions" [9] with "sound, pure words," [10] and to more fully comprehend the written and spoken language of others.

Learning the Science of Conversation

Have you ever had a conversation like the following with a ten-year-old?

You: "How was your day?"

Child: "Fine."

You: "What did you do?"

Child: "Nothing."

You: "Did you and your sister help Grandma pack the Christmas boxes?

Child: "Uh-huh."

You: "What else did you do?"

Child: "I dunno."

You: "You don't know what you did?"

Child: "I dunno."

You: "So, you had a good day?"

Child: "Uh-huh."

You (desperately trying to think of how to get this child to actually communicate with you): "So, what do you think about _____?"

Child: "I dunno."

This type of communication – or lack of communication – is woefully common between parents and their children. But God would not have it thus.

A good portion of an individual's life will be spent in conversation. Even for those who are on the quiet side, conversation is an essential social skill, and our conversations with others have the power to influence lives for better or for worse. This is one reason that "the Lord requires that education should be given in the science of conversation." [11] He desires children to have the ability to communicate well and to use their communication skills for His honor. "This branch of education has been woefully neglected," [12] but this should not be the case.

Children are generally born loving to communicate. From the babbling of babies to the endless questions of toddlers, parents are given numerous opportunities to encourage good communication skills. If a child is provided with a life full of practical experiences in the context of a secure relationship with responsive parents (instead of being confined to a school desk and told to be quiet and listen), good communication skills will develop quite naturally.

Through the example and instruction of their parents in everyday conversations, children learn how to hold pleasant and considerate conversations, to communicate clearly, to look at the individual to whom they are speaking, to be careful to not interrupt, and to ask fitting questions that demonstrate an interest in another's thoughts and opinions. In this same context, a child is taught that a conversation is something to be shared – rather than one person doing all the talking, a conversation is an exchange of thoughts in which all can participate. Parents effectively teach a child this skill when they express an interest in his thoughts, attentively listen to him, and instruct him to do the same for others.

Voice Culture

Another important part of language study is voice culture. "Of all the gifts that God has bestowed upon men, none is more precious than the gift of speech. If sanctified by the Holy Spirit, it is a power for good." [13] "With the voice we convince and persuade, with it we offer prayer and praise to God, and with it we tell others of the Redeemer's love. How important, then, that it be so trained as to be most effective for good." [14]

"The education of the speech must not be neglected." [15] "The power of speech is a talent that should be diligently cultivated," [16] "carefully studied and carefully guarded." [17] "Instruction is to be constantly given to encourage the children in the formation of correct habits in speech, in voice, in deportment." [18] "Education falls short if students do not obtain a knowledge of how to use the faculty of speech, and how to use to the best advantage the education they have obtained." [19]

Voice culture begins with proper breathing.

In order to learn to speak correctly, we must first learn to breathe correctly. Since breathing is something that is automatic for us, we sometimes assume we don't need to be taught to breathe correctly; and this is true to some extent. As babies and toddlers, most of us breathed correctly. But by the time we reached late childhood, many of us were no longer breathing the way our bodies were designed to breathe.

So, what happened between toddlerhood and late childhood? Not enough happened – not enough physical activity, that is. A child's body needs hours and hours of physical activity every day to develop all the organs and their functions properly. But in our modern society, the typical child spends several hours every day sitting. And all this sitting fosters anatomically incorrect breathing. [20] Instead of using the muscles that were designed for breathing to take a breath, the child's body learns to use the shoulder, chest, neck, and back muscles to breathe, which strains muscles that weren't meant to be used for breathing, weakens those that were, and does not supply sufficient air to the bottom of lungs. (Improper breathing also has a negative effect on digestion, cognitive function, the liver, blood circulation, mood and behavior, sleep, and immunity, and can cause back pain and neck pain.)

To breathe correctly, the diaphragm should contract downward, and the lower abdomen should expand. This diaphragmatic breathing draws oxygen down into the bottom of the lungs. Then, as we exhale, the diaphragm should relax back to its original state and the abdomen come back in.

Parents should ensure that their child gets an abundance of outdoor exercise and should avoid requiring him to sit too much. They should also impress upon their child the importance and many benefits of good posture and breathing correctly and deeply. [21]

Voice culture involves learning to speak clearly.

As a child grows older and is able to pronounce words correctly, he should be taught to "speak plainly and clearly, in full, round tones," [22] and "to speak so plainly that the listeners can understand every word." [23] "Every word, every syllable, should be plainly spoken," [24] "every sentence clear and distinct to the very last word." [25]

Voice culture involves learning to read correctly.

"The science of reading correctly and with the proper emphasis, is of highest value. No matter how much knowledge you may have acquired in other lines, if you have neglected to cultivate your voice and manner of speech so that you can speak and read distinctly and intelligently, all your learning will be of but little profit." [26]

A child should be "taught to read and speak slowly and distinctly, with clearness and force, placing the emphasis where it belongs." [27]

If a child has learned to read accordant with God's natural schedule of development (see Chapters 5 and 25), and he has learned to speak distinctly and in clear, full, round tones, then, more often than not, he will *naturally* read out loud with the same distinct, smooth, unhalted, clear expression as he does when he speaks. If this is not the case, the parent should gently help the child to read distinctly and with proper emphasis. However, this type of reading instruction should not be given until after the child has a good foundation for learning and is comfortable with reading. (See Chapters 3 and 4 for how to lay a good foundation.) Rushing instruction on reading properly can cause frustration for the child and foster a dislike for reading.

The Chief Requisite

In the subject of language, there is another consideration of great significance that should in no way be neglected.

The talent of speech is a gift of God, and we must teach our children to use this talent as He wants us to use it. No "useless, meaningless chit-chat," [28] "no evil speaking, no frivolous talk, no fretful repining or impure suggestion, will escape the lips of him who is following Christ." [29] "The Lord is greatly dishonored when cheap, frivolous words fall from the lips." [30] "All frivolity, all cheapness of conversation, all jesting and joking, weakens the soul, and weans the heart from prayer." [31] "Upon every family, upon every individual Christian, is laid the duty of barring the way against corrupt speech. When in the company of those who indulge in foolish talk, it is our duty to change the subject of conversation if possible. By the help of the grace of God we should quietly drop words or introduce a subject that will turn the conversation into a profitable channel." [32] Parents should be intentional in teaching their children this skill.

"God's word condemns also the use of those meaningless phrases and expletives that border on profanity. It condemns the deceptive compliments, the evasions of truth, the exaggerations, the misrepresentations in trade, that are current in society and in the business world. 'Let your speech be, Yea, yea; Nay, nay: and whatsoever is more than these is of the evil one.'" [33]

Gossip and criticism should also be strictly avoided. "This habit reveals a lack of culture and refinement and of true goodness of heart; it unfits one both for the society of the truly cultured and refined in this world and for association with the holy ones of heaven." [34] "Closely allied to gossip is the covert insinuation, the sly innuendo, by which the unclean in heart seek to insinuate the evil they dare not openly express. Every approach to these practices the youth should be taught to shun as they would shun the leprosy." [35]

In addition, we should carefully consider the reading material and other media to which we expose our children. Many Christian books and other seemingly good material for children – such as character-building stories, children's Bible stories (especially those that are dramatized), historical stories, and missionary stories – fall short of the admonition that we have to think on that which is true, pure, and lovely, [36] to speak "only words of gentleness, truth, and purity." [37] To make the stories interesting, sometimes the voices in the stories are rough, unkind, or rude. To teach a moral lesson, the children in the story may speak and act in ways out of harmony with how God would have children speak and act. While these stories may seem innocent enough to our adult senses, this material introduces into the mind of a young child speech that is unbecoming of a Christian.

A Christian's voice "is to be used in talking of those things which increase love for Jesus." [38] "We should speak of the mercy and loving-kindness of God, of the matchless depths of the Saviour's love. Our words should be words of praise and thanksgiving." [39] "Educate your children to speak words that will bring sunshine and joy." [40] "We should do as Christ did. Wherever He was, in the synagogue, by the wayside, in the boat thrust out a little from the land, at the Pharisee's feast or the table of the publican, He spoke to men of the things pertaining to the higher life. ... So it should be with us. Wherever we are, we should watch for opportunities of speaking to others of the Saviour. If we follow Christ's example in doing good, hearts will open to us as they did to Him. Not abruptly, but *with tact* born of divine love, we can tell them of Him who is the 'Chiefest among ten thousand' and the One 'altogether lovely.' Song of Solomon 5:10, 16. This is the very highest work in which we can employ the talent of speech. It was given to us that we might present Christ as the sin-pardoning Saviour." [41] Therefore, one of the main components of the subject of language study should be to learn to "pass easily and courteously from subjects of a temporal nature to the spiritual and eternal." [42] Parents should take the time to teach their children how to tactfully do so.

"Out of the abundance of the heart the mouth speaketh." [43] "If the mind and heart are full of the love of God, this will be revealed in the conversation." [44] "Our words index the state of our heart." [45] "If Christ is abiding in the soul there will come forth from the treasure house of the heart words which are pure and uplifting; if Christ is not abiding there, a satisfaction will be found in frivolity, in jesting and joking, which is a hindrance to spiritual growth and a cause of grief to the angels of God." [46]

"The chief requisite of language is that it be pure and kind and true – 'the outward expression of an inward grace.'" [47]

There is no need to despair if you are in the habit of speaking in a way that does not bring honor to God. By His power we can change. The tongue can and "should be converted; for the talent of speech is a very precious talent. Christ is ever ready to impart of His riches, and we should gather the jewels that come from Him, that, when we speak, these jewels may drop from our lips." [48]

Words of Counsel

"The best school for this language study is the home." [49]

"It is the work of parents to train their children to proper habits of speech." [50]

"Of the Levites who read the Scriptures to the people in the days of Ezra, it is said, 'They read in the book in the law of God distinctly, and gave the sense, and caused them to understand the reading.' Nehemiah 8:8." [51]

"They [parents] should teach them to read the Bible with clear, distinct utterance in a way that will honor God. And let not those who kneel around the family altar put their faces in their hands close down to the chair when they address God. Let them lift up their heads and with holy awe speak to their heavenly Father, uttering their words in tones that can be heard." [52]

"The great responsibility bound up in the use of the gift of speech is plainly made known by the Word of God. 'By thy words thou shalt be justified, and by thy words thou shalt be condemned,' Christ declared." [53]

"We should receive the education essential in the line of conversation that we may know how to speak right words and how to speak in a proper tone, that our words may be a power for good. The truth is no truth to us unless it is brought into the inner courts of the soul. When this is done, our words are a channel through which truth is communicated to others. Sow the seed beside all waters, not knowing which shall prosper, either this or that. But be constantly educating yourself in how to use properly the faculty of speech." [54]

CHAPTER 20

MISSIONARY TRAINING

"The Great Commission is not an option to be considered; it is a command to be obeyed." – Hudson Taylor

THE best education that can be given to children and youth is that which bears the closest relation to the future, immortal life. This kind of education should be given by godly parents, by devoted teachers, and by the church, to the end that the youth in turn may become zealous missionaries for either home or foreign fields."[1] "We are under sacred covenant with God to rear our children for His service. To surround them with such influences as shall lead them to choose a life of service, and to give them the training needed, is our first duty."[2]

"True education is missionary training"[3] and "prepares the student for the joy of service in this world."[4] "Children are to be trained to become missionaries,"[5] "and to fit them for this service should be the object of education."[6]

Do not wait until a child is in his teens before giving him training in missionary work. This training should commence in toddlerhood and continue throughout life. Children "should be trained and educated and disciplined for the service of God in their earliest years."[7] "Every youth, every child, has a work to do for the honor of God and the uplifting of humanity."[8] "Even in their early years they can be missionaries for God."[9] "God has a work for every one of them."[10]

Training a child for missionary service not only benefits others, but it also provides a child with the highest mental, physical, and spiritual development that he can have. "Unselfishness underlies all true development. Through unselfish service we receive the highest culture of *every* faculty."[11]

How to Train Your Child to Be a Missionary

1. Training begins in the home.

While we usually think of missionary training as something that happens at a mission training school, true missionary training begins in the home. When a child gives up a chair for his grandma, gets a glass of water for his mom, or cleans his father's shoes, he is developing the spirit of unselfishness, which underlies all missionary effort. "If they [children] ever learn to do genuine missionary work for others, they must first learn to labor for those at home, who have a natural right to their offices of love. Every child should be trained to bear his respective share of service in the home." [12] This training is the preparatory training for wider service.

Children "should be so educated that it will be their pleasure to relieve the cares of their toil-worn fathers and mothers." [13] "How many hours are wasted by children and youth which might be spent in taking upon their strong young shoulders, and assisting to lift the family responsibilities which someone must bear, thus showing a loving interest in father and mother." [14]

"Fathers and mothers should feel that there is most sacred missionary work to be done in their own home, in their own family, that the members of the family may become missionaries in every sense of the word." [15] "In the home they can be trained to do missionary work that will prepare them for wider spheres of usefulness. Parents, help your children to fulfil God's purpose for them. ... Teach them that God has a part for them in his great work." [16]

2. Include medical missionary training.

An essential component of missionary training involves medical missionary training. "In the work of the gospel, teaching and healing are never to be separated." [17] "Let no line be drawn between the genuine medical missionary work and the gospel ministry." [18] "Genuine medical missionary work is the gospel practiced." [19] "The light God has given on health reform is for our salvation and the salvation of the world." [20] "The work of health reform is the Lord's means for lessening suffering in our world *and* for purifying His church." [21]

Again, this training can be done in the home. Through practical, everyday lessons, teach your children how to live healthfully, how to prevent sickness and disease, how to do basic first aid, and how to treat illnesses with the use of God's natural remedies, such as hydrotherapy, charcoal, and other simple remedies. [22] Show them how to "pray for the sick, ministering to their necessities, not with drugs, but with nature's remedies, and teaching them how to regain health and avoid disease." [23]

3. Make missionary work a priority.

A crucial step in training our children to be missionaries is to teach them that this work is a priority in life. As we place the salvation of souls, including those of our children, far above any temporal concerns and accordingly work earnestly with our children toward that goal, our children will catch the same spirit. If this concern is placed above all others, it will be reflected in the day-to-day decisions we make, such as what we spend our time on, what we train our children to do, how closely we follow God's plan of education, and what careers we encourage our children to choose.

4. Help those in need.

"When our own homes are what they should be, our children will not be allowed to grow up in idleness and indifference to the claims of God in behalf of the needy all about them." [24] Instead, they "should be led to consecrate themselves to God, whose they are by creation and by redemption. They should be taught that all their powers of body, mind, and soul are His. They should be trained to help in various lines of unselfish service." [25]

"The children should be so educated that they will sympathize with the aged and afflicted and will seek to alleviate the sufferings of the poor and distressed. They should be taught to be diligent in missionary work; and from their earliest years self-denial and sacrifice for the good of others and the advancement of Christ's cause should be inculcated, that they may be laborers together with God." [26]

5. Don't wait.

Mission work is not an activity to be done on school breaks or when a child reaches his teen years. Every child, from a young age, should be taught and given experience in self-sacrifice for the good of others in everyday life. [27]

"Whether in the home, the neighborhood, or the school, the presence of the poor, the afflicted, the ignorant, or the unfortunate should be regarded, not as a misfortune, but as affording precious opportunity for service. In this work, as in every other, skill is gained in the work itself. It is by training in the *common* duties of life and in ministry to the needy and suffering, that efficiency is assured. Without this the best-meant efforts are often useless and even harmful. It is in the water, not on the land, that men learn to swim." [28]

True Education

In an article appropriately entitled "Awake Out of Sleep," parents are admonished, "How carefully should the little ones be trained for the service of the Lord." [29] "Children and youth may be trained in such a way as to become workers in the Master's vineyard. The Lord desires them in his service, and looks to parents to train them in such a way as to make them missionaries at home and abroad. ... If parents had not neglected the fulfilling of their responsibilities in doing their parental duties to their children, there would not be so few children and youth enlisted as young soldiers in Christ's army." [30]

"Children are a heritage of the Lord, and are to be trained for His service. This is the work that rests upon parents and teachers with solemn, sacred force, which they cannot evade or ignore." [31] "What excuse can the professed followers of Christ offer for neglecting to train their children to work for Him?" [32]

"Train them to do missionary work." [33]

Words of Counsel

"There is earnest work to be done in this age, and parents should educate their children to share in it." [34]

"Children are to be instructed in the special truths for this time and in practical missionary work." [35]

"Health reform and medical missionary work are to be bound up with the preaching of the gospel." [36]

"If you will educate and train your children here for the future, immortal life, whom do you have to help you? – Christ Himself. He has said, 'Suffer little children to come unto Me, and forbid them not; for of such is the kingdom of heaven.' This is our work. And then, fathers and mothers, you have the children entrusted to you of God, to help you in missionary efforts." [37]

"Not only words, but deeds, not only the affections of the heart, but the service of the life, must be devoted to our Maker." [38]

"God desires them to be taught that they are in this world for useful service, not merely for play." [39]

"Unless we understand the importance of the moments that are swiftly passing into eternity, and make ready to stand in the great day of God, we shall be unfaithful stewards." [40]

CHAPTER 21

SOCIAL SKILLS

"A man that hath friends must shew himself friendly." – *Proverbs 18:24*

L ITTLE four-year-old Hudson has no siblings, lives out in the country with very few neighbors around, has few interactions with children his age, and doesn't go to school. Yet Hudson exhibits some extraordinary social skills for a four-year-old. Though he's not at all outgoing (his natural personality is quiet, humble, and contemplative), he's always the first to say hello, whether being introduced to someone new or seeing a familiar friend at church. He smiles, makes eye contact, and reaches out his hand to whomever he is greeting. At church, he is happy to visit with all ages, and he often makes sure he talks to someone he thinks may be lonely, whether the three-year-old or the eighty-year-old. How did Hudson become such a genuinely kind and friendly young boy? Some may argue that he was naturally that way, but since "children are what their parents make them by their instruction, discipline, and example,"[1] we could logically conclude that his parents had at least some influence on the development of his social skills, and in Hudson's case, our conclusion would be correct. We'll examine what his parents did in a moment, but first, we'll take a look at why the development of social skills is an essential part of true education.

The Importance of Social Skills

How important is it for children to be taught social skills? How important is it that children are well socialized? Is instruction in social competence an essential part of true education?

At its core, socialization has much to do with character development, which is an essential aspect of true education. True social skills include character traits such as consideration, kindness, respectfulness, unselfishness, and politeness. Furthermore, life is largely about relationships, and good social skills enable children and adults to relate well to others and even to be more successful in life. [2]

Most importantly, it is through our social influence and interactions with others that we and our children can work for Christ and win souls for Him.

Christian sociability is a "branch of education [that] should not be neglected or lost sight of." [3] "Especially should those who have tasted the love of Christ develop their social powers, for in this way they may win souls to the Saviour." [4]

How can we properly educate our children in Christian sociability?

Healthy Socialization vs Unhealthy Socialization

Our society, for the most part, is of the opinion that children must be with other children for them to learn to socialize. However, spending the first several years of life primarily with those of one's own age is a narrow, limiting, and restrictive form of socialization, and does not prepare a child for real life because in real life we must be able to interact with those of all ages.

Very young children naturally love to learn from those who have more wisdom and experience than they (hence the millions of questions); but when surrounded by those who are his own age, there is very little that a child can learn since his companions are at about the same maturity level as he is, and they still have much to learn in the area of social graces. Since there is little to learn from one another, children in this environment learn to compete and conform, and the risk of developing peer dependency increases.

In contrast, the socialization that can happen in the context of a loving, warm, stable, Christ-centered family is broad and abundant. As a child lives life with his family, he can learn to relate to people of all ages, not just those who were born in the same year in which he was born. A loving home environment provides a young child with unpressured time to develop emotional security and identity rather than requiring him to be immersed in an environment in which he must compete for a position of acceptance by his peers. In a Christian home, he is encouraged in good behavior and is free from pressure to participate in negative forms of behavior in order to be accepted by the other children. He can be given numerous, real-life opportunities to develop, practice, and improve the social traits in a supportive and loving environment that is void of peer pressure and other negative types of socialization. In this positive social environment, a child can gain social competency without losing his individuality. He can learn to define himself by what God thinks of him instead of by what his peers think of him. He can be taught to think for himself and yet still be considerate of others. He can be taught to honor authority yet not unthinkingly conform to societal norms. Values are handed down from parent to child, not passed on horizontally from child to child. As child psychologist David Elkind, in his book *The Hurried Child*, points out, "The family is a school of human relations in which children learn how to live within a society."⁵ There is no better place for the development of good social skills than in the family.

But My Child Needs Friends!

Yes, your child does need friends. He needs friends who love him deeply, who are wise enough and mature enough to give him good advice, who are consistently a good example to him, who are genuinely interested in his well-being, who accept and love him as he is, and who build rather than hinder the development of emotional security so crucial at his young age. He needs his loving *parents* to be his friends, and until conditioned otherwise, children instinctively look for this valuable friendship from their parents. ⁶

Children have a strong tendency to conform to their environment. God created them this way so that they would readily adopt the values of their parents. But when we place a child with other children, the social needs that God intended to be met by the child's parents are now met by his peers. In this environment, a child, with his immature reasoning skills, judgment, and emotional processing, learns to look to his peers as his behavioral models. He learns to look to them for advice and direction and to use their feedback, instead of that of his parents, as an assessment of his self-worth. Children are naturally prone to be influenced by their companions, and when those companions are those of their same age instead of their parents, it isn't long before they learn to care more about what their peers think than what their parents think. They eventually become averse to being different from their peers, and they develop indifference to family values and resistance to their parents' guidance.

Even if a child is fortunate enough to acquire wholesome friends who are good examples to him, peer dependence is dangerous. Research shows that peer dependency contributes to feelings of insecurity and moral dependence. [7] Just as Joseph and Daniel, to be faithful to God, had to take a stand contrary to everyone around them, so our children will be required to do the same if they will be true to God. "It is the privilege of the young people of today to be as firm and true ... as were the Jewish youths in the kingdom of Babylon." [8] "God honored Daniel, and he will honor every youth who takes the course that Daniel took in honoring God." [9]

It is one of Satan's most well-accepted lies that children should be socialized by other children. Very young children crave connection and friendship with their parents. [10] When parents are willing to put their own desires aside so as "to devote more time and attention to the children," [11] to show an interest in what interests them, to talk with them, to listen to them, to work with them, to be a friend to their children, then a more secure relationship will be formed between parent and child. The more secure the relationship is between parent and child, the more immune the child will be to peer pressure and peer dependence. He will learn to turn to his parents, and ultimately to God, for guidance rather than turning to his peers for direction in his life.

"Burdened with many cares, mothers sometimes feel that they can not take time patiently to instruct their little ones, and give them love and sympathy. But they should remember that if the children do not find in their parents and in their home that which will satisfy their desire for sympathy and companionship, they will look to other sources, where both mind and character may be endangered. Give some of your leisure hours to your children; become acquainted with them; associate with them in their work and in their sports, and win their confidence. Cultivate friendship with them. In this way you will be a strong influence for good," [12] and children can learn healthy socialization within the family.

How To Teach Social Skills

So, how did quiet little Hudson develop such exceptional social skills at such a young age? Here are twelve principles that his parents followed in their child-rearing practices that contributed to the development of such a sweet, friendly boy.

1. Build the proper foundation.

To build a solid house, you must first have a solid foundation. Building social skills is like building a house – a good foundation is essential for the proper development of social competence. The foundation for natural and fluent social ability lies primarily in the development of emotional security and a solid development of self-regulation. [13] Babies who have secure attachments with their mother have larger grey matter volume in the brain regions involved in social and emotional functioning, grow to be more socially competent, and tend to develop better relationships later in life than do those who do not have this attachment. [14]

Interestingly, research also shows that breastfeeding contributes greatly toward the emotional development of a child, and there is a significant positive relationship between *extended* breastfeeding and social development. [15] In the words of the researchers, "there are statistically significant tendencies for conduct disorder scores to decline with increasing duration of breastfeeding." [16] Simply put, breastfeeding well into the toddler years can help a child become more emotionally and socially healthy.

Babies develop emotional security through a close mother-child bond in which the mother is consistently available, nurturing, and responsive, and it is with this secure attachment that the proper foundation for socialization is laid. [17] If a child does not have this secure attachment, he is more likely to exhibit negative behavior like attention-seeking, stubbornness, boasting, incessant talking, or reclusiveness, selfishness, fighting, arguing, and/or temper tantrums. [18] Obviously, none of these behaviors contribute to social competence.

2. Treat your baby with respect and attentiveness.

Social competence involves the ability to communicate and

interact effectively with others, and the foundation for this ability is laid in babyhood primarily through how parents interact with their baby. To encourage the development of good social skills, we should pay attention to how we communicate and interact with our little ones.

Consider this simple interaction I observed between nine-month-old Bethany and her parents. Bethany was contentedly sitting on Dad's lap at the table as he and Mom were enjoying visiting with some friends. Bethany was amusing herself by repeatedly hugging her toy rabbit, placing it on the table, picking it up again, hugging it, and then putting it back on the table. When Robert, her five-year-old brother, called for Dad, Dad handed Bethany to Mom so he could attend to their son. Bethany was content to be with Mom, but when she stretched out her hand for her rabbit, she discovered that it was no longer within reach. Bethany looked up at Mom and reached out her hand again, trying to communicate with her mother that she couldn't reach her rabbit, but though Mom was somewhat attentive to her baby, she was also engaged in conversation with her friends and didn't realize that Bethany was looking up at her. Bethany tried again to reach her rabbit. No success. She looked up at her mom again and made a baby noise that perhaps meant something like, "Mom, could you just scoot a few inches forward to allow me to reach my rabbit?" This baby babble was the beginning of the development of good communication and social skills, but her mom didn't realize this. Instead of trying to understand what her baby was trying to communicate, she smiled at her and then went back to the conversation. Bethany realized Mom wasn't listening, so she tried to squirm out of her mom's arms so she could reach her rabbit. Mom was attentive enough to her little one to interpret the squirming as a desire to reposition, so she turned Bethany around to face Mom. This was frustrating for Bethany because all she wanted was her rabbit, and now she was even farther from it. And perhaps even stronger than the desire for the rabbit was this little one's desire for someone to be attentive and listen to her.

(I want to note here that it is perfectly acceptable for parents to tell their child that he may not have something he desires, but if Mom did not want Bethany to have the rabbit, she should have first given her baby her

full attention, listened to her request, acknowledged her request, kindly explained to her that she didn't want her to play with the rabbit anymore, and suggested something else she could do. But as it was, Bethany's attempt at communicating with her mom was not reciprocated.)

Understandably, Bethany began to whine and squirm some more. Mom looked at her baby and asked her what was wrong. By this time, Bethany had already spent at least five minutes futilely trying to communicate what she wanted and was now too frustrated to try to respond to her mom in a polite manner. When Bethany whined again, Mom said, "I think you're getting tired. You need a nap." This made Bethany even more frustrated, and she started crying. At which point, Mom put the baby in a sleeping position, grabbed Bethany's blanket and her rabbit, and declared, "Time for a nap."

Incidents like this are all too common in parent-baby relationships because parents are typically too distracted, not sufficiently attentive, and do not realize how capable of communicating a baby is. The result is poor behavior on the part of the child as he struggles to make sense of the inconsistencies in his daily social experiences. In the case of Bethany, Mom not only missed an opportunity to model respectfulness and good social skills with Bethany, but she also confused her little one as she wouldn't give her the rabbit upon polite requests (her attempts to let her mom know that she couldn't reach her rabbit), but then *did* give her the rabbit once she whined and cried. She essentially taught Bethany that polite communication is futile and that whining may just be the best way to get what you want.

When parents are attentive to a baby's quiet and subtle communications, responding appropriately to his gestures and facial expressions, listening to him, and looking at him while talking to him, they teach their little one about how healthy and polite communication works. Research shows that mothers who are exceptionally attentive to their babies, who understand that babies' babblings and other expressions have meaning and consistently respond to them appropriately, are more likely to have toddlers who comfortably communicate with adults, have more advanced reasoning skills, better self-regulation skills, more advanced perspective-taking abilities, better understanding of emotions, and better ability to discern the feelings of others [19] – all of which are important for the development of social capability.

3. Do life with your child.

Even though Hudson (the little boy at the beginning of this chapter) had very few interactions with children his age, he did have an abundance of social interaction with his parents as he and his parents lived life together. When parents spend their day with their children in work and recreation, they provide well for their social needs and contribute to the development of social skills. Children "sense that they are integral parts of the family corporation. This feeling of belongingness and of the privilege of helping brings a sound sense of self-worth and altruism which are the crucial foundation stones of positive sociability."[20] Children who have this secure feeling of belongingness tend to relate well to others, even those outside their age group. In addition, they are less likely to become peer dependent.

4. Don't speak for your child.

Parents often make the mistake of acting as their child's interpreter when they are in social settings. I recently met a sweet and very interesting three-year-old boy and was eager to get to know him better, but every time I tried to make conversation with him, his mother would answer for him. His mother was probably trying to be helpful, but she was stealing from him both the need and the opportunity to learn social skills.

Don't speak for your child. Even if you think he doesn't have a response (or the correct response) when someone is addressing him, expect that he will answer for himself. Your expectation will be a stimulus for him to develop good social skills.

5. Provide an age-integrated environment.

Strong intergenerational relationships were the norm for thousands of years. Families – little babies, older siblings, mothers, fathers, aunts, uncles, and grandparents – worked together, played together, ate together, worshiped together, and socialized together. The younger generation cared for the older generation, and the older generation imparted wisdom to the younger generation. In this diverse environment, young children easily and naturally learned many valuable social skills. It is only in the past one hundred years or so that we have begun to use an artificially-contrived sorting mechanism of segregating children by age and compelling children and adults to reside in two separate worlds, inevitably sending the message that shared values and mutual understanding cannot exist between different generations.

Age segregation robs children of social interactions and experiences that cannot be had in an age-integrated environment. It robs the child's mind of the stimulation it can receive from being around people who think from a different perspective. It robs them of true and deep connection and wisdom. It robs them of experiences that teach loving cooperation, humility, and selflessness. It robs them of the gift of *true* socialization.

Give your child opportunities to interact with those of various ages. Seek out an elderly person who could benefit from a visit or help from you and your child. Teach your child how to be a polite listening ear to an elderly person who needs someone to talk to. Teach him to be interested in the lives of others. Encourage your child to start his own small business in which he will have opportunities to interact with others of various ages. Consider becoming a part of an age-integrated family class at church so your child can be exposed to the thoughts and ideas of various ages. Seek out opportunities to help extended family, friends, and neighbors. Children benefit immensely by learning to feel comfortable with all ages – from tiny babies to the elderly.

6. Avoid placing your child in the front.

"Nathan, show Grandma how you can count to twenty."

"Alina, tell Aunty Eva your memory verse."

It's natural for parents to enjoy watching their children demonstrate their abilities and talents in front of others, yet most parents do not realize how damaging it is to a child to be put on display.

Children are especially impressionable when young, and the experiences of their younger years play a significant role in shaping their understanding of their value and identity. When young children are placed in the spotlight, when we encourage them to do special music at church, say their memory verse in front of others, perform at music recitals, and engage in similar activities, they learn to find their identity and worth through the eyes of those who admire them and praise them for their talents and abilities.

This, of course, is very damaging to a young child and can contribute to feelings of insecurity or pride or anxiety. [21] We don't want our children to shape their sense of worth on something so fragile and defective as the praise and opinions of others. Rather, we want our children to see themselves through the eyes of their Creator who loves them in spite of all their mistakes and flaws. We want our children to find their identity in Christ.

"It is not wise to give [children] special notice." [22] We should "leave them as far as possible to the simplicity of their childhood. One great reason why so many children are forward, bold, and impertinent [traits that do not contribute to good social skills], is they are noticed and praised too much." [23] While our society has normalized this behavior, our heavenly Father calls us to teach our children humility. Parents who come to understand the true ideal of character "will not encourage in the youth the desire or effort to display their ability or proficiency. He who looks higher than himself will be humble." [24]

7. Provide social environments that are good for character development.

On this same note, it is common for adults in conversation with a child to flatter or praise him, telling him how "cute" or "smart" he is, instead of simply engaging with him politely and intelligently like they would with an adult. Flattery is damaging to a child and does nothing toward helping him develop good social skills. Do what you can to limit this type of socialization and instead choose for your child social settings in which adults engage with your child intelligently and genuinely.

8. Don't push.

If your child is timid or shy in social situations or simply prefers to be with his parents, do not push him to be more social. While parents should always require politeness of a child, they should remember that a child needs to feel emotionally secure before he can develop true social competence. [25] When Hudson was three years old, he was very attached to his mother, and many of his relatives were quite concerned that he was too dependent on and too attached to her. But his parents were not concerned. They focused on providing emotional security, patiently and consistently taught him good social skills, and helped him to develop at his own pace and in the context of a secure relationship with his family. And Hudson grew to be a kind and friendly young boy.

Children who are provided with a good foundation of emotional security *naturally* develop higher levels of social competence than those who are pushed to be social. [26] "Meeting a child's dependency needs is the key to helping that child achieve independence." [27]

9. Avoid electronic devices.

God created us as social beings, and a child's brain especially seeks relationship. Because electronic devices activate the same neural circuitry and release many of the same brain chemicals as does a relationship, children are attracted to these devices to meet that need for connectedness. But electronic devices do not truly satisfy a child's relationship needs. In addition, the use of electronic devices can cause damage to many areas of the brain. Research reveals a connection between the use of these devices and increased levels of anxiety, depression, and other mental health issues. [28] Electronic devices not only offer nothing in the way of social-emotional development, but they can actually *hinder* good development.

10. Choose quality over quantity.

While we do want our children to have social interactions, we want these interactions to be meaningful and of value. The more people around a child, the fewer meaningful interactions he may have. Children who have fewer, yet deeper and more meaningful friendships, like those that can be found between siblings or between parent and child, tend to have a better sense of self-worth than children who have an abundance of friends.

11. Operate within God's schedule.

Children whose early years are filled with physical activity, practical work, and time with family tend to be more socially adept, have less difficulty with self-regulation, and have fewer emotional and social challenges than those who begin academics before this age. [29] Beginning school before age eight to ten hinders the development of brain areas that are involved with social skills.

Dr. Raymond Moore, in his book *Better Late Than Early*, says, "The child who remains at home with a mother and shares the tasks of the home appears to develop self-respect and a sense of responsibility and values not shared by the child who started school earlier. These values, in turn, seem to bring with them a certain *social and emotional stability* that is difficult otherwise to achieve." [30] (See Chapter 5 for more information on God's schedule.)

12. Remember the purpose of socialization.

Hudson's remarkable social skills did not come about by chance. His parents followed God's divine plan of education, including teaching their little one the true purpose of socialization. While friendships are enjoyable, the purpose of socialization is not only for our own pleasure. Through precept and example, we can teach our children that their social abilities are to be used for the honor of God, for the purpose that "they may win souls to the Saviour." [31] We are not only to be friends with those we like or who make us happy. Children should "be taught the Christlikeness of exhibiting a kindly interest, a social disposition, toward those who are in the greatest need, even though these may not be their own chosen companions." [32] Children must know and understand that "they are not independent atoms, but that each one is a thread which is to unite with other threads in composing a fabric." [33] As Christians, we are not to seek our own good, but to seek to make a positive difference in the lives of others.

An Important Part of True Education

Christian sociability is an important part of true education. And young children, with their immature reasoning abilities and under-developed sense of social-emotional security, were designed to be socialized primarily in the family at least until around eight to ten years of age. While self-centeredness, peer dependence, insecurity, and competition are readily cultivated among children who are so-cialized among their peers, a child who is nurtured within a family setting where he senses that he is a needed part of the functioning of the family is better able to develop the tools he needs for good social skills and "largely avoids the dismal pitfalls and social cancer of peer dependency."[34] Because social skills are important for reaching others for Christ, parents should take care, using God's methods, to help their children to become socially competent.

Words of Counsel

"The family firm is a sacred, social society, in which each member is to act a part, each helping the other."[35]

"The dangers of the young are greatly increased as they are thrown into the society of a large number of their own age."[36]

"The family circle is the school in which the child receives its first and most enduring lessons. Hence parents should be much at home. By precept and example, they should teach their children the love and the fear of God; teach them to be intelligent, social, affectionate, to cultivate habits of industry, economy, and self-denial. By giving their children love, sympathy, and encouragement at home, parents may provide for them a safe and welcome retreat from many of the world's temptations."[37]

CHAPTER 22

CAUSE-TO-EFFECT REASONING

"Teach your children to reason from cause to effect."
– Counsels on Education, 173

I spent some time in the rural countryside of Tanzania, and in the area where I was, most cooking was done outdoors over a fire of wood or charcoal, sometimes under a roof and sometimes not. There were typically one or two young children (under the age of five) working with their mothers around the fire, often poking a very long, wooden spoon into the pot of whatever was cooking. In their laughter and happy activities, the children were often – what seemed to me – precariously close to the fire, and many times I felt my stress level rise as I observed a child just inches from getting burned. Yet, never did I witness a child get hurt, nor did I hear a mother warn her child not to get too close to the fire. Perhaps the admonition had been given to each child months previous when he graduated from the kanga (a wrap that mothers wore and babies seemed to live in for the first two years of life), but there was certainly no continued and repeated instruction from the mother on this subject, and the children were never forbidden to be in the kitchen with their mother (as they perhaps would have been had North American parents been making the rules).

One afternoon, while spending a couple of hours scrubbing potatoes and cleaning pots in one of these outdoor kitchens with a particularly adorable four-year-old, I was contemplating the risks of these small ones being so close to danger. As I thought, I had to admit that even though the children were often too close to the fire for the comfort of my North-American-way-of-thinking brain, it was clear that the little ones were noticeably cautious in their step and careful with their movements. And I had several times witnessed a little one checking the proximity of his clothing to the fire and even feeling it with his little hand to make sure his clothing wasn't too hot.

A year or so later, I was still occasionally contemplating the differences in child-raising methods among various cultures when

I heard a wise, elderly man make a comment during a conversation that involved teaching children. "If we do that," he quietly said after listening to another's plans for a particular type of learning program, "then we will have to help them learn for the rest of their life." This discerning man understood how children learn. He understood that an approach that merely instructs without giving children hands-on, real-life experience, an approach that removes opportunities for children to learn from their mistakes, greatly hinders the development of their thinking abilities, including cause-to-effect reasoning.

Upon reflection, I realized that the mothers of the little children in the outdoor kitchens of Tanzania did not need to tell their children to be careful around the fire. Why? Because they *already* were being careful. How did these children learn to be careful? It wasn't due to the fact that their mothers had nagged them a hundred times until the admonition was so ingrained in their heads that they could not forget it. And (thankfully) it wasn't due to the fact that the children had previously wandered too close to the fire and been burned. Rather, it was due to both the activities and the cultural mindset in which these children were daily immersed from birth. Through babyhood and toddlerhood, these children were continually in an environment in which they were working with their parents and other adults. This type of environment develops in a child the ability and habit to closely observe and to learn through observation. [1] In addition, by age four, these children had already experienced the consequences of being required to carry another pitcher of water back from the well because they had accidentally spilled the water that had been brought earlier that morning. They had already experienced what it felt like to drop a large, heavy piece of wood on their toe because they weren't carrying it carefully. They had already experienced a grumbling stomach when they hadn't started washing the potatoes soon enough, and lunch was consequently delayed.

These little children were well on their way to developing mature cause-to-effect reasoning even at a young age because they daily worked with their parents in real-life activities, and their parents did not constantly warn them or rescue them from the consequences of their actions. And when they were in those little outdoor kitchens with no barrier between them and the fire, they were remarkably attentive to any instruction from their parents (be it verbal instruction or instruction via example), and they were exceptionally careful.

While it is absolutely essential that parents protect their children from serious dangers and injuries (no parent should ever allow their child to play or work by a fire or other potentially dangerous situation if the child does not understand how to be careful), children also must be given experiences in life that will give them the opportunities to develop cause-to-effect reasoning – one of the most valuable skills a child should learn.

Why Should a Child Develop Cause-To-Effect Reasoning?

In the book *Child Guidance*, parents are instructed to teach their "children to study from cause to effect." [2] Natural consequences are a very real part of adult life. If we forget to pay a bill, we might pay a late fee. If we repeatedly don't show up for work, we might get fired. If we eat unhealthy food, our health will suffer. If we don't put fuel in the car when it is nearing empty, we may run out of fuel at an inopportune time. If we procrastinate too much, we might find ourselves very stressed as we try to meet a deadline. Good cause-to-effect reasoning can help us avoid a lot of mistakes and misery in life.

Children who develop solid cause-to-effect reasoning skills also develop strong skills in the areas of self-regulation, problem solving, intelligent observation, risk management, and decision-making. They tend to have above-average foresight, discernment, and the practical wisdom that we call common sense. A young child who has good cause-to-effect reasoning recognizes that if he goes to bed too late, he'll be tired the next morning. If he doesn't keep his room tidy, he may lose something. If he is unkind to others, he may hurt their feelings. If he wastes time, he may not have time to do what is important. Children with this type of reasoning tend to require less discipline from their parents and are apt to be more responsible and make good decisions as teens. In addition, since these savvy reasoning skills are strongly connected to better problem-solving skills, children with good cause-to-effect reasoning tend to do better academically.

Yet perhaps the most important reason for helping a child

develop good cause-to-effect reasoning skills is the spiritual effects of this reasoning. When a child develops solid cause-to-effect reasoning at a young age, this reasoning ability naturally and readily transfers to his spiritual life. The Bible tells us in the book of Galatians, "Whatsoever a man soweth, that shall he also reap." "Man's conduct in this world decides his eternal destiny. As he has sown, so he must reap. Cause will be followed by effect." [3] A lack of cause-to-effect reasoning in childhood may seem of little importance in childhood, but in later years, it can have weighty consequences as a teen or young adult lives for the present and gives very little thought to what eternity will bring.

How to Help Your Child Develop Cause-To-Effect Reasoning

You may not live in a culture like that of rural Tanzania, but no matter where you live, if you teach your child using the heaven-appointed lesson books of useful work, the study of the Scriptures and of nature, and the experiences of life (see Chapter 10), you will find an abundance of opportunities to help your child develop the skill of cause-to-effect reasoning.

Useful Work and Experiences of Life

Useful work and experiences of life are especially helpful in developing the skill of cause-to-effect reasoning. Throughout the day, every day, involve your child in the regular hands-on, practical activities. Most work carries with it built-in natural consequences. If you don't wash the dishes, you'll run out of something to eat off of. If you aren't careful when preparing food, you'll have a mess to clean up. If you don't carry the bucket of water carefully, you may get wet. Involving children in practical activities allows children to develop cause-to-effect reasoning early in life when the consequences are relatively small in comparison to what they would be when they are older. Running out of clean clothes is not as serious as missing an important meeting at work. Cleaning the floor after you wear your muddy shoes in the house is a more manageable consequence than causing an accident after carelessly running a stoplight.

As you go through your day together, take the time to communicate with your child. Answer his questions. Many times, these questions are a child's attempt to make sense of life and can help him connect cause with effect. Be sure to listen to your child. Your two-year-old isn't giving you his long, drawn-out, detailed explanation of what happened when the dog ran into him and knocked him over because he wants to try your patience; rather, this explanation is his brain's method of working out connections. Communications like this engage his mind in ways that other cognitive processes do not.

Allow your child plenty of opportunities to experiment with real life. A child needs an abundance of experiences that have results that affect him on a practical level. He needs to be free to *try* to lift that box that you know is too heavy for him. He needs to *try* to jump the stream that you know is too wide for him and you know he will fall into and get wet. He needs to *try* to spoon out the soup that you know he will spill.

One snowy but sunny winter day, my seven-year-old friend, Aaron, and I were using a couple of small sleds to transport firewood from the woodpile to the house that was on a big hill. We pulled the firewood up the hill, unloaded the wood, and then sat on the empty sleds to have a fun ride down the hill. On one of our first few trips, Aaron pushed his sled aside so we could unload from my sled. But his sled didn't just move a few inches. On the slippery snow, it quickly started to slide down the hill, and within a second or two it was out of his reach. After watching the sled speed to the bottom of the hill with its heavy load, Aaron and I turned to each other with wide eyes, and then laughed at the mistake. Aaron didn't get to ride his sled down the hill on that trip, and he had to pull the same load of wood up twice, but it was an easy and effective lesson in cause-to-effect for Aaron. On every subsequent trip, he secured his sled at the top of the hill so he wouldn't lose it to gravity.

Nature

Children need to spend an abundance of time in nature where they can balance on fallen logs, jump from rock to rock, climb trees, and jump over streams. When children spend most of their day in the indoor environment where the footing is even and life is comparatively controllable, they are deprived of the physical and mental feedback they need for proper development of cause-to-effect reasoning.

Children also need time to observe the rhythms, correlations, and causal relationships in nature, to notice and discover (on his own – not in a two-dimensional book format) how much rain must fall before the ground becomes muddy, how much sun is needed to melt the ice on the puddle, why some plants thrive and others die in a particular environment, and more of the innumerable cause-to-effect lessons that nature can teach.

And perhaps the best way for a child to learn that cause follows effect is through gardening. "In the laws of God in nature, effect follows cause with unerring certainty." [4] If we plant spinach seeds, we'll reap spinach. "The reaping testifies to the sowing. Here no pretense is tolerated. ... [I]n nature there can be no deception. On the unfaithful husbandman the harvest passes sentence of condemnation. And in the highest sense this is true also in the spiritual realm. It is in appearance, not in reality, that evil succeeds." [5]

The Scriptures

And finally, the stories, warnings, and promises in the Bible give unfailing lessons on cause-to-effect. One of the errors that Ancient Israel made in the education of their children was neglecting to use their own history to teach their children to observe the connection between cause and effect. Paul says of the Jews, "I bear them record that they have a zeal of God, but not according to knowledge." [6] Spend an abundance of time learning from the illustrative stories and lofty principles found in God's Word and applying these principles in everyday life.

How to Hinder the Development of Cause-to-Effect Reasoning

Our sedentary, indoor, book- and screen-oriented educational methods that lack practical application are a massive hindrance to the development of cause-to-effect reasoning. When we educate children primarily from books and teach them math, grammar, science, or any other subject out of the context of real-life situations, we are serving up life to them in sliced-up, two-dimensional slivers without regard for how these subjects fit together as a dynamically integrated whole. This artificial way of learning encourages narrow, shallow, and fragmented thinking, causes children to lose a solid sense of connection to a larger whole, and contributes *significantly* to poor cause-to-effect reasoning. The negative effects of this artificial learning tend to appear in a child's later years in both his spiritual discernment and his intellectual abilities. A child needs an abundance of practical experiences that give him the physical and mental feedback he needs to develop thinking skills, good judgment, and cause-to-effect reasoning.

Another hindrance to the development of cause-to-effect reasoning is rescuing a child from poor judgment or excusing him from the effects of his actions. (Parents are especially prone to do this when the child did not realize that his actions would bring about the effects – when the incident was a mistake, not a bad decision.) If a child loses a flashlight on a camping trip, parents should not replace it but rather require that he earn the money to purchase a new one. If he walks into the house with dirty shoes, parents should not reprimand him and then clean the floor for him. The child should be required to stop what he is doing, remove his shoes, and clean the floor. When parents rescue a child from the effects of his actions, the child does not experience in a practical way that his actions have effects. Parents should certainly acknowledge their child's feelings and even sympathize with him when he loses his flashlight or has to clean the floor, but they should not change the results of his actions.

If a child needs help making the connection between cause and effect, parents could ask him questions, such as: "What do you think you could have done to prevent this from happening?" (Parents should also ask *themselves* questions, such as: "Are there inconsistencies in my parenting that are hindering my child's development of cause-to-effect reasoning?") Wisdom will grow as parents help their child to think through situations. That said, parents should be cautious about doing all their child's thinking for him. When parents are consistent in their parenting and do not hinder the development of cause-to-effect reasoning, a child should not have to be reminded, "Don't forget to take off your shoes!" When parents over-manage their child's life by giving him minute-to-minute direction and instruction and reminders, they do not give their child the opportunity to think for himself, to learn through observation, to plan ahead, to problem solve, and to reason from cause to effect. "Too much management is as bad as no management at all."[7] Encourage your child to think. Allow him to make decisions and choices, to experience failure and the results of his actions, and to learn the valuable lessons that disappointment teaches. Be sure you are there to comfort and encourage, yet allow your child the opportunity to become wise through experience.

A Note of Caution

Scraped knees, bruised shins, spilled food, lost items, missed opportunities, and similar consequences allow a child to experience the natural results of his decisions and actions. These experiences are essential for developing cause-to-effect reasoning. However, just as it is the parents' responsibility to help their child to develop this skill, it is also the parents' responsibility to protect their child from serious dangers and injuries. Never should the child be allowed to engage in any type of activity that could bring serious consequences (physical, mental, or emotional). Keeping our children safe is one of our responsibilities as parents.

In addition, parents should not rely on natural consequences when the child's behavior will hurt someone or something else. For example, three-year-old Allie loved holding her grandma's cat, but the feelings were not mutual. The cat was always squirming and trying to escape the grip of her captor. Allie's parents had told their daughter to not pick up the cat, but Allie wasn't heeding her parents' warning. Allowing natural consequences (the cat scratching Allie in her attempts to be free) was not a good solution here. This approach would have been unfair to the cat (and the cat could seriously harm Allie if it scratched her in the eye). Rather, Allie's parents should clearly explain to their daughter why she should not pick up the cat, warn her that she would no longer be allowed to pet the cat if she disobeyed, and then carefully keep an eye on Allie so they could follow through if Allie didn't obey.

An Important Part of True Education

Seven-year-old Jason's mom asked him to take a large bowl of applesauce over to the table. Jason picked up the bowl, took two steps, and tripped over a small rug. The entire bowl of applesauce spilled all over him and onto the floor. Mom looked over at her little boy as his desperate eyes met hers. Jason seemed to be frozen in space, so Mom gave her son a compassionate smile and a few words of sympathy, and then asked him what he thought he should do. "Clean up the mess," Jason replied as he extracted his hand from a puddle of applesauce. Mom smiled again and nodded, and Jason went to change his clothes and then fetch some cleaning cloths. After he cleaned up the mess, he asked his mom what they were going to eat on their toast now. "We'll just eat our toast dry. And later today, I can help you make more applesauce to replace what spilled, so we can have applesauce on our toast tomorrow."

Jason's mom did not withhold sympathy or help, but she didn't completely rescue him from the results of his mishap. When Jason's mom asked *him* what he should do and required that *he* clean up the mess and that *he* make more applesauce to replace the spilled sauce, she not only helped him develop cause-to-effect reasoning, but she also communicated an unspoken message to him that she had confidence in his ability to think for himself and to take responsibility for his mishap.

Cause-to-effect reasoning is an important part of a child's education as it not only strengthens the brain and helps a child with his other academic studies, but it also brings with it numerous practical and spiritual benefits as well. Taking the time to daily nurture this skill in a child provides many rewards.

CHAPTER 23

READING

"Education ... has produced a vast
population able to read but unable to distinguish
what is worth reading." – G. M. Trevelyan

SINCE birth, Samantha's parents read books to her every day. Books about animals, books about numbers, books about colors, simple Bible story books, and wholesome story books. At age four, Samantha's parents started teaching her phonics. Using an excellent phonics curriculum, Samantha learned that the letter *b* says "buh," the letter *e* says "eh," the letter *g* says "guh," and so forth. At age five, Samantha's parents determined that it was time for her to learn to read. They purchased some easy-reader books that read something like this: "This is a pig. The pig is big. The pig has a wig. The big pig likes the wig." Samantha learned quickly and soon could read the entire first book in the easy-reader series – much to the delight of her parents and grandparents. Samantha gradually moved on to other books that introduced different words and eventually learned to read more advanced reading material. By age twelve, she could read well, although she did struggle with some more advanced vocabulary. Her teachers and parents encouraged her to read often to practice her reading skills.

As we can see with Samantha and the countless other children who have gone through this same process, this method works. However, there are several disadvantages to this method that should be considered. We'll come back to those in a moment, but first let's look at another way reading can be taught.

Jonathan, age six, did not know how to read. His daily activities didn't include reading practice, but rather helping his mother with household chores, working in the garden, cooking, disassembling an old lawn mower engine that his grandfather had given him, climbing trees, and exploring the woods near his house. All these activities were done with the companionship of his mother and his two-year old sister. (Yes, even the disassembly of the engine was enjoyed together. His mom said she had no idea what she was doing, but they were having fun learning together.) On the weekends, Jonathan often helped his father with cutting firewood, vehicle maintenance, and doing yard work. The family had daily morning and evening worship in which they sang hymns, read short passages from the Bible and from the book *Patriarchs and Prophets*, and talked about what they had learned from both the hymns and the readings. In all their activities, Jonathan's parents actively engaged in conversation with their children.

On his seventh birthday, Jonathan still didn't know how to read, and he showed no interest in learning to do so; yet his parents were not concerned, nor were they pushing him to read. Two months before his eighth birthday, Jonathan, his mom, and his sister were in the kitchen making soup, and his mother was following a recipe. She pointed to a line in the recipe and said, "We need two carrots." Jonathan retrieved two carrots from the refrigerator, quickly scrambled back up on his stool, his eyes searching the cookbook page. His little fingers pointed to a word in the recipe. "What does that word say?"

"Carrots," replied Mom, and then she pointed to each of the letters in the word as she repeated it more slowly, emphasizing the sound of each letter.

"What does that word say?" Jonathan eagerly asked again.

"Basil," replied Mom with a smile. Jonathan asked his sister if she could get the basil, and then, turning back to the cookbook, he pointed to the next word and repeated his question.

"Celery," replied his mother, slowly pronouncing each letter sound.

Jonathan nodded and then pointed to the next word.

"Potatoes."

When they finished reading the list of ingredients, they put the soup on the stove to cook and went on with their day. That experience *seemed* to be the end of his interest in reading until one rainy morning, about three weeks later, Jonathan emerged from the living room holding a book that he found on the bookshelf. "Mom, this book says that the floppy thing we took off the engine yesterday is a cylinder head gasket. And I think this," he said, holding out an engine part in his hand, "might be called the governor linkage," pronouncing each word correctly.

And just like that, he could read. And he could read well.

Though this story may sound a bit extraordinary, it is quite common among children who are taught using God's method of true education.

In typical educational settings, reading is a school subject. The young child begins with the alphabet, learning the names and sounds of the letters. He is then gradually introduced to easy-reading books that use short, easy-to-sound-out words and overly simplistic vocabulary. Later, he moves on to more challenging books until he eventually can read well.

In true education, the approach to reading is completely different. In fact, reading isn't even a school subject. Rather, a child is given a healthy foundation for learning and grows up in a linguistically-rich, brain-building environment conducive to the development of keen observation abilities and healthy brain circuitry. (See Chapters 3, 4, 8, and 9.) These factors give him the ability to easily make connections between the letters on a page and real words. Accordingly, with relatively minimal instruction, he is enabled to master the skill of reading, and his first reading material may be anything from an instruction manual to a nutrition label on a package of food to a chapter in the Bible. No long, drawn-out formal reading lessons needed.

Children raised with God's methods tend to read more fluently and have better expression and comprehension than do children who learn to read using the traditional methods. And God's method is much more enjoyable for the child.

Though this method is very different from the traditional method of learning to read, a large body of research in the area of neuroscience and child development demonstrates that this is the method by which children learn best and that learning to read at a later age is actually beneficial in many ways. [1]

God's Timing

Reading is a complex task for the eyes and requires more than visual acuity.

As you read the words on this page, your eyes are doing far more than simply moving across the page from one word to the next. Eye engagement during reading is extremely complex and sophisticated, and the eyes perform some stunning acrobatics as you read. [2] To be a proficient reader, to read with fluency, accuracy, and good comprehension, the eyes must move with incredible speed, precision, and coordination, and then send the visual information they gather to the brain to process the data. In the tiny millisecond that the eyes and brain of a proficient reader work at decoding and discerning the meaning of a word, the eyes also use peripheral vision to perceive the other words around it. Each word is rapidly processed, letter-by-letter (so that a reader can distinguish between similarly-spelled words, such as twin and twine, dessert and desert, or casual and causal), and the brain then links the word's sequence of letters with its pronunciation and meaning. And all this happens while the visual attention is strategically planning the next eye movement. For a proficient reader, this speedy processing happens to the tune of about five words per second. That's an average of two-tenths of a second per word! The motor agility of the eyes and the processing skills of the brain are so gracefully coordinated that the reader can easily read long passages with pleasure and understanding.

However, before the age of eight, neither the brain nor the eyes have the capacity to accomplish these acrobatics smoothly and without difficulty. If we try to teach reading before these systems are ready, reading will not only be slow, but the child will struggle with fluidity and comprehension, which can contribute to poor reading habits.

Proficient reading also requires efficient integration of several brain regions as the brain must compare the grammar and word order of sentences, as well the context of what is being read, with its previously-stored information to enable a reader to read a text with fluidity, good expression, at the proper speed, and with good comprehension. Fluent reading is not a result of practice as much as it is a consequence of synaptic reorganization, synaptic pruning, myelination, connectivity, and many other transformations that take place in the brain between birth and age ten. Pushing reading instruction on a child's brain before the various areas of the brain are well integrated and working in synchrony can hinder the development of good reading skills and contribute to poor reading habits. But when we wait until the brain is sufficiently developed, a child is enabled to read proficiently with comprehension and expression from the moment he learns to read.

In addition, as mentioned in Chapter 5, close-up work (such as reading) before the age of eight to nine can cause eye inflammation and elongation, which can lead to myopia (near-sightedness) and permanent damage to the eyes.[3] Research shows that children need to spend several hours a week outside for proper eye development. [4] Outdoor time exposes the eyes to the sunlight required for good development. The uneven terrain and varied scenery in nature that cause the eyes to constantly adjust are also important to strengthen the eye muscles that are needed for reading. One large, in-depth study showed that myopia rates were reduced by 50 percent when children spent an *extra* seventy-six minutes outside per day above the study baseline. [5] Waiting until the eyes have developed before teaching reading or writing significantly reduces the risk of developing myopia.

Not only do the eyes and brain need time and the proper experiences to develop, but the large muscles of the body do as well. Early childhood is a time that God designed for the development of the physical constitution, and children need many years of spending several hours each day climbing trees, running through the fields, working in the garden, digging in the dirt, carrying large rocks, balancing on logs, and engaging in other physical activities that strengthen the large muscles before they are expected to be able to sit still to read or write.

We are counseled that children should learn to read "with full, clear voice and distinct utterance, giving the proper emphasis to each word." [6] Understanding the many prerequisites to reading readiness should help us to see that focusing on reading instruction before the child's physical constitution is ready for reading is not the path to acquiring these skills. Following God's schedule is the best method. (See Chapter 5 for more information on God's schedule.)

There is no need to be concerned that a child will be behind in reading skills if parents wait until his eyes, brain, and muscles are developed sufficiently for close-up, sit-down work. Consider this experiment that Ruth Beechick talks about in her book, *The Three R's*. Kindergartners in a particular school district were divided into two groups. One group received extensive instruction in reading, while the other group of children spent their reading instruction time engaged in hands-on science activities. When tested in the third grade, the children in the science group achieved higher scores in reading than the children who had received reading instruction. Not only was the active, hands-on learning what the young children's brains and bodies needed to engage in at that young age, but the science activities (like growing plants, melting ice, playing with magnets, and other hands-on activities) helped to develop their brain and thinking capacities, as well as expand their vocabulary. Thus, when the children in the science group *did* learn to read (which happened in a fraction of the time that it took for the early readers to learn), they were able to read with better comprehension and able to understand higher-level reading material. Ruth Beechick writes, "This research and others like it are compelling. They drive home the fact that each child has only a limited amount of time in his early years. The time can be squandered in trying to teach reading before the 'optimum' time for it. Or it can be used wisely in teaching 'real stuff' that the child is ready for."[7]

A vast amount of research has been invested in trying to figure out the best way to teach children to read. Countless experiments have been conducted comparing one instruction method to another. Scores of books have been written on this subject. An entire industry has been developed around the marketing and sale of various programs and curricula to help children learn to read. Every supposed advantage is given to children to help them acquire this skill. Yet, year after year, over 60 percent of eighth-grade students consistently test below proficiency level in reading. [8] With all the intervention, why do so many children struggle with reading? The reason that learning to read is so difficult for many children is that reading instruction begins too early. We are expecting children to read before the time God designed them to read.

When we look at the traditional method of reading instruction, which begins the slow and laborious process at age four (or earlier), requires hours and hours of instruction time over the span of five years (or more), and misuses a child's mind on books with oversimplified language and very little depth of meaning, and we contrast this tedious method with God's perfectly simple method in which a child is raised in an enriching environment and then proceeds straight to books with advanced vocabulary, sophisticated sentence structures, and deep and intelligent themes, we can clearly see the advantages of choosing God's method.

When to Worry

In the false system of education, children who are not reading by an arbitrary, predetermined age are often diagnosed or labeled with a reading delay and given interventions to help them catch up. There seems to be an underlying cultural imperative that a child must be able to read by the time he is some predetermined age or he will never be a proficient reader. The truth is that research has found that children may begin to read at a wide range of ages and still become proficient readers. [9] "In many schools, children are identified as 'behind' with reading before they would even have started school in many other countries." [10] Schools in which reading instruction begins at a later age consistently score in the top percentile on the Programme for International Student Assessment (a standardized test given to fifteen-year-olds in sixty-five nations and territories around the world). Many of the best readers learn to read "late" (according to cultural standards). And later readers often tend to have superior thinking abilities, better memorization skills, extraordinary literary ability, and more positive attitudes towards reading than those who learn to read earlier. [11] [12]

It is important for parents to recognize that learning to read later than the typical age does not hinder a child's learning. When a child is raised using the methods of true education as outlined in the first several chapters of this book, a tremendous amount of solid learning happens from a very early age.

Each child is unique, and the way in which he learns to read may be just as unique as he is. Some children learn to read based on things they've memorized. For example, if a child memorizes hymns, he can (usually with help from an adult) follow along with the words in the hymns while singing. This gives him opportunity to connect the written words with verbal ones, and soon he is reading. Some children learn to read because they want to write something like a thank-you card or a note to their friend. Other children learn to read by listening to their parents read to them. As the parents read to their child and the child observes the words on the page, the child's brain gradually begins to connect the written words with the verbal ones. Most children pick up the skill of reading through a combination of methods. Through these varied experiences, a child makes associations between the letters and the sounds of words, and when his brain and eyes have sufficiently matured, he quickly pieces the needed components together and begins reading.

Though each child will learn to read in his own unique way and at his own pace, there is often one common thread among children who teach themselves to read – words like "cat" and "hat" are not the child's first words. Using God's method of learning, children are able to read longer words – and even advanced vocabulary – simply because these are the words that they use in their daily life.

An Environment for Reading

The skill of reading could be compared to a garden plant. It will develop and grow to be strong if given the right conditions or environment.

As mentioned previously, a child can easily learn to read without extensive formal instruction, but giving the child a foundation and environment conducive to reading is key. Just as language skills are developed long before the child begins to actually talk, reading skills are developed long before the child actually starts to read, and a child's environment should be designed to be favorable to this development. Besides following the guidelines found in Chapters 3, 4, 8, and 9 (and, of course, growing up in a literate society surrounded by people who read), there are a few important components for creating an environment to help a child become a good reader.

1. Conversation

The foundation for good reading skills is conversation. Children who engage in regular conversation in their early years receive higher scores on reading tests, even in the absence of reading instruction, than those who are not engaged in frequent conversation. Conversation builds contextual vocabulary, and the development of phonemic representation is more contingent on the size of a child's vocabulary than on his age or on reading instruction. Children with large working vocabularies tend to become more proficient readers. [13]

2. Physical Movement

Research gives unmistakable evidence of an "elaborate interplay of brain and body," [14] and physical movement is critical for the brain development necessary for reading proficiency. Physical activities that use a variety of senses in multiple ways help to develop connections between the different structures of the brain. These connections enable the various areas of the brain to work in cooperation with each other, which is a crucial factor for good reading skills.

Physical activity also helps to develop the vestibular system and the proprioceptive system. Together, these systems assist the eyes to move smoothly across the page as a child reads. They also help a child clearly perceive the top and bottom and left and right arrangement and directionality of letters and words, as well as help the child's eyes trace the exact direction of the lines and curves that make up letters and track the orientation of words on a page. Without good functioning vestibular and proprioceptive systems, a child may skip words when trying to read or reverse letters and numbers. In addition, he may struggle with distinguishing between letters and words that look similar, such as the letter *b* and the letter *d* or the word *saw* and the word *was*.

With a well-developed vestibular and proprioceptive system, most of the physical and mental aspects of reading can very quickly become automatic. But when these systems are weak, the child experiences cognitive overload when trying to read, and because so much of his mental energy is required to decode letters and words, his reading fluency and comprehension suffer.

Proper physical development must *precede* formal academic learning. Strategies such as taking activity breaks during school time, sitting on bouncy balls while reading, or enrolling a child in extra-curricular activities (like gymnastics or sports) do *not* supply a young child with the movement he needs. In order to fully and effectively develop the body systems in the way God intended them to be developed, young children should spend nearly their entire day in real-life, physical activity.

3. Real-Life Experiences

A child's engagement in real-life experiences is also one of the strongest predictors for reading proficiency. A young child's life should be filled with useful and meaningful activities, such as using tools, helping a neighbor, preparing meals, repairing items that are broken, and working in the garden. These experiences lead to synaptic growth in the brain, particularly in the frontal cortex (the part of the brain responsible for higher mental functions). In addition, these experiences create a bank of knowledge in a child's brain that helps him to visualize the meaning of concepts that he will encounter in his reading.

In the context of these real-life experiences, a parent can find many opportunities for helping a child learn basic phonics. For example, when five-year-old Theodore asked what the sign said, his mom responded, "It says stop. The first letter is an *s*, and *s* says 'ssss' like 'ssstop.'" When Jonathan's mom read the recipe ingredients with him, she pointed to each of the letters in the word while emphasizing the letter sounds. When Lily and her dad were building a shelf, Dad pointed to the box of nails and sounded out a couple of the words on the box for Lily. When Ryan and his mom were writing out a meal plan for the week, Mom showed Ryan the word *potato* and told him the sounds of each of the letters. Each lesson was short, incidental, and contextual to their real-life activity, but they provided practical and easy-to-remember phonics learning for the children, thus giving them a basis for deciphering words on a page. This type of incidental phonics instruction is quite helpful in the process of learning to read and is usually better assimilated than formal reading instruction.

4. Quality Reading Material

One essential component to developing good reading skills is good reading material. Don't slow down the growth of your child's mind with picture books or easy-readers with simple words and basic sentence structures that offer nothing beneficial for his language and brain development and don't encourage any deep thinking. With a background of daily engagement in practical life and conversation with their parents, even young children can understand the complex vocabulary and sentence structures of useful books, like inspired writings, how-to manuals, and reference books.

Many families who have followed the methods of true education began reading to their children from the Bible and the *Conflict of the Ages Series* [15] when their children were just toddlers. If the readings are kept short and the reading time includes discussion, explanation (when needed), and application, even the very young child can benefit much from the stories in these writings. Not only can the child gain valuable Biblical knowledge and moral training, but his vocabulary and understanding of language syntax and usage can be so well developed that his transition from listening to reading will be nearly seamless.

I saw a great example of how these useful books can benefit a child in my young friend, David. David and his family had lived in the United States for about six years, but they were originally from another country, and English was not their native language, nor was English spoken much in their home. When David was twelve years old, circumstances required that his family move back to their home country, and this move necessitated that David take a test to determine his level of academic achievement. Though he had not attended any formal schooling, and though the test was in English, David scored very high – far above his grade level – on all of the test subjects, including the English grammar portion! He had grown up being read to from the Bible and *The Conflict of the Ages Series* and had read them himself when he was old enough; and through the lifestyle of true education, he had developed strength of mind that enabled him to far surpass the grade standards of the world even in subjects he had not formally studied.

5. A Reason to Read

Children can be quite logical. They see no sense in wearing a jacket if they are not cold. They don't see why they should bother with a napkin when their shirt does a fantastic job. And they seldom take on the task of learning to read if they have no reason to read. Some children naturally find this reason on their own; other children need their parents to help them find this reason. Either way, children are more apt to learn to read when reading becomes to them a means to some valued end.

For example, Trevor, a bright, active, ten-year-old boy with many interests in life, had spent nearly a year working hard and saving his money to buy a bicycle. When the day finally came that he was able to bring home his new bike, the bike came in a box and needed to be assembled according to specific instructions. Up until then, Trevor couldn't read, but he was now very motivated to read. And, because his brain was reading to learn to read, with some encouragement from his parents, he learned very quickly.

What About Phonics?

Should a child be taught phonics? Though he doesn't need to be able to list from memory all the different ways a long *a* sound can be spelled to know how to read the words *gate*, *mail*, and *pray*, for most children, learning phonics can be beneficial as an understanding of phonics helps the brain to decode words provides a key to the ability to read words that a child has not yet encountered in everyday life.

Most children who are raised using the principles of true education pick up a great deal of phonics on their own without any formal teaching of the subject – saving loads of time and potential frustration. And, as previously mentioned, parents should supplement this learning using an incidental, casual, and practical approach to learning letter sounds. If phonics instruction is short, contextual, and to the point, a child's interest will be maintained, and he will remember what he learned. If parents don't know the rules of phonics well enough to share them with their child, they should obtain a good phonics handbook (for themselves, not for the child) so they can know how to correctly teach their child.

What Should My Child Read?

It was a beautiful Sunday, and Lila was excited. Her grandma had planned a special day at the amusement park with just Lila and Grandma to celebrate Lila's ninth birthday. Lila woke up early that morning, showered, dressed, ate breakfast, and then positioned herself by the front window to watch for Grandma. The minute she saw the blue car turn into the driveway, she raced to hug her parents and older brother and hopped in the car with Grandma.

On their way to the park, Grandma and Lila passed by an ice cream stand and made a quick U-turn to avail themselves of a cold treat to start their fun, summer day. Grandma opted for chocolate ice cream in a cone, and Lila chose vanilla ice cream in a dish topped with strawberry sauce, whipped cream, and chocolate sprinkles. After enjoying their sweet treat, they were back in the car and off to the amusement park. The day was spent riding the rides, playing the games, and eating cotton candy, French fries, and other special treats.

It was late afternoon when Lila arrived home after her entertaining day with Grandma, and she noticed the storm clouds blowing in as her brother and her parents were hurriedly trying to get the yard work done before the impending rain arrived. She thanked her grandma and cheerily greeted her family as she walked past them to go play with the new doll that her grandma had purchased for her at the park.

About forty minutes had passed when heavy raindrops began to fall, and her family scrambled into the house, having just barely put the yard tools away. After a quick cleanup, her father sat down at his desk to pay some bills while her mom and brother started preparing dinner. The minutes passed by quickly as Lila was enjoying her new doll, and before she knew it, her brother was calling the family to dinner. The family sat down at the table to a delicious and healthy meal, but for some reason, Lila wasn't interested in the salad or the beans. And the whole-grain bread – a food she normally enjoyed – had lost its appeal as well. In fact, she wasn't really interested in any of the healthy food on the table.

Just about any thinking parent can quickly discern the reason that Lila had lost her appetite for healthy food, as well as why she was content to allow her family to work while she played. Indulgence is one of the most effective ways to lessen the desire for that which is good. This principle is true not just for food and work, but also for what we read. Just as a diet of cotton candy and French fries weakens the appetite for hearty, wholesome, whole-grain bread, so does entertaining reading weaken the mind's appetite for hearty, wholesome, whole-grain reading – reading that requires thinking and mental chewing. And just as a day full of play diminishes the desire to engage in hard work, so does light reading diminish the desire to engage in reading that requires mental self-discipline.

Light reading and exciting stories – even those with good moral lessons – cripple the mental strength. When the mind feeds upon that which is light and easy, it loses its ability for concentration, focus, and vigorous thought. In contrast, if a child's reading diet has always consisted of wholesome books that require mental effort to understand, then he will be much less likely to crave light, frivolous reading.

"We should endeavor to keep out of our homes every influence that is not productive of good." [16] Light reading, fiction, and other similar reading sow seeds "the harvest of which you will not care to gather. There is no spiritual strength to be gained from such reading. Rather, it destroys the love for the pure truth of the Word." [17]

Beyond Content

We must be concerned about not only what a child reads but also *how* he reads it. "Chasing through books superficially, clogs the mind." [18] "To read daily a certain number of chapters ... without careful thought as to the meaning of the text, will profit but little." [19] When we read in such a way as to only cover the reading material superficially, we do not allow the brain to reflect, organize meaningful ideas, approach a concept from different angles, and make practical application. In other words, we discourage the development of habits of deep thinking.

The book *Education* recommends the following approach to reading the Scriptures: "In daily study the verse-by-verse method is often most helpful. Let the student take one verse, and concentrate the mind on ascertaining the thought that God has put into that verse for him, and then dwell upon the thought until it becomes his own." [20] This approach not only takes time and patience, but it may also require breaking old habits that the false system of education may have instilled – that of covering material for the sake of covering it, as if reading the text were the equivalent of learning it.

The verse-by-verse method encourages depth of thought and helps prevent the shallow, superficial, narrow, emotion-controlled thinking that is so common in our modern society. By precept and example, we can encourage our children to read with the goal of providing food for deep thought. "One passage thus studied until its significance is clear is of more value than the perusal of many chapters with no definite purpose in view and no positive instruction gained." [21]

Start the habit of profound thinking at a young age before your child can read. When you are reading to your child, avoid rushing through the reading material, piling one sentence upon the other. Instead, take the time to pause often and consider with your child the meaning of a sentence or paragraph you've just read, to reflect upon the ideas, thoughts, and principles portrayed within it, and to think about how it can be made applicable and practical in your lives.

Digital vs Printed Page

Does it make a difference whether children read from printed books or from digital ones?

Digitally-based books and other forms of digital learning are increasingly popular, but research using brain scans reveals that the brain processes digital material quite differently than it processes physical material. [22] Physical media leaves a "deeper footprint" [23] in the brain. Reading from print material produces a stronger brain response and generates more activity within several areas of the brain than does reading from a digital device. [24] Readers experience better comprehension, increased learning, and greater internalization of what is read on paper versus a screen (a factor that is of utmost importance when reading the Bible), and readers are better able to connect what is read to previously stored information in the brain. In addition, print material has a greater ability to engage with the brain's spatial memory networks, which means that reading from physical text results in better memory retention than does reading from a digital device. [25] Reading a printed page is also visually less demanding than reading digital text.

While digital devices may, at first, seem to hold the attention better than printed text, over time, the young brain changes to adapt to digital mediums, resulting in shallower processing and reduced ability to focus. The use of digital devices appears to hinder the development of a child's ability to concentrate and contemplate and may even diminish the ability for critical thinking, insight, empathy, and reflection. [26]

If you want to help your child develop strong thinking abilities, it's best to avoid digital devices and stick with real books.

God's Better Way

Pushing reading on children at a young age is not only unnecessary, but it also contributes to eye damage, reading disorders, attention deficit disorders, poor reading comprehension, less than optimal reading ability, and negative attitudes toward reading, as well as stress for both child and parents.

Given the right environment, children who begin to read later actually tend to be more fluent readers and read with better comprehension and expression than those who begin reading early. With true education, a child's first reading material is not limited to beginner reading books. Instead, he'll be able to read books with valuable information that will enrich his mind right from the start. This means he will spend more time reading to learn than learning to read!

CHAPTER 24

GEOGRAPHY

*"God that made the world ... hath made of one
blood all nations of men for to dwell on all the face
of the earth, and hath determined ... the bounds of
their habitation." – Acts 17:24, 26*

A knowledge and understanding of geography do more than simply give a child a comprehension of different places on earth and how they relate to each other. The subject of geography is very much interconnected with history, science, religion, government, economics, and other subjects, and can give a child a deeper, more comprehensive, and more practical understanding of these subjects.

An understanding of geography can also strengthen and broaden a child's thinking skills. A view of other lands and cultures can help him to realize that there are other ways of living, other ways of doing things than those to which he is accustomed. This understanding can deepen his thinking as well as help him gain an appreciation for different countries and cultures.

Perhaps most importantly, a knowledge of geography gives a child a better understanding of his role and responsibility in the great commission. [1] Christ's mission in life was the salvation of others; as His followers, we must have the same mission and impart that mission to our children. "We have the word of God to show that the end is near. The world is to be warned, and as never before we are to be laborers with Christ. The work of warning has been entrusted to us. We are to be channels of light to the world." [2] If we want to reach the various cultures for Christ, we need to learn about and understand those cultures. The better we understand a culture, the better we can share the love of Christ with that culture.

How to Learn Geography

God's lesson book of the experiences of life and the lesson book of the study of the Scriptures provide a good foundation, practical purpose, and application for learning geography.

If you have a world globe and a world map (a large one that hangs on the wall is good), a child can become quite familiar with geography by coupling these resources with events of everyday life. When you sing a hymn written by someone from Germany, when friends travel to Poland, when you hear about a missionary going to Kazakhstan, when you notice your garden tool was made in the Netherlands, when you hear a story of a man from Korea, find these places on the map and talk about them. Take note of how far a place is from where you live. Observe how big or small a country is. Notice what continent it is on. Get out an encyclopedia or other reference book (a book, not a digital source) and learn about the weather, the language, and the culture of that country. As you learn about events in history, use your map to understand how geography may have influenced those events. Learning in this way provides a richer and more contextual understanding of both history and geography.

Get a map that has the countries mentioned in the Bible, and as you read the Bible together, find the countries mentioned on the map. And then compare that map with a modern-day map to discover what that area of the world is now called.

Awaken an interest in learning about the various countries and cultures by finding out about missionaries that are serving Christ around the world, looking up their location on your map, reading reference books about those countries, and supporting those missionaries through financial donations and prayers. "It is acquaintance that awakens sympathy, and sympathy is the spring of effective ministry. To awaken in the children and youth sympathy and the spirit of sacrifice for the suffering millions in the 'regions beyond,' let them become acquainted with these lands and their peoples. In this line much might be accomplished in our schools. Instead of dwelling on the exploits of the Alexanders and Napoleons of history, let the pupils study the lives of such men as the apostle Paul and Martin Luther, as Moffat and Livingstone and Carey, and the present daily-unfolding history of missionary effort. Instead of burdening their memories with an array of names and theories that have no bearing upon their lives, and to which, once outside the schoolroom, they rarely give a thought, let them study all lands in the light of missionary effort and become acquainted with the peoples and their needs." [3]

CHAPTER 25

HISTORY

*"Prophecy and history should form a part of the
studies in our schools." – Christian Education, 212*

A S too often taught, history is little more than a record of the rise
and fall of kings, the intrigues of courts, the victories and defeats
of armies – a story of ambition and greed, of deception, cruelty, and
bloodshed. Thus taught, its results cannot but be detrimental."[1] But
in God's method of education, all subjects may be learned in such
a way as to "tend to the strengthening and upbuilding of character.
Of no study is this true to a greater degree than of history. Let it be
considered from the divine point of view."[2]

"Far better is it to learn, in the light of God's word, the causes
that govern the rise and fall of kingdoms. Let the youth study these
records, and see how the true prosperity of nations has been bound
up with an acceptance of the divine principles. Let him study the
history of the great reformatory movements, and see how often
these principles, though despised and hated, their advocates brought
to the dungeon and the scaffold, have through these very sacrifices
triumphed."[3]

Sources for History Instruction

"The Bible is the most comprehensive and the most instructive
history that men possess. It came fresh from the fountain of eternal
truth; and a Divine hand has preserved its purity through all the
ages. Its bright rays shine into the far-distant past, where human
research seeks vainly to penetrate. In God's word only we find an
authentic account of creation. Here we behold the power that laid
the foundation of the earth, and that stretched out the heavens. In
this word only can we find a history of our race unsullied by human
prejudice or human pride."[4]

"The Bible is the most wonderful of all histories, for it is the
production of God, not of the finite mind. It carries us back through

the centuries to the beginning of all things, presenting the history of times and scenes which would otherwise never have been known." [5]

How to Study History

Instead of studying Western civilization one year, American history another year, European history another year, and so forth, the study of history should be logical and sequential so that the child can see how one event of history leads to another. Not only will this method provide for the child's mind a natural flow of the events in history and make these events come together as a connected whole, but it will also help develop the skill of reasoning from cause to effect.

Begin with the creation of the world (or even before then at the rebellion in heaven) and gradually continue through the history of the world as described in the Bible and expounded on in the *Conflict of the Ages Series*. [6] In the early years, parents can read to their children. If you have children of different ages, all can listen to the readings together and benefit. Interest can be maintained if the readings are kept short and parents encourage thought and discussion regarding what has been read.

"Sacred history was one of the studies in the schools of the prophets. In the record of His dealings with the nations were traced the footsteps of Jehovah. So today we are to consider the dealings of God with the nations of the earth. We are to see in history the fulfilment of prophecy, to study the workings of Providence in the great reformatory movements, and to understand the progress of events in the marshaling of the nations for the final conflict of the great controversy." [7]

Once a child has the foundation of knowing and understanding true history as found in the Bible, deeper and more comprehensive study of the protestant reformation and the growth of the Christian church, as well as prophecy and the fulfillment of prophecy, can be included. [8] Books by J. A. Wylie, such as *The History of Protestantism* or *The History of the Waldenses*, are excellent resources at the appropriate age.

Studied correctly, history can develop the quality of gratitude for the efforts and labors of those who have gone before us. "Such study will give broad, comprehensive views of life. It will help the youth to understand something of its relations and dependencies, how wonderfully we are bound together in the great brotherhood of society and nations, and to how great an extent the oppression or degradation of one member means loss to all." [9]

Tips for History Study

Avoid abstract, disconnected learning; all parts of history should have a connection to other parts of history. Studying history as a connected whole helps a child remember what he's learned and makes the various events of history more relevant to each other.

As much as possible, connect the study of history with the study of geography.

History should be taught from the perspective of the great controversy between God and Satan and, as much as possible, studied in conjunction with Bible history and prophecy.

History should be presented to the child in such a way that he can clearly trace the workings of Jehovah throughout history. Again, the Bible and the *Conflict of the Ages Series* provide the ideal resource for this.

Do not rush through your study of history. Take time to learn about it thoroughly. The goal is not to cover a certain amount of material, but to learn and understand history well.

CHAPTER 26

MUSIC

*"Let us do everything in our power to make music
in our homes, that God may come in." – The Voice
in Speech and Song, 410*

MUSIC carries with it numerous benefits for both brain development and moral development. Listening to and learning music have positive effects on cognitive functions such as memory, attention span, and processing speed, as well as language processing, reading ability, executive function, and more. [1] "Music is of heavenly origin," [2] and "the art of sacred melody" should be "diligently cultivated." [3]

True vs False Music Education

When parents desire their child to learn to play a musical instrument, they typically enroll him in music lessons – and the earlier the better. Then comes the practice. And more practice. Coaxing, rewards, threats, and even crying may also be involved (by both the parents and the child).

While it is true that most children *can* learn music through early lessons and lots of practice, in God's method of education, we find a completely different and more enjoyable model for how children may learn music.

We see an example of God's method of music education in the life of a young boy who became one of the greatest musicians and composers of all time and wrote over seventy well-known, sacred music pieces (and many additional lesser-known pieces). He played music so beautifully that he was chosen to play before royalty. This amazing virtuoso was not only an exceptional musician, but he even designed and built musical instruments. [4] David of the Bible did not become such an amazingly talented musician and composer because his parents purchased a violin for him, enrolled him in music lessons at age five, and diligently made sure that he practiced every day. David became a talented musician because he learned music in God's beautiful way.

How to Develop a Musical Mind

God's way of learning music is much broader and deeper than what is offered through the typical method of music lessons. Not only is the approach to music education completely different in true education, but the results are astoundingly different as well.

Here we will look at six factors for learning music through God's method of learning.

1. Immersion and Exposure

The first step in God's plan of music education is to expose the child to high-quality, sacred music from an early age. This music should include choir music, orchestral music, and four-part harmony, as well as singing in the home. Children who are exposed to high-quality music early in life more easily develop musical talent.

This exposure to good music should primarily be through attentively listening to the music rather than having the music playing in the background. Children develop best in an environment that is quiet and simple (see Chapter 8), and having music playing in the background while a child is engaging in other activities can be overstimulating to a young child's brain.

2. Nature

Nature plays an undervalued yet important role in God's plan for developing musical ability in a child. David was an accomplished musician, yet he did not gain his musical ability by attending music lessons every Monday at 2:30 p.m. and then daily practicing scales for thirty minutes before he was allowed to go out to play. Instead, a natural life of responsibility and active work amidst the beautiful scenes of nature provided David with plentiful "opportunities of contemplation and meditation"[5] and "daily revelations of the character and majesty of his Creator."[6] This environment brought David's young heart into "intimate communion with God"[7] – the Creator of music Himself.

The results? Being surrounded by God's created works caused the musical faculties of David's brain to develop and grow strong. And thus, this simple shepherd boy learned to sing beautifully, to play the harp skillfully, and even to compose music.

Long before any formal musical training begins, we should surround our children with God's beautiful creation where they can hear the cheerful melody of the birds, the chorus of the tree frogs, the whistling of the breeze through the trees, and the song of the brook as it journeys down its path. Exposure to nature tunes the ear to beautiful sounds. A child's heart cannot help but be moved, and his musical talents will begin to develop in harmony with his Creator's plan.

3. Singing

In God's method of education, a child's first training in music is not with a musical instrument but with the voice. "The proper training of the voice is an important feature in education and should not be neglected." [8] "There is something peculiarly sacred in the human voice. Its harmony and its subdued and heaven-inspired pathos exceeds every musical instrument. Vocal music is one of God's gifts to men, an instrument that cannot be surpassed or equaled when God's love abounds in the soul." [9] "The human voice that sings the music of God from a heart filled with gratitude and thanksgiving is far more pleasing to Him than the melody of all the musical instruments ever invented by human hands." [10]

How do we give our children this training of the voice? "Let there be singing in the home, of songs that are sweet and pure." [11] Sing when you are washing dishes, working in the garden, cleaning the house, doing the laundry, and other daily activities.

Parents should teach children the proper way to sing. "Some think that the louder they sing the more music they make; but noise is not music. Good singing is like the music of the birds – subdued and melodious" [12] "without the full volume of [the] voice." [13] "It is soft ... not forced and strained." [14] "The long-drawn-out notes and the peculiar sounds common in operatic singing are not pleasing to the angels. They delight to hear the simple songs of praise sung in a natural tone. The songs in which every word is uttered clearly, in a musical tone, are the songs that they join us in singing. They take up the refrain that is sung from the heart with the spirit and the understanding." [15] God desires us "to cultivate [our] voices so that [we] can speak and sing in a way that all can understand. It is not loud singing that is needed, but clear intonation, correct pronunciation, and distinct utterance. Let all take time to cultivate the voice so that God's praise can be sung in clear, soft tones, not with harshness and shrillness that offend the ear. The ability to sing is the gift of God; let it be used to His glory." [16]

4. Knowledge of God

To learn to be a truly great musician, a child must learn more than the right notes and the right techniques; he must know the Creator of music so he can truly understand music and sing and play with genuine expression. "How can those who have no interest in the word of God, who have never read His word with a sincere desire to understand its truths, be expected to sing with the spirit and the understanding? How can their hearts be in harmony with the words of sacred song?" [17]

Helping your child to truly know God through the avenues described in Chapters 4, 9, 12, and 14 will help him develop true musical talent.

5. God's Timing

I recently heard a conversation that went something like this:

Mom 1: "That was amazing! Just beautiful. All the times you made sure your son practiced his music have certainly paid off."

Mom 2: "Actually, I never had to tell him to practice."

Mom 1: "What?! You never had to tell him to practice?! He must have natural musical talent."

Mom 2: "I wouldn't say that. He has put in many hours of practice to be able to play the piano like that."

Mom 1: "But you never had to tell him to practice? He must

have been an extraordinarily self-disciplined child."

Mom 2: (laughs) "That certainly wouldn't be my first choice of adjectives to describe him. He was a very playful, gregarious child who loved to play outside and struggled quite a bit with scheduling and self-discipline. But music was like play for him – a fun and happy time."

Mom 1: "But to get ... If music was like play ... I don't see ... How... ?"

Mom 2: "Well, I think one of the keys was that I didn't start him in music lessons until he was twelve years old, which was after many years of experiencing the fun and joy of music 'play'. He had learned the enjoyment of music and had developed a love for music long before we ever started lessons. Then, the practice that came along with those lessons became an extension of the enjoyment that music brought to him."

As unique as it may sound, this experience is a common one for parents who have followed God's method of education.

There are direct parallels between the brain's readiness for formal academics and its readiness for formal music learning. Taking music lessons before the brain structures for formal music learning are developed means that the brain has to employ an inferior method of learning that can be detrimental to optimal brain development. In addition, the fine motor skills, which involve the dexterity and coordination of the muscles and nerves of the hands and fingers, do not mature enough for formal music learning until at least ten years of age. The eyes are not developed sufficiently for reading music until around the age of eight to ten. And a young child's intersensory perception (the ability to take information from one of the senses, such as the visual sense, and coordinate it with information from another of the senses, such as the tactile sense) is not ready for the type of actions that music lessons require. Not allowing sufficient time for the full development of these systems causes unhealthy stress and strain on the child and can inhibit proper development in other areas.

Many children learn to hate music lessons because they were forced to sit and practice for several hours a week before their young brain and body were ready. This is an "artificial line of education," [18] and "this course is not wise." [19] According to Jane Healy in her book, *Your Child's Growing Mind*, "Making demands on undeveloped or unprepared brain systems is a mistake. ... [W]e risk frustration, inferior skill development, and an abiding distaste and incompetence for the activity." [20]

Musical ability is developed more naturally and much more easily if God's perfect timing is followed. When we follow God's timing, children not only quickly catch up with (and often surpass) their peers who began formal music training at an earlier age, but they are also more likely to enjoy practicing music.

There is yet another benefit in using God's timing for music learning. Nearly any music instructor will tell you that to be a truly great musician, one must do much more than play the right notes. A digital device can be programmed to play an arrangement of notes, but to understand and feel the music and give it the correct expression is a potential that God gave only to humans. God wants music to "have an influence to subdue the heart and touch the feelings." [21] "The heart must feel the spirit of the song to give it right expression." [22] This ability to naturally understand music and give it true expression is actually more than a feeling, but rather the result of the development of white matter connectivity between sensory processing areas of the brain and emotional processing areas, [23] which better develops when we follow God's plan for music education.

Using God's method of education, a child does not just learn how to sing or play an instrument; rather, his whole brain engages in the music, he deeply understands the music, and he sings and plays with feeling and expression rather than merely in a rote manner. He doesn't just learn to sing or play the right notes; rather, every part of his being resonates with the melody, rhythm, and harmony of a sacred song. He is enabled to intellectually immerse himself in the music, and he learns to make mental predictions about how the music is going to unfold. He learns to correctly discern the power that music holds, and he carries the responsibility of musical talent carefully and reverently. And because of this, he also learns to continually make melody in his heart to God and hold "communion with heaven in song" [24] as Jesus did. All of these factors make the child a better musician, and they help the child bring honor to His Creator through music.

Waiting until the brain and body are sufficiently developed before engaging in formal music lessons does not mean the young child is not actively engaged in learning music. As I previously mentioned, there are many benefits to raising a child in a musically-rich environment. When a child is exposed to quality music from babyhood, when there is both spontaneous and scheduled singing in the family environment, when an abundance of time is spent surrounded by the sounds of nature, and when the child is daily coming into a deeper relationship with his Creator, musicality will develop as naturally in a child as did his ability to speak his native language. In this environment, a solid foundation is laid and numerous brain connections are made that facilitate and enhance later learning. This means that when the child does begin formal music lessons, his musical ability will grow by leaps and bounds – especially compared with the slow and tedious process experienced in traditional music learning.

6. Musical Instruments

A child benefits by having musical instruments in the home to allow for music exploration, experimentation, and enjoyment. If possible, the family should have a keyed instrument (such as a piano), as keyed instruments provide a visual and tactile representation of the structure of music and help to train the ear. If the family is not able to have a piano, other types of instruments can still provide a child with opportunities for enjoying listening to and experimenting with music.

Parents should spend time with their child experimenting with their musical instrument and enjoying casual, incidental learning. They can listen to or sing melodies and then take turns trying to figure out the melody on the instrument.

In addition, the child should be taught to properly handle and care for the instrument.

What parents often do not think about when they place their child in music lessons is that no amount of prodding or coercion can make a child love music, and a love for music is an essential part of being a truly good musician. Using the six factors mentioned here, along with the other principles of God's method of education outlined in the earlier chapters of this book, nurtures the development of true musical ability as well as a love for music. Parents should encourage a love of music so that when a child eventually does take music lessons, music learning is a joy to the child, not a lesson in drudgery. "True education is not the forcing of instruction on an unready and unreceptive mind. The mental powers must be awakened, the interest aroused." [25] With an interest awakened, the mind more readily learns anything new.

Correct vs Incorrect Use of Music

God, the creator of music, has given us instruction concerning the proper and improper use of music, and God desires that parents teach their children accordingly.

In Its Proper Place

Once children begin music lessons, a common mistake is to spend too much time on music practice. "It is one of the great temptations of the present age to carry the practice of music to extremes." [26] Music is the idol that many professed Christians worship. [27] While music is indeed an important part of true education, it should never be permitted to usurp time that should be devoted to other important activities of life, such as practical work, household duties, maintaining a well-ordered home, time outdoors, missionary endeavors, and prayer. [28] "Music, when not abused, is a great blessing; but when put to a wrong use, it is a terrible curse." [29]

Music Performance

Adults typically love to hear children perform special music in church, and some parents believe that such activities are a help in the child's Christian walk. But parents should consider the effect of performing special music, as well as recitals and similar activities, on a child's character. Children should "be educated in childlike simplicity" [30] and humility. [31] Their lives should be "quiet and simple." [32] "Musical talent too often fosters pride and ambition for display." [33] Placing children up front to sing or play an instrument puts them in the spotlight and brings praise and attention to them, but "it is not wise to give children special notice." [34]

"Music was made to serve a holy purpose, to lift the thoughts to that which is pure, noble, and elevating, and to awaken in the soul devotion and gratitude to God"; [35] but the attention a child receives when he performs in front of others has a tremendous potential to gradually shift the child's focus and attention away from his Creator and toward himself, and the child can easily learn to use the gift of music "to exalt self, instead of using it to glorify God." [36]

The parent who understands the true ideal of character will not allow their child to be put on display, but rather encourage humility, simplicity, and quietness in the life of a child. [37] "The most sacred lessons of modesty and humility are to be taught to the children." [38]

The Type of Music

We should use great care when choosing what music we expose ourselves to, as research shows that music has direct access to the limbic system, an area of the brain that is involved in emotional processing, memory, the formation of habits and addictions, and the regulation of certain behaviors.

God gave us the precious gift of music "to uplift the thoughts to high and noble themes, to inspire and elevate the soul," [39] and to prepare us to sing the songs of heaven. [40] Frivolous, light, and trifling music and songs without meaning do not serve the purpose God intended when He created music. [41] No "flippant song that should extol man and divert the attention from God" [42] should have a place in a child's developing mind. Parents should especially consider this principle when a child begins music lessons, as much of the music for beginners is of this nature.

That which is not good should always be replaced with something better. [43] From birth, children should be exposed to Christian hymns, and a variety of hymns should be sung often in the home until the child learns them well. While there is nothing wrong with some Christian songs that are not hymns, hymns play a special role in the Christian life and are uniquely valuable for not only a child's music learning but also his language development, reading comprehension, spiritual development, social development, and more.

Here are a few reasons why children can and should learn to sing hymns from a young age.

1. Hymns help develop an appreciation for well-written music.

The music for almost all of the older hymns is better written and has richer harmony than contemporary music and can help a child develop an appreciation for well-written music.

2. Hymns are a benefit for voice training.

The melodies of most hymns are simple and predictable, yet they cover a wide range of notes and intervals. These components combined are exactly what a child needs for effective voice training.

3. Learning hymns cultivates excellent language development.

The language in many of the older hymns is rich and deeply meaningful. Early exposing children to the poetic language, sentence structure, and vocabulary found in these hymns greatly enriches and strengthens their language skills. Good language development will translate to better reading comprehension and writing skills as a child gets older. In addition, children who are exposed to profound language as found in hymns tend to become deeper thinkers.

4. Hymns help children feel more involved in the worship service.

When parents regularly sing a variety of hymns with their child in the home, by the time the child is four years old, he may have fifty or more hymns memorized. When children learn hymns at an early age, even children who cannot read can participate in the worship service, which, in turn, will help them to be more interested in the worship service. In addition, if children learn hymns when they are young, they do not need to learn a whole new set of songs when they are older.

Speaking of her childhood, missionary and author Elisabeth

Elliot said, "[W]e sang a hymn every single morning after breakfast. Because of that, we children learned hymns by heart without any effort whatsoever."

5. Most hymns teach solid theology.

By learning hymns, good theology is ingrained in the child's developing mind. "The value of song as a means of education should never be lost sight of." [44]

6. Many hymns teach history and enhance the study of history.

Some children grow up in the church knowing little, if anything, about how God has led the church throughout history. Hymns can give insight into our heritage. Many hymns have fascinating stories behind them and rich history lessons. Learning hymns and the circumstances that prompted the writing of those hymns greatly enriches the study of history. For example, the beautiful hymn "A Mighty Fortress" written by Martin Luther during the darkest period of his experience during the Protestant Reformation praises and exalts God for His mighty power, love, and protection during this time of trial. The hymn "I Saw One Weary" by Annie R. Smith gives us a glimpse into the hardships, sacrifice, and commitment to a cause greater than self. It gives us insight concerning the patient endurance and the hope that Advent Christians experienced in the early days of a movement that was driven by mostly young people.

Be sure to sing all the stanzas of a hymn with your children so as to not miss the full message or story in the hymn.

7. Hymns cultivate spiritual maturity in children.

Because of the rich, deep, and powerful messages found in the older hymns, children who learn them begin to acquire a knowledge of what it means to be a mature Christian at a young and impressionable age. Often, adults underestimate a young child's ability to comprehend the profound expressions found in hymns; however, research shows that exposing children to this complex and meaningful language at a young age enables them to better appreciate these concepts as their mind grows and develops.

8. Hymns encourage breadth and depth of thought.

When a child sings songs that contain rich language, teach good theology, and remind them of solid, time-tested truths in God's Word, it inevitably encourages deep and broad thinking.

9. Hymns invest in a child's future spiritual well-being.

Music that is learned in early childhood gets impressed upon the brain more deeply and is retrieved more easily than music learned later in life. This fact enables a child to benefit significantly from hymns that he learned when he was young. When struggling with temptation, the powerful words, "I hear the Savior say, 'Thy strength indeed is small; Child of weakness, watch and pray, Find in Me thine all in all,'" [45] will probably offer more help and encouragement than will the song, "The Happy Little Duck Says Quack."

10. Hymns unite Christians.

While contemporary songs vary depending on generation, location, and culture, hymns are more constant. Even when the language is different, the tune of a traditional hymn can be recognized.

11. Hymns narrow the gap and build connections between the young and the old.

When the younger generation and the older generation sing together, especially when the songs have rich spiritual meaning, a subtle bond is developed between them.

12. Hymns have endured the test of time.

Just like a quality piece of furniture, the older hymns have endured the test of time. Many traditional hymns have been around for hundreds of years.

There is no need for special learning time or special books or activities to help children learn hymns. A young child will pick up the words and melodies of hymns remarkably fast when they are incorporated into the daily activities. "Let there be singing in the home." [46] Parents can sing while they play with their children, while they travel in the car, while they prepare a meal, while they wash the dishes, while they do laundry. "Make your work pleasant with songs of praise." [47]

"As the children of Israel, journeying through the wilderness, cheered their way by the music of sacred song, so God bids His children today gladden their pilgrim life." [48] "There is great power in music," [49] and music should be a regular and happy part of a child's life.

Words of Counsel

"The history of the songs of the Bible is full of suggestion as to the uses and benefits of music and song." [50]

"Happy the father and mother who can teach their children God's written Word with illustrations from the open pages of the book of nature; who can gather under the green trees, in the fresh, pure air, to study the Word and to sing the praise of the Father above. By such associations parents may bind their children to their hearts, and thus to God, by ties that can never be broken." [51]

"Music forms a part of God's worship in the courts above, and we should endeavor, in our songs of praise, to approach as nearly as possible to the harmony of the heavenly choirs." [52]

"When human beings sing with the spirit and the understanding, heavenly musicians take up the strain and join in the song of thanksgiving." [53] "How can the heavenly choir join in music that is only a form?" [54]

The talent of singing "should be cultivated; for the human voice in singing is one of God's entrusted talents to be employed to His glory." [55]

CHAPTER 27

SCIENCE

"In the study of the sciences ... we are to obtain
a knowledge of the Creator." – Patriarchs and
Prophets, 599

STUDIES clearly show that curiosity and the skills of observation and objective analysis are crucial factors for science learning. [1] A student must be able to keenly observe, analyze what he has observed, generate objective thoughts, and make intelligent experimental predictions about what he observes (which may sometimes be quite different from the beliefs generally held). He then must be able to test those predictions and build on what he learns. And since data doesn't mean much unless it has a practical application, a good science student must be able to make accurate analyses and decisions about the interpretation of data. Without these traits and abilities, scientific knowledge will be of little benefit. When we help our children develop these traits and skills, they will learn science much better than they ever will by reading a science textbook.

The good news is that the methods of true education, as outlined in the earlier chapters of this book, naturally develop these skills in children. They also cultivate a child's natural, inborn curiosity and love of learning.

Another important factor in the study of science is practical, hands-on learning, [2] especially in the context of nature. [3] The world of nature is active and alive, and significant learning can take place in the areas of ecology, biology, botany, zoology (such as ornithology, ichthyology, and entomology), earth science, astronomy, physical science, and chemistry (and more) in God's creation. In addition, the effects that experiential learning in nature has on the development of the brain are astounding. An abundance of hands-on time in nature will help your child excel in science. (See Chapters 11 and 12.)

Studies demonstrate that being in nature "stimulates children's interest in science." [4] Studies also show "that children's encounters with nature and natural elements (e.g., plants, insects, rocks) facilitate their question-asking," [5] and a child's question-asking is a powerful catalyst for his learning and understanding. [6] This approach is in line with God's method of education, in which emphasis is placed on brain development, thinking skills, awakening the interest, the skill of observation, character development, and the education of the whole child rather than simply conveying information. When parents use true education, "the children generally will be inquisitive to learn the things of nature. They will ask questions in regard to the things they see and hear, and parents should improve the opportunity to instruct, and patiently answer these little inquiries. They can, in this manner, get the advantage of the enemy, and fortify the minds of their children, by sowing good seed in their hearts, leaving no room for the bad to take root." [7]

For the best science learning, spend a lot of time outside in nature. Show an interest in what your child observes and what he is interested in. Occasionally, ask a question or two. This type of interaction increases a child's natural desire to learn and explore.

As a child grows, the parent and child can conduct field studies to further science learning. A field study involves collecting data about plants and animals in their natural environment without changing or disturbing the setting or any part of what one is observing. In addition to all the interesting things that a child can learn, field studies greatly encourage the development of observational and thinking skills, as well as the character traits of patience and perseverance. Some examples of field studies that often interest children include observing how the weather affects the color of the autumn leaves, observing the process through which a bird builds a nest, observing how the time of day affects the number of worms or insects that birds feed their babies, and observing whether the characteristics of spider webs change depending on where the web is built. Use a notebook to record your observations. If your child has been raised using the methods of true education, his innate curiosity will prompt questions that can lead to more ideas for field studies.

In addition to field studies, you and your child can conduct some scientific experiments in the garden. Experiment with different seeds to see which ones sprout the fastest under equal conditions. You could also experiment to see how moisture and heat affect the rate at which they sprout. Or compare the growth of plants in various light conditions or with different types of soil. Be sure to document your observations so you can refer to them later when you want to use the data for practical purposes or to conduct other experiments.

When science learning is approached in this practical way, time in nature will prompt a child who has been raised using methods of true education to do more science learning on his own. And when the child is older and does read a book on science, he will better grasp the information in the book because he's already had many years of extensive personal experience with science in real life. What he learns from books will "stick" because his brain can connect the information in the books with his previous observations and experiences.

True Science

"Too often the minds of students are occupied with men's theories and speculations, falsely called science and philosophy. They need to be brought into close contact with nature. Let them learn that creation and Christianity have one God. Let them be taught to see the harmony of the natural with the spiritual." [8]

In God's method of education, the study of science helps us to "obtain a knowledge of the Creator. All true science is but an interpretation of the handwriting of God in the material world. Science brings from her research only fresh evidences of the wisdom and power of God. Rightly understood, both the book of nature and the written word make us acquainted with God by teaching us something of the wise and beneficent laws through which He works." [9]

"All true science is in harmony with his works; all true education leads to obedience to his government." [10]

Words of Counsel

"The student should be led to see God in all the works of creation. Teachers should copy the example of the Great Teacher, who from the familiar scenes of nature drew illustrations that simplified His teachings and impressed them more deeply upon the minds of His hearers. The birds caroling in the leafy branches, the flowers of the valley, the lofty trees, the fruitful lands, the springing grain, the barren soil, the setting sun gilding the heavens with its golden beams – all served as means of instruction." [11]

CHAPTER 28

MATHEMATICS

"Mathematics is the language with which God has
written the universe." – Galileo

GOD is the creator of all true mathematics, and a knowledge
and understanding of mathematics is tremendously useful in
our everyday lives. Unfortunately, many learn to hate math because
it is typically taught in a rote and formulaic manner – completely
contrary to how the brain was designed to learn this subject. False
education does not lead a student to truly learn and understand math;
rather, it trains him to memorize and execute procedures.

But learned correctly, mathematics is interesting, beautiful, creative, meaningful, useful, practical, fascinating, and even fun!

Real-Life Math

In traditional education, many children grow up learning algebra,
trigonometry, and calculus, yet they don't have a basic knowledge of
how to budget or practice financial responsibility, balance a check-
book, figure distance and cost for travel, measure and multiply or
divide measurements, and use math to do calculations for time management or price comparison. In God's math class, a child learns all
these very useful and practical skills – and more! Using God's lesson
books of useful work and the experiences of life (see Chapters 11 and
13), a child is enabled to learn a much wider range of mathematical
concepts than he would ever learn even with the best curriculum.

Peter Gray, PhD, research professor at Boston College, notes that
"when children are ... solving real-world problems that involve math,
they acquire these skills more deeply, in ways that make sense and are
remembered, than when they are doing them as school assignments."
[1] Children can enjoy math and excel at it when they learn it as God
intends them to learn it.

A plethora of math skills can be learned just in the kitchen alone.

A toddler can learn to count as he counts how many potatoes are needed for the soup or how many berries will fit in a measuring cup. He can learn to count backwards when he needs to stir something for ten seconds and you and he count backwards from ten. A child will learn the use of ordinal numbers as you talk to him about the first, second, third, and fourth steps in a recipe. He learns addition when you ask him how many carrots are in the salad if he adds two carrots to the three that are already in it. He very practically and concretely learns measurement units like grams, ounces, quarts, gallons, and liters as he uses them in cooking. He'll naturally learn multiplication when doubling or tripling a recipe, and he will learn division when dividing a recipe in half. He will learn fractions when using measuring spoons and measuring cups or when cutting an apple into fourths, sixths, or eighths. And he'll learn all these skills much more efficiently and at a more advanced level than he ever could with pencil and paper.

But math learning isn't limited to the kitchen. A child can learn math when measuring in the garden, using highway mile markers to figure road distances, calculating the amount of material needed for a building project, calculating percentages (tithes, tax on purchases, discount sales, etc.), and comparing prices at stores. From a young age, a child can be taught how to create a budget and keep a record of his finances. (More on this in the next chapter.) "In the study of figures the work should be made practical. Let every youth and every child be taught, not merely to solve imaginary problems, but to keep an accurate account of his own income and outgoes." [2] All these opportunities give a child experience in learning math at a practical level, which is far better than the linear approach to math that you find in a math workbook.

When Should Math Be Taught?

In God's method of education, even toddlers can begin to learn practical mathematics. But parents should remember that God designed children to learn in a practical way, not with pencil, paper, and books – and this especially applies to the subject of mathematics. Until the age of ten to twelve, the areas of a child's brain that are involved with correctly understanding the abstract concepts needed for pencil-and-paper math are not developed sufficiently. (See Chapter 5.) In addition, several years of real-life experiences are necessary to develop logical and analytical thinking, spatial understanding, problem-solving skills, and reasoning abilities, which are necessary for a child to readily grasp mathematical concepts in a way that he will learn them well. According to mathematics educator and consultant, Dr. Maria Droujkova, "Calculations kids are forced to do are often so developmentally inappropriate, the experience amounts to torture."[3]

In addition, experiments have shown that teaching children mathematics before they have reached sufficient maturity (in age and experience) may hinder a child's mathematical learning. For example, in one experiment conducted by educator Louis Paul Bénézet, math class was omitted from the curriculum for several classrooms below the sixth-grade level. The children were occasionally given a few practical, incidental experiences with numbers, such as estimating lengths and distances, telling time, and calculating change, but the school time regularly allocated to math class was replaced with a time for discussion and conversation about topics that were interesting to them. The results? The no-math-class students outperformed the math-class students at word problems and were even adept at solving very complex word problems. They also had a better conception and comprehension of distance, heights, lengths, and areas. (In addition, their knowledge of geography, as well as their communication and reading skills, far surpassed those of the math-class students.) By the end of sixth grade, after receiving just one year of math instruction, the no-math-class children were able to do regular computational math just as well as, if not better than, the traditionally-taught students. According to Bénézet, the early introduction of arithmetic dulls a child's reasoning facilities, and children would excel in math if teachers would just wait until a child is at least in the seventh grade before teaching this subject. "The whole subject of arithmetic could be postponed until the seventh year of school, and it could be mastered in two years' study by any normal child."[4]

Taking the time to build a foundation of practical, real-life experiences develops in a child a true understanding of the concepts of math so that, when he is older, he can compute mathematical problems on paper with understanding and skill.

Mathematics in the Bible and Nature

As a child grows older, after he has developed a solid understanding of math concepts through practical experiences of life, a more advanced understanding of mathematics can be gained through God's other lessons books, the study of the Scriptures and of nature. [5] (See Chapters 12 and 14.)

In the Bible, there are over one hundred references to arithmetic and geometry, and the prophecies of the Bible require the use of mathematics to calculate them. If a family is actually studying the *Bible* (rather than a man-made guide to the Scriptures), and the child is being educated using the methods of true education, his active and inquisitive mind will naturally notice and be drawn to explore the math found in the Scriptures. (A guide or a curriculum can hinder this learning. As I mentioned in Chapter 7, when a child becomes accustomed to a curriculum telling him what he should learn, he has little need to discover knowledge on his own, and he does not have to understand what he is doing and why he is doing it; he only needs to give the right answers and complete the assignment. Consequently, his thinking skills are weakened.)

Mathematics is also involved in nearly all functions of nature, such as the movement of planets, in the nature of light, and even in the growth of a tree. Nature presents many repeating number sequences and mathematical patterns, such as the spiral of a seashell, the pattern in the center of the sunflower, and the structure of a pinecone. Fractals – patterns that repeat themselves on smaller scales – are found in many places in nature, such as in snowflakes and the fronds and leaves of a fern. Older children with a good foundation in true education often enjoy exploring the advanced mathematics found in nature.

Memorizing vs Learning

Should children memorize multiplication tables and other math facts?

While some may find the memorization of math facts to be helpful, for most, it isn't necessary, and it can hinder learning. Some of the world's leading mathematicians (such as software performance expert Daniel Lemire, who holds three degrees in mathematics and ranks among the top 2 percent of scientists globally [6]) don't have their multiplication (or addition) tables memorized. Dr. Maria Droujkova, who won several math and science Olympiads, says, "I never memorized addition facts; 8 plus 4 still goes, 8 -> 10 and 2 extra -> 12 in my mind, albeit lightning-fast." [7] Individuals who are exceptionally adept at math typically didn't learn math through memorization, flashcards, worksheets, timed tests, and other conventional ways of learning. More often than not, they were allowed to explore math in practical ways, taking information from real-life context, quantifying it, and developing their own methods and strategies for calculating and solving. According to Jo Boaler, researcher of mathematics education, "Extensive research demonstrates that kids readily understand math when they develop the ability to use numbers flexibly." [8] Memorizing does not equal thinking, nor is it conducive to true understanding. Studies show that learning math naturally through real-life experiences involves completely different pathways in the brain than does learning through memorization, and children who learn practically instead of through memorization learn math facts more securely and are more adept at applying them. [9] This practical, real-life approach not only helps a child learn math better, but it also helps him see the relevance of math to life, which completely eliminates the complaining question, "When will I ever use this?"

When using God's lesson books for math learning, there is no need for a curriculum or page after page of boring, impractical, and repetitive mathematical instruction. Children learn math very efficiently and solidly in God's method of true education. When a child has a background in learning mathematical skills in a practical way from God's lesson books, all further learning will happen quickly and efficiently.

CHAPTER 29

BOOKKEEPING AND BUDGETING

"Beware of little expenses; a little leak will sink a great ship." – Benjamin Franklin

BOOKKEEPING has strangely dropped out of school work in many places but this should be regarded as a study of primary importance."[1] "Bookkeeping should stand as one of the most important branches of education."[2] "A knowledge of bookkeeping should be considered as important as a knowledge of grammar."[3] "Children should be educated ... to understand figures, to keep their own accounts."[4]

Bookkeeping and budgeting are key to helping a child learn to be financially responsible. They also help a child improve the skills of decision-making, planning, prioritizing, and delayed gratification.

How and When to Learn Bookkeeping and Budgeting

A child can learn the skill of budgeting and bookkeeping as early as three or four years of age. Label some jars or envelopes with budget categories such as tithe, offering, helping the needy, savings, and spending. Teach your child that ten percent of his income is to be given as tithe, another percentage is to be given to other areas of the Lord's work, another percentage to help the needy, and another is to be saved for his future needs. The remainder is his spending money that he may spend in a way that the Lord approves. This method gives a child a very practical, hands-on understanding of budgeting and financial responsibility.

Once a child is older and has been using this hands-on method for a few years and has a solid grasp of how to allocate his income, parents can then teach him how to use a pencil and paper for bookkeeping. As the child places money in his jar or envelope, parents can show their child how to record the corresponding figures in his budgeting book. At first, the parent may want to do this with their child, but as the child gets older, he can gradually take on more and more of the responsibility of recording the numbers in his record book and doing the required math.

In connection with the instruction on budgeting and bookkeeping, a child should be given lessons on financial responsibility and earning his own money. Even a child as young as four years of age can do jobs like weeding a neighbor's garden, selling garden produce, or making bread to sell. (See Chapter 13 for more about teaching a child to earn his own money.) "Money which comes to the young with but little effort on their part will not be valued,"[5] but children who earn money by working with their own hands learn to appreciate the value of money. They "generally prize their abilities, improve their privileges, and cultivate and direct their faculties to accomplish a purpose in life. They frequently develop characters of industry, frugality, and moral worth, which lie at the foundation of success in the Christian life."[6] "It is possible for the children... to be able to help in buying their own clothes, and they should be encouraged to do this."[7] "How much safer are those youth who know just where their spending money comes from, who know what their clothing and food costs, and what it takes to purchase a home!"[8]

Education for a Purpose

In the creation of a budget, parents should, by little lessons often repeated, instill in the mind of their children that money is a trust from God. Children "should be taught that the money which they earn is not theirs to spend as their inexperienced minds may choose, but to use judiciously and to give to missionary purposes. They should not be satisfied to take money from their father or mother and put it into the treasury as an offering when it is not theirs. They should say to themselves, 'Shall I give of that which costs me nothing?' [2 Samuel 24:24]"[9] "There are many ways in which children can earn money themselves and can act their part in bringing thank offerings to Jesus, who gave His own life for them."[10] "Many a child ... can have a little plot of land where he can learn to garden. He can be taught to make this a means of securing money to give to the cause of God. Both boys and girls can engage in this work; and it will, if they are rightly instructed, teach them the value of money and how to economize." [11]

Children should also be given thorough and practical lessons in stewardship. They should be taught that "we are to be careful not to spend our precious time and money unwisely." [12] Why? Because money is given to the Christian for a purpose. "In the hands of God's children it is food for the hungry, and clothing for the naked. It is a defense to the oppressed, a means of health to the sick, a means of preaching the gospel to the poor," [13] and furthering the work of the Lord. For the Christian, every dollar is "of value, not to gratify his taste or lust, not for him to hide in the earth, but to do good with, to help win souls to the truth, to build up the kingdom of Christ. His enjoyment is the same as that of Christ, – in seeing souls saved." [14]

"Parents are to instruct their children in lessons of economy, in order that the younger members of the flock may learn to share the responsibility of supporting the cause of God." [15] We are to "teach our children to deny self and become the Lord's helping hands in dispensing His blessings." [16] When we teach our children self-denial and economy for Christ's sake, we enable them to be *personally* involved in the Lord's work.

Children naturally tend to adopt the consumer attitudes of their parents, and they learn financial stewardship best through the everyday example of their parents. Search your heart and ask yourself what your priorities are regarding finances and what example you are setting for your child. Do your financial goals focus on that which will only fade, or do your goals have eternal value? Children watch what parents purchase, and they notice when their parents are careful to not spend money on items that are not needed and to not be wasteful. When you choose to get your older vehicle repaired (or learn to repair it yourself) instead of buying a newer one so you can give more money to support the Lord's work, your child notices. You may think that it's a bother to put that small amount of leftover food in the refrigerator instead of throwing it away, but little eyes are watching how you manage the gifts that God has given you. When you decide to send money to a missionary instead of purchasing a new phone, your child will learn what should be his priorities in life as well.

Involve your child in your practical, day-to-day purchasing decisions as well as the planning for purchases (large and small). Discuss what factors are involved in making those decisions. These activities give opportunities to discuss stewardship responsibilities, the difference between wants and needs, how to balance saving money with purchasing items of quality, and how to avoid the pitfalls and dangers of borrowing money. "Expend your money carefully and let your daily example teach lessons of frugality, self-denial, and economy to your children. They need to be educated by precept and example." [17]

When we teach our children to be economical so they can invest in the work of the Lord, we are not only teaching them budgeting and mathematics, but we are also teaching them good investment practices as they learn to invest in riches that will never fade.

Words of Counsel

"Money is a needed treasure; let it not be lavished upon those who do not need it. Someone needs your willing gifts." [18]

"Every dollar used unnecessarily deprives the spender of a precious opportunity to do good." [19]

"How careful should fathers and mothers be to teach economy by precept and example to their children!" [20]

"Money is to be regarded as a gift entrusted to us of God to do His work, to build up His kingdom, and the youth should learn to restrict their desires. Teach that none may prostitute their powers in self-pleasing and self-gratification." [21]

CHAPTER 30

SPELLING

"To spell correctly, to write a clear, fair hand, and to keep accounts, are essential accomplishments." – *The Review and Herald, October 4, 1898*

RESEARCH shows that the best spellers are those who have exceptional observational and pattern-learning skills. [1] Excellent spellers can see words briefly and ever after know how to spell those words. How do they do this? When they see a word, their brain quickly and adeptly observes how the word is spelled, extricates patterns in its spelling, compares the patterns with the spelling patterns in others words it has already observed, and classifies and organizes the word according to its patterns of spelling, and thus creates connections and neural pathways that enable it to remember the spelling of that word with just that brief exposure.

We can easily see that observational and pattern-learning skills are valuable skills to possess. Interestingly, all babies are born with a keen desire to observe and to recognize patterns [2] and will solidly develop these skills throughout childhood if given the right environment. Unfortunately, several factors in our modern culture and in the false system of education have a strong tendency to squelch their development. In addition, because traditional spelling curricula rely heavily on rote memorization, which uses the lower parts of the brain, the skills of observing, thinking, and noticing patterns are not strengthened when using conventional methods. Research shows that an emphasis on memorization does very little to help students become good spellers overall. [3] The brain *prefers* to learn spelling by observing patterns [4] rather than by memorizing words.

God's method of education not only helps a child retain these natural abilities of observing and pattern-learning, but it also helps him develop them. A simple, quiet, and orderly environment that excludes the use of electronic devices and allows the expression of a child's natural curiosity (see Chapter 8); [5] the development of true learning and whole-brain thinking (see Chapter 7); an abundance of time in nature (see Chapter 12); a generous amount of practical work in the family environment (see Chapter 13); the development of cause-to-effect reasoning (see Chapter 22); and the many other factors in God's method of education all cultivate the skills of observant learning and pattern learning and help a child become an excellent speller.

Parents can support a child's learning by gradually teaching him various spelling rules as they become useful to the child. To be used correctly, these rules do not need to be memorized. Rather, a child can use these rules to help him better detect patterns in spelling. Because spelling is so effectively learned through keen observation and pattern detection, and because children must have a practical use of knowledge to truly learn it, there is no sense in teaching spelling rules until a child has a need for learning those rules. If parents don't know the rules of spelling, they should get a good spelling handbook (for themselves, not for the child) so they can know how to correctly teach their child.

With his inquisitive and active mind, a child may also be interested in learning about word origins (etymology), and exploration along these lines should be encouraged. Not only can the study of word origins be fascinating, but it will also strengthen pattern detection and spelling skills. Learning the rules of spelling and the principles and reasons *behind* those rules – which can be greatly helped through an exploration of etymology – uses the higher brain functions involved with problem-solving and reasoning skills and exercises the thinking abilities. These factors, coupled with his pattern-detection skills, will help a child recognize patterns in spelling, which will help him figure out how to spell words that he has never previously seen or heard.

Some may argue that the English language has many irregularly spelled words, and spelling rules have so many exceptions that pattern-detection cannot possibly be used for learning spelling. However, spelling research shows that English spelling is, in fact, "a predictable, logical, and rule-based language system," [6] and the great majority of English words are spelled according to a predictable pattern. The problem is not that the spelling of English words does not follow a pattern, but that there are a great number of patterns, and without strong pattern-detection skills, those patterns are easily missed.

A book of basic spelling rules and a large, high-quality dictionary (to learn etymology) can be very helpful, but they should be used for reference, not as textbooks. Spelling should not be treated as a separate subject, isolated to a weekly list of spelling words learned out of natural context without application or authentic and meaningful uses of the word. Even children with good observational and pattern-detection skills will not learn to spell well in this way. Rather, learning to spell should be integrated into all other academic subjects and all areas of practical, everyday life. However, while learning to spell can be naturally incorporated into a child's everyday life, parents must be intentional in teaching their child. This subject should not be neglected, as the ability to spell correctly is an important skill.

When children learn to spell using God's methods of true education, learning is more effective and more enjoyable.

CHAPTER 31

FOREIGN LANGUAGES

*"To learn a language is to have one
more window from which to look at the
world." – Chinese Proverb*

L EARNING more than one language brings with it some remarkable cognitive advantages. The brain of a child who learns
a second language looks and functions differently than the brain
of a monolingual child. We see higher density of the grey matter
and a more active prefrontal cortex in the brains of bilingual and
multilingual children. Children who speak more than one language
tend to have advanced decision-making skills, problem-solving skills,
reasoning abilities, and cognitive flexibility compared to those who
don't. [1] And bilingual and multilingual children are often able to
process information faster and score higher on memory tests than
children who speak only one language.

But there is an even more valuable reason to learn another language. "A familiarity with the languages of the different nations
is a help in missionary work," [2] and "true education *is* missionary
training." [3] Many areas of the Lord's work are in great need of the
assistance of those who know more than one language, and your child
can be a wonderful blessing to others if he gains this skill.

When to Learn a Second Language

When is the best time to learn a second language?

I've had the privilege of meeting many toddlers and young children around the world who were proficient in two and even three
languages, yet who had never taken a single language class. It has
always fascinated me that a little three-year-old who could not yet tie
his shoes was able to chat away with me in English, ask his mom a
question in Spanish, and then translate the conversation into French
for his grandmother. How did this child become completely fluent
in three languages in only three years, while many adults who took

four years of foreign language in high school can barely communicate on a basic level?

The brains of babies and toddlers are primed for language learning, and a young child quickly and thoroughly learns his first language simply through exposure. The same holds true for a second language. No flashcards. No word lists. No workbook. No vocabulary drills. Just simple exposure.

Very young children are able to learn languages more easily than those who are older because language acquisition for the young child happens in both hemispheres of the brain (thus giving him a more holistic grasp of the language), while in most adults, language learning is mostly limited to only one hemisphere (which makes language learning more difficult). [4] As a child gets older, his language-learning abilities begin to decrease. This does not mean that an older child cannot learn a second language, but that the learning gradually becomes more difficult as the child gets older.

How To

The very best way for a child to learn a second (or third) language is through immersion at a young age.

If both parents speak the same second language, they can communicate with their child primarily in that second language. The child will absorb the language of the country in which they live through other social interactions, such as at church. For example, if the family lives in the United States and both parents speak Korean, they should speak to their child primarily in Korean. The child will learn English through his interactions with others since he lives in an English-speaking country.

If only one parent speaks a second language, that parent can speak to the child only in the second language. For example, if the family lives in England, and the father speaks German while the mother speaks English, the father should speak to the child only in German.

What can you do if neither parent knows another language? Choose a language that you would like your child to learn, and then do your best to provide him with frequent exposure to that language.

Research shows that frequent exposure to a second language at a young age is still superior to classes, vocabulary memorization, and grammar drills. [5]

There are several ways you can increase your child's exposure to a second language. Perhaps you can make friends with someone who speaks another language. Ask them to speak to your child in that language and to teach you various words and how to use them. You can also obtain recordings of hymns in the second language, listen to them, and learn to sing along. And you can listen to the Bible, *Christ's Object Lessons,* [6] or the books in the *Conflict of the Ages Series* [7] in the second language. [8] (Listening is preferable to reading as listening allows you to hear how the words should be pronounced.) As you become familiar with the language, attending a church service in the language you want to learn may also be helpful.

Learning through exposure can have many other benefits besides excellent language learning. Philip and his family learned Japanese when they befriended an elderly lady who was originally from Japan. She and Philip became the best of friends, and the benefits went far beyond learning another language. The young boy learned to communicate with, relate to, and respect others not of his age group. And the frequent visits from Philip and his family shed a cheery light on the lonely life of the elderly woman.

You can boost language learning by learning specific words that you can practice using in your everyday speech. "Emily, could you please hand me a *toalla*?" "We are having *maçãs* for breakfast." "*Guten Morgen!*" It's alright if you make mistakes. Don't worry if your patched-together sentences wouldn't make sense to a native. Simply attempting to include the second language in your day creates connections in your child's brain that make later language learning easier and more efficient.

What if your child is older and would like to learn another language? Learning a second language as an older child or teen is still easier than learning it as an adult. Lydia learned Portuguese by taking about an hour to study a few basics of the language and then daily listening to the book *Patriarchs and Prophets* in Portuguese. [9] She chose that book because it was a book that she was already very familiar with in her native tongue, and it's full of stories, which lend themselves well to language learning. At first, she understood nothing, but within a few months, she could follow the stories quite well. Through this process, she developed a solid foundation in Portuguese, which enabled her to branch out in other ways of Portuguese learning, and she quickly became fairly fluent.

Again, to learn a second language well and to prevent the learning from becoming drudgery, avoid the mundane drills of verb conjugations and vocabulary lists, and skip the memorization of mostly useless phrases, such as "Where is the bathroom?" (Okay, that phrase could come in handy at some point, but it isn't a phrase that a child will use regularly in everyday life as he communicates with his family.) Instead, adopt the language learning technique that has been successfully used for thousands of years – and the one your child used to learn his native language. Use the language daily in your home, talking about what you would normally talk about.

Learning another language can be both fun and useful, and young children can learn a language so quickly that many of them even surpass their parents in fluency.

Note: The learning of another language, while useful in life and beneficial for the brain, should never overshadow the necessity for a child to learn his mother tongue well. As discussed in Chapter 19, children should be able to speak their native language correctly, using proper grammar and good articulation. [10]

Words of Counsel

"Young men should be qualifying themselves by becoming familiar with other languages, that God may use them as mediums to communicate His saving truth to those of other nations." [11]

"If young women who have borne but little responsibility would devote themselves to God, they could qualify themselves for usefulness by studying and becoming familiar with other languages. They could devote themselves to the work of translating." [12]

SECTION VI
THE PARENTS' EDUCATION

CHAPTER 32

A Curriculum for True Education

"The grace of Jesus Christ will give wisdom to all
who follow the Lord's plan of true education." –
Testimonies for the Church 9:177

WHEN my first child was born, I didn't know anyone who homeschooled, nor did I know very much about homeschooling.
And I certainly had never heard the term *true education*. I just knew
that I loved having my little one with me, and there was no way I
was going to send him to school. So, I decided – amidst plenty of
alarm and opposition – that I was going to teach him at home rather
than send him to school.

This was before the days of the internet, and I couldn't do an
online search about how to homeschool. I didn't have a curriculum.
How would I know what to teach him? I felt that I needed some
help – a curriculum or something to guide me – and I didn't know
where to turn, so I used the only resource I knew of. I prayed. I barely
knew God at the time, but I somehow knew that He could help me
know how to teach this child. Just a few days after that fumbling
prayer, someone shared some books with me. I don't think, at that
time, that I saw these books as an answer to prayer, but I now know
they were. As I read those books, [1] I learned a whole new way of
thinking. I felt like my eyes were being opened. And as I continued to
study and pray, I suddenly came to a realization that forever changed
my understanding of education.

Is There a Curriculum for True Education?

My friend, Gina, was putting together a large, complex puzzle
with thousands of pieces. The picture was of a beautiful nature scene,
and I enjoyed watching it come together. As she worked on the puzzle, she kept coming across a particular puzzle piece that just didn't

seem to fit anywhere. She tried to fit it here and tried to fit it there, but she had to keep setting it aside because the fit was never quite right. It became a bit humorous to us as she found herself repeatedly picking it up, thinking it was just the piece that she was looking for, only to find that, once again, it did not fit. At one point, I saw her pick up that puzzle piece, look at it, and mumble something about "forcing you to fit," but of course, she didn't do that as the beautiful scene at the end would have marred. Eventually, the puzzle was completed, and as we stood back to admire the gorgeous picture, I noticed that the one perplexing puzzle piece that never seemed to fit anywhere was still sitting off to the side. It never fit in the puzzle because it wasn't even part of that particular puzzle! It belonged to a different puzzle.

Educational methods are like puzzles. There are many pieces to an educational method – the teachers, the students, the different subjects studied, the various methods used to teach each subject, the environment, and so forth. In traditional methods of education, a curriculum is seen as an essential piece to the educational puzzle. It is part of completing the picture – a picture that parents and teachers will find difficult, if not impossible, to complete without the curriculum to tell them what to teach and how to teach it. When we look at how God designed our children to be educated, however, a curriculum doesn't have that place. In fact, a curriculum doesn't fit the methods of true education at all. If forced into the picture, it will mar the beautiful scene.

Here are just a few of the reasons I have found, through my study and prayer, why a curriculum doesn't fit into true education.

1. A curriculum author doesn't know God's plan for your child.

The Lord has a very specific plan for your child. Even the very best curriculum – no matter how flexible and adaptable it is, no matter how much Biblical information it includes, no matter how closely it purports to follow true education – was designed by someone who has no idea what God's life plan is for your child, and therefore is incapable of writing an educational guide that will give your child what he needs to follow God's plan for him.

I made many mistakes in my children's education (because I didn't always understand and follow God's beautiful ways), but not nearly as many mistakes as I would have made had I followed a curriculum instead of God's direction for my child. When we follow a curriculum, we inevitably bring aspects into a child's education that God, in His original plan, would not have brought in and undoubtedly neglect other aspects that would not have been neglected were He our guide. When we turn to God for constant guidance, an amazing exchange takes place – instead of a curriculum guiding our children's education, the Lord of the universe, the greatest Educator this world has ever known, guides their education.

God's workings with us are custom-made to our specific needs. There is no curriculum that can be so precisely tailored to a child. Nor can there ever be. Why would we pass by this amazing opportunity to be guided by our Creator and settle for being led by someone who doesn't even know our children?

2. A curriculum teaches us to rely on man for guidance.

It can be scary to suddenly be responsible for the education of a little human without something material or tangible to tell us what to do, but to follow someone else's program, even if the program claims to be based on God's methods of education, defeats one of the main purposes of true education – "to enable us to understand the voice of God." [2]

True education is not a step-by-step program that can be contained in a curriculum. True education is not a program that you work your way through. True education is connecting yourself and your child with the Source of wisdom.

"God desires to bring men into direct relation with Himself. ... He seeks to encourage a sense of personal dependence and to impress the need of personal guidance. ... Satan works to thwart this purpose. He seeks to encourage dependence upon men." [3] "We cannot depend for counsel upon humanity. The Lord will teach us our duty just as willingly as He will teach somebody else." [4]

Jesus has invited us to come unto Him and be guided by Him. [5] He has given us an abundance of instruction regarding true education in books such as *Education* and *The Ministry of Healing*, in the older, inspired writings of "The Review and Herald," and more. As you turn to God for instruction and learn from Him instead of turning to man for guidance, your child will notice, and you will be teaching him *through your own example* how to turn to and learn from the great God of heaven.

3. Curricula weaken thinking abilities.

When God created man in His image, He created him with the ability to *think*. God wants us to cultivate this ability in our children.

The false system of education is not designed to produce strong thinkers but rather mere reflectors of others' thoughts. In this system, the student's responsibility is not to think but to follow a predetermined learning sequence.

Following a curriculum perpetuates this lack-of-thinking problem. The curriculum determines *what* a child supposedly needs to learn, tells the parent *how* to teach it, and even tells the parent *when* to teach it. And the "better" the curriculum is, the less we have to think. Using the methods of false education, we are gradually conditioned to be dependent upon something else to do the thinking for us. And the full and proper intellectual growth that God desires us to have is stunted.

"False influences have checked the development of the intellect." [6] But "it is the work of true education to develop this power, to train the youth to be thinkers." [7] Accordingly, one of the most important responsibilities of parents is not to impart knowledge to their child, but rather to strengthen their child's mind so he can "think for himself." [8] God wants the mind to be "trained to think." [9]

How can parents teach their child to think?

The first and most important step in teaching a child to think is to lead by example. If parents want to educate their child according to God's method and thus encourage him to be a thinker, parents cannot have someone else or something else doing their thinking for them.

Some parents may feel that the information given in this book doesn't give enough specific and detailed steps to take for educating their child. But if the book did that, it would no longer be about true education. Each child is different, and parents must seek the Lord and learn to understand His guidance to know God's plan for their child.

Don't be concerned if you were raised in the false system of education and feel like you don't know what to do. God is ready and waiting to help you. Ask for wisdom, trust that God will give it to you, and then begin by following God's instruction that has already been revealed to you. Don't worry if you don't know everything. As you obey what God has shown you – though it seems very small to you – He will reveal more, and step-by-step He will guide you. The more you follow His ways, the more your mind will "expand and strengthen by exercise,"[10] and both you and your children will learn to reason well and think well.

"The education that should be given to all is, that they should exercise faith, that they should go to God in earnest prayer, and *learn to think* for themselves. To meet difficulties and plow through them by the help of God is a lesson of the highest value. If men and women do this, they realize that their help has not come from a human source, but from the living God, and that, having sought wisdom of God, they have not sought in vain. It is the privilege of every soul to go to God for himself, and to have a personal connection with the Source of all power. Then the lips can speak forth the praises, not of men [and not of a curriculum], but of God."[11]

4. A curriculum cannot develop character.

Character development is an important aspect of true education. There are a handful of curricula that emphasize character development, but character can never be truly developed at the heart level through a curriculum. True character development for children occurs best in the real-life, practical, everyday activities (such as cooking and working in the garden) as the parent spends time with the child, seeking the Lord for guidance, studying the child's character, and cooperating with God. (See Chapter 6 for more about character development.)

5. Curricula crowd out real-life learning.

As we saw in Chapter 11, learning in the practical, everyday activities of life is an essential part of true education. Experiential learning means that the child is actively engaged in his learning instead of relying on a curriculum to tell him what he should learn.

Not only does real-life learning result in the development of better thinking skills and observational skills, but when a child is learning through his involvement in daily activities, he learns lessons that could never be planned by a curriculum.

6. Curricula stifles curiosity and suppresses a child's natural love of learning.

Curiosity drives learning. [12] The book *Education* calls attention to this fact when it tells us that awakening the interest of a child is one of the first steps for true learning. "True education is not the forcing of instruction on an unready and unreceptive mind. The mental powers must be awakened, the interest aroused." [13]

Anyone who has taken a two-year-old for a walk in nature can attest to the fact that children are born with curiosity and the love of learning. No matter how much the adult would like to hurry through the walk, there is no rushing the two-year-old as he lies down to greet the beetles, stoops to smell each and every dandelion, picks up a stick to examine it, whisks it through the dead leaves to hear what that sounds like, investigates every stone to see if it is throw-worthy and then pauses to test his theories. Until we condition him otherwise, a child has an innate sense of curiosity. Sadly, curricula shift the focus away from interest- and curiosity-based learning to following the schedule that the curriculum dictates.

When eight-year-old William noticed the frogs that he had been observing all summer stopped croaking when the cold weather came, he was intensely curious about what happened to the frogs. His curiosity led him to the family's set of encyclopedias, then to the library, to more observation, to some record-keeping, more research, some experimentation, and then application of the knowledge he gained through his learning adventure. What would have happened had his parents been using a curriculum? What would have happened had the curriculum instructed William to learn about the life cycle of frogs two years before he had noticed the frogs in their pond? William's curiosity had not yet been aroused, and he may not have been interested in the lesson. Because a child's interest level, depth of thinking, level of creativity, retention of information, level of perseverance, and learning goals are all affected by his level of curiosity, William's learning would have been stunted. He would have missed out on the rich experience he had as he was learning to observe, to ask questions, to research, to problem-solve, to experiment, and to apply what he had learned. And he most certainly would not have remembered what he had learned as well as he did when he learned in a natural, real-life setting in response to his own curiosity and interest.

It is a child's internal desire to learn that leads to greater academic success over the long term. This desire can be awakened using God's methods (covered in earlier chapters), but a curriculum does little to rouse the love of learning.

It's fine to be able to accomplish an assignment that someone else has set for you, but to choose to set a lofty goal for yourself and have the motivation, the innovation, and the drive to meet that goal is when true learning happens.

7. Most curricula absent relationship from the learning process.

When we understand that true education is not based on information but rather on relationship, when we understand that true education is about spending time with a child and connecting his heart with ours so that we can connect him to Christ, when we realize that we must really *know* a child to effectively shape his character, we discover that curricula cannot provide this essential component for us. True education cannot be confined to a book or a piece of paper; true education is experienced.

When we educate as God intended us to educate, we are working for the redemption of our children. Don't allow a curriculum to usurp the beautiful and priceless place you have in your child's life.

8. Most curricula do not follow God's schedule of child development.

Very few curricula progress in sync with how a child's mind develops. Even if a curriculum recommends that first grade not begin until age eight to ten, there is generally still too much close-up work, sit-down time, indoor activity, and artificial learning for a child. (For more information about God's schedule, see Chapter 5.)

9. Most curricula do not tend to "the more quiet and simple" life.

"The more quiet and simple the life of the child, the more favorable it will be to both physical and mental development." [14]

Even some of the most wholesome, character-focused, Bible-based curricula use lots of colorful charts, posters, crafts, coloring sheets, activity books, and worksheets. This approach is perhaps used to keep the attention of the child or to make the curriculum more attractive to the parents; but in the process, it transforms the simple educational journey that God has designed for us into one big attention-grabbing, entertaining process.

However morally sound these educational aids may seem to the parents, they do not aid in providing the quiet and simple life that the Lord directs us to give to our children. "Parents should by their example encourage the formation of habits of simplicity, and draw their children away from an artificial to a natural life." [15] "[God] would have us cultivate purity and simplicity." [16]

To many parents, God's uncomplicated, no-frills methods of education – an education in which parents and children learn naturally from everyday life, spend several hours a day outdoors in God's creation, learn through relationship and through applying the principles of God's Word in the everyday activities – seems far too simple. How will my child learn what he needs to learn with such simple, humble, unsophisticated methods?

God knows what He's doing.

A Reasonable Solution at a Cost

In the days of Samuel the prophet, the Israelites began to grow dissatisfied with the way in which the nation was headed. Samuel's sons, who were in leadership positions, were not following the ways of the Lord. There were internal dissensions among the tribes. And the nation was continually dealing with invasions from their heathen enemies. Understandably, the people wanted these problems remedied. Something needed to change. In searching for a solution to their problems, they observed the nations around them and noticed that the strong and prosperous nations were such because they were ruled under a unifying administration. Israel came "to believe that in order to maintain their standing among the nations, the tribes must be united under a strong central government." [17] So, logically, they asked for a king.

This request did not seem unreasonable to them. They needed a solution to their difficulties. To have guidance under a strong leadership seemed like a wise decision. It worked for others. It was logical. But this choice was not in harmony with God's will for them. "God desired His people to look to Him alone as their Law-giver and their Source of strength. Feeling their dependence upon God, they would be constantly drawn nearer to Him. They would become elevated and ennobled, fitted for the high destiny to which He had called them as His chosen people. But when a man was placed upon the throne, it would tend to turn the minds of the people from God. They would trust more to human strength, and less to divine power." [18]

The tendency to look to man for guidance and help is a common mistake among God's people. We want to follow God's ways, but it is so much easier to have a human tell us what to do than to earnestly persevere to learn to understand God's unusual ways, meekly and humbly depend upon Him, and follow Him in faith.

Turning to a man-made curriculum for guidance tends to direct our minds toward human help instead of the help we can receive directly from God. Rather than looking to man for guidance, God wants us to feel our dependence on Him so that we will "be constantly drawn nearer to Him," [19] so that we may educate according to His direction and our children may "become elevated and ennobled, fitted for the high destiny to which He had called them." [20]

When the Israelites were granted a king, they were given the guidance for which they were seeking, but this guidance came at a cost – a literal financial cost and also a cost to their comparatively free condition. Once the king was in place, they would serve the king. Similarly, a curriculum may give us the guidance for which we are seeking, but this guidance comes at a cost – a literal financial cost and also a cost to the child's opportunity and capacity to learn well and learn freely. Once the curriculum is in place, the child learns to serve the curriculum, and he learns to learn in the way in which it dictates.

The Israelites were warned that "once a monarchy was established, they could not set it aside at pleasure."[21] Once a child has been learning through the traditional methods in which he is told what to learn and how to learn it, he begins to lose his capacity for self-motivated learning and strong thinking, and he becomes dependent upon something or someone to guide him. Dispensing with that system to begin learning in the way in which God designed can be challenging (not impossible, but challenging).

Connecting Your Child with the Source of Wisdom

Thousands have successfully educated their children without a man-made curriculum. Elisha, Daniel, Joseph, and Moses are just a few of the "many noble examples of men whose characters were formed under divine direction."[22] Throughout history, God's curriculum-free education has produced young people who were both spiritually strong and highly intelligent, and who grew to fill responsible positions in this world – great statesmen, wise legislators, and faithful reformers – "men whose lives were a blessing to their fellow men and who stood in the world as representatives of God."[23] These young people didn't need a curriculum because "God Himself was their teacher."[24] Their parents weren't brilliant or extraordinarily talented. They didn't possess certain special abilities. They simply followed the instructions in the book of Deuteronomy – first, they connected with the Source of wisdom themselves, then they connected their children with the Source of wisdom.[25] And true education will help you connect your child with the Source of wisdom, also. When you work in harmony with God, you have the promise: "Thy children shall be taught of the Lord; and great shall be the peace of thy children."[26] In fact, this is really the only way that anyone, whether they follow true education or not, can reach their fullest potential. "There can be a full development of mind and heart *only* by having a living connection with the Source of all wisdom, power, and holiness." [27]

There is no need to worry, parent. The Master of the universe, the One who designed the solar system and holds the stars in space, the One who knows all from eternity past to eternity future, the Source of all wisdom, knows how to educate your child, and He is willing – more than willing, He is desirous – to give this wisdom to you, the parent. His method of education perfectly fits your child. It cooperates with how a child's mind develops, nurtures rather than inhibits a child's natural curiosity and desire to learn, takes into account the individual ways in which he learns, builds a beautiful character, and strengthens thinking in both parent and child.

God is to His people wisdom and fullness and power. To follow His direction is to choose the path of true success.

Words of Counsel

"We are not to go through human wisdom, which is termed foolishness, to seek true wisdom." [28]

"Satan exults as he sees men looking to men, and trusting in men to be wisdom for them." [29]

"Now, as never before, we need to understand the true science of education. If we fail to understand this, we shall never have a place in the kingdom of God." [30]

"If parents seek to obey the word of God, in bringing their children up in the nurture and admonition of the Lord, they find a work before them requiring thought, resolution, and trust in God. Difficulties will arise on every hand which seem almost impossible to be overcome; but the parents must have continual communion with God in their trials and efforts, and have their souls stayed on him. He will not turn a deaf ear to their prayers, but will impart to them wisdom and strength." [31]

"That education that brings the student into close relation with the Teacher sent from God, is true education." [32]

CHAPTER 33

The Parents' Education

"The training of children puts the parents as well as the children to school." – The Signs of the Times, March 30, 1891

WHEN God brought the children of Israel out of Egypt, He desired to reestablish His perfect plan of education among them. But first, the parents themselves needed instruction. So it is with us today. With a mindset cultivated in conventional educational methods, we tend to think that education is for the children, forgetting the first and most vital step in true education – the education of the *parents*.

True education does not begin with the children. True education starts with us, the parents, because "success in education depends on fidelity in carrying out the Creator's plan."[1] As parents, we must educate ourselves to understand God's plan, trust His plan, and be obedient to His plan. We must educate ourselves to reason according to God's wisdom and not our own.

Success Through Unlikely Methods

After God brought the Israelites into Canaan, he gave them specific instructions regarding their new life there. However, instead of diligently following all the instructions that the Lord had given them, they chose an easier course. To follow the Lord's instructions meant they needed to put forth effort to understand and follow His ways, which were so different from what they were accustomed to, and it was much easier to just live their comfortable life. But their lack of diligence led them, little by little, to associate with the nations around them. These nations had an influence over the thoughts, daily habits, and the educational methods of the Israelites. Little by little, the Israelites set aside God's methods and adopted those of the other nations. The result? "His strength was removed from them, and they could no longer prevail against their enemies."[2]

At one point in Israel's history, the Midianites "came swarming into the land, with their flocks and herds. Like a devouring plague, they spread over the country. ... They came as soon as the harvests began to ripen, and remained until the last fruits of the earth had been gathered. They stripped the fields of their increase and robbed and maltreated the inhabitants. ... For seven years this oppression continued, and then, as the people in their distress gave heed to the Lord's reproof, and confessed their sins, God again raised up a helper for them."[3] That helper's name was Gideon.

God instructed Gideon that he was to deliver his people from the oppression of the Midianites. After Gideon was assured that God would be with him, this young man then proceeded to gather an army to go to battle against the Midianites. But God was about to use a very unusual method, an approach very different from conventional methods, for giving His people victory. Despite the fact that Gideon's army was terribly small compared with that of the enemy, God instructed Gideon to reduce his army from thirty-two thousand men to a mere three hundred men.

How could they possibly win this battle with only three hundred men?

God further instructed Gideon to give every man a trumpet and a torch concealed in an earthen pitcher and to divide the men into three groups. [4] What an extremely unconventional way to go into battle! Any intelligent person would agree that this is not a normal, or even logical, way for an army to go to battle. But Gideon's success was not dependent upon his numbers or his strategy. His success was dependent upon God's power, which was promised to him upon obedience to God's instructions.

"In the dead of night, at a signal from Gideon's war horn, the three companies sounded their trumpets; then, breaking their pitchers and displaying the blazing torches, they rushed upon the enemy."[5] "The sleeping army was suddenly aroused. Upon every side was seen the light of the flaming torches. In every direction was heard the sound of trumpets, with the cry of the assailants. Believing themselves at the mercy of an overwhelming force, the Midianites were panic-stricken. With wild cries of alarm they fled for life, and, mistaking their own companions for enemies, they slew one another." [6]

Through Gideon's obedience to God's plan, "the power of the Midianites was broken, so that they were never again able to make war upon Israel." [7] "The simple act of blowing a blast upon the trumpet ... by Gideon's little band about the hosts of Midian, was made effectual, through the power of God, to overthrow the might of His enemies." [8]

God's method for giving victory to Israel was unconventional; it was very different. God's method of education is also unconventional; it is very different. [9] Gideon did not achieve success through conventional methods; he achieved it through obedience to God. Obedience to God will produce success for us just as it did for Gideon. "The most complete system that men have ever devised, apart from the power and wisdom of God, will prove a failure, while the most unpromising methods will succeed when divinely appointed and entered upon with humility and faith." [10]

This lesson of following God's plan with humility and faith is an essential part of the parents' education.

Learning and Obeying God's Plan

Gideon did *not* reduce his army to three hundred men, give each man a trumpet, a torch, and a pitcher, and divide the men into three groups because it sounded like a good idea to him. He did so because he was following the Lord's plan. "With us, as with Israel of old, success in education depends on fidelity in carrying out the Creator's plan." To faithfully follow the Lord's plan, we must learn God's plan. "Says the wise man, 'Train up a child in the way he should go: and when he is old, he will not depart from it.' ... To perform this work aright, parents and teachers must themselves understand 'the way the child should go.'" [11]

Just as Gideon needed to be attentive to God's instructions to know how to carry out God's plan, so must we. If parents will commit to taking a few minutes every day to read and study the instruction God has given, He will give them wisdom.

And just as Gideon needed to follow every small detail of God's plan to have success, so must we. To follow God's method of true education, we must educate the *whole* child, we must follow all the details of His health laws, we must provide the child with emotional security through a loving relationship with him, we must prioritize character development, we must educate according to God's schedule, we must live a simple and orderly life, we must teach our children to work – we must use the *entire* plan that God has given us.

Taking Down the Idols

God gave a miraculous victory to Gideon and his tiny army, but before He did so, God gave Gideon a very important job to do. "Gideon's father, Joash, who shared in the apostasy of his countrymen, had erected at Ophrah, where he dwelt, a large altar to Baal, at which the people of the town worshiped."[12] The first task Gideon was commanded to fulfill was to destroy this altar and build an altar to God. Gideon obeyed, and his obedience was essential to his success.

As we step out in faith to follow God's methods of education, we must first remove all idols from our lives, including the idols of our own opinions. [13] Exchanging our thoughts and methods for those of the Lord is an essential part of our education as parents. "Wrong maxims and methods of teaching, which have been looked upon as wholly essential"[14] must be given up. We must ask the Lord to open our eyes to "the worthlessness of those things that men regarded as life's great essentials." [15]

When God tells us in the third chapter of Proverbs to not lean on our own understanding, He is being serious. Our own understanding is flawed. It does not see the big picture. It often (unknowingly) mingles truth with error. It does not always understand the full ramifications of our choices, plans, and actions. It cannot see the future. It is often in error without our realization. "It is a fact widely ignored, though never without danger, that error rarely appears for what it really is. It is by mingling with or attaching itself to truth that it gains acceptance. The eating of the tree of knowledge of good and evil caused the ruin of our first parents, and the acceptance of a mingling of good and evil is the ruin of men and women today."[16] To follow God's plan, we must set aside the idols of our own opinions, ideas, philosophies, methods, and preferences.

We can make an idol of what people think of us. We may want our child to be able to read by age six because we are concerned about what others will think if he cannot. We may be concerned about what others will think if we follow a method of education that is very different from that which others use. A desire to not be different can be an idol. We notice what other children have accomplished and are concerned if our children have not accomplished the same. We see other children involved in certain activities and wonder if our children should be as well.

It's normal for the culture we live in to sway our thinking, and there is a natural, and usually unintentional, tendency to "reason after the manner of the world and copy its plans and imitate its customs." [17] When the people of ancient Israel asked for a king, one of their reasons was so they could be like the other nations. "The Israelites did not realize that to be in this respect unlike other nations was a special privilege and blessing. God had separated the Israelites from every other people, to make them His own peculiar treasure." [18] "The longing to conform to worldly practices and customs exists among the professed people of God. ... But all who pursue this course thereby separate from the Source of their strength." [19]

"Let parents study less of the world and more of Christ; let them put forth less effort to imitate the customs and fashions of the world, and devote more time and effort to molding the minds and character of their children according to the divine Model." [20]

"Very different" [21] from false methods of education is God's method, and to be successful in following God's plan, parents must embrace this fact. His plan "will necessitate opposition to the fashions, customs, practices, and maxims of the world." [22] As parents, we must educate ourselves to abandon the ways of the world and trust that God's ways are best. "In the education of our children a different order of things must be brought in." [23]

"Parents and children alike belong to God to be ruled by Him. ... God's will must be paramount. The question for us to ask is not: What have others done? What will my relatives think? or, What will they say of me if I pursue this course? but, What has God said? Neither parent nor child can truly prosper in any course excepting in the way of the Lord." [24]

We must be willing to give up the approval of others in exchange for the approval of God. No matter how essential a subject or method of education may seem to us or to those around us, we must remember that "we are not at liberty to teach that which shall meet the world's standard or the standard of the church, simply because it is the custom to do so." [25] As difficult as it may be, a child needs his parents to be courageous and conscientious enough to do what is best for him even if it means they must go against the grain of society (including the society of family and church family). It isn't easy to swim upstream, but "when the Lord requires us to be distinct and peculiar, how can we crave popularity or seek to imitate the customs and practices of the world?" [26]

God urges us, "Now, as never before, we need to understand the true science of education." [27] Parents have this duty. They "must study Christ's lessons and the character of His teaching. They must see its freedom from formalism and tradition, and appreciate the originality, the authority, the spirituality, the tenderness, the benevolence, and the practicability of His teaching." [28] "By conforming entirely to the will of God, we shall be placed upon vantage ground, and shall see the necessity of decided separation from the customs and practices of the world. We are not to elevate our standard just a little above the world's standard; but we are to make the line of demarcation decidedly apparent." [29]

God Will Help You

When God told Gideon to go fight against the Midianites with an army of only three hundred men, Gideon did not understand how he could possibly achieve victory. He didn't know how God would work everything out. Gideon didn't need to know. He only needed to move forward with what God had already asked him to do.

If you feel like you don't understand all of God's ways, your first steps are to do that which He has already revealed to you and to look to God for help. The Christian walk requires faith. Often, we must be obedient to that which God has already shown us before He will give us the answers to our questions. If you will but take one step of faith, doing that very small thing that you know through His counsel to be true, then the next step will become clear. "The obstacles that hinder our progress will never disappear before a halting, doubting spirit. Those who defer obedience till every shadow of uncertainty disappears and there remains no risk of failure or defeat, will never obey at all." [30] If by faith we advance step by step in the right way, following the Great Leader, more and more light will shine along our pathway. "However great the obstacles, all who are determined to obey God will find the way opening as they go forward." [31]

When God sent Gideon to fight the Midianites, He didn't just give Gideon instructions and then send him on his way with a pat on the back and a cheery, "Good luck!" No, after God gave Gideon the method with which he was to work, all of heaven went to work alongside Gideon. God will do the same for you! God "is just as willing to work with the efforts of His people now and to accomplish great things through weak instrumentalities. All heaven awaits our demand upon its wisdom and strength." [32] "All heaven is watching the efforts of the Christian parent." [33] All heaven wants to help you. No one loves you as much as He does, and no one wants to help you as much as He does. No one knows your child's heart like He does. No one knows the temptations you will face during the day like He does. Only God knows your child's future and how to prepare him for it. He knows how to take the work you do for your child and transform it into a soul-saving influence that will extend beyond the few short years you are with him. God is "able to do exceeding abundantly above all that we ask or think." [34]

"If today we would take time to go to Jesus and tell Him our needs, we should not be disappointed; He would be at our right hand to help us. We need more simplicity, more trust and confidence in our Saviour." [35]

Though God's educational methods may seem like unpromising ones, they will succeed beautifully if we follow them in humility and faith.

Words of Counsel

"If the mother will but heed with care the instructions *already* given in the sacred word, she will receive further light and knowledge as she shall have need." [36]

"God would have parents enter upon their work with energy and courage, and prosecute it with fidelity. Whatever he has made it their duty to do, he will give them wisdom and strength to accomplish." [37]

"The Lord can work most effectually through those who are most sensible of their own insufficiency, and who will rely upon Him as their leader and source of strength. He will make them strong by uniting their weakness to His might, and wise by connecting their ignorance with His wisdom." [38]

"God requires of us nothing that we cannot in his strength perform; nothing that is not for our own good and the good of our children. He does not call woman to engage in any work that will lead her to neglect the physical, mental, and moral training of her own children. She may not shift this responsibility upon others, and leave them to do her work." [39]

"In the education of her children, the mother needs the wisdom which God alone can give her. ... The customs and habits of the world in regard to the training of children should not turn a Christian mother from her course." [40]

"The training of children puts the parents as well as the children to school. The dependent children look to father and mother to have their wants supplied, and in this is a lesson to the parents of their own dependence upon their heavenly Father. The children look to the parents for precept and example, and for reproof, for correction, for instruction in righteousness, and the parent sees himself as dependent upon God for wisdom and knowledge. ... Oh, what need there is that parents flee to God in order to obtain his grace and power to train their children in the way of the Lord!" [41]

"Parents have a great and responsible work to do, and they may well inquire: "Who is sufficient for these things?" But God has promised to give wisdom to those that ask in faith, and He will do just as He said He would. He is pleased with the faith that takes Him at His word." [42]

CHAPTER 34

LEARNING THE DIVINE PATTERN

"Those things you learn without joy you will forget easily." – Finnish saying

THIRTEEN and a half feet!" exclaimed nine-year-old Ethan.

"I've never seen a bed so enormous!" declared his older sister, Meghan. "It must have been quite heavy since it was made of iron. Have you ever tried carrying iron, Elliot?" Meghan asked her little brother.

"I've carried Mama's cast iron skillet," little five-year-old Elliot replied. "It was sooo heavy!"

"Stainless steel is 98 percent iron, so we've probably all carried iron," Ethan proposed.

"The people of Bashan were giant people. That must be why King Og's bed was so enormous," suggested Meghan, referring back to the Bible story her dad had been reading. The children were thoughtful for a moment when Meghan whispered, "That must have tested the Israelites' courage and faith in God."

The Davis family were having family worship, and Dad was reading about King Og in the Bible when he read that this giant king's bed was nine cubits long.

"How long is nine cubits?" Meghan had asked.

"I think the back of my Bible tells how long that is," volunteered Ethan as he quickly thumbed through the pages. "Yes, here it is! A cubit is eighteen inches." You could almost see the wheels start turning in the siblings' heads as they were mentally figuring out how many inches were in nine cubits.

Ethan, who loved math and was quite proficient at it, was the first to declare the answer. "That's 162 inches!"

The Davis children loved to learn and were always looking for learning opportunities. But it had not always been that way. You may remember Ethan from the beginning of this book. Every day was a struggle between Mom and her easily distractible boy as she tried to teach him the best she knew how. School had become so distasteful to Ethan that he regularly declared that he hated learning. His younger brother, Elliot, was quickly catching this negative attitude. And his older sister, although she enjoyed school, had become rebellious and disinterested in anything related to God.

But things had changed in the Davis family since that day when we first met Ethan. Ethan's parents had learned about true education, and they immediately determined to follow God's ways.

Mr. and Mrs. Davis began by talking with their children about God's plan, the benefits of it, and why they were choosing to follow it. Elliot and Ethan were all in favor, but Meghan was resistant. Mom and Dad did what they could to gain the confidence of their children, and, realizing that relationship was an essential element of true education, they took plenty of time to reconnect with their children and lay a foundation of love, trust, and unity within the family.

They also recognized that the children needed a "reset" from the effects of traditional learning methods, so they put away the workbooks and all other academic material, and, for the first year, they spent several hours every day together outside in nature. Setting aside the academics also gave them the time they needed to make other changes as well.

Through patient and clear instruction and examples, they helped their children see how their diet and other lifestyle habits were affecting their thinking, their emotions, and their behavior. They enlisted their children's involvement by asking them for their thoughts and ideas for making changes. They also sought out creative and fun ways to implement the changes and gave each child a specific responsibility in facilitating changes for the family.

They also recognized the need to bring order to their home and their schedule. Once again, they talked over the need with their children and encouraged their cooperation by asking for their thoughts and ideas on the matter. Together with their children, they created a detailed plan for how to bring organization to their lives. They worked through the difficult task of weeding out some of the activities in their lives that were making maintaining an orderly life difficult. They discussed how to better distribute the workload and how they could work together as a family more. And they created a schedule that prioritized what was truly important.

Through all the adjustments, Mom and Dad demonstrated a cheerfully positive attitude and often rehearsed the benefits of God's ways.

Changes were not made overnight, but so as to impress upon the children the importance of obedience to the Lord and the solemnity of His commands, there was no delay in making changes either.

At the beginning of their journey, Meghan constantly complained. She was bored when they went outside, she didn't like the new way of eating, and she didn't see why she should have to help wash dishes. Mom and Dad prayerfully worked to reach Meghan's heart, and in the process, realized that their hearts needed work too. They began spending more time with their daughter, showing an interest in what she was interested in, and truly listening to her. They helped her to see the benefits of the changes and even brainstormed with her about her strengths and ways that *she* could help make the changes more enjoyable (a step which helped give Meghan the sense of control she felt like she was losing in this change). After some time, Meghan's heart began to soften. Little by little, Mom and Dad saw a spark reignite in their daughter. She became more patient, less rebellious, more loving toward her brothers, and more interested in the activities of the family.

Ethan was less resistant. He loved the outdoor time but was not at all happy to help with any of the chores. But, as his parents did the chores *with* him and used this time for bonding as well as helping Ethan to see the benefits of working, he soon became more cooperative. And buried deep beneath a pile of workbooks, learning activities, and curricula, Mom and Dad eventually found the love of learning that God had built into Ethan.

Elliot didn't have as much trouble adapting, but he wasn't too happy about not being allowed to play all day anymore. Anytime Mom and Dad turned around, he would suddenly disappear to play with his toy cars. His parents solved this problem by being more attentive to Elliot and replacing the toys with more useful activities that would keep his interest. When a lamp broke, they gave Elliot a screwdriver and allowed him to take it apart and see if he could figure out what was wrong with it. They started gardening and involved Elliot (and their other children) in all the aspects of planning and planting the garden. They involved him in all the daily activities, and as Elliot's day was full of work and play with his family, he no longer missed his toys.

Today, Ethan, Meghan, and their little brother Elliot "do life" with their parents – they energetically and enthusiastically learn through useful work, real-life experiences, nature, and the Bible. Ethan and his siblings have developed a keen ability to think on their own, and they've become competent, active agents of their own education. If you were to visit their home today, you may find these three eager-to-learn children researching how bridges are engineered, learning the German language for fun, practicing sign language so they can communicate with the deaf woman at church, working on a long division problem involving numbers in the trillions (again, just for fun), playing the piano and singing, repairing a broken vacuum cleaner, learning about the muscles in the body, helping their neighbor with her garden, and operating their own highly-successful business growing and selling strawberries. When they finish learning about bridge engineering, Ethan wants to learn about the different types of biomes that exist around the world.

Children are born with a natural desire to learn. "God has given inquiring minds to youth and children," [1] and, in the right environment, children who are educated according to God's perfect methods will pursue learning and find pleasure in the process. They will have "an inward love of thought," [2] and with proper instruction and encouragement, they will use their minds for the glory of God.

The Only Safe Guide

There is no educational method that functions as beautifully as the one designed by the Creator of a child's mind. For thousands of years, God has been successfully educating young people for greatness – young people who were true, firm, and noble and had a high a sense of the claims of God, [3] who were influential even in their youth, [4] who grew to be moral and intellectual giants, [5] who were capable leaders [6] and honest, noble, brave, and talented rulers of nations, [7] who were pure, kind, generous, obedient, and respectful, and maintained their Christian character amidst negative influences, [8] and who were missionaries for God and ministers of mercy to the world. [9] There is no other system of education so perfectly suited for your child.

Though we may not completely understand the beauty, depth, and interconnected complexities of true education, we can know that it is the method perfectly designed for our needs and the needs of our children. "He only who created the mind and ordained its laws can perfectly understand its needs or direct its development. The principles of education that He has given are the only safe guide." [10] "Defeat comes in depending on human methods, human inventions, and placing the divine secondary." [11] But if we follow God's methods and depend on Him, "Christ will conduct His battles in ways that will surprise the greatest powers of earth!" [12]

"Our people are now being tested as to whether they will obtain their wisdom from the greatest Teacher the world ever knew, or seek to the god of Ekron. Let us determine that we will not be tied by so much as a thread to the educational policies of those who do not discern the voice of God." [13] To raise godly children, we must embrace God's methodologies.

"True education is to know and to do the will of God. This education is as lasting as eternity." [14]

FINAL NOTE

Because true education was created by the One who is infinite in wisdom, knowledge, and understanding, it is impossible for this mere book to fully encapsulate the infinitely broad, deep, and far-reaching principles and methods of true education. If it were possible for finite man to attain to a full understanding of God's perfect ways, then once they did, they would have no need for God's guidance, no need for growth, no need for further development of the mind and heart.

It is my desire that this book provide an introduction to God's beautiful methods of education and an explanation of some of the principles involved with God's method. But this book is only a beginning. There is much more to learn. And God intends for His people, with the simplicity and humility of little children, to be continually learning of His ways and faithfully obeying His leadings, that His truths may be ever unfolding to His people through the illumination of His Holy Spirit. As we do so, more truth and greater understanding will unfold day by day. The more we learn of the wisdom, love, and power of God, the more we will come to understand His plan and His ways.

"Blessed are those who trust in the Lord, whose trust is the Lord." [1]

Enjoy the journey. Enjoy growing and learning with your child.

Notes

How to Use This Book

1 Ellen White, *Testimonies for the Church* 9:284
2 Ellen White, *Testimonies for the Church* 9:177
3 Ellen White, "The Treasures of God's Word," *The Review and Herald*, July 3, 1900

Chapter 1

1 Deuteronomy 28:13 KJV
2 Ellen White, "His Glory Shall Be Seen," *The Signs of the Times*, May 7, 1902
3 Ellen White, *The Ministry of Healing*, 283; "The Education of Israel," in *Education*
4 Ellen White, "Education of Israel," in *Education*
5 Ellen White, *Testimonies for the Churh* 6:127
6 Ellen White, "The True Ideal for Our Youth," *The Review and Herald*, August 12, 1912
7 Ellen White, "Important Duties in Home Life," *The Signs of the Times*, April 17, 1884
8 Ellen White, *Mind, Character, and Personality* 1:53
9 Ellen White, *Education*, 20
10 Ellen White, *Testimonies for the Church* 6:142
11 Ellen White, *Fundamentals of Christian Education*, 387
12 Ellen White, *Education*, 13
13 Ellen White, "The Schools of the Ancient Hebrews," *The Review and Herald*, October 30, 1900
14 Ellen White, "The Schools of the Ancient Hebrews," *The Review and Herald*, October 30, 1900
15 Ellen White, *Patriarchs and Prophets*, 592
16 Deuteronomy 6:7-9
17 Ellen White, "The Responsibilities of Parents and Teachers," *Sabbath-School Worker*, April 1, 1889
18 Stephen N. Haskell, *The Story of Daniel the Prophet*, 15
19 Ellen White, "Parents as Character Builders," *The Review and Herald*, October 5, 1911
20 Ellen White, "The Responsibilities of Parents and Teachers," *Sabbath-School Worker*, April 1, 1889
21 Ellen White, *Education*, 45
22 Ellen White, "The Schools of the Ancient Hebrews," *The Review and Herald*, October 30, 1900
23 Proverbs 22:6
24 Ellen White, *Education*, 55; Ellen White, *Fundamentals of Christian Education*, 95
25 Stephen N. Haskell, *The Story of Daniel the Prophet*, 20; Ellen White, 12 Letters and Manuscripts, Manuscript, no 122
26 Daniel 1:17 KJV
27 Ellen White, *Education*, 55
28 Ellen White, *Education*, 55
29 Ellen White, *Education*, 54
30 Ellen White, *Education*, 54
31 Ellen White, "Parental Responsibility," *The Signs of the Times*, January 31, 1884
32 Ellen White, *Education*, 51; Ellen White, "Parental Responsibility," *The Signs of the Times*, January 31, 1884; Ellen White, *Education*, 52; Ellen White, *Patriarchs and Prophets*, 222
33 Ellen White, *Christian Education*, 50
34 Ellen White, *Education*, 77
35 Ellen White, *Education*, 50
36 Ellen White, *Education*, 276
37 Ellen White, *Testimonies for the Church* 6:145

Chapter 2

1 Ellen White, *Education*, 13
2 Ellen White, *Fundamentals of Christian Education*, 57
3 Carla Hannaford, *Smart Moves: Why Learning Is Not All in Your Head* (Great Ocean Publishers, 2005), 60

4 Ellen White, "Education," *Good Health*, May 1, 1889
5 Ellen White, "Proper Education," *The Review and Herald*, July 14, 1885; Ellen White, *Education*, 114
6 2 Corinthians 5:14
7 Ellen White, *The Ministry of Healing*, 402
8 Ellen White, *Christian Education*, 20
9 Ellen White, *Education*, 195
10 Ellen White, *Fundamentals of Christian Education*, 27 (emphasis supplied)
11 Ellen White, "Daniel a Temperance Reformer," *The Signs of the Times*, March 2, 1882
12 Ellen White, *Patriarchs and Prophets*, 601
13 Ellen White, *Education*, 195
14 Ellen White, *Education*, 15
15 Ellen White, *Patriarchs and Prophets*, 45, 50; "Redemption," *The Review and Herald*, February 24, 1874
16 Ellen White, *Education*, 15
17 Ellen White, *Education*, 15
18 Ellen White, *Education*, 30
19 Ellen White, *Christ's Object Lessons*, 330
20 Ellen White, *Christian Education*, 33
21 Ellen White, *Fundamentals of Christian Education*, 71
22 Ellen White, *Fundamentals of Christian Education*, 27
23 Ellen White, *The Ministry of Healing*, 398
24 Mark 12:30 KJV
25 Ellen White, *Testimonies for the Church* 4:197

Chapter 3

1 Ellen White "Sanctification," *The Review and Herald*, January 25, 1881
2 Ellen White, *Counsels on Diet and Foods*, 230
3 Ellen White "Sanctification," *The Review and Herald*, January 25, 1881
4 Ellen White, *Counsels on Diet and Foods*, 244
5 Ellen White, *Counsels on Diet and Foods*, 244
6 Ellen White "Sanctification," *The Review and Herald*, January 25, 1881
7 Ellen White "Sanctification," *The Review and Herald*, January 25, 1881
8 Ellen White, "The Need of a Deeper Knowledge of God," *The Review and Herald*, December 3, 1889
9 Ellen White, 12 Letters and Manuscripts Manuscript, no 122
10 Stephen N. Haskell, *The Story of Daniel the Prophet*, 19
11 Ellen White, *Temperance*, 190
12 Ellen White, "Lessons from the Life of Daniel," *The Youth's Instructor*, June 4, 1903
13 Ellen White "Sanctification," *The Review and Herald*, January 25, 1881
14 Ellen White "Sanctification," *The Review and Herald*, January 25, 1881
15 Ellen White "Sanctification," *The Review and Herald*, January 25, 1881
16 Ellen White "Sanctification," *The Review and Herald*, January 25, 1881
17 Ellen White "Sanctification," *The Review and Herald*, January 25, 1881
18 Ellen White, *Prophets and Kings*, 485
19 Ellen White "Sanctification," *The Review and Herald*, January 25, 1881
20 Ellen White, "Striking Examples of Prayer," *The Signs of the Times* August 14, 1884
21 Ellen White "Sanctification," *The Review and Herald*, January 25, 1881 (emphasis supplied)
22 Ellen White, *Temperance*, 191
23 Ellen White, *Prophets and Kings*, 489
24 Ellen White, *Prophets and Kings*, 490
25 Ellen White, *Temperance*, 191
26 Ellen White, *Education*, 208
27 Ellen White "Sanctification," *The Review and Herald*, January 25, 1881
28 Ellen White, *The Ministry of Healing*, 315 (emphasis supplied)
29 Ellen White, *The Ministry of Healing*, 135
30 Ellen White, "The Mother a Missionary," *The Signs of the Times*, September 29, 1881
31 Ellen White, "Christian Courtesy," *The Review and Herald*, September 1, 1885
32 Ellen White, *Christian Temperance and Bible Hygiene*, 120

33 Ellen White, *Christian Temperance and Bible Hygiene*, 134
34 Ellen White, *Patriarchs and Prophets*, 599
35 Ellen White, *Patriarchs and Prophets*, 599
36 Ellen White, *The Ministry of Healing*, 147
37 Ellen White, *The Ministry of Healing*, 283 (emphasis supplied)
38 Ellen White, *Education*, 107
39 Kevin P. Madore, Ph.D., Anthony D. Wagner Ph.D., "Multicosts of Multitasking," *Cerebrum* 2019; Daniel J. Levitin, *The Organized Mind: Thinking Straight in the Age of Information Overload* (Dutton Penguin Random House, 2014)
40 Ellen White, *The Ministry of Healing*, 381
41 François Trudeau, Roy J Shephard, "Physical Education, School Physical Activity, School Sports and Academic Performance," *The International Journal of Behavioral Nutrition and Physical Activity* 2008; E Haapala, "Physical Activity, Academic Performance and Cognition in Children and Adolescents," *Baltic Journal of Health and Physical Activity* 2012; Harold W. Kohl III, Heather D. Cook, *Educating the Student Body: Taking Physical Activity and Physical Education to School* (National Academies Press, 2013); Fred L. Martens, "Daily Physical Education - A Boon to Canadian Elementary Schools," *Journal of Physical Education, Recreation and Dance* 1982; Caitlin Lees, Jessica Hopkins, "Effect of Aerobic Exercise on Cognition, Academic Achievement, and Psychosocial Function in Children," *Preventing Chronic Disease* 2013
42 Ellen White, "A Neglected Work," *The Review and Herald*, October 9, 1900; Ellen White, "Counsel to Teachers," *The Review and Herald*, 1909
43 Ellen White, *Special Testimonies on Education*, 32
44 Ellen White, *The Ministry of Healing*, 238
45 Hongying Zhu, et al. "Moderate UV Exposure Enhances Learning and Memory by Promoting a Novel Glutamate Biosynthetic Pathway in the Brain," *Cell* 2018; Lynne Chantranupong, Bernardo L Sabatini, "Sunlight Brightens Learning and Memory," *Cell* 2018
46 Ellen White, *The Ministry of Healing*, 238
47 Ellen White, *Child Guidance*, 339
48 Ellen White, *Child Guidance*, 342
49 Richard M. Ryan, et al. "Vitalizing Effects of Being Outdoors and in Nature," *Journal of Environmental Psychology* 2010
50 Ellen White, *The Ministry of Healing*, 273
51 Trisha A. Jenkins, et al. "Influence of Tryptophan and Serotonin on Mood and Cognition with a Possible Role of the Gut-Brain Axis," *Nutrients* 2016
52 U Haverinen-Shaughnessy, D J Moschandreas, R J Shaughnessy, "Association Between Substandard Classroom Ventilation Rates and Students' Academic Achievement," *Indoor Air* 2011; Pawel Wargocki, David Wyon, "The Effects of Outdoor Air Supply Rate and Supply Air Filter Condition in Classrooms on the Performance of Schoolwork by Children," *Hvac&R Research* 2007; Santosh Gaihre, et al. "Classroom Carbon Dioxide Concentration, School Attendance, and Educational Attainment," *The Journal of School Health* 2014
53 Ellen White, *The Ministry of Healing*, 382
54 Ellen White, *Testimonies for the Church* 1:701
55 Ellen White, *The Ministry of Healing*, 261
56 Ellen White, *The Ministry of Healing*, 263
57 Ellen White, *Education*, 208
58 Sheldon Cohen, et al. "Positive Emotional Style Predicts Resistance to Illness After Experimental Exposure to Rhinovirus or Influenza A Virus," *Psychosomatic Medicine* 2006; "Emotional Style and Susceptibility to the Common Cold," *Psychosomatic Medicine* 2003; Emily C Willroth, et al. "Being Happy and Becoming Happier as Independent Predictors of Physical Health and Mortality," *Psychosomatic Medicine* 2020; J Smyth, et al. "Stressors and Mood Measured an a Momentary Basis are Associated with Salivary Cortisol Secretion," *Psychoneuroendocrinology* 1998; Elizabeth M. Lawrence, PhD, Richard G. Rogers, PhD, Tim Wadsworth, PhD, "Happiness and Longevity in the United States," *Social Science & Medicine* 2015; Ilona Papousek, et al. "Trait and State Positive Affect and Cardiovascular Recovery From Experimental Academic Stress," *Biological Psychology* 2010; Anthony D Ong, et al. "Positive Affect and Sleep," *Sleep Medicine Reviews* 2017
59 Ellen White, *The Ministry of Healing*, 241

60 Ellen White, *The Ministry of Healing*, 387

61 Ellen White, *The Ministry of Healing*, 281

62 Ellen White, "Family Prayer," *The Signs of the Times*, August 7, 1884

63 Ellen White, *Testimonies for the Church* 7:43

64 Agatha M. Thrash, M.D., "Circadian Rhythms – 1" Ucheepines.org, ucheepines.org/circadian-rhythms-1; "Circadian Rhythms – 2" Ucheepines.org, ucheepines.org/circadian-rhythms-2; Ellen White, *Christian Temperance and Bible Hygiene*, 50

65 Ellen White, "Words to Students," *The Youth's Instructor*, May 31, 1894

66 Ellen White, *Fundamentals of Christian Education*, 150

67 Darcia Narvaez, PhD, "Normal, Human Infant Sleep: Feeding Method and Development," *Psychology Today* (2013) psychologytoday.com/us/blog/moral-landscapes/201302/normal-human-infant-sleep-feeding-method-and-development

68 E. L. Ardiel, C. H. Rankin, "The Importance of Touch in Development," *Paediatrics & Child Health* 2010; Darcia Narvaez, et al. "The Importance of Early Life Touch for Psychosocial and Moral Development," *Psicologia: Reflexão e Crítica* 2019; Ruth Feldman, et al. "Comparison of Skin-To-Skin (Kangaroo) and Traditional Care: Parenting Outcomes and Preterm Infant Development," *Pediatrics* 2002; L. Casler, "The Effects of Extra Tactile Stimulation on a Group of Institutionalized Infants," *Genetic Psychology Monographs* 1965; T M Field, et al. "Tactile/Kinesthetic Stimulation Effects on Preterm Neonates," *Pediatrics* 1986; J. Tuulari, et al. "Neural Correlates of Gentle Skin Stroking in Early Infancy," *Developmental Cognitive Neuroscience* 2019; Bruce Cushing, Kristin Kramer, "Mechanisms Underlying Epigenetic Effects of Early Social Experience," *Neuroscience and Biobehavioral Reviews* 2005

69 Sonia J. Lupien, et al. "Effects of Stress Throughout the Lifespan on the Brain, Behaviour and Cognition," *Nature Reviews Neuroscience* 2009; C. Sue Carter, "Developmental Consequences of Oxytocin," *Physiology & Behavior* 2003

70 Evan L Ardiel, MSc, Catharine H Rankin, PhD, "The Importance of Touch in Development," *Paediatrics & Child Health* 2010; Ian C G Weaver, Michael J Meaney, Moshe Szyf, "Maternal Care Effects on the Hippocampal Transcriptome and Anxiety-Mediated Behaviors in The Offspring That Are Reversible in Adulthood," *Proceedings of the National Academy of Sciences of the United States of America* 2006

71 Alison B. Wismer Fries, et al. "Early Experience in Humans Is Associated with Changes in Neuropeptides Critical for Regulating Social Behavior," *Proceedings of the National Academy of Sciences* 2005

72 S. Yoshida, H. Funato, "Physical Contact in Parent-Infant Relationship and Its Effect on Fostering a Feeling of Safety," *iScience* 2021; Gunther Meinlschmidt, Christine Heim, "Sensitivity to Intranasal Oxytocin in Adult Men with Early Parental Separation," *Biological Psychiatry* 2007

73 Myron A. Hofer, "Hidden Regulators in Attachment, Separation, and Loss," *Monographs of the Society for Research in Child Development* 1994; Denis Pereira Gray, Diana Dean, Philip M Dean, "Childcare Outside the Family for the Under-Threes: Cause for Concern?" *Journal of the Royal Society of Medicine* 2020; M L Laudenslager, et al. "Total Cortisol, Free Cortisol, And Growth Hormone Associated with Brief Social Separation Experiences in Young Macaques," *Developmental Psychobiology* 1995; Chris Murgatroyd, et al. "Dynamic DNA Methylation Programs Persistent Adverse Effects of Early-Life Stress," *Nature Neuroscience* 2009; John Bowlby, *Attachment and Loss*, Vol. 1. 2nd ed (Hogarth Press, 1982); National Scientific Council on the Developing Child, "Excessive Stress Disrupts the Architecture of the Developing Brain: Working Paper 3" (2005/2014); "Stress in Small Children Separated from Their Parents May Alter Genes," *ScienceDaily* 2020

74 Dr. Raymond Moore, "Synopsis," Moore Academy, mooreacademy.org/articles/synopsis; Jan Kunzler, Katharina Braun, Joerg Bock, "Early Life Stress and Sex-Specific Sensitivity of the Catecholaminergic Systems in Prefrontal and Limbic Systems of Octodon Degus," *Brain Structure and Function* 2015

75 Ellen White, *The Ministry of Healing*, 271

76 Ellen White, *The Ministry of Healing*, 271

77 Ellen White, *The Ministry of Healing*, 293

78 Ellen White, *The Ministry of Healing*, 382

79 Ellen White, *The Ministry of Healing*, 276

80 Faraco G, et al. "Water Deprivation Induces Neurovascular and Cognitive Dysfunction Through Vasopressin-Induced Oxidative Stress," *Journal of Cerebral Blood Flow and Metabolism* 2014

81 David Benton, et al. "Minor Degree of Hypohydration Adversely Influences Cognition," *American Journal of Clinical Nutrition* 2016; Barry M. Popkin, Kristen E. D'Anci, Irwin H. Rosenberg, "Water, Hydration, and Health," *Nutrition Reviews* 2010; Matthew J Kempton, et al. "Dehydration Affects Brain Structure and Function in Healthy Adolescents," *Human Brain Mapping* 2011

82 Ellen White, *The Ministry of Healing*, 237

83 Ellen White, *Child Guidance*, 461

84 Ellen White, *The Ministry of Healing*, 276

85 Ellen White, *Education*, 204

86 Ellen White, *Counsels on Diet and Foods*, 243

87 Ellen White, "Faithfulness in Health Reform," *The Review and Herald*, March 3, 1910

88 Ellen White, *Fundamentals of Christian Education*, 143; Ellen White, *The Ministry of Healing*, 129-131

89 Ellen White, *Testimonies for the Church* 2:399

90 Ellen White, *Counsels on Diet and Foods*, 230

91 Ellen White, *Testimonies for the Church* 9:156

92 Ellen White, *The Ministry of Healing*, 296 (emphasis supplied)

93 Katríona E. Lyons, et al. "Breast Milk, a Source of Beneficial Microbes and Associated Benefits for Infant Health," *Nutrients* 2020; Kelsey Fehr, et al. "Breastmilk Feeding Practices Are Associated with the Co-Occurrence of Bacteria in
Mothers' Milk and the Infant Gut," *Cell Host & Microbe* 2020; Xuyao Zhang, et al. "The Composition and Concordance of Lactobacillus Populations of Infant Gut and the Corresponding Breast-Milk and Maternal Gut," *Frontiers in Microbiology* 2020; Lieke W J van den Elsen, et al. "Shaping the Gut Microbiota by Breastfeeding: The Gateway to Allergy Prevention?" *Frontiers in Pediatrics* 2019; Anders Bergström, et al. "Establishment of Intestinal Microbiota during Early Life: A Longitudinal, Explorative Study of a Large Cohort of Danish Infants," *Applied and Environmental Microbiology* 2014; S M O'Mahony, et al. "Serotonin, Tryptophan Metabolism and the Brain-Gut-Microbiome Axis," *Behavioural Brain Research* 2015; Jane A Foster, Karen-Anne McVey Neufeld, "Gut–Brain Axis: How the Microbiome Influences Anxiety and Depression," *Trends in Neurosciences* 2013; Trisha A. Jenkins, et al. "Influence of Tryptophan and Serotonin on Mood and Cognition with a Possible Role of the Gut-Brain Axis," *Nutrients* 2016

94 Alecia-Jane Twigger, et al. "Gene Expression in Breastmilk Cells is Associa- ted with Maternal and Infant Characteristics," *Scientific Reports* 2015; Foteini
Hassiotou, et al. "Breastmilk is a Novel Source of Stem Cells with Multilineage Differentiation Potential," *Stem Cells* 2012; Alecia-Jane Twigger, et al. "From Breast Milk to Brains: The Potential of Stem Cells in Human Milk," *Journal of Human Lactation* 2013

95 Sean C L Deoni, et al. "Breastfeeding and Early White Matter Development," *Neuroimage* 2013

96 Abraham Englard, "Cognitive Effects of Breastfeeding," *The Science Journal of the Lander College of Arts and Sciences* 2016

97 Katriina Heikkilä, et al. "Breastfeeding and Educational Achievement at Age 5" *Maternal & Child Nutrition* 2014; Hyungmin Lee, et al. "Effect of Breastfeeding Duration on Cognitive Development in Infants: 3-Year Follow-up Study," *Journal of Korean Medical Science* 2016; Michael S. Kramer, MD, et al. Promotion of Breastfeeding Intervention Trial (PROBIT) Study Group, "Breastfeeding and Child Cognitive Development," *Archives of General Psychiatry* 2008; Mandy Brown
Belfort, "The Science of Breastfeeding and Brain Development," *Breastfeeding
Medicine* 2017; Mandy B Belfort, et al. "Breast Milk Feeding, Brain Development, and Neurocognitive Outcomes," *The Journal of Pediatrics* 2016; Maria A Quigley, et al. "Breastfeeding is Associated with Improved Child Cognitive Development," *The Journal of Pediatrics* 2012; Wendy H Oddy, et al. "Breastfeeding Duration and Academic Achievement at 10 Years," *Pediatrics* 2011

98 Cristina Lucía Sánchez, et al. "Evolution of the Circadian Profile of Human Milk Amino Acids During Breastfeeding," *Journal of Applied Biomedicine* 2013; Shikha Pundir, et al. "Variation of Human Milk Glucocorticoids Over 24 Hour Period," *Journal of Mammary Gland Biology and Neoplasia* 2017; Olivia Ballard, JD, PhD, Ardythe L. Morrow, PhD, MSc, "Human Milk Composition: Nutrients and Bioactive Factors," *Pediatric Clinics of North America* 2013; Jennifer Hahn-Holbrook, et al. "Human Milk as 'Chrononutrition': Implications for Child Health and
Development," *Pediatric Research* 2019

99 Shikha Pundir, et al. "Variation of Human Milk Glucocorticoids Over 24 Hour Period," *Journal of Mammary Gland Biology and Neoplasia* 2017

100 David Katzer, MD, et al. "Melatonin Concentrations and Antioxidative Capacity of Human Breast Milk

According to Gestational Age and the Time of Day," *Journal of Human Lactation* 2016; J Cubero, V Valero, et al. "The Circadian Rhythm of
Tryptophan in Breast Milk Affects the Rhythms of 6-Sulfatoxymelatonin and Sleep in Newborn," *Neuro Endocrinology Letters* 2005

101 Darcia Narvaez, PhD, "Normal Infant Sleep: Night Nursing's Importance," *Psychology Today* 2013 psychologytoday.com/us/blog/moral-landscapes/201303/normal-infant-sleep-night-nursings-importance

102 Matthew P Walker, Robert Stickgold, "Sleep, Memory, and Plasticity," *Annual Review of Psychology* 2006; Agatha M. Thrash, M.D., "Effect of Diet on Thinking," Ucheepines.org, ucheepines.org/effect-of-diet-on-thinking; James McKenna, *Safe Infant Sleep: Expert Answers to Your Cosleeping Questions* (Platypus Media, LLS, 2020); M Baringa, "Neuroscience. To sleep, Perchance to ... Learn? New Studies Say Yes," *Science* 1994

103 Darcia Narvaez, PhD, "Normal Infant Sleep: Night Nursing's Importance," *Psychology Today* 2013 psychologytoday.com/us/blog/moral-landscapes/201303/normal-infant-sleep-night-nursings-importance

104 Michelle G. Brenner, M.D., IBCLC, E. Stephen Buescher, M.D., "Breastfeeding: A Clinical Imperative," *Journal of Women's Health* 2011

105 Ellen White, *The Ministry of Healing*, 383. Note that Ellen White uses the word "infant" to refer to children up to the age of seven. See Ellen White, *Child Guidance*, 300

106 Agatha M. Thrash, M.D. "Feeding the Baby and Toddler - 1", Ucheepines.org, ucheepines.org/feeding-the-baby-and-toddler-1 (emphasis supplied); Audrey J. Naylor, Ardythe L. Morrow (ed.), "Developmental Readiness of Normal Full Term Infants to Progress from Exclusive Breastfeeding to the Introduction of Complementary Foods: Reviews of the Relevant Literature Concerning Infant Immunologic, Gastrointestinal, Oral Motor and Maternal Reproductive and Lactational Development," 2001; Børresen HC, "Diskutabel Veiledning Om Fast Føde Til Brystbarn," *Tidsskr nor Laegeforen* 1994

107 Throughout history, babies were breastfed for at least three years and as long as five years. For a sampling of research on this subject, see: "A History of Infant Feeding," *The Journal of Perinatal Education* 2009; "A History of Infant Feeding. Primitive Peoples: Ancient Works: Renaissance Writers," *Archives of Disease in Childhood* 1953; "Factors Affecting Initiation and Duration of Breastfeeding Among Off-Reserve Indigenous Children in Canada," *The International Indigenous Policy Journal* 2019; "The History of Nursing Profession in Ancient Egyptian Society," *International Journal of Africa Nursing Sciences* 2019; The American Academy of Family Physicians states that children weaned before two years of age are at increased risk of illness. (AAFP 2008)

108 E E Gulick, "The Effects of Breast-Feeding on Toddler Health," *Pediatric Nursing* 1986

109 Maryanne T Perrin, et al. "A Longitudinal Study of Human Milk Composition in the Second Year Postpartum: Implications for Human Milk Banking," *Maternal & Child Nutrition* 2017; Dror Mandel, et al. "Fat and Energy Contents of Expressed Human Breast Milk in Prolonged Lactation," *Pediatrics* 2005

110 Maryanne T Perrin, et.al. "A Longitudinal Study of Human Milk Composition in the Second Year Postpartum: Implications for Human Milk Banking," *Maternal & Child Nutrition* 2017

111 Institute of Medicine (US) Committee on Nutritional Status During Pregnancy and Lactation, *Nutrition During Lactation* (National Academies Press 1991); A S Goldman, R M Goldblum, C Garza, "Immunologic Components in Human Milk During the Second Year of Lactation," *Acta Paediatrica Scandinavica* 1983; Maryanne T Perrin, et al. "A Longitudinal Study of Human Milk Composition in the Second Year Postpartum: Implications for Human Milk Banking," *Maternal and Child Nutrition* 2017

112 Foteini Hassiotou, et al. "Maternal and Infant Infections Stimulate a Rapidleukocyte Response in Breastmilk," *Clinical & Translational Immunology* 2013; Arieh Riskin, et al. "Changes in Immunomodulatory Constituents of Human Milk in Response to Active Infection in the Nursing Infant," *Pediatric Research* 2012

113 H. Lee, et al. "Effect of Breastfeeding Duration on Cognitive Development in Infants: 3-Year Follow-up Study," *Journal of Korean Medical Science* 2016

114 Wendy H Oddy, et al. "The Long-Term Effects of Breastfeeding on Child and Adolescent Mental Health: A Pregnancy Cohort Study Followed For 14 Years," *The Journal of Pediatrics* 2010; D M Fergusson, L J Horwood, F T Shannon, "Breastfeeding and Subsequent Social Adjustment in Six- to Eight-Year-Old Children," *Journal of Child Psychology and Psychiatry* 1987

115 Amy Bentley, *Inventing Baby Food* (University of California Press, 2014), 159

116 M. Hamosh, K. Dewey, C. Garza, Institute of Medicine, *Nutrition During Lactation*, (National Academy Press, 1991)

117 Evan L Ardiel, MSc, Catharine H Rankin, PhD, "The Importance of Touch in Development," *Paediatrics and Child Health* 2010

118 Amanda C. Trofholz, MPH, RD, Anna K. Schulte, Jerica M. Berge, PhD, MPH, LMFT, CFLE, "How Parents Describe Picky Eating and Its Impact on Family Meals," *Appetite* 2017; Paulina Łoboś, Anna Januszewicz, "Food Neophobia in Children," *Pediatric Endocrinology, Diabetes, and Metabolism* 2019

119 Agatha M. Thrash, M.D. "The Long Cooking of Grains", Ucheepines.org, ucheepines.org/the-long-cooking-of-grains/; Agatha M. Thrash, M.D., "Feeding the Baby and Toddler - 1" (See note 107.); Ellen White, *The Ministry of Healing*, 301

120 Ellen White, *The Ministry of Healing*, 296

121 A. Wise, "Nutrition Abstracts and Reviews Series A: Human and Experimental" 1980

122 Ellen White, *Counsels on Diet and Foods*, 228

123 A. Nyaradi, et al. "Prospective Associations Between Dietary Patterns and Cognitive Performance During Adolescence," *The Journal of Child Psychology and Psychiatry* 2014; Ellen White, *Counsels on Health*, 114

124 Caffeine is part of a family of methylxanthine compounds that includes theobromine, phenylethylamine, theophylline, and others.

125 Agatha M. Thrash, M.D., "Learning and What Interferes with It"

126 Jessica E. Beilharz, Jayanthi Maniam, Margaret J. Morris, "Diet-Induced Cognitive Deficits: The Role of Fat and Sugar, Potential Mechanisms and Nutritional Interventions," *Nutrients* 2015; Heather Francis, Richard Stevenson, "Higher Reported Saturated Fat and Refined Sugar Intake is Associated with Reduced Hippocampal-Dependent Memory and Sensitivity to Interoceptive Signals," *Behavioral Neuroscience* 2011; Molteni, R. et al. "A High-Fat, Refined Sugar Diet Reduces Hippocampal Brain-Derived Neurotrophic Factor, Neuronal Plasticity, and Learning," *Neuroscience* 2002

127 Clara Seira Oriach, et al. "Food for Thought: The Role of Nutrition in the Microbiota-Gut–Brain Axis," *Clinical Nutrition Experimental* 2016; Guy E. Townsend, et al. "Dietary Sugar Silences a Colonization Factor in a Mammalian Gut Symbiont," *Proceedings of the National Academy of Sciences* 2019; Shahanshah Khan, et al. "Dietary Simple Sugars Alter Microbial Ecology in the Gut and Promote Colitis in Mice," *Science Translational Medicine* 2020; Joe Alcock, Carlo C Maley, C Athena Aktipis, "Is Eating Behavior Manipulated by the Gastrointestinal Microbiota?," *BioEssays: News And Reviews in Molecular, Cellular and Developmental Biology* 2014

128 Ellen White, "An Earnest Plea," *The Review and Herald*, January 7, 1902

129 Amin Salehi Abargouei, et al. "Refined Carbohydrate Intake in Relation to Non-Verbal Intelligence Among Tehrani Schoolchildren," *Public Health Nutrition* 2012; Agatha M. Thrash M.D., "Feeding the Baby and Toddler - 1" (See note 107.); P. J. Ong, et al. "Effect of Fat and Carbohydrate Consumption on Endothelial Function," *Lancet* 1999; Misty A W Hawkins, Natalie G Keirns, Zachary Helms, "Carbohydrates and Cognitive Function," *Current Opinion in Clinical Nutrition and Metabolic Care* 2018; Sarah J. Spencer, et al. "Food for Thought: How Nutrition Impacts Cognition and Emotion," *NPJ Science of Food* 2017; Agatha M. Thrash M.D., "Learning and What Interferes with It"; Caldwell B Esselstyn Jr, "Is Oil Healthy?," *International Journal of Disease Reversal and Prevention* 2019; Michael Greger M.D. FACLM, "Olive Oil & Artery Function.," NutritionFacts.org nutritionfacts.org/video/olive-oil-and-artery-function

130 Ellen White, *The Ministry of Healing*, 296

131 Ellen White, *The Ministry of Healing*, 311

132 Ellen White, *The Ministry of Healing*, 316

133 Ellen White, *The Ministry of Healing*, 271

134 Bonnie L. Beezhold, Carol S. Johnston, "Restriction of Meat, Fish, And Poultry in Omnivores Improves Mood: A Pilot Randomized Controlled Trial," *Nutrition Journal* 2012; Debbie MacLellan, Jennifer Taylor, Kyla Wood, "Food Intake and Academic Performance Among Adolescents," *Canadian Journal of Dietary Practice and Research* 2008; Steven C. Masley, MD, FAAFP, CNS, FACN, Lucas V. Masley; C. Thomas Gualtieri, MD, "Cardiovascular Biomarkers and Carotid IMT Scores as Predictors of Cognitive Function," *Journal of the American College of Nutrition* 2014; Lawrence A David, et al. "Diet Rapidly and Reproducibly Alters the Human Gut Microbiome," *Nature* 2014; J. Zimmer, et al. "A Vegan or Vegetarian Diet Substantially Alters the Human Colonic Faecal Microbiota," *European Journal of Clinical Nutrition* 2012

135 Ellen White, "Faithfulness in Health Reform," *The Review and Herald*, March 3, 1910

136 Ellen White, *Testimonies for the Church* 2:68

137 Agatha M. Thrash, M.D., Calvin L. Thrash, M.D., *Nutrition for Vegetarians* (NewLifestyle Books, 1996), 79-81; Andrew Chang, Alan Rosani, Judy Quick, *Capsaicin* (StatPearls Publishing, 2020)

138 Yu-Heng Chen, et al. "High Spicy Food Intake and Risk of Cancer," *Chinese*

Medical Journal 2017; Eman Mohamed Mahfouz, et al. "The Role of Dietary and Lifestyle Factors in the Development of Colorectal Cancer," *Central European Journal of Public Health* 2014; Yanmin Wu, et al. "Analysis of Risk Factors
Associated with Precancerous Lesion of Gastric Cancer in Patients from Eastern China," *Journal of Cancer Research and Therapeutics* 2013; L López-Carrillo, M Hernández Avila, R Dubrow, "Chili Pepper Consumption and Gastric Cancer in Mexico" *American Journal of Epidemiology* 1994; R K Phukan, et al. "Role of Dietary Habits in the Development of Esophageal Cancer in Assam, the North-Eastern Region of India," *Nutrition and Cancer* 2001

139 Agatha M. Thrash, M.D., Calvin L. Thrash, M.D., *Nutrition for Vegetarians* (NewLifestyle Books, 1996), 80

140 Emeran A. Mayer, et al. "Symposium: Gut Microbes and the Brain," *The Journal of Neuroscience* 2014; Livia H. Morais, Henry L. Schreiber IV, Sarkis K. Mazmanian, "The Gut Microbiota–Brain Axis in Behaviour and Brain Disorders," *Nature Reviews Microbiology* 2020

141 While some spices may have limited use as a remedy for certain health issues, they should not be used as a part of the regular diet as they are irritating to the body system.

142 Ellen White, *The Ministry of Healing*, 325; Miguel A. Alvareza, M. Victoria Moreno-Arribas, "The Problem of Biogenic Amines in Fermented Foods and the Use of Potential Biogenic Amine-Degrading Microorganisms as a Solution," *Trends in Food Science & Technology* 2014; Jeongseon Kim, et al. "Fermented and Non-Fermented Soy Food Consumption and Gastric Cancer in Japanese and Korean
Populations," *Cancer Science* 2011; Hong-Mei Nan, et al. "Kimchi and Soybean Pastes are Risk Factors of Gastric Cancer," *World Journal of Gastroenterology* 2005; Rup Kumar Phukan, et al. "Dietary Habits and Stomach Cancer in Mizoram, India," *Journal of Gastroenterology* 2006; Jian-Song Ren, et al. "Pickled Food and Risk of Gastric Cancer," *Cancer Epidemiology, Biomarkers & Prevention* 2012; Wang C, et al. "Case-Control Study on Risk Factors of Laryngeal Cancer in Heilongjiang Province," *Lin Chuang er bi yan hou tou Jing wai ke za zhi* 2011; Hyejin Yu, et al. "Vegetables, but not Pickled Vegetables, are Negatively Associated with the Risk of Breast Cancer," *Nutrition and Cancer* 2010; F. Islami, et al. "Pickled Vegetables and the Risk of Oesophageal Cancer," *British Journal of Cancer* 2009; Hyun Ja Kim, et al. "Fresh and Pickled Vegetable Consumption and Gastric Cancer in Japanese and Korean Populations," *Cancer Science* 2010

143 Agatha M. Thrash, M.D., "Diet, Disease, and Behavior"

144 Elizabeth Jane Hall, Poliana V. Vale, M.D., "Natural Remedies for Peptic Ulcer," WildwoodHealth.com (2020) wildwoodhealth.com/blog/natural-remedies-for-peptic-ulcer/; Jiyeon Chang, et al. "Corrosive Esophageal Injury due to a Commercial Vinegar Beverage in an Adolescent," *Clinical Endoscopy* 2020; Y Nobuhara, K Takeuchi, S Okabe, "Vinegar is a Dietary Mild Irritant to the Rat Gastric Mucosa," *Japanese Journal of Pharmacology* 1986; A Molster, K Svanes, S Tonjum, "Changes in Vascular Permeability Associated with Acetic Acid-Induced Gastrin Ulcer in Rats," *Europaische chirurgische Forschung. Recherches chirurgicales europeennes* 1976; Agatha M. Thrash, M.D., Calvin L. Thrash, M.D., *Nutrition for Vegetarians* (NewLifestyle Books, 1996), 80

145 Ellen White, *Child Guidance*, 357

146 Ellen White, *The Ministry of Healing*, 300; Agatha M. Thrash, M.D., Calvin L. Thrash, M.D., *Nutrition for Vegetarians* (NewLifestyle Books, 1996), 108

147 Ellen White, *The Ministry of Healing*, 303

148 Hiroaki Oda, "Chrononutrition," *Journal of Nutritional Science and Vitaminology* 2015; Victoria A. Acosta-Rodríguez, et al. "Importance of Circadian Timing for Aging and Longevity" *Nature Communications* 2021

149 Joseph Bass, Joseph S Takahashi, "Circadian Integration of Metabolism and
Energetic," *Science* 2010; Andrew W McHill, et al. "Later Circadian Timing of Food Intake is Associated with Increased Body Fat," *The American Journal of Clinical Nutrition* 2017; Lauren Pickel, Hoon-Ki Sung, "Feeding Rhythms and the Circadian Regulation of Metabolism," *Frontiers in Nutrition* 2020; Hiroaki Oda, "Chrononutrition," *Journal of Nutritional Science and Vitaminology* 2015

150 Ellen White, *The Ministry of Healing*, 384

151 Agatha M. Thrash, M.D., Calvin L. Thrash, M.D., *Nutrition for Vegetarians* (NewLifestyle Books, 1996), 91

152 Agatha M. Thrash, M.D., "Eating Between Meals," Ucheepines.org, ucheepines.org/eating-between-meals

153 Agatha M. Thrash, M.D., "Effect of Diet on Thinking," Ucheepines.org, ucheepines.org/effect-of-diet-on-thinking

154 Ellen White, *Special Testimony for the Battle Creek Church*, 16

155 Ellen White, *Christian Temperance and Bible Hygiene*, 50

156 Ellen White, *Testimonies for the Church* 2:400

157 Ellen White, *Counsels on Diet and Foods*, 173
158 Keith A. Wesnes, et al. "Breakfast Reduces Declines in Attention and Memory Over the Morning in School-children," *Appetite* 2003; J.M. Murphy, et al. "The Relationship of School Breakfast and Psychosocial and Academic Functioning," *Archives of Pediatric and Adolescent Medicine* 1998
159 Ellen White, *The Ministry of Healing*, 303
160 Rahul Jandial, MD, PhD, *Neurofitness: A Brain Surgeon's Secrets to Boost Performance and Unleash Creativity* (Houghton Mifflin Harcourt, 2019); J Lee, et al.
"Dietary Restriction Increases the Number of Newly Generated Neural Cells, and Induces BDNF Expression, in the Dentate Gyrus of Rats," *Journal of Molecular Neuroscience* 2000, Jaewon Lee, Kim B. Seroogy, Mark P. Mattson, "Dietary Restriction Enhances Neurotrophin Expression and Neurogenesis in the Hippocampus of Adult Mice," *Journal of Neurochemistry* 2002; Sebastian Brandhorst, et al. "A Periodic Diet that Mimics Fasting Promotes Multi-System Regeneration, Enhanced Cognitive Performance, and Health Span," *Cell Metabolism* 2015
161 Wang Man-Man, et al. "The Relationship Between Autophagy and Brain Plasticity in Neurological Diseases," *Frontiers in Cellular Neuroscience* 2019
162 A. V. Witte, et al. "Caloric Restriction Improves Memory in Elderly Humans," *Proceedings of the National Academy of Sciences* 2009; Mark P. Mattson, et al. "Intermittent Metabolic Switching, Neuroplasticity and Brain Health" *Nature Reviews Neuroscience* 2018; Donald K. Ingram, et al. "Dietary Restriction Benefits Learning and Motor Performance of Aged Mice," *Journal of Gerontology* 1987; Matthew C. L. Phillips, "Fasting as a Therapy in Neurological Disease," *Nutrients* 2019; Liaoliao Li, Zhi Wang, Zhiyi Zuo, "Chronic Intermittent Fasting Improves Cognitive Functions and Brain Structures in Mice," *PLoS ONE* 2013; Ángela Fontán-Lozano, et al. "Caloric Restriction Increases Learning Consolidation and Facilitates Synaptic Plasticity Through Mechanisms Dependent on NR2B Subunits of the NMDA Receptor," *Journal of Neuroscience* 2007
163 Agatha M. Thrash, M.D. "Effect of Diet on Thinking," Ucheepines.org, ucheepines.org/effect-of-diet-on-thinking
164 Ellen White, *The Ministry of Healing*, 321
165 Ellen White, *The Ministry of Healing*, 321
166 Ellen White, *Counsels on Diet and Foods*, 178
167 Ellen White, Manuscript 14, no 155 (1899)
168 Agatha M. Thrash, M.D. "Effect of Diet on Thinking", Ucheepines.org, ucheepines.org/effect-of-diet-on-thinking; Ellen White, Manuscript 155 (1899); Ellen White, *The Ministry of Healing*, 306-307
169 Ellen White, "Disease and Its Causes," *The Review and Herald*, August 1, 1899
170 Ellen White, *Fundamentals of Christian Education*, 143 (emphasis supplied)
171 Ellen White, *Medical Ministry*, 273
172 Ellen White, *Testimonies for the Church* 4:515 (emphasis supplied)
173 Ellen White, *Child Guidance*, 461 (emphasis supplied)
174 Ellen White, "Christian Temperance," *The Signs of the Times*, January 6, 1876
175 Ellen White, *The Ministry of Healing*, 295
176 Evelyn Medawar, et al. "The Effects of Plant-Based Diets on the Body and the Brain," *Translational Psychiatry* 2019
177 Ellen White, *Healthful Living*, 96
178 Ellen White, *Testimonies for the Church* 5:311
179 Tülin Yürdem, Funda İfakat Tengiz, "Interaction of REM and Non-REM Sleep with Memory," *Demiroglu Science University Florence Nightingale Journal of Medicine* 2021; Björn Rasch, Jan Born, "About Sleep's Role in Memory," *Physiological Reviews* 2013; Ernesto Durán, et al. "Sleep Stage Dynamics in Neocortex and Hippocampus," *Sleep* 2018
180 Katrin Ivars, et al. "Development of Salivary Cortisol Circadian Rhythm and Reference Intervals in Full-Term Infants," *PLoS ONE* 2015
181 Jennifer Hahn-Holbrook, et al. "Human Milk as 'Chrononutrition'," *Pediatric Research* 2019
182 Sawa Kikuchi, et al. "The Influence of Feeding Method on a Mother's Circadian Rhythm and on the Development of her Infant's Circadian Rest-Activity Rhythm," *Early Human Development* 2020
183 Yvonne Harrison, "The Relationship Between Daytime Exposure to Light and Night-Time Sleep in 6-12-Week-Old Infants," *Journal of Sleep Research* 2004; Shao-Yu Tsai, et al. "Light is Beneficial for Infant Circadian Entrainment: An Actigraphic Study," *Journal of*

Advanced Nursing 2012

184 K. Wulff, R. Siegmund, "Der Einfluss der elterlichen Tagesrhythmik vor und nach der Geburt auf die Entwicklung der Tagesrhythmik beim Säugling," *Zeitschrift für Geburtshilfe und Neonatologie* 2002; Rodrigo Jose Custodio, et al. "The Emergence of the Cortisol Circadian Rhythm in Monozygotic and Dizygotic Twin Infants," *Clinical Endocrinology* 2007

185 Darcia Narvaez, PhD, "Normal, Human Infant Sleep: Feeding Method and Development," *Psychology Today* (2013) psychologytoday.com/us/blog/moral-landscapes/201302/normal-human-infant-sleep-feeding-method-and-development

186 Marie-Hélène Pennestri, et al. "Uninterrupted Infant Sleep, Development, and Maternal Mood," *Pediatrics* 2018

187 James J, McKenna, Thomas McDade, "Why Babies Should Never Sleep Alone: A Review of the Co-Sleeping Controversy in Relation to SIDS, Bedsharing and Breast Feeding," *Paediatric Respiratory Reviews* 2005; Sarah Mosko, et al. "Infant Sleep Architecture During Bedsharing and Possible Implications for SIDS," *Sleep* 1996; James J. McKenna, "Sudden Infant Death Syndrome (SIDS or Cot Death) Infant Sleep, Breast Feeding, and Infant Sleeping Arrangements," *Encyclopedia of Medical Anthropology*, (Springer, 2004); Darcia Narvaez, PhD, "Normal, Human Infant Sleep: Feeding Method and Development," *Psychology Today* (2013) psychologyto-day.com/us/blog/moral-landscapes/201302/normal-human-infant-sleep-feeding-method-and-development

188 Ronbei and Arm's Reach are popular brands.

189 Barak E Morgan, Alan R Horn, Nils J Bergman, "Should Neonates Sleep Alone?," *Biological Psychiatry* 2011

190 James J. Mckenna, Lee T. Gettler, "Mother-Infant Cosleeping with Breastfeeding in the Western Indus-trialized Context," 2007; James J. McKenna, Edmund P. Joyce, "Cosleeping and Biological Imperatives: Why Human Babies Do Not and Should Not Sleep Alone," Neuroanthropology.net, neuroanthropology.net/2008/12/21/cosleeping-and-biological-imperatives-why-human-babies-do-not-and-should-not-sleep-alone/; James J. McKenna, Helen L. Ball, Lee T. Gettler, "Mother–Infant Cosleeping, Breastfeeding and Sudden Infant Death Syndrome," *Yearbook of Physical Anthropology* 2007

191 Malcom W. Stewart, Lara A. Stewart, "Modification of Sleep Respiratory Patterns by Auditory Stimulation: Indications of Techniques for Preventing Sudden Infant Death Syndrome?," *Sleep* 1991; Anneliese F. Korner, Evelyn B. Thoman, "The Relative Efficacy of Contact and Vestibular-Proprioceptive Stimulation on Soothing Neonates," *Child Development* 1972

192 For more information, I recommend the book, *Safe Infant Sleep: Expert Answers to Your Cosleeping Questions* by James McKenna; K. Sankaran, et al. "Sudden Infant Death Syndrome (SIDS) and Infant Care Practices in Saskatchewan Canada," Program and Abstracts, Sixth SIDS International Conference, Auckland, New Zealand, 2000; M. A. Kibel, M. F. Davies, "Should the Infant Sleep in Mother's Bed?," Program and Abstracts, Sixth SIDS International Conference, Auckland, New Zealand, 2000; Pranee Liamputtong, *Childrearing and Infant Care Issues: A Cross-cultural Perspective* (Nova Science Publishers 2007), 6-8; D. P. Davies, "Cot Death In Hong Kong: A Rare Problem?," *The Lancet* 1985; Natalie N Y Lee, et al. "Sudden Infant Death Syndrome in Hong Kong: Confirmation of Low Incidence," *British Medical Journal* 1999; S. Fukai, F. Hiroshi, "1999 Annual Report, Japan SIDS Family Association", Sixth SIDS International Conference, Auckland, New Zealand, 2000; Elizabeth Wilson, "Sudden Infant Death Syndrome (SIDS) and Environmental Perturbations in Cross-Cultural Context," Master's thesis, University of Calgary, 1990; M. Macintyre, J. Yelland, S. Gifford, "Explanatory Models About Maternal and Infant Health and Sudden Infant Death Syndrome Among Asian-Born Mothers," *Asian Mothers, Australian Birth: Pregnancy, Childbirth and Childrearing: The Asian Experience in an English-Speaking Country* (Ausmed Publications, 1994), 175-191

193 Huilan Xu, et al. "Associations of Outdoor Play and Screen Time with Nocturnal Sleep Duration and Pattern Among Young Children," *Acta Paediatrica* 2016

194 M. Nathaniel Mead, "Benefits of Sunlight: A Bright Spot for Human Health," *Environmental Health Perspectives* 2008

195 Christian Cajochen, et al. "Evening Exposure to a Light-Emitting Diodes (LED)-Backlit Computer Screen Affects Circadian Physiology and Cognitive Performance," *Journal of Applied Physiology* 2011; Mari Hysing, et al. "Sleep and Use of Electronic Devices in Adolescence: Results from a Large Population-Based Study," *BMJ Open* 2015; Huilan Xu, et al. "Associations of Outdoor Play and Screen Time with Nocturnal Sleep Duration and Pattern Among Young Children," *Acta Paediatrica* 2016

196 Lauren Hale, PhD, Stanford Guan, MPH, "Screen Time and Sleep Among School-Aged Children and Ado-

lescents," *Sleep Medicine Reviews* 2015

197 Ellen White, Letter 85, 1888

198 Christoph Randler, "Proactive People are Morning People," *Journal of Applied Social Psychology* 2009; Matthew Walker, *Why We Sleep* (Scribner, 2018); Renee Biss, Lynn Hasher, "Happy as a Lark: Morning-Type Younger and Older Adults are Higher in Positive Affect," *Emotion* 2012

199 Ellen White, *The Ministry of Healing*, 130

200 Ellen White, *The Ministry of Healing*, 128

201 Ellen White, "Temperance in the Family," *The Signs of the Times*, September 22, 1881

202 Ellen White, Manuscript 155 (1899)

203 Ellen White, *Christ's Object Lessons*, 349

204 Ellen White, *The Ministry of Healing*, 335

205 Ellen White, *The Ministry of Healing*, 310

Chapter 4

1 Michael Lewis, Jeannette M. Haviland-Jones, Lisa Feldman Barrett, *Handbook of   Emotions*, 3rd ed. (Guilford, 2008)

2 Katherine Rand, Amir Lahav, "Maternal Sounds Elicit Lower Heart Rate in Preterm Newborns in the First Month of Life," *Early Human Development* 2014; A J DeCasper, W P Fifer, "Of Human Bonding: Newborns Prefer Their Mothers' Voices," *Science* 1980

3 Ellen White, *Testimonies for the Church* 2:536

4 Ellen White, *Testimonies for the Church* 2:536

5 Eun Joo Kim, Blake Pellman, Jeansok J. Kim, "Stress Effects on the Hippocampus," *Learning & Memory* 2015; Joan L. Luby, et al. "Maternal Support in Early Childhood Predicts Larger Hippocampal Volumes at School Age,"
Proceedings of the National Academy of Sciences 2012; A Rifkin-Graboi, et al. "Maternal Sensitivity, Infant Limbic Structure Volume and Functional Connectivity: A Preliminary Study," *Translational Psychiatry* 2015

6 Élizabel Leblanc, et al. "Attachment Security in Infancy: A Preliminary Study of Prospective Links to Brain Morphometry in Late Childhood" *Frontiers in Psychology* 2017

7 Amanda S. Hodel, "Rapid Infant Prefrontal Cortex Development and Sensitivity to Early Environmental Experience," *Developmental Review* 2018

8 N.K. Mackes, et al. "Early Childhood Deprivation is Associated with Alterations in Adult Brain Structure Despite Subsequent Environmental Enrichment" *Proceedings of the National Academy of Sciences* 2020; A Rifkin-Graboi, et al. "Maternal Sensitivity, Infant Limbic Structure Volume and Functional Connectivity: A Preliminary Study," *Translational Psychiatry* 2015; Li Xin Zhang, et al. "Maternal Deprivation Increases Cell Death in the Infant Rat Brain," *Developmental Brain Research* 2002; Lane Strathearn, "Maternal Neglect: Oxytocin, Dopamine and the Neurobiology of Attachment," *Journal of Neuroendocrinology* 2011; Gail Gross, *How to Build Your Baby's Brain: A Parent's Guide to Using New Gene Science to Raise a Smart, Secure, and Successful Child* (Skyhorse, 2019)

9 Wanêssa Lacerda Poton, et al. "Breastfeeding and Behavior Disorders Among Children and Adolescents," *Revista de Saude Publica* 2018; Lisa-Christine Girard, Chamarrita Farkas, "Breastfeeding and Behavioural Problems," *BMJ Open* 2019; Wendy H Oddy, et al. "The Long-Term Effects of Breastfeeding on Child and Adolescent Mental Health," *The Journal of Pediatrics* 2010; Jeffry A. Simpson, W. Andrew Collins, Jessica E. Salvatore, "The Impact of Early Interpersonal Experience on Adult Romantic Relationship Functioning," *Current Directions in Psychological Science* 2011; Kathleen. M. Krol, Tobias Grossmann, "Psychological Effects of Breastfeeding on Children and Mothers," *Bundesgesundheitsblatt, Gesundheitsforschung, Gesundheitsschutz* 2018

10 M Nachmias, et al. "Behavioral Inhibition and Stress Reactivity: The Moderating Role of Attachment Security," *Child Development* 1996; M L Laudenslager, et al. "Total Cortisol, Free Cortisol, and Growth Hormone Associated with Brief Social Separation Experiences in Young Macaques," *Developmental Psychobiology* 1995; Nikolaos P. Daskalakis, et al. "Immediate Effects of Maternal Deprivation on the (Re)Activity of the HPA-Axis Differ in CD1 and C57Bl/6J Mouse Pups," *Endocrinology* 2014; Naima Lajud, Luz Torner, "Early Life Stress and Hippocampal Neurogenesis in the Neonate: Sexual Dimorphism, Long Term Consequences and Possible Mediators," *Frontiers in Molecular Neuroscience* 2015; P Rosenfeld, et al. "Maternal Regulation of the Adrenocortical Response in Preweanling Rats," *Physiology & Behavior* 1991

11 M.A. Smith as reported by John Travis, *Science News* 1997; Eun Joo Kim, Blake Pellman, Jeansok J. Kim, "Stress Effects on the Hippocampus," *Learning & Memory* 2015; Amanda S. Hodel, "Rapid Infant Prefrontal Cortex Development and Sensitivity to Early Environmental Experience," *Developmental Review* 2018; J. Raber, "Detrimental Effects of Chronic Hypothalamic-Pituitary-Adrenal Axis Activation," *Molecular Neurobiology* 1998

12 Colwyn Trevarthen, "Making Sense of Infants Making Sense," *Intellectica* 2002

13 Colwyn Trevarthen, "Making Sense of Infants Making Sense," *Intellectica* 2002

14 Katharina Braun, Bock Jörg, "The Experience-Dependent Maturation of Prefronto-Limbic Circuits and the Origin of Developmental Psychopathology," *Developmental Medicine and Child Neurology* 2011 ; Allan Schore, "The Experience-Dependent Maturation of a Regulatory System in the Orbital Prefrontal Cortex and the Origin of Developmental Psychopathology," *Development and Psychopathology* 1996; E. Meins, et al. "Rethinking Maternal Sensitivity: Mothers' Comments on Infants' Mental Processes Predict Security of Attachment at 12 Months," *Journal of Child Psychology and Psychiatry, and Allied Disciplines* 2001; Elizabeth Meins, "The Effects of Security of Attachment and Material Attribution of Meaning on Children's Linguistic Acquisitional Style," *Infant Behavior and Development* 1998

15 Cynthia A. Stifter, Tracy L. Spinrad, "The Effects of Excessive Crying on the Development of Emotion Regulation," *Infancy* 2002

16 Elise A. Piazza, et al. "Infant and Adult Brains are Coupled to the Dynamics of Natural Communication," *Psychological Science* 2020

17 Julie Gros-Louis, et al. "Mothers Provide Differential Feedback to Infants' Prelinguistic Sounds" *International Journal of Behavioral Development* 2006; Victor J. Bernstein, Sydney L. Hans, Candice Percansky, "Advocating for the Young Child in Need Through Strengthening the Parent-Child Relationship," *Journal of Clinical Child Psychology* 1991

18 Evan L Ardiel, MSc, Catharine H Rankin, PhD, "The Importance of Touch in Development," *Paediatrics & Child Health* 2010

19 Darcia Narvaez, et al. "The Importance of Early Life Touch for Psychosocial and Moral Development," *Psicologia: Reflexão e Crítica* 2019

20 Ellen White, "The Work of Parents," *Good Health*, March 1, 1880; Ellen White, "The Home and the School," *The Review and Herald*, March 21, 1882; Ellen White, "The Position and Responsibility of a True Educator," *The Signs of the Times*, March 14, 1900; Ellen White, *Counsels to Parents, Teachers, and Students*, 76, 124

21 Ellen White, *The Ministry of Healing*, 203

22 Ellen White, *Education*, 237

23 Ellen White, *Fundamental of Christian Education*, 304

24 Pam Leo, Connection Parenting: Parenting Through Connection Instead of Coercion, Through Love Instead of Fear (Wyatt-MacKenzie Publishing; 2nd edition 2007), 87

25 Ellen White, Manuscript 79 (1901)

26 Ellen White, Testimonies for the Church 3:528

27 Ellen White, Manuscript 79 (1901)

28 Ellen White, Manuscript 79 (1901)

29 Ellen White, Manuscript 79 (1901)

30 Linda Luecken, "Childhood Attachment and Loss Experiences Affect Adult Cardiovascular and Cortisol Function," *Psychosomatic Medicine* 1998; J. Raber, "Detrimental Effects of Chronic Hypothalamic-Pituitary-Adrenal Axis Activation," *Molecular Neurobiology* 1998; Bruce Cushing, Kristin Kramer, "Mechanisms Underlying Epigenetic Effects of Early Social Experience: The Role of Neuropeptides and Steroids," *Neuroscience and Biobehavioral Reviews* 2005

31 Vincent J Felitti MD, FACP, et al. "The Adverse Childhood Experiences (ACE) Study - Relationship of Childhood Abuse and Household Dysfunction to Many of the Leading Causes of Death in Adults," *American Journal of Preventive Medicine* 1998; J. Raber, "Detrimental Effects of Chronic Hypothalamic-Pituitary-Adrenal Axis Activation," *Molecular Neurobiology* 1998

32 James McKenna, Safe Infant Sleep: Expert Answers to Your Cosleeping Questions (Platypus Media, LLS, 2020), 46; Tiffany M. Field, "Touch Therapy Effects on Development," *International Journal of Behavioral Development* 1998

33 Ellen White, *Fundamentals of Christian Education*, 65

34 Ellen White, *Patriarchs and Prophets*, 579 (emphasis supplied)

35 Ellen White, *Testimonies for the Church* 5:326

36 Ellen White, "The Parents' Work," *The Review and Herald*, August 30, 1881

37 Ellen White, "The Parents' Work," *The Review and Herald*, August 30, 1881
38 Ellen White, "Co-operation Between the School and the Home," *The Review and Herald*, April 21, 1904
39 Ellen White, "Happy and Unhappy Homes," *The Signs of the Times*, October 2, 1884
40 Ellen White, "The Home-Life," *The Signs of the Times*, April 8, 1903
41 Elizabeth N. Baldwin, "Extended Breastfeeding and the Law," *Mothering* (Spring 1993); See also Hong, Yoo Rha, Jae Sun Park, "Impact of Attachment, Temperament and Parenting on Human Development," *Korean Journal of Pediatrics* 2012; Becker-Stoll, et al. "Is Attachment at Ages 1, 6 and 16 Related to Autonomy and Relatedness Behavior of Adolescents in Interaction towards Their Mothers?," *International Journal of Behavioral Development* 2008
42 Yoo Rha Hong, MD, Jae Sun Park, MD, "Impact of Attachment, Temperament and Parenting on Human Development," *Korean Journal of Pediatrics* 2012
43 Victor J. Bernstein, Sydney L. Hans, Candice Percansky, "Advocating for the Young Child in Need Through Strengthening the Parent-Child Relationship," *Journal of Clinical Child Psychology* 1991
44 Diane Benoit, "Infant-Parent Attachment: Definition, Types, Antecedents, Measurement and Outcome," *Paediatrics & Child Health* 2004; P. Heron, "Non-Reactive Cosleeping and Child Behavior: Getting a Good Night's Sleep All Night, Every Night" Master's thesis, Department of Psychology, University of Bristol (1994)
45 Ellen White, "Child-Training," *The Signs of the Times*, April 23, 1902
46 Ellen White, Manuscript 8 (1875)
47 Ellen White, "Our Children and Youth Demand Our Care," *The Review and Herald*, February 13, 1913
48 Ellen White, Manuscript 79 (1901)

Chapter 5

1 U.S. Department of Education, National Center for Education Statistics, Reading Literacy in the United States 1996
2 K. Durkin, et al. "Effects of a Statewide Pre-Kindergarten Program on Children's Achievement and Behavior Through Sixth Grade," *Developmental Psychology* 2022
3 The information in this paragraph is based on a large body of research in the area of child development and developmental neuroscience. To learn more, one may study Piaget's stages of development, Dr. Raymond Moore's research on school entrance age, or books and research by authors such as Dr. Jane Healy, Dr. Susan Johnson, Dr. Linda Bryant Caviness, Dr. Carla Hannaford, Dr. Peter Grey, Erika Komisar, and Dr. David Elkind.
4 Ellen White, *Counsels to Parents, Teachers, and Students*, 80
5 Ellen White, "Disease and Its Causes," *The Review and Herald*, August 1, 1899
6 Dr. Raymond Moore, "Synopsis," Moore Academy, mooreacademy.org/articles/synopsis; Carla Hannaford, *Smart Moves: Why Learning Is Not All in Your Head* (Great Ocean Publishers, 2005), 104 - 106
7 Susan R Johnson MD, FAAP, "A Developmental Approach Looking at the Relationship of Children's Foundational Neurological Pathways to their Higher Capacities for Learning," 2017
8 Nancy Carlsson-Paige, Joan Almon, Geralyn Bywater Mclaughlin, "Reading in Kindergarten: Little to Gain and Much to Lose," *The Alliance for Childhood* 2015
9 Ellen White, *Education*, 208
10 Cédric M.P. Koolschijn, Eveline A. Crone, "Sex Differences and Structural Brain Maturation from Childhood to Early Adulthood," *Developmental Cognitive Neuroscience* 2013
11 Allan N. Schore, "All our Sons: The Developmental Neurobiology and Neuroendocrinology of Boys at Risk," *Infant Mental Health Journal* 2017
12 Ephesians 5:22-26
13 Dr. Raymond Moore, "Synopsis," Moore Academy, mooreacademy.org/articles/synopsis
14 Joshua White, "The Case for Delayed Formal Education" 2011
15 Dr. Raymond Moore, Dorothy Moore, *Better Late than Early* (Reader's Digest Association, 1979), 206
16 Caroline Sharp of the National Foundation for Educational Research, quoted in "Do We Send Our Children to School Too Young" *The Times* 2007
17 Joshua White, "The Case for Delayed Formal Education" 2011
18 Ellen White, *Testimonies for the Church* 3:145
19 "[P]arents should improve the opportunity to instruct, and patiently answer these little inquiries. They can, in this manner, get the advantage of the enemy, and fortify the minds of their children, by sowing good seed in

their hearts, leaving no room for the bad to take root." Ellen White, *The Review and Herald*, August 1, 1899

20 Ellen White, *Education*, 41

21 Ellen White, "Work Out Your Own Salvation," *The Signs of the Times*, September 25, 1901

Chapter 6

1 Ellen White, *Testimonies for the Church* 5:329

2 Ellen White, "Disease and Its Causes," *The Review and Herald*, December 5, 1899; Manuscript 64 (1899); Diane Benoit, "Infant-Parent Attachment: Definition, Types, Antecedents, Measurement and Outcome," *Paediatrics & Child Health* 2004; Jay Belsky, "The Effects of Infant Day Care Reconsidered," *Early Childhood Research Quarterly* 1988

3 "What the child sees and hears is drawing deep lines upon the tender mind, which no after circumstances in life can entirely efface.... Repeated acts in a

given course become habits. These may be modified by severe training, in after life, but are seldom changed. The whole future course of thousands is determined by the education received from the parents in childhood." Ellen White, "Appeal to Mothers," *Good Health*, January 1, 1880; Deborah J. Laible, Ross A. Thompson, "Mother-Child Discourse, Attachment Security, Shared Positive Affect, and Early Conscience Development," *Child Development* 2000; Ellen White, "Disease and Its Causes," *The Review and Herald*, December 5, 1899; For more information, I recommend the books *Better Late than Early* and *School Can Wait* by Dr. Raymond and Dorothy Moore.

4 Ellen White, "Appeal to Mothers," *Good Health*, January 1, 1880

5 Ellen White, "Home Training," *The Review and Herald*, December 5, 1899 (emphasis supplied)

6 Ellen White, "Home Training," *The Review and Herald*, December 5, 1899

7 Ellen White, *Fundamentals of Christian Education*, 156 (emphasis supplied)

8 Ellen White, *Christ's Object Lessons*, 332

9 Ellen White, *Testimonies for the Church* 5:306

10 Ellen White, "Praise Due to the Creator," *The Review and Herald*, April 21, 1885

11 Ellen White, *Testimonies for the Church* 5:306

12 Ellen White, *The Desire of Ages*, 307

13 Ellen White, *The Ministry of Healing*, 450

14 Ellen White, *Special Testimonies on Education*, 71

15 Psalm 119:11

16 Ephesians 6:11 KJV

17 Revelation 1:1

18 Jay Belsky, "The Effects of Infant Day Care Reconsidered," *Early Childhood Research Quarterly* 1988

19 D. J. Laible, R. A. Thompson, "Mother-Child Discourse, Attachment Security, Shared Positive Affect, and Early Conscience Development," *Child Development* 2000; Winston Seegobin, "The Parent-Child Relationship," In: "Christianity and Developmental Psychopathology: Foundations and Approaches" *Faculty Publications – Grad School of Clinical Psychology* 2014

20 Winston Seegobin, "The Parent-Child Relationship," In: "Christianity and Developmental Psychopathology: Foundations and Approaches" *Faculty Publications – Grad School of Clinical Psychology* 2014

21 Ellen White, *Patriarchs and Prophets*, 596

22 Ellen White, *Patriarchs and Prophets*, 599

23 Ellen White, *Patriarchs and Prophets*, 599

24 Ellen White, *The Ministry of Healing*, 241

25 Ellen White, *Education*, 195

26 Ellen White, *Testimonies for the Church* 4:197

27 Ellen White, *The Ministry of Healing*, 130

28 Ellen White, "The Home and the School," *The Review and Herald*, March 21, 1882

29 Ellen White, *Testimonies for the Church* 6:93

30 Ellen White, "Education from a Christian Stand-Point," *Good Health*, July 1, 1889

31 Ellen White, "Work Out Your Own Salvation," *The Signs of the Times*, September 25, 1901

32 Ellen White, "The Duties of a Mother," *The Signs of the Times*, August 30, 1877; "Home Training," *The Review and Herald*, December 5, 1899

33 Ellen White, Manuscript 8, no 654

34 Ellen White, "Education from a Christian Stand-Point," *Good Health*, July 1, 1889

35 Ellen White, Manuscript 64 (1899)
36 Ellen White, "Disease and Its Causes," *The Review and Herald*, August 1, 1899
37 Ellen White, *Fundamentals of Christian Education*, 69
38 Ellen White, "The Mother's First Duties," *The Signs of the Times*, August 5, 1875
39 Ellen White, "The Mother's Duty - Christ her Strength," *The Health Reformer*, August 1, 1877
40 Ellen White, "The Mother's Duty - Christ her Strength," *The Health Reformer*, August 1, 1877
41 Ellen White, *Education*, 30
42 Ellen White, *Patriarchs and Prophets*, 595; *Education*, 225
43 Ellen White, *Counsels to Parents, Teachers, and Students*, 49
44 Ellen White "The Christian's Work," *The Signs of the Times*, July 13, 1888
45 Ellen White, *Child Guidance*, 184
46 Ellen White, "The Mother's Duty - Christ her Strength," *The Health Reformer*, August 1, 1877
47 Ellen White "The Christian's Work," *The Signs of the Times*, July 13, 1888
48 Ellen White, *Testimonies for the Church* 4:650
49 Ellen White, Letter 28, 1890

Chapter 7

1 Ellen White, *Fundamentals of Christian Education*, 17
2 Ellen White, *Education*, 230
3 Ellen White, *Education*, 230
4 Ellen White, *Fundamentals of Christian Education*, 16
5 Ellen White, *Fundamentals of Christian Education*, 16
6 Ellen White, *Fundamentals of Christian Education*, 16
7 Ellen White, *Education*, 17
8 Ellen White, *Education*, 17
9 Ellen White, *Education*, 17
10 Ellen White, *Education*, 17
11 Barbara Rogoff, "How do People Learn Without Being Taught?," (2011)
   psychology.ucsc.edu
12 Ellen White, *Education*, 17
13 Ellen White, *Fundamentals of Christian Education*, 17
14 Ellen White, *Education* 220
15 Carla Hannaford, *Smart Moves: Why Learning Is Not All in Your Head* (Great Ocean Publishers, 2005), 97
16 Ellen White, *Education* 230
17 Ellen White, *Special Testimonies on Education*, 112
18 Ellen White, *Education*, 202
19 Ellen White, *Testimonies for the Church* 3:142

Chapter 8

1 Ellen White, *Education*, 107
2 Anna V. Fisher, et al. "Visual Environment, Attention Allocation, and Learning in Young Children: When Too
   Much of a Good Thing May Be Bad," *Psychological Science* 2014
3 Ellen White, *Education*, 248; See also *Education*, 202
4 Ellen White, *Testimonies for the Church* 3:144
5 Ellen White, *Testimonies for the Church* 3:144
6 Emilia Campayo-Muñoz, Alberto Cabedo-Mas, David Hargreaves, "Active Listening, Expressive Communication and Cooperation in Music Learning," *Australian Journal of Music Education* 2021
7 Carly Dauch, et al. "The Influence of the Number of Toys in the Environment on Toddlers' Play," *Infant Behavior and Development* 2018
8 Ellen White, *The Ministry of Healing*, 366
9 Deuteronomy 29:10-13 and 31:12,13; Joshua 8:35; Joel 2:15-16; 2 Chronicles 20:13
10 Penelle Chase, Jane Doan, *Full Circle: A New Look at Multiage Education*
   (Heinemann 1994)
11 Ellen White, *Education*, 189
12 Ellen White, *Education*, 189
13 Pam A. Mueller, Daniel M. Oppenheimer, "The Pen Is Mightier Than the Keyboard: Advantages of Longhand

Over Laptop Note Taking," *Psychological Science* 2014; Keita Umejima, et al. "Paper Notebooks vs. Mobile Devices: Brain Activation Differences During Memory Retrieval," *Frontiers in Behavioral Neuroscience* 2021

14 Dimitri A. Christakis, et al. "Early Television Exposure and Subsequent Attentional Problems in Children," *Pediatrics* 2004; Jenny S. Radesky, MD, et al. "Infant Self-Regulation and Early Childhood Media Exposure," *Pediatrics* 2014; Dimitri A. Christakis, et al. "How Early Media Exposure May Affect Cognitive Function," *Proceedings of the National Academy of Sciences* 2018

15 Ellen White, *The Ministry of Healing*, 386

16 Ellen White, *The Ministry of Healing*, 388

17 Ellen White, "Home Thoughts," *The Signs of the Times*, August 23, 1877

18 Ellen White, *The Ministry of Healing*, 367

Chapter 9

1 H. Rudolph Schaffer, *Social Development* (Oxford, Blackwell, 1998); Dr. Raymond Moore, "The Dangers of Early Schooling: The Need to Reexamine Our Motives and Methods," Hewitt Research Center 1973; Haena Lee, Markus Schafer," Are Positive
   Childhood Experiences Linked to Better Cognitive Functioning in Later Life?," *Jour
   nal of Aging and Health* 2021; Karen J. Bos, et al. "Effects of Early Psychosocial Depri
   vation on the Development of Memory and Executive Function," *Frontiers in
   Behavioral Neuroscience* 2009; X. Xiong, L. Deng, H. Li, "Is Winning at the Start Im
   portant: Early Childhood Family Cognitive Stimulation and Child Development,"
   Children and Youth Services Review 2020; M.B. Bibok, J.I.M. Carpendale, U. Müller,
   "Parental Scaffolding and the Development of Executive Function," *New Directions
   for Child and Adolescent Development* 2009

2 Ellen White, *Education*, 231

3 Ellen White, *The Ministry of Healing*, 389

4 Ellen White, *The Ministry of Healing*, 203

5 Ellen White, *Education*, 16

6 Ellen White, *Education*, 33

7 Exodus 25:8 KJV; Ellen White, *Education*, 35

8 Ellen White, *Education*, 84

9 Ellen White, *Education*, 84

10 Ellen White, *Gospel Workers 1892*, 404

11 "Young hearts yearn for sympathy and tenderness, and if they do not obtain it from their parents, they will seek it from sources that may endanger both mind and morals." Ellen White, *Christian Education* 169

12 "Satan tempts children to be reserved to their parents, and choose their young and inexperienced companions as their confidants; such as cannot help them, or give them good advice." Ellen White, "Parents as Counselors," *The Signs of the Times*, June 6, 1878

13 Ellen White, *Testimonies for the Church* 6:93

14 Ellen White, *The Desire of Ages*, 250

15 Ellen White, *Education*, 14

16 "Great is the honor and the responsibility placed upon fathers and mothers, in that they are to stand in the place of God to their children." Ellen White, *The Ministry of Healing*, 375. See also Ellen White, "Home Training,"; Ellen White, "Disease and Its Causes" *The Review and Herald*, December 5, 1899; Ellen White "Work Out Your Own Salvation," *The Signs of the Times*, September 25, 1901; Ellen White "The Parents' Work," *The Review and Herald*, August 30, 1881.

17 Ellen White, *Testimonies for the Church* 6:93

18 Ellen White, *Education*, 84

19 Ellen White, *Education*, 114

20 Ellen White, "The Pearl of Great Price," *The Review and Herald*, August 1, 1899

21 Ellen White, "The Training of Children," *The Signs of the Times*, April 10, 1884

22 Ellen White, "The Training of Children," *The Signs of the Times*, April 10, 1884

23 Ellen White, "Work Out Your Own Salvation," *The Signs of the Times*, September 25, 1901

Chapter 10

1 Ellen White, "Thoughts on Education," *The Review and Herald*, January 10, 1882

2 Ellen White, *Education*, 77
3 Luke 2:40 KJV
4 Luke 4:32 RSV
5 Ellen White, *Education*, 81
6 Ellen White, *Special Testimonies on Education*, 159
7 Ellen White, *Education*, 77
8 Ellen White, *Education*, 77
9 Ellen White, *Education*, 77
10 Ellen White, *Education*, 276

Chapter 11

1 Karen Stromswold, in M. Gazzaniga (ed.), The cognitive and neural bases of
   language acquisition (MIT Press 1995), 855-867
2 Peter Gray, PhD, "Coronavirus School Closures: An Educational Opportunity," *Psychology Today*, psychologyto-
   day.com/us/blog/freedom-learn/202003/coronavirus-school-closures-educational-opportunity
3 Inge Bolin, *Growing Up in a Culture of Respect* (University of Texas Press, 2006)
4 A. D. Schliemann, D. W. Carraher, B. M. Brizuela, "From Quantities to Ratio, Functions, and Algebraic Relations," 2000 AERA Meeting, New Orleans, LA
5 Sylvia Scribner, "Head and Hand: An Action Approach to Thinking," Office of Educational Research and
   Improvement 1988
6 Ellen White, "Among the Churches," *The Signs of the Times*, February 9, 1882
7 Ellen White, *Testimonies for the Church* 8:316
8 Ellen White, *Christian Education*, 246
9 James 1:22
10 James 4:17
11 We see this law referenced in the article entitled, "Proper Education," *The Health Reformer*, May 1, 1873. The
   context of this article is the benefits of manual labor, but the law applies to other areas of life as well.
12 Ellen White, "A Neglected Work," *The Review and Herald*, October 9, 1900
13 Ellen White, *The Ministry of Healing*, 499
14 Ellen White, *Education*, 238
15 Ellen White, *Education*, 238
16 Ellen White, *Education*, 238
17 Charles Spurgeon, *The Complete Works of C. H. Spurgeon* (Delmarva Publications, 2015)
18 Ellen White, *Testimonies for the Church* 5:22
19 Ellen White, *Counsels on Health*, 178
20 Ellen White, *Counsels to Parents, Teachers, and Students*, 388

Chapter 12

1 Acts 13:22 KJV
2 Ellen White, *Patriarchs and Prophets*, 641
3 Ellen White, *Patriarchs and Prophets*, 641
4 Ellen White, *Patriarchs and Prophets*, 642
5 Ellen White, *Patriarchs and Prophets*, 642
6 Ellen White, *Special Testimonies on Education*, 57
7 Ellen White, *Christian Education*, 143 (emphasis supplied)
8 Ellen White, "The Position and Responsibility of a True Educator," *The Signs of the Times*, March 14, 1900
9 Ellen White, *Education*, 211
10 Ellen White, *The Ministry of Healing*, 52
11 Ellen White, *Special Testimonies on Education*, 158
12 Ellen White, *Education*, 81
13 Ellen White, *The Ministry of Healing*, 52
14 Ellen White, *The Ministry of Healing*, 54
15 Ellen White, *Steps to Christ*, 85
16 Ellen White, *Education*, 102
17 Ellen White, *Education*, 102
18 Ellen White, *Fundamentals of Christian Education*, 60

19 Ellen White, *Special Testimonies on Education*, 37
20 Ellen White, *Education*, 102
21 Ellen White, *Education*, 100
22 Ellen White, *Special Testimonies on Education*, 62
23 Ellen White, *Education*, 100
24 Ellen White, "The Position and Responsibility of a True Educator," *The Signs of the Times*, March 14, 1900
25 Ellen White, "The Treasures of God's Word," *The Review and Herald*, July 3, 1900
26 Job 12:8 KJV
27 Job 12:7 KJV
28 Job 12:8 KJV
29 Ellen White, *Education*, 117
30 Ellen White, "Nature Speaks of God," *The Signs of the Times*, December 6, 1905
31 Ellen White, *Testimonies for the Church* 8:261
32 Ellen White, Manuscript 20, no 1454
33 Ellen White, "Nature Speaks of God," *The Signs of the Times*, December 6, 1905
34 Ellen White, "Nature Speaks of God," *The Signs of the Times*, December 6, 1905
35 Ellen White, *Our High Calling*, 251
36 Ellen White, *Education*, 100
37 Lara S. Franco, Danielle F. Shanahan, Richard A. Fulle, "A Review of the Benefits of Nature Experiences: More Than Meets the Eye," *International Journal of Environmental Research and Public Health* 2017
38 Nancy M. Wells, "At Home with Nature: Effects of 'Greenness' on Children's Cognitive Functioning," *Environment and Behavior* 2000; Stephen C. Van Hedger, et al. "Of Cricket Chirps and Car Horns: The Effect of Nature Sounds on Cognitive Performance," *Psychonomic Bulletin & Review* 2019; Marc G. Berman, John Jonides, Stephen Kaplan, "The Cognitive Benefits of Interacting with Nature," *Psychological Science* 2008; Ellen White, *Counsels on Health*, 164; Mikaël J. A. Maes, et al. "Benefit of Woodland and Other Natural Environments for Adolescents' Cognition and Mental Health," *Nature Sustainability* 2021
39 Ellen White, "Words to the Young", *The Youth's Instructor*, July 13, 1893
40 Andrea Faber Taylor, Frances E. Kuo, William C. Sullivan, "Views of Nature and Self-Discipline: Evidence from Inner City Children," *Journal of Environmental Psychology* 2001
41 Frances E. Kuo, William C. Sullivan, "Aggression and Violence in the Inner City: Effects of Environment via Mental Fatigue," *Environment and Behavior* 2001
42 Gregory N. Bratman, et al. "Nature and Mental Health: An Ecosystem Service Perspective," *Science Advances* 2019
43 Ellen White, Manuscript 8, no 582
44 Ellen White, *Testimonies for the Church* 3:333
45 Ellen White, "The Primal Object of Education," *The Review and Herald*, July 11, 1882
46 Junsung Woo, C. Justin Lee, "Sleep-Enhancing Effects of Phytoncide via Behavioral, Electrophysiological, and Molecular Modeling Approaches," *Experimental Neurobiology* 2020; Emi Morita, et al. "A Before and After Comparison of the Effects of Forest Walking on the Sleep of a Community-Based Sample of People with Sleep Complaints," *BioPsychoSocial Medicine* 2011, Kenneth P Wright J, et al. "Entrainment of the Human Circadian Clock to the Natural Light-Dark Cycle," *Current Biology* 2013
47 Ellen White, *Counsels on Health* 177
48 Ellen White, *Fundamentals of Christian Education*, 159
49 Ellen White, *Steps to Christ*, 85
50 Ellen White, *Education*, 119
51 Ellen White, "The Great Controversy Between Christ and His Angels and Satan and His Angels - The Flood," *The Signs of the Times*, February 27, 1879
52 Ellen White, *Counsels on Health*, 164
53 Romans 1:20
54 Ellen White, "The Primal Object of Education," *The Review and Herald*, July 11, 1882
55 Ellen White, *The Desire of Ages*, 281
56 Ellen White, *Steps to Christ*, 85
57 Ellen White, *Christ's Object Lessons*, 25
58 Ellen White, *Our High Calling*, 250
59 Shuyu Xiong, et al. "Time Spent in Outdoor Activities in Relation to Myopia Prevention and Control,"

Acta Ophthalmologica 2017; Charlotte Mason, *Home Education* (Start Publishing LLC, 2013), 44; Angela J. Hanscom, Balanced and Barefoot: How Unrestricted Outdoor Play Makes for Strong, Confident and Capable Children (New Harbinger Publications, 2016)

60 Ellen White, "Dress Reform," *The Health Reformer*, January 1, 1873

61 Ellen White, *Testimonies for the Church* 6:126

62 Ellen White, *Special Testimonies on Education*, 60

63 Ellen White, "Battle Creek College," *The Signs of the Times*, February 7, 1878

64 Ellen White, *Christian Education*, 8

65 Ellen White, "Nature Speaks of God," *The Signs of the Times*, December 6, 1905

66 Ellen White, *Thoughts from the Mount of Blessing*, 96

67 Ellen White, *The Ministry of Healing*, 294

68 Ellen White, "Seek First the Kingdom of God," *The Review and Herald*, October 27, 1885

69 Ellen White, "Seek First the Kingdom of God," *The Review and Herald*, October 27, 1885

70 Ellen White, *The Adventist Home*, 146

71 Ellen White, *Testimonies for the Church* 6:185

Chapter 13

1 Ilona Bidzan-Bluma, Małgorzata Lipowska, "Physical Activity and Cognitive Functioning of Children," *International Journal of Environmental Research and Public Health* 2018; Laura Chaddock, et al. "A Functional MRI Investigation of the Associa tion Between Childhood Aerobic Fitness and Neurocognitive Control," *Biological Psychology* 2012; Anya Doherty, Anna Forés Miravalles, "Physical Activity and Cog nition: Inseparable in the Classroom," *Frontiers in Education* 2019

2 Phillip D Tomporowski, et al. "Exercise and Children's Intelligence, Cognition, and Academic Achievement," *Educational Psychology Review* 2008

3 John Best, "Effects of Physical Activity on Children's Executive Function," *Developmental Review* 2010; Ellen White, *Special Testimonies on Education*, 39

4 Ellen White, *Special Testimonies on Education*, 40 (emphasis supplied)

5 Ellen White, *Messages to Young People*, 179

6 Ellen White, *The Ministry of Healing*, 366

7 Ellen White, *The Ministry of Healing*, 366

8 Ellen White, *Testimonies for the Church* 6:179 (emphasis supplied)

9 Elizabeth M. White, Mark D. DeBoer, Rebecca J. Scharf, "Associations Between Household Chores and Child hood Self-Competency," *Journal of Developmental & Behavioral Pediatrics* 2019; Nobue Nakahori, et al. "The Relationship between Home Environment and Children's Dietary Behaviors, Lifestyle Factors, and Health," *Japanese Journal of Public Health* 2016; Richard Rende, *Raising Can-Do Kids* (TarcherPerigee, 2015)

10 Ellen White, "The Training of Children," *The Signs of the Times*, April 10, 1884; Dr. Raymond Moore, Dorothy Moore, *Better Late than Early* (Reader's Digest Association, 1979), 56

11 Marty Rossmann, "Involving Children in Household Tasks: Is It Worth The Effort?," University of Minnesota publication 2002; Elizabeth M. White, Mark D. DeBoer, Rebecca J. Scharf, "Associations Between Household Chores and Childhood Self-Competency," *Journal of Developmental & Behavioral Pediatrics* 2019

12 Dr. Franz E. Weinert, "Lehren und Lernen für die Zukunft - Ansprüche an das Lernen in der Schule," *MaxPlanck-Institut für psychologische Forschung* 2000

13 Ellen White, "Elements of Success," *Atlantic Union Gleaner*, January 6, 1904

14 Marty Rossmann, "Involving Children in Household Tasks: Is It Worth The Effort?," University of Minnesota publication 2002

15 Michal Zivan, et al. "Screen-Exposure and Altered Brain Activation Related to Attention in Preschool Chil dren: An EEG Study," *Trends in Neuroscience and Education* 2019; Renata Maria Silva Santos, "The Association Between Screen Time and Attention in Chil dren," *Developmental Neuropsychology* 2022

16 Ellen White, "Mothers and their Daughters," *The Signs of the Times*, August 19, 1875

17 Ellen White, "Parents as Counselors," *The Signs of the Times*, June 6, 1878

18 Ellen White, *Testimonies for the Church* 3:122

19 Ellen White, "Proper Education," *The Signs of the Times*, September 6, 1877

20 Ellen White, *Education*, 212

21 Ellen White, "The Parents' Work," *The Review and Herald*, August 30, 1881

22 Ellen White, *Testimonies for the Church* 2:348

23 Ellen White, *Fundamentals of Christian Education*, 36 (emphasis supplied)

24 Ellen White, "Parents as Counselors," *The Signs of the Times*, June 6, 1878

25 Ellen White, *Special Testimonies on Education*, 38

26 Ellen White, "A Neglected Work," *The Review and Herald*, October 9, 1900

27 Ellen White, *Testimonies for the Church* 6:180

28 Ellen White, "Proper Education," *The Signs of the Times*, September 6, 1877

29 Ellen White, *Testimonies for the Church* 3:122

30 Ellen White, *Testimonies for the Church* 4:410

31 Ellen White, *Special Testimonies on Education*, 32

32 Ellen White, *Education*, 220

33 Ellen White, *Christian Temperance and Bible Hygiene*, 96

34 Ellen White, *Education*, 33

35 Ellen White, *Education*, 34

36 Ellen White, *Special Testimonies on Education*, 38

37 Ellen White, *Special Testimonies on Education*, 38

38 Ellen White, "Parents in the Sabbath-School," *The Signs of the Times*, June 23, 1881

39 Ellen White, *Fundamentals of Christian Education*, *417*

40 Ellen White, *Testimonies for the Church* 9:185

41 Ellen White, *Fundamentals of Christian Education*, 417

42 Ellen White, "Parents in the Sabbath-School," *The Signs of the Times*, June 23, 1881

43 Ellen White, *The Ministry of Healing*, 366

44 Ellen White, *The Ministry of Healing*, 366 (emphasis supplied)

45 Ellen White, *Christian Temperance and Bible Hygiene*, 134

46 Ellen White, "The Home School," *The Review and Herald*, January 12, 1911

47 Ellen White, *Special Testimonies on Education*, 37

48 Marty Rossmann, "Involving Children in Household Tasks: Is It Worth The Effort?," University of Minnesota publication 2002

49 Ellen White, *The Ministry of Healing*, *388*

50 Barbara Rogoff, *The Cultural Nature of Human Development* (Oxford University Press, 2003), 361

51 Andrew Dayton, Itzel Aceves-Azuara, Barbara Rogoff, "Collaboration at a Microscale: Cultural Differences in Family Interactions," *British Journal of Developmental Psychology* 2022; Rebeca Mejía-Arauz, et al. "Collaborative Work or Individual Chores: The Role of Family Social Organization in Children's Learning to Collaborate and Develop Initiative," *Advances in Child Development and Behavior* 2015

52 Lucia Alcalá, Cervera Montejano, Y.S. Fernandez, "How Yucatec Maya Children Learn to Help at Home," *Human Development* 2021

53 Ellen White, "The Work of Parents," *The Review and Herald*, June 24, 1890 (emphasis supplied)

54 Ellen White, "Education from a Christian Stand-Point," *Good Health*, July 1, 1889

55 Ellen White, "The Home-Life," *The Signs of the Times*, April 8, 1903

56 Ellen White, "The Importance of Early Training," *The Health Reformer*, June 1, 1877

57 Ellen White, "The Parents' Work," *The Review and Herald*, August 30, 1881

58 Andrew D. Coppens, et al. "Children's Contributions in Family Work: Two Cultural Paradigms," In: *Families, Intergenerationality, and Peer Group Relations* (Springer, Singapore 2016)

59 Sara R Jaffee, et al. "Chaotic Homes and Children's Disruptive Behavior: A Longitudinal Cross-Lagged Twin Study," *Psychological Science* 2012

60 Ellen White, "Proper Education," *The Review and Herald*, July 14, 1885

61 Ellen White, "Proper Education," *The Review and Herald*, July 14, 1885

62 Ellen White, "Proper Education," *The Review and Herald*, July 14, 1885

63 Ellen White, "Proper Education," *The Review and Herald*, July 14, 1885

64 Ellen White, "Proper Education," *The Review and Herald*, July 14, 1885

65 Ellen White, "Lessons from the Past," *The Review and Herald*, December 17, 1903

66 Ellen White, "Early Life of Samuel," *The Signs of the Times*, November 3, 1881

67 Ellen White, "The Importance of Home Training," *The Review and Herald*, June 6, 1899

68 Ellen White, "Lessons from the Past," *The Review and Herald*, December 17, 1903 (emphasis supplied)

69 Eelix Warneken, Michael Tomasello, "Extrinsic Rewards Undermine Altruistic Tendencies in 20-Month-

Olds," *Developmental Psychology* 2008; David Greene, Mark R. Lepper, "Effects of Extrinsic Rewards on Children's Subsequent Intrinsic Interest," *Child Development* 1974

70 R. A. Fabes, et al. "Effects of Rewards on Children's Prosocial Motivation," *Developmental Psychology* 1989

71 Ellen White, *The Adventist Home*, 387

72 Bernardo J. Carducci, *The Psychology of Personality: Viewpoints, Research, and Applications* (Wiley, 2009), 443; George Lowenstein, *Choice Over Time* (Russell Sage Foundation, 1992); Louise Twito, et al. "The Motivational Aspect of Children's Delayed Gratification: Values and Decision Making in Middle Childhood," *Frontiers in Psychology* 2019; Walter Mischel, et al. "Willpower Over the Life Span: Decomposing Self-Regulation," *Social Cognitive and Affective Neuroscience* 2011

73 Ellen White, "The Duties of a Mother," *The Signs of the Times*, August 30, 1877

74 Ellen White, "Proper Education," *The Health Reformer*, July 1, 1873 (emphasis supplied)

75 Ellen White, *Counsels to Parents, Teachers, and Students*, 308

76 Ellen White, *Fundamentals of Christian Education*, 369

77 Ellen White, *Daughters of God*, 205

78 Ellen White, "Words for Mothers," *The Signs of the Times*, March 23, 1891

79 Ellen White, "Proper Education," *The Health Reformer*, June 1, 1873

80 Ellen White, *Messages to Young People*, 178

81 Ellen White, *Special Testimonies on Education*, 39

82 Ellen White, "The Apostle Paul and Manual Labor," *The Review and Herald*, March 13, 1900

83 Ellen White, *Testimonies for the Church* 6:180

Chapter 14

1 Ellen White, *Education*, 125

2 Ellen White, "The Treasures of God's Word," *The Review and Herald*, July 3, 1900

3 Rick Weissbourd, Stephanie Jones, "The Children We Mean to Raise: The Real Messages Adults Are Sending About Values," *Making Caring Common, Harvard Graduate School of Education* 2014

4 OECD, "United States" in *Education at a Glance 2019: OECD Indicators*, (OECD Publishing, Paris 2019)

5 Ellen White, *Patriarchs and Prophets*, 596

6 Ellen White, "The Need of Reform in Our Educational Work," *General Conference Daily Bulletin*, March 6, 1899

7 Ellen White, "Parental Responsibility," *The Signs of the Times*, January 31, 1884

8 Ellen White, *Testimonies for the Church* 5:321

9 Ellen White, *Education*, 124

10 Ellen White, *Fundamentals of Christian Education*, 165

11 Ellen White, *Christian Education*, 58

12 Ellen White, *Counsels to Parents, Teachers, and Students*, 422

13 Ellen White, *Testimonies for the Church* 8:319

14 Ellen White, "Importance of Education," *The Review and Herald*, August 19, 1884

15 Ellen White, "The Position and Responsibility of a True Educator," *The Signs of the Times*, March 14, 1900

16 Ellen White, *Christ's Object Lessons*, 42

17 Ellen White, *Patriarchs and Prophets*, 599

18 Ellen White, *The Desire of Ages*, 70

19 Ellen White, *Education*, 185

20 Ellen White, *Education*, 187

21 Ellen White, *Testimonies for the Church* 6:43

22 Psalm 119:97 KJV

23 D. J. Laible, R. A. Thompson, "Mother-Child Discourse, Attachment Security, Shared Positive Affect, and Early Conscience Development," *Child Development* 2000; Winston Seegobin, "The Parent-Child Relationship," In: "Christianity and Developmental Psychopathology: Foundations and Approaches" *Faculty Publications – Grad School of Clinical Psychology* 2014

24 Ellen White, *Testimonies for the Church* 5:158

25 Ellen White, *Our High Calling*, 105

26 Ellen White, *The Desire of Ages*, 455

27 Ellen White, Manuscript 141, 1903

28 Quoted by Ellen White in "Appeal to Mothers," *Good Health*, January 1, 1880

29 D. J. Laible, R. A. Thompson, "Mother-Child Discourse, Attachment Security, Shared Positive Affect, and

Early Conscience Development," *Child Development* 2000
30 Ellen White, "Parents and Children," *The Review and Herald*, January 20, 1863
31 Ellen White, "Home Religion," *The Signs of the Times*, March 3, 1909
32 2 Timothy 3:5
33 Ellen White, *Testimonies for the Church* 5:159
34 Ellen White, *The Adventist Home*, 381
35 Ellen White, "The Treasure with Which to Store the Mind," *The Review and Herald*, November 24, 1891
36 Ellen White, *Testimonies for the Church* 4:611
37 Ellen White, *Education*, 47
38 Ellen White, *Patriarchs and Prophets*, 504; *Steps to Christ*, 58
39 Ellen White, "Parents in the Sabbath-School," *The Signs of the Times*, June 23, 1881
40 Ellen White, *The Desire of Ages*, 515
41 Ellen White, *Steps to Christ*, 58
42 Ellen White, "Thoughts on Education," *The Review and Herald*, January 10, 1882
43 Ellen White, "The Training of Children," *The Signs of the Times*, April 10, 1884
44 Ellen White, *Education*, 185 (emphasis supplied)
45 *Christ's Object Lessons*, a book on the parables of Jesus, is authored by Ellen White.
46 The Conflict of the Ages series consists of the books *Patriarchs and Prophets*,
   Prophets and Kings, *The Desire of Ages*, *The Acts of the Apostles*, and *The Great Controversy*. These books cover the
   time from the rebellion in heaven to the end of the world and the second coming of Jesus.
47 Deuteronomy 6:5
48 Ellen White, "Appeal to Mothers," *Good Health*, January 1, 1880
49 Ellen White, *Child Guidance*, 41 (emphasis supplied)
50 Ellen White, *Testimonies for the Church* 5:329
51 Ellen White, "The Parents' Work," *The Review and Herald*, August 30, 1881
52 Ellen White, "The Parents' Work," *The Review and Herald*, August 30, 1881
53 Ellen White, "Have You Oil in Your Vessels with Your Lamps?," *The Review and Herald*, September 17, 1895
54 Ellen White, "The Responsibilities of Parents and Teachers," *Sabbath-School
   Worker*, April 1, 1889
55 Ellen White, *Mind, Character, and Personality* 2:593
56 Ellen White, *The Ministry of Healing*, 460
57 Ellen White, "Bible Study," *The Signs of the Times*, September 26, 1895
58 Ellen White, *Child Guidance*, 147
59 Ellen White, *Education*, 186
60 1 John 4:8
61 Ellen White, *Christ's Object Lessons*, 114
62 Ellen White, "Notes of Travel," *The Review and Herald*, October 21, 1884
63 Ellen White, *Education*, 186
64 Ellen White, *Education*, 186
65 Ellen White, *Testimonies for the Church* 6:174
66 Ellen White, "Family Prayer," *The Signs of the Times*, August 7, 1884
67 Ellen White, *Education*, 186
68 Ellen White, *Education*, 186
69 Ellen White, *Testimonies for the Church* 6:175
70 Ellen White, *Testimonies for the Church* 6:131
71 Ellen White, *Testimonies for the Church* 5:329
72 Ellen White, *Testimonies for the Church* 6:166
73 Ellen White, *Testimonies for the Church* 8:311
74 Ellen White, *Fundamentals of Christian Education*, 541
75 Ellen White, *Christian Education*, 85
76 Ellen White, *The Ministry of Healing*, 459
77 Ellen White, "The Truth as it is in Jesus," *The Signs of the Times*, June 16, 1898

Chapter 15
1 Ellen White, *Testimonies for the Church* 6:142

2.Ellen White, *Testimonies for the Church* 6:141

3 Ellen White, *Testimonies for the Church* 6:141

4 Ellen White, "A Wise Reply," *The Signs of the Times*, July 21, 1881

5 Ellen White, *Testimonies for the Church* 5:22

6 Ellen White, *Fundamentals of Christian Education*, 288 (emphasis supplied)

7 Ellen White, *Testimonies for the Church* 6:153

8 Genesis 1:27; *The Desire of Ages*, 37

9 Ellen White, *Education*, 195

10 Ellen White, "True Education," *Christian Educator*, August 1, 1897

11 Ellen White, *Special Testimonies on Education, 149*

12 Ellen White, *Counsels to Parents, Teachers, and Students, 208*

13 Ellen White, "The Bible in Our Schools," *The Review and Herald*, August 17, 1897

14 Ellen White, *Education*, 77

15 Ellen White, *Counsels to Parents, Teachers, and Students,* 64

16 Ellen White, *Counsels to Parents, Teachers, and Students,* 444

Chapter 16

1 Ellen White, "Our Duty to Our Children," *Gospel Medical Messenger*, October 15,
   1913

2 Ellen White, *Testimonies for the Church* 6:183

3 Ellen White, *Testimonies for the Church* 6:179

4 Ellen White, *Education*, 111

5 Amy E. Dirks, Kathryn Orvis, "An Evaluation of the Junior Master Gardener Program in Third Grade Classrooms," *HortTechnology* 2005; Irene Canaris, "Growing Foods for Growing Minds: Integrating Gardening and
   Nutrition Education into the Total Curriculum," *Children's Environments* 1995

6 Ellen White, *Counsels to Parents, Teachers, and Students,* 126

7 Ellen White, *Christ's Object Lessons,* 289

8 Ellen White, *Education*, 111

9 Ellen White, *Education*, 111

10 Ellen White, *Fundamentals of Christian Education,* 375

11 Ellen White, *Fundamentals of Christian Education,* 375

12 Ellen White, *Counsels to Parents, Teachers, and Students,* 187

13 Ellen White, *Testimonies for the Church* 6:185; See also Hosea 10:12

14 Ellen White, *Testimonies for the Church* 6:185

15 Ellen White, *Testimonies for the Church* 6:185

16 Ellen White, "Week of Prayer in Australia," *The Review and Herald*, October 18, 1898

17 Ellen White, *Testimonies for the Church* 6:187

18 Ellen White, *Testimonies for the Church* 6:181

19 Ellen White, *Testimonies for the Church* 6:187

20 Ellen White, *Special Testimonies on Education,* 60

21 Ellen White, *Testimonies for the Church* 6:185

22 Ellen White, *Testimonies for the Church* 6:186

23 Ellen White, *Testimonies for the Church* 6:186

24 Ellen White, *Testimonies for the Church* 6:192

25 Ellen White, *Education*, 219

26 Ellen White, *The Ministry of* Healing, 200

27 Ellen White, *Education*, 219

28 Ellen White, *The Adventist Home,* 142

29 Ellen White, *Counsels to Parents, Teachers, and Students,* 311

30 Ellen White, *Fundamentals of Christian Education,* 322

31 Ellen White, *Testimonies for the Church* 6:178

32 Ellen White, *Testimonies for the Church* 6:181

33 Ellen White, *Testimonies for the Church* 6:177

34 Ellen White, *Fundamentals of Christian Education,* 326

35 Ellen White, *Testimonies for the Church* 6:192

36 Ellen White, *Fundamentals of Christian Education,* 325

37 Ellen White, *Education*, 219
38 Ellen White, *Education*, 219

Chapter 17
1 Ellen White, *Medical Ministry*, 221
2 Ellen White, *Education*, 195
3 Ellen White, *Patriarchs and Prophets*, 601
4 Ellen White, *Counsels to Parents, Teachers, and Students*, 125
5 Ellen White, *Christ's Object Lessons*, 348
6 Ellen White, *Education*, 196
7 Ellen White, *Education*, 196
8 Ellen White, *Patriarchs and Prophets*, 599
9 Ellen White, "Right Methods in Education," *The Signs of the Times*, August 26, 1886
10 Ellen White, "Earnest Words to Mothers," *The Health Reformer*, January 1, 1873
11 Ellen White, *Counsels on Diet and Foods*, 327
12 *The Health Reformer* is authored by Ellen White.
13 Ellen White, *Testimonies for the Church* 7:63
14 Ellen White, "Proper Education," *The Health Reformer*, September 1, 1872
15 Ellen White, Manuscript 20, no 1420
16 Ellen White, *The Ministry of Healing*, 127 (emphasis supplied)
17 Ellen White, *The Ministry of Healing*, 237
18 Ellen White, *The Ministry of Healing*, 237
19 Ellen White, Manuscript 21, no 1559
20 Ellen White, Manuscript 21, no 1559 This is referring to activated charcoal, which is different from the charcoal that may be used for cooking.
21 Ellen White, *The Ministry of Healing*, 127 (emphasis supplied)
22 Ellen White, *The Ministry of Healing*, 128 (emphasis supplied)
23 Ellen White, *Education*, 196
24 Ellen White, "The Duty of Parents to Children," *The Review and Herald*, June 27, 1899
25 John 7:17
26 Ellen White, "Importance of Good Cooking," *The Review and Herald*, August 14, 1894
27 Ellen White, "Faithfulness in Health Reform," *The Review and Herald*, March 3, 1910
28 Ellen White, *Testimonies for the Church* 6:375
29 Ellen White, *Testimonies for the Church* 6:369
30 Ellen White, "The Position and Responsibility of a True Educator," *The Signs of the Times*, March 14, 1900
31 Ellen White, *Counsels to Parents, Teachers, and Students*, 125
32 Ellen White, "Disease and Its Causes," *The Review and Herald*, August 8, 1899
33 Ellen White "Proper Education," *The Health Reformer*, June 1, 1873
34 Ellen White, *Testimonies for the Church* 9:160
35 Ellen White, *Christ's Object Lessons*, 348
36 Ellen White, "Importance of Physical Training," *The Signs of the Times*, June 29, 1882
37 Ellen White, "Proper Education," *The Health Reformer*, September 1, 1872

Chapter 18
1 Ellen White, *Medical Ministry*, 270
2 Ellen White, *Counsels to Parents, Teachers, and Students*, 312
3 Ellen White, *Counsels to Parents, Teachers, and Students*, 313
4 Ellen White, *Medical Ministry*, 271
5 Ellen White, "Importance of Good Cooking," *The Review and Herald*, August 14, 1894
6 Ellen White, "Importance of Good Cooking," *The Review and Herald*, August 14, 1894
7 Ellen White, *Christian Temperance and Bible Hygiene*, 48
8 Ellen White, "Importance of Good Cooking," *The Review and Herald*, August 14, 1894
9 Ellen White, *Medical Ministry*, 270
10 Ellen White, *The Ministry of Healing*, 302
11 Ellen White, *The Ministry of Healing*, 301
12 Grains should either be browned (as is the case when making bread) or have several hours of cooking. For more information, see Jennifer White "Are Grains Healthy?" jenniferskitchen.com/whole-grains-should-you-

avoid-grains; *The*
Ministry of Healing, 301; and Agatha M. Thrash M.D. "The Long Cooking of Grains," Ucheepines.org, uch-eepines.org/the-long-cooking-of-grains/
13 Ellen White, *Child Guidance*, 376
14 Ellen White, *Child Guidance*, 376
15 Ellen White, Manuscript 16, no 1194
16 Ellen White, *Testimonies for the Church* 1:682
17 Ellen White, "Importance of Good Cooking," *The Review and Herald*, August 14, 1894

Chapter 19

1 Ellen White, *Counsels to Parents, Teachers, and Students*, 216
2 Ellen White, *Counsels to Parents, Teachers, and Students*, 217
3 Ellen White, *Counsels to Parents, Teachers, and Students*, 216
4 Sue Roulston, et al. "Investigating the Role of Language in Children's Early Educational Outcomes," Research Report DFE-RR134 2011
5 Ellen White, *Counsels to Parents, Teachers, and Students*, 216
6 Ellen White, *Counsels to Parents, Teachers, and Students*, 219
7 Ellen White, *The Voice in Speech and Song*, 33
8 Ellen White, *The Voice in Speech and Song*, 175
9 Ellen White, *Christian Education*, 123
10 Ellen White, *Christian Education*, 123
11 Ellen White, *The Voice in Speech and Song*, 30
12 Ellen White, *The Voice in Speech and Song*, 31
13 Ellen White, *Testimonies for the Church* 6:337
14 Ellen White, *Christ's Object Lessons*, 305
15 Ellen White, "Our Words," *The Review and Herald*, January 25, 1898
16 Ellen White, *Christ's Object Lessons*, 305
17 Ellen White, Manuscript 77 (1897)
18 Ellen White, *Fundamentals of Christian Education*, 267
19 Ellen White, *The Voice in Speech and Song*, 43
20 Other factors (such as being overweight or wearing tight clothing) can contribute to improper breathing, but too much sitting is the most common cause.
21 Ellen White, *Education*, 198
22 Ellen White, *Testimonies for the Church* 6:380
23 Ellen White, *Testimonies for the Church* 6:381
24 Ellen White, Manuscript 69, (1903)
25 Ellen White, *The Voice in Speech and Song*, 187
26 Ellen White, *The Voice in Speech and Song*, 187
27 Ellen White, Manuscript 69, (1903)
28 Ellen White, *The Voice in Speech and Song*, 65
29 Ellen White, *Christ's Object Lessons*, 337
30 Ellen White, "Godliness in the Every-day Life," *The Review and Herald*, December 31, 1901
31 Ellen White, *The Voice in Speech and Song*, 126
32 Ellen White, *Christ's Object Lessons*, 337
33 Ellen White, *Education*, 236 (quoting Matthew 5:37, R.V.)
34 Ellen White, *Education*, 235
35 Ellen White, *Education*, 236
36 Philippians 4:8
37 Ellen White, *Christ's Object Lessons*, 337
38 Ellen White, *The Voice in Speech and Song*, 15
39 Ellen White, *Christ's Object Lessons*, 338
40 Ellen White, "Godliness in the Every-day Life," *The Review and Herald*, December 31, 1901
41 Ellen White, *Christ's Object Lessons*, 338-339 (emphasis supplied)
42 Ellen White, "Disseminating Temperance Principles," *The Review and Herald*, June 18, 1908
43 Matthew 12:34 KJV
44 Ellen White, *Christ's Object Lessons*, 338

45 Ellen White, *Sons and Daughters of God*, 180
46 Ellen White, *Testimonies for the Church* 6:173
47 Ellen White, *The Voice in Speech and Song*, 133
48 Ellen White, *Testimonies for the Church* 6:173
49 Ellen White, *Education*, 235
50 Ellen White, *Christ's Object Lessons*, 337
51 Ellen White, *Christ's Object Lessons*, 335
52 Ellen White, *The Voice in Speech and Song*, 183
53 Ellen White, "Our Words," *The Youth's Instructor*, July 26, 1900
54 Ellen White, *The Voice in Speech and Song*, 189

Chapter 20

1 Ellen White, "The Best Education and Its Purpose," *The Review and Herald*, November 21, 1893
2 Ellen White, *The Ministry of Healing*, 396
3 Ellen White, "Training the Youth to Be Workers," *The Review and Herald*, May 16, 1912
4 Ellen White, *Education*, 13
5 Ellen White, *Counsels to Parents, Teachers, and Students*, 168
6 Ellen White, "Training the Youth to Be Workers," *The Review and Herald*, May 16, 1912
7 Ellen White, Manuscript 5 (1896)
8 Ellen White, *Education*, 58
9 Ellen White, *Christ's Object Lessons*, 345
10 Ellen White, *Patriarchs and Prophets*, 574
11 Ellen White, *Education*, 16 (emphasis supplied)
12 Ellen White, *Testimonies for the Church* 6:429
13 Ellen White, "How Parents Should Discipline Their Children," *The Signs of the Times*, August 13, 1896
14 Ellen White, *Testimonies for the Church* 6:429
15 Ellen White, Manuscript 64 (1899)
16 Ellen White, "How Lay Members May Help," *The Review and Herald*, December 8, 1910
17 Ellen White, *The Ministry of Healing*, 140
18 Ellen White, *Testimonies for the Church* 6:291
19 Ellen White, *Testimonies for the Church* 8:168
20 Ellen White, *Testimonies for the Church* 7:136
21 Ellen White, *Testimonies for the Church* 9:112 (emphasis supplied)
22 There are many counterfeit health messages today. For solid information on natural remedies, I recommend obtaining books by Agatha M. Thrash, M.D., the book *The Ministry of Healing*, and the periodicals *The Health Reformer* and *Good Health* by Ellen White.
23 Ellen White, *Testimonies for the Church* 9:172
24 Ellen White, *Testimonies for the Church* 6:430
25 Ellen White, *Testimonies for the Church* 7:63
26 Ellen White, *Testimonies for the Church* 6:429
27 Ellen White, *Counsels to Parents, Teachers, and Students*, 545
28 Ellen White, *Education*, 268 (emphasis supplied)
29 Ellen White, "Awake Out of Sleep," *The Review and Herald*, February 21, 1893
30 Ellen White, "How Parents Should Discipline Their Children," *The Signs of the Times*, August 13, 1896
31 Ellen White, *Special Testimonies on Education*, 72
32 Ellen White, *Testimonies for the Church* 6:430
33 Ellen White, Manuscript 5 (1896)
34 Ellen White, "Parental Responsibility," *The Signs of the Times*, January 31, 1884
35 Ellen White, *Testimonies for the Church* 6:203
36 Ellen White, *Testimonies for the Church* 8:168
37 Ellen White, "Christ's Mission of Love," *The Bible Echo*, November 19, 1894
38 Ellen White, "The Primal Object of Education," *The Review and Herald*, July 11, 1882
39 Ellen White, "How Lay Members May Help," *The Review and Herald*, December 8, 1910
40 Ellen White, *Testimonies for the Church* 6:407

Chapter 21

1 Ellen White, *Testimonies for the Church* 5:37
2 Damon E. Jones, Mark Greenberg, Max Crowley, "Early Social-Emotional Functioning and Public Health: The Relationship Between Kindergarten Social Competence and Future Wellness," *American Journal of Public Health* 2015
3 Ellen White, *Testimonies for the Church* 6:172
4 Ellen White, *Testimonies for the Church* 6:172
5 David Elkind, *The Hurried Child* (Addison-Wesley Publishing Co. 1981), 120
6 John C. Condry, Michael L. Siman, "Characteristics of Peer- and Adult-Oriented Children," *Journal of Marriage and Family* 1974
7 Dr. Raymond Moore, "Synopsis," Moore Academy, mooreacademy.org/articles/synopsis; John C. Condry, Michael L. Siman, "Characteristics of Peer- and Adult-Oriented Children," *Journal of Marriage and Family* 1974
8 Ellen White, "I Have Written Unto You, Young Men," *The Youth's Instructor*, October 25, 1894
9 Ellen White, "I Have Written Unto You, Young Men," *The Youth's Instructor*, October 25, 1894
10 John C. Condry, Michael L. Siman, "Characteristics of Peer- and Adult-Oriented Children," *Journal of Marriage and Family* 1974
11 Ellen White, "The Parents' Work," *The Review and Herald*, August 30, 1881
12 Ellen White, "Parent and Child," *The Review and Herald*, May 26, 1910
13 Manuela Veríssimo, et at. "Associations Between Attachment Security and Social Competence in Preschool Children," *Merrill–Palmer Quarterly* 60 no 1
14 Élizabel Leblanc, et al. "Attachment Security in Infancy: A Preliminary Study of Prospective Links to Brain Morphometry in Late Childhood," *Frontiers in Psychology* 2017; L. Alan Sroufe, "Attachment and Development: A Prospective, Longitudinal Study from Birth to Adulthood," *Attachment & Human Development* 2005; Donald L. Pastor, "The Quality of Mother-Infant Attachment and Its Relationship to Toddlers' Initial Sociability with Peers," *Developmental Psychology* 1981; Linda Rose-Krasnor, "The Relation of Maternal Directiveness and Child Attachment Security to Social Competence in Preschoolers," *International Journal of Behavioral Development* 1996
15 C Baumgartner, "Psychomotor and Social Development of Breast-Fed and Bottle-Fed Babies During Their First Year of Life," *Acta Paediatrica Hungarica* 1984; Wendy H Oddy, et al. "The Long-Term Effects of Breast-feeding on Child and Adolescent Mental Health: A Pregnancy Cohort Study Followed for 14 Years," *The Journal of Pediatrics* 2010; Paulita Duazo, Josephine Avila, Christopher W. Kuzawa, "Breastfeeding and Later Psychosocial Development in the Philippines," *American Journal of Human Biology* 2010
16 D M Fergusson, L J Horwood, F T Shannon, "Breastfeeding and Subsequent Social Adjustment in Six- to Eight-Year-Old Children," *Journal of Child Psychology and Psychiatry* 1987
17 Gordon Neufeld, Gabor Maté, *Hold on to Your Kids: Why Parents Need to Matter More Than Peers* (Ballantine Books, 2006); Allan N. Schore, "Effects of a Secure Attachment Relationship on Right Brain Development, Affect Regulation, and Infant Mental Health," *Infant Mental Health Journal* 2001
18 Gordon Neufeld, Gabor Maté, *Hold on to Your Kids: Why Parents Need to Matter More Than Peers* (Ballantine Books, 2006); Kim B Burgess, et al. "Infant Attachment and Temperament as Predictors of Subsequent Behavior Problems and Psychophysiological Functioning," *Journal of Child Psychology and Psychiatry and Allied Discipline* 2003
19 Elizabeth Meins, "The Effects of Security of Attachment and Material Attribution of Meaning on Children's Linguistic Acquisitional Style," *Infant Behavior and Development* 1998; Elizabeth Meins, et al. "Rethinking Maternal Sensitivity: Mothers' Comments on Infants' Mental Processes Predict Security of Attachment at 12 Months," *Journal of Child Psychology and Psychiatry, and Allied Disciplines*, 2001; Jessica Laranjo, et al. "The Roles of Maternal Mind-Mindedness and Infant Security of Attachment in Predicting Preschoolers' Understanding of Visual Perspective Taking and False Belief," *Journal of Experimental Child Psychology* 2014; Luna Centifanti, Elizabeth Meins, Charles Fernyhough, "Callous-Unemotional Traits and Impulsivity: Distinct Longitudinal Relations with Mind-Mindedness and Understanding of Others," *Journal of Child Psychology and Psychiatry* 2016; Elizabeth Meins, C Fernyhough, "Linguistic Acquisitional Style and Mentalising Development: The Role of Maternal Mind-Mindedness," *Cognitive Development* 1999;

Annie Bernier, et al. "Social Factors in the Development of Early Executive Functioning: A Closer Look at the Caregiving Environment," *Developmental Science* 15 2012

20 Dr. Raymond Moore, Dorothy Moore, *Home Grown Kids* (Word Books, 1981), 40

21 Seth J. Schwartz, et al. "Daily Dynamics of Personal Identity and Self-Concept Clarity," *European Journal of Personality* 2011

22 Ellen White, *Education*, 237

23 Ellen White, "Among the Churches," *The Signs of the Times*, February 9, 1882

24 Ellen White, *Education*, 237

25 Hong, Yoo Rha, Jae Sun Park, "Impact of Attachment, Temperament and Parenting on Human Development," *Korean Journal of Pediatrics* 2012; Becker-Stoll, et al. "Is Attachment at Ages 1, 6 and 16 Related to Autonomy and Relatedness Behavior of Adolescents in Interaction towards Their Mothers?," *International Journal of Behavioral Development* 2008

26 Yoo Rha Hong, MD, Jae Sun Park, MD, "Impact of Attachment, Temperament and Parenting on Human Development," *Korean Journal of Pediatrics* 2012

27 Elizabeth N. Baldwin, "Extended Breastfeeding and the Law," *Mothering* (Spring 1993)

28 Kira E. Riehm, MS, et al. "Associations Between Time Spent Using Social Media and Internalizing and Externalizing Problems Among US Youth," *JAMA Psychiatry* 2019; Russell M Viner, PhD; et al. "Roles of Cyberbullying, Sleep, and Physical Activity in Mediating the Effects of Social Media Use on Mental Health and Wellbeing Among Young People in England," *The Lancet* 2019

29 Thomas S. Dee, Hans Henrik Sievertsen, "The Gift of Time? School Starting Age and Mental Health," *Health Economics* 2018

30 Dr. Raymond Moore, Dorothy Moore, *Better Late Than Early* (Reader's Digest Association 1975) 92

31 Ellen White, *Testimonies for the Church* 6:172

32 Ellen White, *Testimonies for the Church* 6:172

33 Ellen White, *Testimonies for the Church* 6:172

34 Dr. Raymond Moore, "Synopsis," Moore Academy, mooreacademy.org/articles/synopsis

35 Ellen White, "Lessons from the Past," *The Review and Herald*, December 17, 1903

36 Ellen White, *Testimonies for the Church* 4:650

37 Ellen White, "The Home and the School," *The Review and Herald*, March 21, 1882

Chapter 22

1 Katie G Silva, Maricela Correa-Chávez, Barbara Rogoff, "Mexican-Heritage Children's Attention and Learning from Interactions Directed to Others," *Child Development* 2010; Maricela Correa-Chávez, Barbara Rogoff, "Children's Attention to Interactions Directed to Others: Guatemalan Mayan and European American Patterns," *Developmental Psychology* 2009

2 Ellen White, *Child Guidance*, 104

3 Ellen White, *The Ministry of Healing*, 180

4 Ellen White, *Christ's Object Lessons*, 84

5 Ellen White, *Education*, 108

6 Romans 10:2 KJV

7 Ellen White, "Child-Training," *The Signs of the Times*, April 23, 1902

Chapter 23

1 Warwick B. Elley, Judith Langer, "In Praise of Incidental Learning: Lessons from Some Empirical Findings on Language Acquisition," 2021

2 E.J. Paulson, K.S. Goodman, Re-reading eye movement research: Support for transactional models of reading (Routledge, 2011)

3 Dr. Raymond Moore, "Synopsis," Moore Academy, mooreacademy.org/articles/synopsis; Carla Hannaford, Smart Moves: Why Learning Is Not All in Your Head (Great Ocean Publishers, 2005), 104 - 106

4 Amanda N French, et al. "Risk Factors for Incident Myopia in Australian Schoolchildren: The Sydney Adolescent Vascular and Eye Study," *Ophthalmology* 2013

5 Shuyu Xiong, et al. "Time Spent in Outdoor Activities in Relation to Myopia Prevention and Control," *Acta Ophthalmologica* 2017

6 Ellen White, "Week of Prayer in Australia," *The Review and Herald*, 1898

7 Ruth Beechick, *The Three R's* (Mott Media, 2006)

8 The National Assessment of Educational Progress

9 U.S. Department of Education, National Center for Education Statistics, *Reading Literacy in the United States* 1996; Sebastian P. Suggate, Elizabeth A. Schaughency, Elaine Reese, "Children Learning to Read Later Catch Up to Children Reading Earlier," Early Childhood Research Quarterly 2013

10 "Hard Evidence: At What Age Are Children Ready for School?" theconversation.com/hard-evidence-at-what-age-are-children-ready-for-school-29005

11 "Hard Evidence: At What Age Are Children Ready for School?" theconversation.com/hard-evidence-at-what-age-are-children-ready-for-school-29005

12 Linda Bryant Caviness, "Educational Brain Research as Compared with E.G. White's Counsels to Educators" 2000

13 National Academies of Sciences, Engineering, and Medicine, *Preventing Reading Difficulties in Young Children* (The National Academies Press, 1998); Sebastian Suggate, et al. "From Infancy to Adolescence: The Longitudinal Links Between Vocabulary, Early Literacy Skills, Oral Narrative, and Reading Comprehension," Cognitive Development 2018

14 Claude Fredericks, Shirley Kokot, Susan Krog, "Using a Developmental Movement Programme to Enhance Academic Skills in Grade 1 Learners," *South African Journal for Research in Sport, Physical Education and Recreation* 2006

15 The Conflict of the Ages series consists of the books, *Patriarchs and Prophets, Prophets and Kings, The Desire of Ages, The Acts of the Apostles*, and *The Great Controversy*. They cover the time from the rebellion in heaven to the end of the world and the second coming of Jesus.

16 Ellen White, "Parents as Character Builders," *The Review and Herald*, October 5, 1911

17 Ellen White, "Parents as Character Builders," *The Review and Herald*, October 5, 1911

18 Ellen White, *Christian Education*, 204

19 Ellen White, "Able to Make Us Wise unto Salvation," *The Signs of the Times*, May 1, 1907

20 Ellen White, *Education*, 189

21 Ellen White, *Education*, 189

22 Michal Zivan et al. "Higher Theta-Beta Ratio During Screen-Based vs. Printed Paper is Related to Lower Attention in Children," *PLoS One* 2023

23 Millward Brown Case Study, "Using Neuroscience to Understand the Role of Direct Mail"

24 Millward Brown Case Study, "Using Neuroscience to Understand the Role of Direct Mail"

25 L. M. Singer, P.A. Alexander, "Reading on Paper and Digitally: What the Past Decades of Empirical Research Reveal," *Review of Educational Research* 2017; Millward Brown Case Study, "Using Neuroscience to Understand the Role of Direct Mail"; J.M. Noyes, K.J. Garland, "VDT Versus Paper-Based Text," International Journal of Industrial Ergonomics 200

26 Maryanne Wolf, *Reader, Come Home, The Reading Brain in a Digital World* (Harper, 2018)

Chapter 24

1 Matthew 28:19-20

2 Ellen White, *Testimonies for the Church* 6:329

3 Ellen White, *Education*, 269

Chapter 25

1 Ellen White, *Education*, 238

2 Ellen White, *Education*, 238

3 Ellen White, *Education*, 238

4 Ellen White, "The Primal Object of Education," *The Review and Herald*, July 11, 1882

5 Ellen White, *Special Testimonies on Education*, 217

6 The Conflict of the Ages series consists of the books *Patriarchs and Prophets, Prophets and Kings, The Desire of Ages, The Acts of the Apostles*, and *The Great Controversy*. These books proceed through history from creation to the end of the world and uncover some of the beautiful details of the Scriptural accounts in a way that can help keep the child's interest.

7 Ellen White, *Testimonies for the Church* 8:307

8 Ellen White, "Prophecy and history should form a part of the studies in our schools" *Christian Education*, 212

9 Ellen White, *Education*, 238

Chapter 26

1 "Music on Our Minds: The Rich Potential of Music to Promote Brain Health and Mental Well-Being" Global Council on Brain Health 2020; Clara E. James, et al. "Musical Training Intensity Yields Opposite Effects on Grey Matter Density in Cognitive Versus Sensorimotor Networks," *Brain Structure and Function* 2014; Muriel T Zaatar, et al. "The Transformative Power of Music: Insights into Neuroplasticity, Health, and Disease," *Brain, Behavior, & Immunity - Health* 2023; Ewa A. Miendlarzewska, Wiebke J. Trost, "How Musical Training Affects Cognitive Development: Rhythm, Reward and Other Modulating Variables," *Frontiers in Neuroscience* 2013; Corneliu Toader, et al. "Cognitive Crescendo: How Music Shapes the Brain's Structure and Function," *Brain Sciences* 2023
2 Ellen White, *The Voice in Speech and Song*, 424
3 Ellen White, "The Schools of the Ancient Hebrews," *The Review and Herald*, October 30, 1900
4 2 Chronicles 7:6; 1 Chronicles 23:5
5 Ellen White, *Patriarchs and Prophets*, 642
6 Ellen White, *Patriarchs and Prophets*, 641
7 Ellen White, *Patriarchs and Prophets*, 641
8 Ellen White, *Patriarchs and Prophets*, 594
9 Ellen White, *The Voice in Speech and Song*, 425
10 Ellen White, *Evangelism*, 506
11 Ellen White, *Education*, 168
12 Ellen White, *The Voice in Speech and Song*, 415
13 Ellen White, *The Voice in Speech and Song*, 424
14 Ellen White, *The Voice in Speech and Song*, 423
15 Ellen White, *The Voice in Speech and Song*, 416
16 Ellen White, *Testimonies for the Church* 9:143
17 Ellen White, *Testimonies for the Church* 9:143
18 Ellen White, *Counsels to Parents, Teachers, and Students*, 145
19 Ellen White, *Counsels to Parents, Teachers, and Students*, 145
20 Jane Healy, *Your Child's Growing Mind* (Broadway, 2004), 85-86
21 Ellen White, *The Voice in Speech and Song*, 424
22 Ellen White, *Patriarchs and Prophets*, 594
23 Matthew E. Sachs, et al. "Brain Connectivity Reflects Human Aesthetic Responses to Music," *Social Cognitive and Affective Neuroscience* 2016; Noelia Martínez-Molina, et al. "White Matter Microstructure Reflects Individual Differences in Music Reward Sensitivity," *Journal of Neuroscience* 2019
24 Ellen White, *The Desire of Ages*, 73
25 Ellen White, *Education*, 41
26 Ellen White, "Co-operation with Ministers," *The Review and Herald*, July 24, 1883
27 Ellen White, *Testimonies for the Church* 1:505
28 Ellen White, *The Voice in Speech and Song*, 419; Ellen White, "The Need of Home Religion," *The Review and Herald*, June 22, 1905
29 Ellen White, *Testimonies for the Church* 1:497
30 Ellen White, *Christ's Object Lessons*, 83
31 Ellen White, "The Two Ways," *The Signs of the Times*, April 1, 1880
32 Ellen White, *Education*, 107
33 Ellen White, *The Voice in Speech and Song*, 422
34 Ellen White, *Christ's Object Lessons*, 83
35 Ellen White, *Patriarchs and Prophets*, 594
36 Ellen White, *Patriarchs and Prophets*, 594
37 Ellen White, *Education*, 237
38 Ellen White, "The Responsibilities of Parents and Teachers," *Sabbath-School Worker*, April 1, 1889
39 Ellen White, *Education*, 167
40 Ellen White, *Testimonies for the Church* 2:265
41 Ellen White, *Messages to Young People*, 295; Ellen White, *The Voice in Speech and Song*, 419; Ellen White, *Testimonies for the Church* 1:510

42 Ellen White, *Fundamentals of Christian Education*, 97
43 Ellen White, *Education*, 296
44 Ellen White, *Education*, 168
45 From the hymn "Jesus Paid It All" by Mrs. Elvina M. Hall and John T. Grape
46 Ellen White, *Education*, 168
47 Ellen White, *The Voice in Speech and Song*, 410
48 Ellen White, *Education*, 167
49 Ellen White, *The Voice in Speech and Song*, 424
50 Ellen White, *Education*, 167
51 Ellen White, *Education*, 251
52 Ellen White, *Patriarchs and Prophets*, 594
53 Ellen White, *Testimonies for the Church* 9:143
54 Ellen White, *Testimonies for the Church* 9:143
55 Ellen White, *The Voice in Speech and Song*, 408

Chapter 27

1 Alison Gopnik, "Scientific Thinking in Young Children," *Science* 2012; Jamie J.
Jirout, "Supporting Early Scientific Thinking Through Curiosity," *Frontiers in
Psychology* 2020; "Character Traits: Scientific Virtue," *Nature* 2016
2 Ö. Sadi, J. Cakiroglu, "Effects of Hands-On Activity Enriched Instruction on Students' Achievement and Attitudes Towards Science," *Journal of Baltic Science Education* 2011
3 Ming Kuo, Michael Barnes, Catherine Jordan, "Do Experiences with Nature Promote Learning? Converging
Evidence of a Cause-and-Effect Relationship," *Frontiers in Psychology* 2019
4 I. Skalstad, E. Munkebye, "Young Children's Questions About Science Topics when Situated in a Natural
Outdoor Environment: A Qualitative Study from Kindergarten and Primary School," *International Journal of
Science Education* 2021
5 I. Skalstad, E. Munkebye, "Young Children's Questions About Science Topics when Situated in a Natural
Outdoor Environment: A Qualitative Study from Kindergarten and Primary School," *International Journal of
Science Education* 2021
6 Michelle. M. Chouinard "Children's Questions: A Mechanism for Cognitive
Development," *Monographs of the Society for Research in Child Development* 2007
7 Ellen White, "Disease and Its Causes," *The Review and Herald* 1899
8 Ellen White, *Christ's Object Lessons*, 24
9 Ellen White, *Patriarchs and Prophets*, 599
10 Ellen White, "Science and the Bible in Education," *The Signs of the Times* 1884
11 Ellen White, *Patriarchs and Prophets*, 599

Chapter 28

1 Peter Gray, "Coronavirus School Closures: An Educational Opportunity," *Psychology
Today*, psychologytoday.com/us/blog/freedom-learn/202003/coronavirus-school-clo
sures-educational-opportunity
2 Ellen White, *Education*, 238
3 Dr. Maria Droujkova, "5-Year Olds Can Learn Calculus" *The Atlantic* 2014
4 Benezet, L. P., "The Teaching of Arithmetic: The Story of an Experiment,"
Humanistic Mathematics Network Journal 1991, Article 4
5 Ellen White, *Education*, 77
6 Stanford/Elsevier 2024; lemire.me/blog/about-me
7 Dr. Maria Droujkova, naturalmath.com/2023/05/multiplication-and-jo-boaler
8 Jo Boaler, "Why Math Education in the U.S. Doesn't Add Up," *Scientific American Mind* 2016
9 Margarete Delazer, et al. "Learning by Strategies and Learning by Drill: Evidence from an fMRI Study," *Neuro-
Image* 2005

Chapter 29

1 Ellen White, *Counsels to Parents, Teachers, and Students*, 218
2 Ellen White, Manuscript 2, no 143

3 Ellen White, *Counsels to Parents, Teachers, and Students*, 218
4 Ellen White, *Counsels to Parents, Teachers, and Students*, 168
5 Ellen White, *The Adventist Home*, 387
6 Ellen White, *Testimonies for the Church* 3:122
7 Ellen White, *The Adventist Home*, 388
8 Ellen White, *The Adventist Home*, 387
9 Ellen White, *The Adventist Home*, 387
10 Ellen White, *The Adventist Home*, 387
11 Ellen White, *The Adventist Home*, 388
12 Ellen White, *Child Guidance*, 134
13 Ellen White, *The Ministry of Healing*, 287
14 Ellen White, "Missionary Work," *The Review and Herald*, October 6, 1891
15 Ellen White, *Child Guidance*, 134
16 Ellen White, *Testimonies for the Church* 6:465
17 Ellen White, *The Adventist Home*, 376
18 Ellen White, *Testimonies for the Church* 6:451
19 Ellen White, *Testimonies for the Church* 4:645
20 Ellen White, *Counsels for the Church*, 154
21 Ellen White, *Testimonies for the Church* 6:214
1

Chapter 30

1 Pattern learning is when one detects patterns and learns from the patterns; P. M.
  Cunningham, *Phonics They Use: Words for Reading and Writing* (Allyn and Bacon, 2004)
2 S. Dehaene, *Reading in the Brain* (Viking, 2009)
3 Rebecca Putman, "Using Research to Make Informed Decisions About the
  Spelling Curriculum," *Texas Journal of Literacy Education* 2017
4 P. M. Cunningham, *Phonics They Use: Words for Reading and Writing* (Allyn and Bacon, 2004)
5 Digital devices condition the child's brain to expect high levels of stimulation which lead to lower observation skills.
6 P. R. Hanna, et al. *Phoneme-Grapheme Correspondences as Cues to Spelling Improvement* (U.S. Office of Education Cooperative Research, 1966)

Chapter 31

1 Boaz Keysar, Sayuri L Hayakawa, Sun Gyu An, "The Foreign-Language Effect: Thinking in a Foreign Tongue Reduces Decision Biases," *Psychological Science* 2012; A. Mechelli, et al. "Structural Plasticity in the Bilingual Brain," *Nature* 2004
2 Ellen White, *Counsels to Parents, Teachers, and Students*, 518
3 Ellen White, *The Ministry of Healing*, 395
4 Olumide A. Olulade, et al. "The Neural Basis of Language Development: Changes in Lateralization over Age," *The Proceedings of the National Academy of Sciences* 2020
5 Elley, Warwick, "In Praise of Incidental Learning: Lessons from Some Empirical Findings on Language Acquisition" 1997
6 *Christ's Object Lessons*, a book on the parables of Jesus, is authored by Ellen White.
7 The Conflict of the Ages series consists of the books *Patriarchs and Prophets*, *Prophets and Kings*, *The Desire of Ages*, *The Acts of the Apostles*, and *The Great Controversy*. These books cover the time from the rebellion in heaven to the end of the world and the second coming of Jesus.
8 Audio recordings of the Bible and the Spirit of Prophecy can be found online (usually at no cost).
9 *Patriarchs and Prophets* is authored by Ellen White
10 Ellen White, *Counsels to Parents, Teachers, and Students*, 207
11 Ellen White, *Counsels to Parents, Teachers, and Students*, 508
12 Ellen White, *Counsels to Parents, Teachers, and Students*, 508

Chapter 32

1 There is a treasure trove of parenting and educational advice in the periodical "The Review and Herald," as well as the books *The Ministry of Healing*, *Education*, those in the *Conflict of the Ages Series*, and others.

2 Ellen White, "True Education," *Christian Educator*, August 1, 1897
3 Ellen White, *The Ministry of Healing*, 242
4 Ellen White, *The Desire of Ages*, 668
5 Ellen White, "Look to God for Wisdom," *The Review and Herald*, August 14, 1894
6 Ellen White, *Fundamentals of Christian Education*, 27
7 Ellen White, *Education*, 17
8 Ellen White, *Counsels to Parents, Teachers, and Students*, 434
9 Ellen White, "I Have Written Unto You, Young Men," *The Youth's Instructor*, October 25, 1894
10 Ellen White, "Proper Education," *The Review and Herald*, July 14, 1885
11 Ellen White, "Look to God for Wisdom," *The Review and Herald*, August 14, 1894 (emphasis supplied)
12 Prachi E. Shah, et al. "Early Childhood Curiosity and Kindergarten Reading and Math Academic Achievement," *Pediatric Research* (2018)
13 Ellen White, *Education*, 41
14 Ellen White, *The Ministry of Healing*, 381
15 Ellen White, "Happy and Unhappy Homes," *The Signs of the Times*, October 2, 1884
16 Ellen White, *Christian Education*, 54
17 Ellen White, *Patriarchs and Prophets*, 603
18 Ellen White, *Patriarchs and Prophets*, 606
19 Ellen White, *Patriarchs and Prophets*, 606
20 Ellen White, *Patriarchs and Prophets*, 606
21 Ellen White, *Patriarchs and Prophets*, 606
22 Ellen White, *Education*, 51
23 Ellen White, *Education*, 51
24 Ellen White, *Prophets and Kings*, 486
25 Ellen White, *Education*, 33
26 Isaiah 54:13 KJV
27 Ellen White, "The Necessity of Sympathy and Love," *Sabbath-School Worker*, July 1, 1889 (emphasis supplied)
28 Ellen White, *Special Testimonies on Education*, 15
29 Ellen White, "Look to God for Wisdom," *The Review and Herald*, August 14, 1894
30 Ellen White, "True Education," *Christian Educator*, August 1, 1897
31 Ellen White, "A Few Words to Parents," *The Signs of the Times*, December 19, 1878
32 Ellen White, "The Essential in Education," *The Review and Herald*, October 24, 1907

Chapter 33

1 Ellen White, *Education*, 50
2 Ellen White, *Patriarchs and Prophets*, 544
3 Ellen White, *Patriarchs and Prophets*, 545
4 Judges 7:16
5 Ellen White, *Patriarchs and Prophets*, 550
6 Ellen White, *Patriarchs and Prophets*, 550
7 Ellen White, *Patriarchs and Prophets*, 553
8 Ellen White, *Patriarchs and Prophets*, 554
9 Ellen White, "The Position and Responsibility of a True Educator," *The Signs of the Times*, March 14, 1900
10 Ellen White, *Patriarchs and Prophets*, 554
11 Ellen White, "Thoughts on Education," *The Review and Herald*, January 10, 1882
12 Ellen White, *Patriarchs and Prophets*, 547
13 Ellen White, Manuscript 21, no 1557
14 Ellen White, *Daughters of God*, 90
15 Ellen White, *Education*, 77
16 Ellen White, *Education*, 230
17 Ellen White, *Testimonies for the Church* 5:22
18 Ellen White, *Patriarchs and Prophets*, 607
19 Ellen White, *Patriarchs and Prophets*, 607
20 Ellen White, *Testimonies for the Church*, 5:29
21 Ellen White, "The Position and Responsibility of a True Educator," *The Signs of the Times*, March 14, 1900
22 Ellen White, *Testimonies for the Church* 6:146

23 Ellen White, *Testimonies for the Church* 6:126
24 Ellen White, *Testimonies for the Church* 5:548
25 Ellen White, *Testimonies for the Church* 6:142
26 Ellen White, *Testimonies for the Church* 5:26
27 Ellen White, *Mind, Character, and Personality* 1:53
28 Ellen White, *Testimonies for the Church* 6:160
29 Ellen White, *Fundamentals of Christian Education*, 288
30 Ellen White, *Patriarchs and Prophets*, 290
31 Ellen White, *Testimonies for the Church* 5:182
32 Ellen White, *Patriarchs and Prophets*, 554
33 Ellen White, "The Mother's Work," *The Review and Herald*, September 15, 1891
34 Ephesians 3:20
35 Ellen White, *The Desire of Ages*, 363
36 Ellen White, "The Mother a Missionary," *The Signs of the Times*, September 29, 1881 (emphasis supplied)
37 Ellen White, "The Mother a Missionary," *The Signs of the Times*, September 29, 1881
38 Ellen White, *Patriarchs and Prophets*, 553
39 Ellen White, "Among the Mountains," *The Signs of the Times*, February 2, 1882
40 Ellen White, "The Duties of a Mother," *The Signs of the Times*, August 30, 1877
41 Ellen White, "Words for Mothers," *The Signs of the Times*, March 30, 1891
42 Ellen White, *Testimonies for the Church* 5:322

Chapter 34

1 Ellen White, *Special Testimonies on Education*, 222
2 Ellen White, *Christian Education*, 12
3 Daniel (*The Youth's Instructor*, June 25, 1903)
4 Timothy (*The Acts of the Apostles*, 205)
5 Daniel (*The Signs of the Times*, November 4, 1886)
6 Elisha (*Education*, 58); Moses (*Patriarchs and Prophets*, 243)
7 Joseph (*Patriarchs and Prophets*, 213-223); David (*Patriarchs and Prophets*, 643-648; 2 Samuel 5:10)
8 Samuel (*Patriarchs and Prophets*, 572-574); (*The Signs of the Times*, October 27, 1881)
9 The Little Maid (*Patriarchs and Prophets*, 244-246)
10 Ellen White, *Education*, 276
11 Ellen White, *Testimonies for the Church* 6:140
12 Ellen White, *Testimonies for the Church* 6:218
13 Ellen White, *Counsels to Parents, Teachers, and Students*, 255
14 Ellen White, "True Education," *The Youth's Instructor*, August 31, 1899

Final Note
Jeremiah 17:7 NRSV

www.ingramcontent.com/pod-product-compliance
Lightning Source LLC
Chambersburg PA
CBHW070016100426
42740CB00013B/2515